W9-CID-467

HEALTH CARE AND THE SOCIAL SERVICES

SOCIAL WORK PRACTICE IN HEALTH CARE

HEALTH CARE AND THE SOCIAL SERVICES

SOCIAL WORK PRACTICE IN HEALTH CARE

Edited and compiled by

RICHARD J. ESTES

University of Pennsylvania

WARREN H. GREEN, INC.
St. Louis, Missouri, U.S.A.

Published by

WARREN H. GREEN, INC.
8356 Olive Blvd.
St. Louis, Missouri 63132, U.S.A.

ISBN No. 0-87527-266-5

Printed in the United States of America

CONTRIBUTORS

RICHARD J. ESTES, M.S.W., D.S.W., is Associate Professor of Social Work and Director of Doctoral Education, University of Pennsylvania, Philadelphia, Pennsylvania. Dr. Estes has authored numerous articles on various aspects of health care and has written several books including *The Social Progress of Nations* (Praeger, 1984), *The Directory of Social Welfare Research Capabilities* (Dorrance, 1981), and *The Social Work Calendar, 1982* (National Association of Social Workers, 1982). At the time of this volume's completion Dr. Estes was Visiting Professor of Social Research and Planning at the School of Social Work, University of Hawaii at Manoa, Honolulu, Hawaii.

ANNE-LINDA FURSTENBERG, M.S.S., Ph.D., is Assistant Professor of Social Work, University of Pennsylvania, Philadelphia, Pennsylvania. Dr. Furstenberg has had extensive experience in family and medical social work and has a special interest in the health needs of older persons. Dr. Furstenberg has presented papers at national conferences in aging, health and social work and has given workshops and seminars on aspects of aging and social work in health settings. Her publications include articles and book chapters on social work in health care and health behavior of older people.

JUDITH FRANK HIRSCHWALD, M.S.W., is Director of Social Services, Magee Rehabilitation Hospital, Philadelphia, Pennsylvania, and Patient Systems Coordinator, Delaware Valley Regional Spinal Cord Injury Center, Thomas Jefferson University, Philadelphia, Pennsylvania. Mrs. Hirschwald has served frequently as a consultant to regional and national organizations and groups on issues related to the care and rehabilitation of physically disabled persons. She holds lecturer status with two universities and is a member and officer in several national social work and social welfare organizations.

JOANNE MANTELL received her M.S. from Columbia University School of Social Work and her M.S.P.H. and Ph.D. from UCLA School of Public Health. She was a Visiting Lecturer at the U.C.L.A. School of Social Welfare and is currently Research Assistant Professor at the University of Southern California, School of Social Work and Senior Lecturer in Health Administration at Columbia University, School of Public Health. Dr. Mantell is co-Principal Investigator on a study of "Assessment Ethnic Variations in Social Support Networks and Coping Patterns with Cancer".

MARJORIE McKINNEY CASHION, M.S.W., is currently Coordinator of the Family Resource Center, Family and Child Services Agency, Birmingham, Alabama. At the time of the chapter's preparation Ms. McKinney was a clinical social worker with the Clinical Center of the National Institutes of Health, Bethesda, Maryland. Ms. McKinney's areas of expertise include family therapy, grief and loss, crises counselling and psychosocial care for cancer patients.

ARTHUR F. MOFFA, Jr., M.S.W., is the Adult Service Director, Crozer-Chester Community Mental Health Center, and Adjunct Assistant Professor, Widener University, Chester, Pennsylvania. He also is in private practice, Media, Pennsylvania. Mr. Moffa received his Master's Degree in Social Work from the University of Pennsylvania, and he has advanced training in individual psychotherapy, family therapy and management. Mr. Moffa has taught in the Social Work/Community Psychology Department of Widener University both in the clinical and social welfare sequences. He is presently the President of the Brandywine Valley Division of the National Association of Social Workers.

SUSAN C. MOINESTER, M.S.W., lives in Memphis, Tennessee. She is widely recognized for her expertise on occupational health and safety issues and presents papers on this topic regularly at a variety of national health and social welfare conferences. Ms. Moinester has published extensively on this topic. At the time of the chapter's writing Ms. Moinester was Assistant Director of the Occupational Health Program, College of Pharmacy, University of Tennessee, Memphis, Tennessee.

EDGAR A. PERRETZ, M.S.W., prior to his death in 1983, was Professor of Social Work at the University of Pennsylvania. He served on the faculties of Michigan State University, Ohio State University, the University of Toronto, and the staff of the National Institute of Mental Health in Bethesda, Maryland. In addition, he held a number of administrative, consultant, and direct service positions in the field of mental health, including the Columbus Psychiatric Receiving Hospital (OSU), Toronto Psychiatric Hospital, Ontario Department of Health, and the West Virginia Department of Health.

IRENE SUE POLLIN, M.S.W., L.C.S.W., is Executive Director of the Linda Pollin Institute, Chevy Chase, Maryland. Mrs. Pollin's innovative work in medical crises counselling and community-based health social services have earned her a national reputation. Mrs. Pollin has conducted seminars and workshops on a variety of health related topics.

WILLIAM SILVER, M.S.W., D.S.W., is a senior faculty member of the Training Center and Director of Social Work Training at the Philadelphia Child Guidance Clinic. He serves part-time on the faculties of the University of Pennsylvania School of Social Work and Rutgers University School of Social Work. Dr. Silver has travelled nationally, lecturing on many aspects of family therapy, practice, supervision, and consultation. He is a graduate of the University of Pennsylvania School of Social Work.

S. REID WARREN, III, M.S.W., at the time this chapter was written was Director of Social Services, Northwestern Institute of Psychiatry, Fort Washington, Pennsylvania. He has since been appointed as Director of Mental Retardation Services at the hospital. Mr. Warren received his Master's Degree in Social Work from the University of Pennsylvania. His previous positions have been as Director of Social Services Extended Care Section of Haverford State Hospital, Mental Health/Mental Retardation Consultant with the Commonwealth of Pennsylvania, Coordinator of Mental Retardation Services and Grants Management Specialist, West Philadelphia Mental Health Consortium, and Director of Mental Health/Mental Retardation Services Inc. of Chester County.

TO THE MEMORY OF

My father and first mentor,
Lebert L. Estes

and

My friend and valued colleague,
Edgar A. Perretz

ACKNOWLEDGMENTS

Many persons have contributed to the preparation of this volume. Alvin Gardner, Editor-in-Chief of the Warren H. Green, Inc. Allied Health Handbook Series, is thanked for the opportunity to add this volume to the series. Louise Shoemaker, Dean of the University of Pennsylvania School of Social Work, is acknowledged for the encouragement and administrative support that she provided in helping the volume get started. My colleagues in that School's Health Specialization — James Carpenter, Joan Bonner Conway, Anne-Linda Furstenberg, Edgar Perretz, Eleanor Ryder, Robert Schoenberg, and Peter Vaughan — stimulated many of the ideas contained in the book. Anne-Linda Furstenberg and Edgar Perretz are acknowledged particularly for their willingness to author two of the volume's foundational chapters.

While working as research assistants with the Center for the Study of Social Work Practice, Stephen Betchen and John McQueen undertook the sample statistical survey of social workers employed in health settings summarized in the volume's *Introduction*. Their careful attention to detail, and overall enthusiasm for the project, made what would have been an otherwise difficult task much easier.

Mary Ann Keenan and David Garrity, staff members of the National Association of Social Workers (NASW), provided critically needed, and timely, information concerning national trends in the staffing and regulation of health social services. Their promptness and cooperation in responding to each of several requests was deeply appreciated. Jacqui Atkins, NASW Publications Director, is thanked, too, for granting the Association's permission to reprint the several NASW health/social service policy documents contained in the volume's appendixes.

Dean Daniel Sanders, my good friend and much respected colleague, is thanked for the time and opportunity that he made available to me to complete the volume's final editorial tasks while I was Visiting Professor of Social Work with the University of Hawaii at Manoa. Mahalo nui loa, Dan!

Finally, special acknowledgement is given to Dr. Warren H. Green without whose foresight and commitment to an interdisciplinary view of health care practice the present series, including this volume, would not have been possible. His patience in awaiting the volume's final manuscript as it progressed through various stages of development was deeply appreciated.

Richard J. Estes, D.S.W.
Philadelphia, Pennsylvania

CONTENTS

HEALTH CARE AND THE SOCIAL SERVICES

SOCIAL WORK PRACTICE IN HEALTH CARE

Chapter 1

SOCIAL WORKERS IN HEALTH CARE*

RICHARD J. ESTES, D.S.W.

INTRODUCTION

Approximately 60,000 of the 150,000 professionally qualified social workers, or two out of every five, currently working in the United States practice in the health field.[1] The majority of these health-oriented social service professionals (63%) are employed by mental health agencies, by psychiatric hospitals or clinics or, in increasing numbers, provide mental health services privately. Some 22,000 social workers are employed by acute and long-term medical care facilities as well. A growing number of social workers are employed part-time as human service specialists in group medical care practices, or offer private crisis counseling services in conjunction with these practices.

Whatever their particular area of specialization, health social workers offer a wide range of psycho-social services that are needed to help patients and their families deal effectively with the often difficult requirements of treatment and patient care. Social workers in all types of care settings routinely serve as consultants in the psycho-social aspects of health care; as such, they are integral members of the clinical interdisciplinary health care team. The necessary social services that they offer are provided throughout *all* phases of patient care and are not restricted either to periods of acute stress for patients or to the special problems encountered by or with patients during their admission to or discharge from health care facilities.

*Bonnie Clause is thanked for her editorial assistance with this chapter.

[1] The source of these social work health manpower estimates is described in the next section of this Introduction.

Health-care-related social services emerged during the last half of the 19th century as one response to the problems of fragmentation created by a rapidly expanding, specialty-oriented system of institutionally based health services. Today, the social services are an integral and increasingly more essential component in the delivery of comprehensive health services. Health social workers, for example:

- Participate actively in all aspects of clinical case assessment, planning, treatment, service management, and patient follow up;
- Function as specialists in the psycho-social aspects of health care;
- Serve as consultants to practitioners of other health disciplines in helping to better understand and impact more effectively upon the complex psycho-social factors that directly affect patient care;
- Link patients and their families to the full spectrum of in-patient, out-patient and community-based health services;
- Facilitate patient and family access to the even greater array of health-related services available to them from literally thousands of human service agencies located in communities all across the United States.

Social workers also function as health educators, patient advocates and ombudsmen, as public relations officers for hospitals and clinics, and as program development specialists who generate the resources needed to implement new or innovative programs of health service delivery. In many settings, social workers function as providers of primary health services — especially of mental health services — and, in doing so, contribute directly to the financial support of these programs and specialized service areas.

Social workers also are active in the delivery of primary, secondary, and tertiary public health services. Some of these services are performed by social workers exclusively or primarily (e.g., organizing and facilitating the work of community health councils) but most are offered in collaboration with professionals in other health disciplines (e.g., well-baby clinics, immunization campaigns, rodent control efforts, occupational safety and health inspections, environmental protection programs, etc.). Social workers also perform vital public health services during occurrences of natural and man-made disasters, helping victims recover quickly from the awesome physical, social, emotional, and financial problems that result from these unexpected tragedies.

Health social workers also contribute to the direct management of health care agencies and organizations. Indeed, the policy-making authority and administrative responsibilities of health social workers have increased substantially over the past several decades. In addition to carrying continuing responsibility for the day-to-day management of departments of social service located within health facilities, for example, social workers now regularly serve as chief executive officers for many hospitals and clinics. They function, too, as key members of health agency boards of directors. Social workers participate extensively in the peer review, service audit, and related quality assurance activities of most health organizations. Frequently, they serve as members of external review and health facility accreditation bodies.

Because of their unique training — and especially because of the emphasis they place on an integrated approach to human service delivery — social workers often carry considerable influence in the formulation of health policy at all levels of government and in the private health service sector as well. This influence is most visible in the large number of social workers who serve as members of various national, state, and local health and welfare planning councils, commissions, and specialized community-based health-oriented coalitions and task force groups. It also is apparent in the critical decision-making role that many social workers carry on the boards of directors of private philanthropic organizations, governmental grant-giving agencies, community United Ways and similar types of human service funding organizations. Even when not functioning as members of the boards of directors of these organizations, social workers do influence their financial support decisions by serving as program consultants, as reviewers of funding proposals and, often, as members of their professional staffs. Through all of these roles, social workers exert a powerful influence on the service activities of individual health agencies and on the development of broad-based social policies which, ultimately, affect service delivery in the context of community-wide, state and national health programs.

Throughout all of their activities in the health field social workers share with other health professionals a single concern for the provision of the highest possible quality of health services to patients and their families. To that end, they have applied all of their specialized knowledge and technical skills; over the decades social workers have earned for themselves positions of respect, responsibility and authority as providers of essential services in the health care system. Health social workers, however, also carry a special commitment, one that they share with their colleagues in all other systems of human service, i.e., that of assuring access to quality human services for society's most vulnerable, often economically dependent, populations — the poor, the aged, the physically and emotionally handicapped, racial and ethnic minorities, women, etc. Not surprisingly, in their colleagues in health care, social workers have found valuable allies who share this commitment and who, together, are working to humanize further the existing system of health services so as to make it more responsive to the special health needs of these often ignored people in American society.

SOCIAL WORK MANPOWER IN HEALTH SERVICES

A precise enumeration of professionally qualified social workers currently practicing in the United States is not available. The estimation problems created by the lack of such a census are compounded by the inclusion of some 400,000 human service workers under the "social worker" occupational classification system used by the U.S. Bureau of Labor Statistics. The vast majority of these workers are employed by community health and welfare agencies as "counselors," "recreation specialists," "family workers," "community organizers," "fundraisers," "planners," and the like. Less than half of these persons (40-45 percent), have received formal professional training of any type from an accredited program of social work education.

A better estimate of the number of currently active, professionally qualified, social workers is to be found in the statistics published annually by the Council on Social Work Education, the sole accreditation body for professional social work education in the United States. Over the 31-year period 1950-1981, for example, the Council reported that 149,000 Master of Social Work (M.S.W., M.S.S.W., M.S.S.A., M.A. in S.W.) and 2,490 Doctor of Social Work (D.S.W., Ph.D.) degrees were awarded by American colleges and universities to graduates of 85 accredited graduate programs (12). Persons graduating from the 315 recently accredited undergraduate programs of professional social work education (B.S.W., B.A. in S.W.) number about 8,000 annually (13). Prior to 1950 many fewer professional social work degrees were awarded.

Allowing for deaths and retirements, and for the relatively small number of pre-1950 graduates who continue to practice social work at least part-time, a more reasonable estimate of the current professional social work manpower pool is approximately 150,000 persons, or about 38% of the total number of persons currently classified by the U.S. Department of Labor as "social workers." The majority of these persons are women (65%), and most are employed in systems of human service other than health care (e.g., child welfare, schools, criminal and juvenile justice, public welfare, etc.).

In an effort to arrive at a more accurate estimate of the number of professional social workers engaged in *health-care* related practice, the author undertook a limited sample survey of the members of the National Association of Social Workers (NASW). The NASW is the nation's largest organization of professionally qualified social workers, with a membership in excess of 85,000 persons in 1982. The survey involved a 5% probability sample of all social workers listed in the Association's *Professional Social Workers Directory* (26). Through an examination of the 1977 occupational information contained in the *Directory*, data were ascertained with respect to member level of educational attainment, current employment status, area of practice specialization, and auspices of then current employment.[2] The major results obtained from analysis of these data are summarized in Tables 1 and 2.

The survey established that of the 75,000 professional social workers listed in the *Directory*, approximately 28,000, or 38%, identified themselves as practicing either exclusively or primarily in health settings. As seen in Table 1, the majority of these persons (62.6%) practice in mental health settings. Many health social workers, however, are employed by medical care (19.3%), physical rehabilitation (2.6%), public health (1.0%), developmental disability (0.8%) and similar centers of physical health care. Social workers also are employed as health planners (0.9%), as health educators (4.5%), and as occupational safety and health inspectors (0.1%). Extrapolating these data to include the additional 75,000 otherwise professionally qualified social workers who are *not* members of the NASW, this author conservatively estimates that about 57,000 social workers engage in full- or part-time practice in the health field.

Based on the above data, the largest employers of health social workers are community mental health centers (19.5%), hospital-based inpatient and outpatient medical care departments (15.0%), inpatient and outpatient departments of psychiatry, psychiatric day centers

[2] The author acknowledges with appreciation the research assistance provided by John McQueen and Stephen Betchen during the data collection stage of this survey.

TABLE 1.
SOCIAL WORKERS IN HEALTH CARE BY FIELDS OF PRACTICE AND LEVEL OF PROFESSIONAL EDUCATION, 1977 Estimated (N = 28,320)[1]

Fields of Practice in Health Care	*Level of Professional Education*			*Totals*	
	Bachelor's Degree % (N)	*Master's Degree % (N)*	*Post-Master's Degree % (N)*	*% Row (N)*	*% Column*
MEDICAL CARE SETTINGS	1.8%(100)	96.7(5250)	1.5(80)	100.0(5430)	19.3%
Hospital-Based	1.4%(60)	97.2(4140)	1.4(60)	100.0(4260)	(15.0)
Community-Based	4.8%(40)	95.2(800)	—	100.0(840)	(3.0)
Consultants	—	75.0(60)	25.0(20)	100.0(80)	(0.3)
Others	—	100.0(280)	—	100.0(280)	(1.0)
MENTAL HEALTH CARE SETTINGS	1.5%(260)	97.6(17280)	0.9(160)	100.0(17700)	62.6
Hospital-Based	—	100.0(1800)	—	100.0(1800)	(6.4)
Inpatient-Outpatient	2.5%(100)	97.0(3860)	0.5(20)	100.0(3980)	(14.1)
Community Mental Health Centers	0.7%(40)	98.9(5460)	0.4(20)	100.0(5520)	(19.5)
Full-Time Private Practice	2.7%(60)	96.5(2180)	0.9(20)	100.0(2260)	(8.0)
Family Service Association Agencies	1.7%(60)	95.5(3400)	2.8(100)	100.0(3560)	(12.6)
Other	—	100.0(580)	—	100.0(580)	(2.0)
OTHER HEALTH SETTINGS	—	—	—	100.0(5190)	18.2
PHYSICAL REHABILITATION SETTINGS	5.4%(40)	91.9(680)	2.7(20)	100.0(740)	2.6
DEVELOPMENTAL DISABILITIES SETTINGS	9.1%(20)	81.8(180)	9.1(20)	100.0(220)	0.8
PUBLIC HEALTH SETTINGS	7.2%(20)	92.9(260)	—	100.0(280)	1.0

TABLE 1.
SOCIAL WORKERS IN HEALTH CARE BY FIELDS OF PRACTICE AND LEVEL OF PROFESSIONAL EDUCATION, 1977 Estimated (N = 28,320)[1] (continued)

	Level of Professional Education			*Totals*	
	BSW % (N)	*MSW* %(N)	*Post-MSW* %(N)	% *Row (N)*	% *Column*
HEALTH PLANNING SETTINGS	—	92.3(240)	7.7(20)	100.0(260)	0.9
OCCUPATIONAL HEALTH AND SAFETY SETTINGS	—	50.0(20)	50.0(20)	100.0(40)	0.1
HEALTH EDUCATION SETTINGS, including Universities and Colleges	—	76.6(980)	23.4(300)	100.0(1280)	4.5
VETERANS ADMINISTRATION HOSPITALS & CLINICS	4.1%(60)	95.9(1420)	—	100.0(1480)	5.2
ALL OTHER HEALTH & HEALTH RELATED SETTINGS, (not elsewhere counted)[2]	—	93.3(830)	6.7(60)	100.0(890)	3.1
TOTAL ALL HEALTH SETTINGS	1.8%(500)	95.8(27140)	2.4(680)	100.0(28320)	100.0

[1] Estimates based on a five percent (5%) probability sample of social workers listed in the *Professional Social Workers Directory* (Washington, D.C.: National Association of Social Workers, 1978).
[2] Includes part-time private practitioners in mental health whose full-time professional practice is in a human service field other than health care, e.g., probation, child welfare, etc.

TABLE 2.
PATTERNS OF PRIVATE PRACTICE AMONG SOCIAL WORKERS IN HEALTH CARE, 1977 estimated (N = 28320)[1]

Type of Practice	*Level of Professional Education*			*Totals*	
	Bachelor's Degree % (N)	*Master's Degree % (N)*	*Post-Master's Degree % (N)*	*% Row (N)*	*% Column*
Full-time Private Practice	2.7%(60)	96.5(2180)	0.1(20)	100.0(2260)	8.0
Part-time Private Practice	—	92.0(5540)	8.0(480)	100.0(6020)	21.3
Salaried Employment Only	2.2%(440)	96.9(19420)	0.1(180)	100.0(20040)	70.8
TOTALS	1.8%(500)	95.8(27140)	2.4(680)	100.0(28320)	100.0%

[1] Estimates based on a five percent (5%) probability sample of social workers listed in the *Professional Social Workers Directory* (Washington, D.C.: National Association of Social Workers, 1978).

and hospitals (14.1%), Family Service Association of America[3] agencies (12.6%), and Veterans Administration hospitals and clinics (5.2%). Substantial numbers of health social workers also are employed by colleges and universities either as health educators or as full-time faculty members (4.5%). Frequently, these positions include appointments to the behavioral science faculties of schools of medicine, nursing and other health disciplines.

In addition to paid employment with established centers of health care, a substantial number of social workers engage in private clinical practice. Indeed, the survey confirmed that 29% of all health social workers engage in private practice to some extent (see Table 2). The majority of these practices (73%) are only part-time in nature, however, and most are restricted to the provision of psychiatric counselling and medical crisis outpatient services.

The trend for social workers to engage in private practice is new, but one that is likely to continue for some time into the future. This will be the case as social workers continue to be granted state licenses to practice independently and achieve recognition from third party reimbursers of health services as autonomous vendors of the quality psycho-social services that they provide. Increasingly, social workers are joining with other health care providers in forming new joint ventures and other interdisciplinary partnerships that, over the long term, promise to alter significantly current patterns of health service delivery that exist in the United States, especially with respect to those health services that can be offered outside of hospitals and clinics.

THE EDUCATION OF HEALTH SOCIAL WORKERS

Not unlike the early stages of nursing education, the initial preparation of health specialists in social work took place within large, usually university affiliated, urban hospitals. These "in-service" training programs emphasized the community orientation of social services and prepared social workers for a multiplicity of roles in case finding, information and referral, hospital discharge planning, and often, preventive care (1,17,19,30). Social workers also were trained

[3] Social workers employed by FSAA agencies were grouped with other providers of mental health services because of the unique mental health counseling function that many of these workers perform in FSAA agencies. In any event, the majority of FSAA social workers identify themselves as "counsellors," "therapists," or as "psychiatric social workers" and a good many are licensed to operate part-time mental health practices apart from their full-time responsibilities as FSAA employees.

as "case managers" and, through their knowledge of and relationship with workers in other segments of the social welfare system, worked to prevent unnecessary or repeated patient admissions to hospitals and other clinical centers (3,18). The earliest health social workers also engaged in carefully planned and implemented social and political action efforts aimed at reducing the high rates of communicable and infectious diseases, infant and maternal mortality, and similar massive health problems that characterized much of urban life in America during the early 19th century (22,28,33).

Beginning in 1903, responsibility for the education of social workers shifted from hospitals and social agencies to universities (5). In that year the Chicago School of Civics and Philanthropy (now the University of Chicago School of Social Administration) was founded. A year later the New York School of Philanthropy (now the Columbia University School of Social Work) was established. By 1929, centers of professional social work education had been organized in some 25 colleges and universities, located primarily in the Eastern and Midwestern regions of the United States (31). Today, there are more than 435 formally accredited programs of professional social work education (baccalaureate, 315; master's, 85; doctoral, 35) in some 350 colleges and universities located in all parts of the United States, Puerto Rico, Guam, and the U.S. Virgin Islands (14,15). Another seven hundred programs of social work education exist in universities located in other nations of the world (21).

While the curricula of many of the early schools retained features characteristic of agency-oriented apprenticeship training programs, most schools gradually adopted a principles approach to education that better reflected the diversity and status of social work as a new, and rapidly developing, human service profession (4,6,20,25,29). By 1927, sufficient clarity concerning the nature, content, and organization of social work education existed such that the American Association of Schools of Social Work could be charged with responsibility for formulating and maintaining standards for social work education. The Association implemented its accreditation standards in 1932, a function subsequently transferred to and carried forward by its successor organization since 1952, the Council on Social Work Education. Throughout all of this history, the curricula of schools of social work included extensive preparation of social workers for a multiplicity of specialized roles and functions in health care.

The "Core" Social Work Curriculum

Today, curricula of professional social work education programs are well established. All accredited programs require students to demonstrate expertise in a minimum of five "core" knowledge and skill areas (9,10):

The History and Philosophy of American Social Work
Social Policy
Methods of Social Work Research
Principles of Human Behavior in the Social Environment
Methods of Social Work Intervention.

The core social work curriculum includes required and elective courses on the organization of health and welfare services, social administration, and patterns of racial, ethnic, and cultural diversity in the United States. A significant number of courses in the core curriculum offer specialized training in the dynamics of individual and collective human behavior and psycho-social processes. Specialized practice skill courses in methods of individual, family, group, organization, and community intervention also are found in the core curricula of all programs of social work education.

Always, social work students divide their education between formal course work and carefully structured and supervised field practica. Through a pattern of concurrent field and classroom learning, social work students learn to integrate more effectively the theory of social work with the realities of its practice in actual field settings (11,32). In this way, social work graduates usually demonstrate a high level of theoretical and intervention skill often absent in persons graduating from programs that are based either completely, or primarily, on classroom learning only.

The "Specialized" Social Work Curriculum

Because of the extraordinarily diverse nature of social work practice, students also are expected to select an area of concentration[(4)] for in-depth specialization. Specializations may be chosen on the basis of *practice setting* (e.g., health care, mental health, criminal justice, child welfare, rehabilitation, etc.), *population group* (e.g., the aged,

---

(4) Although the terms "concentration" and "specialization" have come to have precise meanings in social work education, here they are used interchangeably.

women, physically disabled, children, etc.), or social work *practice modalities* (e.g., case work, group work, community organization, research, administration, etc.). Specializations usually are accomplished through a series of well-integrated required and elective courses that are completed after the requirements of the core curriculum have been satisfied. Students also must complete carefully structured and supervised field practice experiences in practice settings closely associated with their area of specialization (e.g., hospitals, clinics, prisons, schools, social agencies. etc.).

Current patterns of graduate student preferences regarding areas of specialization in social work are summarized in Tables 3 and 4 (12). The reader should note, for example, the considerable diversity of specializations in social work and the disproportionate number of students choosing to concentrate in one or another area of social work practice. During academic year 1981-1982, 41% of first-year and 58% of second-year students chose method concentrations related to the provision of direct (i.e., "hands-on") services to individuals, families, and groups (Table 3). During the same year, only 28% of all graduate social work students, by contrast, selected concentrations in social administration or other indirect service methods.

TABLE 3
FULL-TIME MASTER'S STUDENTS ENROLLED 11/1/81
BY YEAR AND TYPE OF CONCENTRATION

	First-Year		*Second-Year*	
Type of Concentration	*No.*	*%*	*No.*	*%*
Generic, Multi-Method	2,965	39.5	1,221	13.5
Casework	1,039	13.8	1,361	15.1
Micro, Direct Service, Clinical	1,842	24.5	3,562	39.4
Groupwork	209	2.8	336	3.7
Community Organization, Planning Development	262	3.5	496	5.5
Administration, Management, Social Policy	331	4.4	614	6.8
Mezzo/Macro Intervention	237	3.2	498	5.5
Social Problems	169	2.2	576	6.4
Research or Evaluation	6	0.1	36	0.4
Other, no concentration, not reported	454	6.0	338	3.7
Total	7,514	100.0	9,038	100.0

Source: Council on Social Work Education, 1982:34. Reprinted with permission.

Student preferences for specializations that have a more "clinical approach" to social work practice are reflected further in the data summarized in Table 4. These data show that 38% of first-year and 57% of second-year graduate students elect specialized concentrations in health (i.e., mental health, community mental health, health, alcohol, drug and substance abuse services, mental retardation, rehabilitation) and health-related (i.e., family services) fields of social work practice.

Students, through their choice of specialization, clearly reflect the profession's historical — and continuing — commitment to personal services to individual clients and client groups experiencing a broad range of social, emotional, and physical ills. Student preferences for

TABLE 4
FULL-TIME MASTER'S STUDENTS ENROLLED 11/1/81,
BY YEAR AND FIELD OF PRACTICE IN PRACTICUM

	First Year		*Second Year*		*Total*	
Field of Practice	*No.*	*%*	*No.*	*%*	*No.*	*%*
Mental Health/ Community Mental Health*	1,172	15.6	2,442	27.0	3,614	21.8
Health*	672	8.9	1,185	13.1	1,857	11.2
Family Services*	615	8.2	1,125	12.4	1,740	10.5
Child Welfare	594	7.9	637	7.0	1,231	7.4
Services to the Aged	331	4.4	346	3.8	677	4.1
School Social Work	301	4.0	292	3.2	593	3.6
Public Assist./Welfare	311	4.1	260	2.9	571	3.4
Community Planning	166	2.2	401	4.4	567	3.4
Corrections/Criminal Justice	209	2.8	217	2.4	426	2.6
Group Services	196	2.6	212	2.3	408	2.5
Alcohol, Drug, Substance Abuse Services*	187	2.5	212	2.3	399	2.4
Mental Retardation*	126	1.7	130	1.4	256	1.5
Rehabilitation*	103	1.4	102	1.1	205	1.2
Combined Fields	182	2.4	79	0.9	261	1.6
Other	489	6.5	487	5.4	976	5.9
None or not yet assigned	1,860	24.8	911	10.1	2,771	16.7
Total	7,514	100.0	9,038	100.0	16,552	100.0

Source: Council on Social Work Education, 1982:35. Reprinted with permission.
*Indicates health & health-related field practica.

"clinical" and health concentrations reflect, too, the enhanced status that "medical" and "psychiatric" social workers long have enjoyed through their collaboration with members of other health disciplines and professions. Recent gains in the granting of state-regulated licenses to social workers, and recognition by insurance companies of social workers as independent vendors of psycho-social services, no doubt, also are reflected in the current specialization preferences of graduate-level students.

The Social Work "Health" Curriculum

Nearly all of the nation's 85 graduate schools of social work offer health or health-related concentrations to their students (13). Most concentrations are available as part of the student's second year of specialized study though, increasingly, some schools encourage students to begin specialization studies during their first year of professional education as well. In general, both graduate and undergraduate social work students specializing in health care are able to spend their two years of required field practice in health settings of particular interest to them (e.g., hospitals, outpatient departments, community health clinics, health planning agencies, etc.). In order to assure student familiarity with the full spectrum of health social services, however, the majority of programs require that students divide their field practice experiences among different systems of health care (e.g., medical care vs. mental health care) and various institutional forms of health service delivery (e.g., inpatient vs. outpatient vs. community-based services). Students also are expected, at least initially, to provide services to a heterogeneous population of health clients, albeit the majority of students choose early in their education to work with one or another patient population group (e.g., children, the aged, women, or persons afflicted with a particular type of illness, disability, or other health problem).

Because of the widespread interest in health care practice that long has existed among social work students, the health curricula of graduate schools of social work are rich (27). Considerable variation is to be found in the specialization requirements of each school, however, such that no single program, at least at the present time, can be used to represent all programs of health social service education. Nonetheless, health specialization curriculum requirements parallel those of the core curriculum (i.e., required courses in social policy, research, human behavior, and practice methods) though specialization courses focus on a variety of topics unique to the delivery of health social services rather than on issues of more general interest to the broader social work community.

As an example of one university's approach to health social service education, Table 5 contains a partial listing of health specialization courses available to students enrolled at the University of Pennsylvania School of Social Work. This school was one of the nation's first to develop a fully integrated program of health social service education (16). Of 16 courses identified, 6 to 7 are taken by health-specialization students during their second year of study. Three courses are required of all health students and three may be taken as electives. Electives are chosen on the basis of an "Individualized Educational Plan" developed by students with their academic advisors toward the end of their first year of professional education.

TABLE 5
ILLUSTRATIVE REQUIRED AND ELECTIVE
HEALTH SPECIALIZATION COURSES

Health Services Policy Courses
- *The Organization of Medical and Psychiatric Services
- Alternative Approaches to Health Social Services

Health Services Research Courses
- Principles of Epidemiology
- Health Services Research
- Methods of Clinical Research

Health and Human Behavior Courses
- *Psycho-Social Dynamics of Health and Illness
- Diagnosis and Assessment
- The Health Needs of Specialized Populations (e.g., women, racial/ethnic minorities, homophiles)
- Death and Dying
- Human Sexuality

Health Intervention Courses
- *Advanced Methods in Social Work Practice
- Principles of Psychotherapy
- Principles of Behavior Modification
- Crisis Intervention
- Family Intervention
- *Collaborative Methods

*Indicates required courses. All other courses are electives and may be selected by students on the basis of specialty interest, career goals, and discrete learning objectives.

Students also choose a year-long field placement in a health agency, hospital, or clinic consistent with the practice learning objectives of the student's educational plan. During the last semester of study, students complete a specialization supervised course of independent study that ends with the writing of a report, equivalent in quality and length to a graduate-level thesis.

Though not all programs offer the same degree of rigor or comprehensiveness in the education of their health specialization students, most do require some combination of mandatory and elective courses — ranging from two to six in number. All programs require specialization-related field practice for their students. Many, however, do not require their health specialization students to undertake independent research on, or to write master's theses about, health or health-related social service issues. Despite these variations this author does expect that, in the near future, the health specialization curricula of at least the graduate programs of social work education will more closely approximate one another. Significant efforts in this direction already have begun (2,7,8,23,24).

REGULATION OF SOCIAL WORK PRACTICE

Formal regulation of professional social work began in 1961 with the establishment of the Academy of Certified Social Workers (ACSW). Originally organized as an independent corporation operating under the general supervision of the National Association of Social Workers, the Academy now is an integral professional credentialing unit within the Association. The Academy imposes a set of rigorous educational and experiential requirements on its members. Today, candidates are admitted to the Academy once annually following successful completion of a standardized written competency examination, administered by an independent national testing organization (currently the Educational Testing Service in Princeton, New Jersey). Once admitted to the Academy, individual practitioners are qualified to add the "A.C.S.W." initials after their names. They also are qualified to supervise graduate social work students and, in many practice settings, the A.C.S.W. serves as a prerequisite for promotion to higher administrative ranks.

Since 1975 the National Association of Social Workers also has sought to recognize those social workers who, because of their special credentials and unique practice experience, are especially qualified to be designated as "clinical social workers." In that year the Association created a registry of clinical social workers and, since then, some 9,000 of the Association's 90,000 members have earned the special distinction of being classified as "clinical social workers." Inclusion in the *Register of Clinical Social Workers* is possibly only upon formal application to the Association and after a careful review of the applicant's qualifications by an independent Board of Directors. The *Register of Clinical Social Workers* is updated frequently and serves as a valuable resource for referring clients to properly qualified clinical social workers.

Social work practice also is regulated through a well-articulated code of professional ethics (reprinted in its entirety as Appendix IV of this volume). Like the norms of ethical behavior developed by most human service disciplines to govern the professional activities of their practitioners, the social work *Code of Ethics* serves as a powerful standard for guiding the ethical responsibiities of individual social workers toward their clients. Unlike the ethical codes of many disciplines, however, the social work *Code of Ethics* imposes an additional set of normative requirements on the ethical responsibilities of social workers toward their colleagues, toward their employers and employing organizations, toward the social work profession, and even more generally, toward society itself. Adherence to the ethical principles contained in the Code are monitored through a system of local, state, and national grievance bodies and committees on ethical conduct. The current version of the social work *Code of Ethics* was adopted by the 1979 Delegate Assembly of the National Association of Social Workers.

As of March 1983, 29 states and the territories of Puerto Rico and the Virgin Islands legally regulate the practice of social work within their communities (see Appendix V, Table 1). State laws governing social work practice generally take the form of granting licenses to social workers to practice independently (N=15) or have created a statewide system of legal registration (N=14) that certifies individuals as competent practitioners within the discipline. Colorado and Maine administer a dual system of licensure and registration that grants either one or the other form of recognition to social workers on the basis of their training and years of professional experience. Mandatory continuing professional education requirements exist in 19 of the 31 states and territories that legally regulate social work practice (see Appendix V, Table 3, for a complete listing of these requirements by state).

The majority of states regulating social work require candidates seeking recognition as independent practitioners to pass a state-administered competency examination. Examination Review Committees are interdisciplinary in composition and consist of social workers, practitioners of other licensed or registered disciplines, and members of the general public. In all states the legal regulation of social work is assigned to either an independent review board (N=13) or to an appropriate state consumer protection or professional regulatory body (N=18).

The trend toward increased legal regulation of social work no doubt will continue into the future. The granting of licenses to social workers as independent practitioners has had a profound impact on the legal status of the profession. It also has contributed significantly to the general public's recognition of social work as a mature discipline. Legal regulation also has assured for social workers a place in the care-giving community as practitioners that share in the rights, privileges, and responsibilities already granted to other disciplines during earlier decades (e.g., privileged communication, legal protection of titles and functions, recognition by insurance companies of social workers as independent vendors of reimbursable services, etc.). The legal regulation of social workers has assured for the general public increased control over the nature, quality and competence of persons presenting themselves as social workers. Through the licensure of social workers, both the special professional interests of social workers and the broader consumer protection concerns of the wider community are being served well.

REFERENCES

1. American Association of Schools of Social Work: *Education for the Public Social Services: A Report of the Study Committee.* Chapel Hill: University of North Carolina Press, 1942.
2. Appel, Y.H.: *Social Work and Health Care in the Future: The Challenge of Change.* New Brunswick, N.J.: Rutgers University, 1973.
3. Bartlett, H.M.: *Medical Social Work: A Study of Current Aims and Methods in Medical Social Work.* Washington, D.C.: American Association of Medical Social Workers, 1934.
4. Bartlett, H.M.: *The Common Base of Social Work Practice.* New York: National Association of Social Workers, 1963.
5. Bernard, L.D.: "Education for Social Work," in *Encyclopedia of Social Work.* 17th Edition. 2 Volumes: 290-305. Washington, D.C.: National Association of Social Workers, 1977.
6. Boehm, W.W.: *Objectives of the Social Work Curriculum of the Future,* "Social Work Curriculum Study," Volume 1. New York: Council on Social Work Education, 1959.
7. Bracht, N.F. (ed.): *Social Work in Health Care.* New York: Haworth Press, 1978.

8. Caroff, P. and Mailick, M.: *Social Work in Health Services: An Academic Practice Partnership*. New York: Prodist, 1980.
9. Council on Social Work Education: *Manual of Accrediting Standards for Graduate Professional Schools of Social Work*. New York: CSWE, 1971.
10. Council on Social Work Education: *Standards for the Accreditation of Baccalaureate Degree Programs in Social Work*. New York: Council on Social Work Education, 1974.
11. Council on Social Work Education. *The Dynamics of Field Instruction: Learning Through Doing*. New York: CSWE, 1975.
12. Council on Social Work Education: *Statistics on Social Work Education in the United States, 1981*. New York: CSWE, 1982.
13. Council on Social Work Education: *Statistics on Social Work Education in the United States, 1981*. New York: CSWE, 1982, Table 207, pp. 69-70.
14. Council on Social Work Education: *Schools of Social Work with Accredited Master's Degree Programs*. New York: CSWE, 1982.
15. Council on Social Work Education: *Colleges and Universities with Accredited Undergraduate Social Work Programs*. New York: CSWE, 1982.
16. Estes, R.J.: *Health Specialization Handbook*. Philadelophia: University of Pennsylvania School of Social Work (xerox).
17. Flexner, A.: "Is Social Work a Profession?" in *Studies in Social Work*, Volume 4. New York: New York School of Philanthropy, 1915.
18. French, L.M.: *Psychiatric Social Work*. New York: Commonwealth Fund, 1940.
19. Hagerty, J.E.: *The Training of Social Workers*. New York: McGraw-Hill, 1931.
20. Hollis, E.V. and Taylor, A.L.: *Social Work Education in the United States*. New York: Columbia University Press, 1951.
21. International Association of Schools of Social Work: *Member Schools and Associations*. Vienna, Austria: 1981.
22. Joint Commission of the Association of American Medical Colleges. *Widening Horizons in Medical Education: A Study of the Teaching of Social and Environmental Factors in Medicine*. A Report of the Joint Committee of the Association of American Medical Colleges and the American Association of Medical Social Workers. New York: Commonwealth Fund, 1948.
23. Kerson, T. (ed.): *Social Work in Health Settings*. New York: Longman, 1982.
24. Kumabe, K. *et al.*: *A Handbook for Social Work Education and Practice in Community Health Settings*. Honolulu: University of Hawaii Press, 1977.
25. Milford Conference: *Social Casework: Generic and Specific*. New York: American Association of Social Workers, 1929.
26. National Association of Social Workers: *Professional Social Workers Directory*. New York: NASW, 1978.
27. Perretz, E.A.: "Social Work Education for the Field of Health," *Social Work in Health Care*. 1(3): 357-65, 1976.
28. Reynolds, B.C.: "Between Client and Community: A Study of Responsibility in Social Casework," *Smith College Studies in Social Work*, V, 1934, pp. 5-28.
29. Reynolds, B.C.: *Learning and Teaching in the Practice of Social Work*. New York: Farrar and Rinehart, 1942.
30. Tufts, J.H.: *Education and Training for Social Work*. New York: Russel Sage Foundation, 1923.
31. Turner, J.B. (ed.): "Demographic and Social Welfare Trends," Table 50, in *Encyclopedia of Social Work*. 17th Edition, 2 Volumes: 1669. Washington, D.C.: National Association of Social Workers, 1977.

32. Wilson, S.J.: *Field Instruction: Techniques for Supervisors*. New York: Free Press, 1981, pp. 5-15.
33. Wittman, M.: "The Social Worker in Preventive Services," in *The Social Welfare Forum*. New York: Columbia University Press, 1962, pp. 136-147.

Chapter 2

SOCIAL WORK IN MEDICAL CARE SETTINGS

ANNE-LINDA FURSTENBERG

INTRODUCTION

From the start, social work brought to medical settings the profession's ability to view people within their social environments. During the late 19th century, social work had moved from an individualistic and moral interpretation of people's troubles to the recognition of economic, social, and environmental sources of the problems observed. When Dr. Richard Cabot first invited social workers into Massachusetts General Hospital in 1905, he did so out of his awareness that family, housing, and working conditions were all implicated in the crushing amount of illness encountered in the hospital's clinics. Medical treatment alone could not achieve its aims without taking account of the forces in the patient's total situation (31).

Social work had developed new professional skills of careful diagnosis of the client's life situation and identification of the social and economic factors creating problems. Social workers could use their understanding of the patient's social situation to help them carry out the steps necessary for their recovery and to promote changes in their environment that would keep them well. Social workers could also be expected to humanize the hospital system and to educate the physicians with whom they worked (3,31). This early vision correctly anticipated the potential influence of social work within the medical care system.

Today, social workers in medical care settings have actualized this potential. They carry a major responsibility for integrating into medical treatment attention to the psychological and social needs of patients and for providing a bridge between the medical setting and the patient's home. In doing so, social workers prevent the pressures of family and environmental difficulties from reversing what medical science has achieved.

Social work services in medical care are mandated by major Federal health care programs, as well as by the accrediting body for hospital care, and the Joint Commission on the Accreditation of Hospitals (9,28). As a result, social work is probably now represented in the majority of hospitals. Of hospitals reporting in the annual survey conducted by the American Hospital Association (not all of which are accredited), 80.7% provide social work help for their patients. Nearly all of the larger hospitals that responded to the survey, those with 100 beds and over, include social work services (54).

This chapter will describe in detail the role of social workers in medical care settings. To provide the context, it will first review the way the medical care system is organized in this society. From this will follow the discussion of social work in medical settings, both its central role in the delivery of social services to individuals and families, and other ways in which it carries out its professional mandate. Finally, the discussion will turn to some of the important issues shaping the current delivery of social work services.

Organization of the Medical Care System

It is difficult to characterize the organization of the medical care system, as there is no uniform and overall structure of medical services (18). There are various ways of beginning to categorize by sources of funds, location of services, type of illness, auspices and types of facilities, to give some examples. One way of classifying care might be from the point of view of the patient and problem and the type of care needed. In this perspective, care can be described as *primary care, secondary or specialty care*, and *tertiary or hospital care.*

In *primary care*, patients are seen by a primary physician — pediatrician, internist or general practitioner for preventive procedures and checkups, diagnosis and, when possible, treatment of illness. This, then, constitutes the first line of health promotion and maintenance. (Routine gynecological care, though delivered by a specialist, fits this description of primary care.) Primary care physicians refer patients to specialists for *secondary care*, i.e., the treatment of conditions that are best managed by a physician with specialized expertise, in surgery, psychiatry or dermatology, for example.

Both primary and specialty care can be provided as ambulatory or outpatient services, but may extend, when required, into the hospital. Patients are admitted (usually) when their condition is serious enough to require intensive surveillance and treatment, or the type of treatment procedure is deemed best carried out within a hospital. Fig. 1 depicts the basic structure of medical care in the U.S.

FIGURE 1

FLOW OF MEDICAL CARE IN U.S.A.

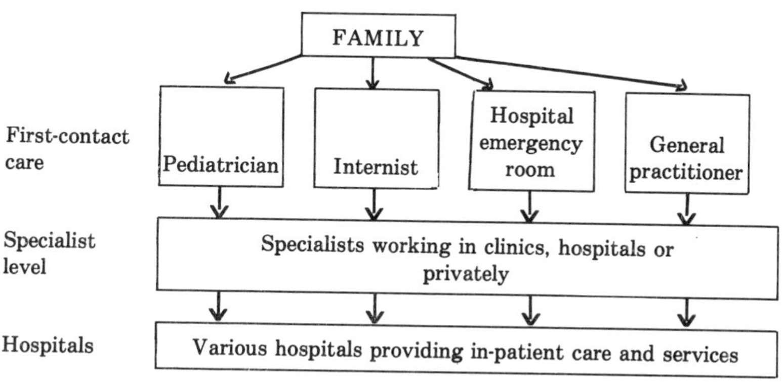

Source: Fry, John: *Medicine in Three Societies*. New York: Elsevier, 1970.

While these categories describe *types* of care, the site in which medical services are delivered, and the way practitioners are organized are other variable factors. Ambulatory (outpatient) care is rendered by physicians in private offices, clinics or health centers, sometimes within a hospital facility, as well as in hospital emergency rooms. Physicians may practice privately alone (solo practice) or in groups, may be part of a Health Maintenance Organization or other prepaid group practice or may be salaried staff in a program funded under some other institutional auspices. As of 1974. approximately 30% of practicing physicians were hospital-based (39).

Hospital Care is supervised by physicians in various types of relationships to the facility: trainees (interns and residents), physicians with "visiting privileges," i.e., they are granted access for admitting patients, or paid staff and attending physicians. Of course, much of the actual physical care is delivered by nurses and other types of professional staff such as physical and occupational therapists, technicians of many sorts, pharmacists and nutritionists. The type of physician, and the way the physicians and other staff are administered and organized leads to considerable variability in the style and quality of care.

Finally, hospitals must be distinguished by their *auspices* — who sponsors and pays for them. Proprietary hospitals are run for profit; voluntary non-profit hospitals, which make up the largest proportion of all hospitals, may be sponsored either by local communities or church groups. Municipalities and counties may own and administer general and specialty hospitals for the medically indigent, and state hospitals care for the chronically ill, mostly those with mental conditions (18). Finally, Federal agencies operate a system of hospitals mainly for the military and veteran populations.

Voluntary hospitals can be divided into two rough categories. 1) Community hospitals, usually local and small, serve patients in the local area and are staffed by local, office based physicians. 2) Teaching hospitals are larger (500-2000 beds) with intensive residency programs and often with medical school affiliations. These offer highly specialized, advanced and even experimental kinds of care. A teaching hospital may serve a large region and draw problem cases referred from many community hospitals surrounding it (39). To such a hospital would be channelled patients with less frequently occurring conditions requiring unusual treatments. Specialized treatment for such conditions as burns, cancer, or rare neurological conditions is organized in some places so that one main center provides care for the surrounding region.

Another distinction must be drawn between the general hospital, which offers many kinds of care, and the specialty setting such as an eye hospital or cancer center. With changes in the system of payment for care (such as Medicare and Medicaid) and the changing economic resources for governmental hospitals, the functioning, relationships among, and quality of these institutions is in almost constant flux.

The way medical care is paid for, like the system of care itself, has no overall organization. Direct payment by consumers and third party payments, public expenditures, private health insurance, and contributions by industry and philanthropic institutions, provide the two categories of funds that pay for American health care. Public expenditures come from federal, state and local government and include programs for specified beneficiaries, such as veterans or crippled children, women's compensation benefits and Medicare and

Medicaid which fund medical care for the elderly, disabled and poor. Public funds supported 40.6% of all health care expenditures in 1978 while private funds paid 59.4%. Third party payments — all of those not paid *directly* by the consumer — amounted to 67.1% of all personal health care expenditures; 38.7% paid by public funds, 27.0% by private health insurance carriers and 1.3% by philanthropy and industry (55). While the payment by consumers of 22.9% of the costs (over and above their investment in private insurance) might appear just, it must be remembered that all but the very poorest pay something toward their care, as each system of underwriting costs leaves residual charges to the consumer, in the form of deductibles, co-payments for a portion of expenditures, the cost of medications, and other such items. Such costs fall unfairly on the elderly with fixed incomes, and others of the economically disadvantaged groups more in need of health care. Health care costs equalling 20.4% of the income of older people are not covered by Medicare, as of 1982, and the beneficiaries themselves pay the major share of these (56).

An important facet of payment for care is whether it is organized on the basis of "fee for service," in which the patient or a third party is billed for each specific procedure or visit, or "prepaid" with a set premium covering contractually agreed on categories of services. The fixed premium of the Health Maintenance Organizations, for example, covers both inpatient and outpatient services (8).

Not surprisingly, given its haphazard organization, analysts identify a number of problems afflicting the American health care system. The cost of health care represents a vexing and persistent crisis, particularly in the face of the current, grim economic situation. Total health expenditures in 1978 reached $192.4 billion, more than doubling during the decade of the 70's. The public portion of these expenditures (40.6%) increased at a disproportionately high rate, stabilizing in the late 70's to annual increased of 13-13.5% (55). The Medicare program cost $50 billion in 1982 and projections set 1987 levels at $100 million (40).

There are many reasons for these startling increases: rising demand, due in part to the enlargement of the elderly portion of the population; over-utilization of the hospital for diagnostic procedures; lack of incentives for physicians to keep costs down, and the expansive if not exploitative use of the Medicare system by some physicians, to name a few. Finally, prices of just about every element of medical care, drugs, supplies, facilities, salaries and other fees, have been increasing steadily (55).

In response to the growing alarm over the skyrocketing cost of care, in the early 1970's Congress enacted legislation creating three different health care cost control mechanisms. Professional Standards Review Organizations (PSRO's—1972) were designed to hold down hospital utilization by reviewing the appropriateness and adequacy of care. Health Maintenance Organizations (HMO's—1973) built in incentives for physicians to limit patient visits, laboratory and other tests, and hospitalization, through use of a fixed prepaid premium. Health Systems Agencies (HSA's—1974) were mandated to review and control the distribution of services and facilities, cutting costs by promoting ambulatory rather than the much more expensive hospital care, and by checking competitive and wasteful duplication of resources within an area (7,43).

At this point, the crisis has merely deepened. An anti-regulatory federal administration is in the process of weakening or eliminating the HSA's. At the same time, pressures to cut expenditures for social programs, while the defense budget swells, have led to painful cutbacks in Federal funds for health programs and threats to the Medicare program (and the entire Social Security system). In an era of increasing prices and decreasing dollar power, American consumers can afford less of the health care they need.

Inevitably, financial woes compound the difficulties American consumers experience in gaining access to medical care. In the current economic situation, many Americans have no doubt contracted their use of medical services, at the same time that the stress of unemployment and the threat of it increase the amount of illness. Other problems of access result from maldistribution of health resources between underserved rural and over-supplied urban areas, as well as from geographic remoteness of health facilities from poor neighborhoods. Finally, there are social and psychological barriers to optimal care, in the form of cultural differences, an impersonal system and discriminatory practices.

Many other issues in the organization of medical care compromise its quality. Medical services may be fragmented, uncoordinated, and incomplete. One person may receive care in several different facilities, or in different specialties within one facility, with no one provider taking responsibility for coordination or overall supervision of the individual's care. Patients may as a result receive incompatible medications and conflicting instructions; families may be treated in an atomized fashion, as though the baby's illness or the father's unemployment had nothing to do with the mother's ulcer, headaches, or mental illness. Dividing the patient among a series of specialists, who never communicate with one another, is still the mode. As a result, most medical facilities fall short of the ideal of comprehensive, coordinated, continuous, family centered care, a form of care that takes account of the whole patient rather than treating him/her as a disconnected set of diseases.

The health care system also suffers from a heavy emphasis on glamorous, expensive, high-technology treatments of acute conditions, because of the nature of medical training and of the way the medical professional assigns prestige and status among its members. Physicians as a group devote little attention to programs of prevention, such as altering life-style patterns of diet, exercise or smoking, and even less to environmental pressures and poisons creating illness (34). While the prestige follows the skilled and decisive intervention in acute conditions, chronic illness consumes the bulk of medical treatment; older people suffer much of that chronic illness. Chronic illness, particularly that of elderly people, receives little medical research attention. The treatment of the chronically ill elderly may in addition be colored by stereotyped attitudes that result in a feeling of apathy and hopelessness on the part of medical professionals.

The following picture emerges. American medical care has evolved a system geared mainly to treating disease and neglecting prevention. It has failed to check costs or to institute rational coordination. It has organized in such a way as to promote fragmented care focused on diseases rather than on patients. This description of the medical care system serves as a background to examining the role of social workers within that system.

Social work is a profession, the purposes of which are to:

1. To enhance the problem-solving capacities of people.
2. To link people with the systems that provide them with resources, services and opportunities.
3. To promote the effective and humane operations of these systems.
4. To contribute to the development and improvement of social policy (45).

The bulk of this chapter will describe in the many ways in which social workers, providing direct services to individuals and families, support problem-solving and link people to resources, both within and outside of the medical setting. It will also show how they promote the humane and effective operation of the system. Other roles of social workers in medical care settings will then be briefly described. Social workers also fill roles as administrators, planners and resource developers, educators, advocates and researchers. Each of these roles extends the capacity of social workers to promote more effective health policies.

It should be noted that social workers are not distributed evenly throughout the medical care system. Most social workers in medical care settings are concentrated in large general and teaching hospitals, usually 100 beds or larger (54). Thus their attention focuses around the treatment of illness and in particular the inpatient population in need of discharge planning (9). Hospitals devote fewer social work resources to outpatient care, and very few social workers are employed anywhere in primary care settings (26). Not surprisingly, jobs emerge where the system experiences and perceives problems that cost money, e.g., inpatient care and discharge planning. The section on indirect social work roles will make clear the ways in which professional social workers can demonstrate the need for their services in additional areas.

SOCIAL SERVICES TO INDIVIDUALS AND FAMILIES

Now, as in the past, the central task of social work in medical care settings is the delivery of social services to patients and their families. Such social work help most commonly has as its goals: 1) the facilitation of the patient's access to care and effective use of care; 2) the alleviation of emotional distress of patient and family over health problems; and 3) the resolution of problems created by the patient's illness or condition. These goals will be illustrated in more detail below.

How social workers and patients come into contact with each other varies from setting to setting. In some facilities, patients are referred to social workers by physicians or other professionals only when problems manifest themselves. Some circumstances which might lead to referral are conflict between the patient and the physician, signs of overwhelming emotional distress, or the inability of a patient to care for himself or herself on returning home. In other settings, social workers may routinely contact all patients in certain categories, such as all renal dialysis patients, all who are over 65, or those with other characteristics that have been found to be associated with problems. Social workers covering a specific clinic or medical service may screen or review all charts for signs of incipient difficulties. Planning prior to admission to the hospital may be structured into the system so that problems affecting entry and discharge can be anticipated and resolved. The earlier in the patients' care the social worker begins to work with them, the better the chances of finding timely solutions to problems. For this reason, the method used to find cases and establish contact has serious consequences for the adequacy of social work service delivery. In a later section, this issue will be examined more closely.

Professional social work practice includes a number of phases. These are:

1) Assessment
2) Social service planning
3) Service delivery
4) Evaluation, termination and follow-up

The distinctions among these phases are analytical ones and the processes are not necessarily carried out in clearly separated stages. Assessment, for example, will continue throughout the social worker-patient relationship as new information comes to light. In the same way, social worker and patient may evaluate, at many steps along the way, the results of actions they have just carried out. Each of the phases of social work help will be described.

Assessment

In the assessment process, the social worker gathers several kinds of information that have bearing on how the patient will deal with the condition that has brought him/her for medical care. Social worker and patient review together how the patient understands the condition and is responding to it. They identify problem areas and explore the sources of the problems. When the social service contact has resulted from problems already pressing and obvious, such as discharge planning, these become the starting point for assessment. The social worker also elicits background information that will be important for understanding the patient's situation and reactions. Finally, social worker and patient explore possible resources that can be brought to bear on the problems that have been identified.

How broad or detailed the assessment is depends on the nature of the setting, the kind of problem and the likely duration of the contact with the patient. Assessment may of necessity be limited and focused if a hospitalized patient requires short-term crisis intervention for overwhelming anxiety. In contrast, the social worker will carry out a more comprehensive assessment of a patient's total social situation when the patient is going to require help with long term medical treatment and extensive adjustments to drastically changed physical functioning.

Social workers gather information through interviewing and through observation. While they conduct the assessment with the patient and family, they also collect important data from the physician, other health care professionals, or the medical record. Their attention must be given to the functioning of the patient and the family in relation to their total social situation. The social worker must also observe the patient's transactions with the health care system and weigh how well the patient's needs are being met. The social worker will explore, as appropriate, the common issues affecting patients in health care settings.

Three categories of problems can be distinguished (see Fig. 2). Managing entry to the health care system creates one set of problems (35). Patients may bring their problems in getting to the medical care setting directly to the social worker, but more commonly social workers become aware of problems indirectly. When patients have difficulties in travelling to a medical facility and in being able to use it, these problems manifest themselves in delays in seeking care, broken appointments, resistance to hospitalization, or failure to follow through on prescribed regimens. In such situations, the social worker must establish contact with the patient and explore the nature of the difficulties interfering with the use of care.

Physical access may be made difficult by deficiencies in the health care system or in a particular health care facility. For example, a health care institution may be located far from the neighborhood of the people requiring the care. Money for transportation may be scarce, and there may be little organized provision for such situations. Transportation may become a particularly critical issue when patients must make frequent visits for treatments such as radiation.

Payment for medical care services may be another reason for not using care. Medical Assistance pays for the medical care of the "medically indigent" (those below a set income level) and public assistance recipients. Medicare funds the health care of older people and the disabled. Others are covered by health insurance. Some patients and families, however, fall between these systems because they earn too much to be considered medically indigent, but not enough to finance health insurance or pay for their care directly. In addition, each scheme for financing care has its inadequacies. Each plan excludes certain categories of care from its coverage; some plans require deductibles or co-payments that create problems for patients.

FIGURE 2

PROBLEMS PATIENTS FACE

1. ENTRY TO SYSTEM (outpatient or inpatient)
   A. Access to services (patient's eligibility for services and ability to pay, availability of services)
   B. Transportation
   C. Ability to negotiate a confusing system
   D. Other impediments, i.e., dependent children or parents at home
2. REACTIONS TO THE ILLNESS
   A. Emotional impact of illness on patient and family
      1. Anxiety and fear
      2. Anger
      3. Depression
      4. Long-term adjustments in self-image
   B. Practical impact of illness on the patient's functioning and family's functioning.
      1. Earning a living
      2. Physical care of dependents
      3. Emotional well being of family members
   C. Practical needs of treating an illness
      1. Medicine
      2. Equipment
      3. Regimens
   D. Planning for discharge
      1. Home care
      2. Convalescent care
      3. Rehabilitative care
3. DEALING WITH THE SYSTEM
   A. Dysfunctional transactions with medicare care system
      1. Poor communication
      2. Traumatic impact of hospitalization

Paying for care is still a source of considerable stress for many families and often a barrier to the optimal use of care.

The nature of the system confronting patients may also interfere with their use of health care services. The way in which entry to the system is organized may be confusing, difficult to negotiate, impersonal or even outright hostile. In contrast, an accessible health facility will present to patients an orderly, comprehensible system, and humane dignified treatment. Such aspects of the setting may have important consequences for the ease or difficulty with which patients present themselves for care.

For some patients, it is not the health care system, but the home situation that makes the use of health care services difficult. Some may find it impossible to give up home or family responsibilities long enough to seek needed outpatient or in-hospital care. A wage earner may require surgery, but find no alternative support available for his family. A mother may have no one to care for her children while she receives prenatal care or enters the hospital for delivery. An elderly woman may have no one to care for her mentally impaired husband when she requires treatment in the hospital. Patients suffering serious social problems such as drug addiction or alcoholism may neglect their medical needs because they fear rejection or discrimination because of their stigmatized condition. All of these difficulties can lead to irregular or delayed use of care.

Finally, patients' own beliefs and attitudes sometimes stand in the way of their constructive use of health services. They may neither know that care is needed nor believe that it can help. Some patients are afraid to enter the unfamiliar setting and to deal with strangers. Others fear being told that something is seriously wrong with them. Their past experiences have not taught them to expect effective help.

Reactions to the illness create a second set of difficulties (5,36,46). While merely managing entry to the medical care system may pose a number of problems to patients, all patients with conditions of any consequence face another set of problems in adjusting to their illness or condition. Patients are often referred to social work because their reactions are interfering with care or because their responses are so strong or atypical that they are taken as evidence of severe difficulties. Because this is a central focus of social work help, the social worker must always assess how the patient is responding to the condition.

Illnesses can be seen as posing two kinds of problems for patients and families: internal, emotional problems and external, environmental problems. All illness arouses powerful emotional responses. A life-threatening condition may arouse feelings of vulnerability, anxiety, grief, depression, anger, or all of these at once. A pregnancy may be greeted with joy or consternation, and in either case requires enormous adjustments in the mother's identity of self-image. Patients suffering chronic illness or permanent injury must accomplish a series of internal adjustments to "work through" the grief and anger surrounding the condition, and to integrate the changed physical capacities into their self-image. Family members too experience strong emotional reactions to the patient's condition; they, too, must make emotional adjustments to the changed circumstances of the patient, whether temporary or permanent.

Emotional responses manifest themselves in various ways. Patients and families sometimes experience a period of disbelief, shock, and horror. Unti they have time to assimilate the "bad news," people may appear unconcerned or apathetic. They may lash out in anger at the health professionals attempting to care for them. They may simply be so upset and overwhelmed that they are unable to begin to take the necessary actions. Patients and family members can have difficulties in coping with their emotional reactions; without intervention, these may hinder the optimal use of care, or lead to long-term damage to family coping patterns.

Patients and families also have to accomplish external adjustments, i.e., specific behavioral changes to cope with the period of acute illness, the demands of treatment regimens or the long-term changes in life-style and functioning. Illnesses have an impact on the patient's functioning in work and family roles. A family must find a way to pay the bills when the wage earner is incapacitated, for example. Child care or housekeeping needs must be managed while one of the parents is hospitalized. A pregnancy requires planning for the confinement period and provision for the care of the infant. An illness affects the total functioning of the patient's family, and family members may experience difficulty in other aspects of their lives as they deal with the serious illness of one of their members. For example, a wife's work life may suffer due to the demands placed on her by her husband's incapacitation.

Patients and family members also have to solve problems in carrying out the treatment of the illness. Patients and families play a role in the treatment of most illness and only rarely, for example during surgery, is treatment totally in the hands of the health care professionals. Patients need to procure medicines and equipment (such as walkers or commodes), and to learn their proper use. They must also learn new regimens for dealing with the illness — daily exercises, or a special way of preparing food. These needs can create practical problems, when patients don't have money for needed items, or have difficulty in learning or adjusting to a regimen.

Finally, the patient's need for physical care may prove difficult to manage. If patients are physically weak, or confined to bed or home, others must meet the requirements of daily living for them. For those living alone, or living with people unable to assume these responsibilities, these needs may pose problems. When there is no one to care for an incapacitated patient during the period of convalescence, or when rehabilitative services are required, then the necessary facilities must be found to provide these services.

Reactions to the health care system itself constitute a third source of difficulties. Emotional discomfort is exacerbated when patients don't understand what is wrong or what is going to be done to them. Problems in communicating this information can arise from several sources (17,36). Professionals use technical knowledge and technical language to describe conditions and procedures. Patients are not always able to translate into lay terms. Health care providers sometimes forget to provide necessary information to patients about what is happening to them. Even when the information is given, patients may be too anxious to assimilate it. When patients receive insufficient information about their condition and about procedures, they are less equipped to cope with their situation. They may exhibit feelings of helplessness and lack of control in the form of hostility, apathy, or withdrawal, as well as diminished capacity for working at solving problems.

Patients who enter the hospital face additional difficulties (32,40). Simply being in the hospital can undermine coping capacities and lead the patient to feel overwhelmed. There are many stressful features of hospital care, over and above the threat from illness. The demands of hospital routines, added to whatever loss of physical functioning the illness itself imposes, frequently force hospitalized patients to relinquish control over many aspects of their usual behavior and daily routines. Confined to a small room, dressed in hospital gown or other sleeping clothes, the patient often is cut off from the means of presenting himself or herself as a competent, well functioning, *whole* person. The patient's behavior must conform to the routines of the hospital, rather than to personal inclination as to when to take a bath, eat, get out of bed, etc. Separation from family or other usual companions — their presence limited to visiting hours and their number restricted — compounds the sense of alienation. Even telephone contact with loved ones may be difficult.

The painful, alienating, and frightening procedures to which patients must submit add to the trauma of hospitalization. Patients are wheeled about, often in a prone position, to wait in unfamiliar surroundings until an x-ray or other type of procedure can be carried out. Surgery is followed by a period of pain, helplessness, sometimes frightening changes in the body, insertion of tubes, and a variety of assaults on the physical integrity.

Some age groups are more vunerable than others to these stressful features of the hospital. The traumatic impact of hospitalization on children has been widely recognized (53), but elderly people also evidence a special vulnerability (37). Because of changes in their capacity to adapt and the slowing of their cognitive functioning, older persons may be more dependent on familiar surroundings and more prone to become disoriented while hospitalized (12).

Overt discriminatory treatment of older people, and of racial and ethnic minority patients may add to the difficulties of hospitalization. Members of low status groups are more likely to be ignored or mistreated. Even without overt discrimination, age or cultural difference may separate hospital staff and patients, interfere with communication, and aggravate feelings of alienation, rejection, and being judged negatively. Such groups also may be less sophisticated about what to expect in the hospital.

These features of hospitalization, separately and in combination with one another, frequently undermine rather than support the coping capacities of patients. A social worker dealing with a hospitalized patient will assess the patient's response to being in the hospital, and look for factors in the situation which might be intensifying the patient's distress. Figure 2 sums up the problems confronting patients in medical care settings.

Several kinds of background information about patients are used in assessment (see Fig. 3). The social situation of the patient provides important information. In the course of assessment, social workers observe or elicit information they think will have bearing on the patient's ability to cope with his or her present situation. Basic data about the patient's social situation will yield several valuable kinds of information. A picture of the family configuration and family functioning will reveal areas such as child care, in which strains may develop, or from which support will be forthcoming, such as a strong sibling or extended family network. Information about the patient's and family's occupational work life yields the same dual focus: possible strains and the availability of support in the form of financial resources or of friends and workmates. The social groupings to which the family relates, such as the church or neighborhood, can be possible sources of help; they also reflect the patient's level of social functioning.

Certain characteristics of patients such as their ethnic background and social class also produce some of the variations in how they respond to illness. Members of an ethnic group are socialized to perceive and respond to illness in the characteristic ways shared by that group. Jews and Italians, for example, have been observed to be more sensitive to pain and more expressive of their feelings about being in pain; persons of "old American" extraction tend to be more stoical and detached about pain. Moreover, Jews' concern about pain focuses on its diagnostic and prognostic meanings, and its implications for their future achievement, while Italians dwell on the present discomfort itself (60). Ethnic differences also account for variations in attitudes toward and behavior within the medical care setting (23).

FIGURE 3

SOCIAL WORKERS GATHER BACKGROUND INFORMATION ABOUT THE PATIENT

1) Social Situation
   - Family
   - Work
2) Demographic Characteristics
   - Race
   - Sex
   - Ethnicity
   - Social Class
3) Developmental Stage
4) Past History and Past Coping Patterns

While ethnic groups within the larger society socialize their members to understand and act in distinctive ways, the resources commanded by those in a specific status also shape the manner in which they respond to illness. The concept of "social class" designates the variations in financial, educational, and other resources, determined to a large extent by occupation. First and foremost, of course, having money enables people to pay for medical care; the very fact that care is accessible influences them to define illness as intolerable and requiring treatment. Social class, however, provides not only money but also linguistic and social ease, supportive social networks and other resources that facilitate use of medical services. Like class and ethnicity, race and sex also influence attitudes and resources for dealing with illness.

The social worker will also note the age and developmental stage of the patient and make some observations about how the patient is dealing with the developmental tasks of the particular stage.

Health conditions have different implications at different stages, for the developmental tasks of a stage both complicate and are complicated by the impact of the condition (46). For example, adolescents' conflicting dependency and autonomy needs might interfere with their acceptance of parental supervision of regimens. An illness throws them back into greater dependence precisely when they are striving for independence. Other illustrations are easy to find: responsibilities of mature adults as parents of young children are most disrupted by an illness. A person in old age will be readier to give up occupational roles than a young adult just entering the work world, and this may compromise his/her motivation to recover. The developmental stage also, of course, influences the patterns of supportive social resources and material wherewithal available to the sick person.

The situations patients have faced in the past and their usual ways of dealing with problems will have an important bearing on their present coping resources. Experience with the condition, or with illness in general, will color the patient's emotional response. This may or may not be helpful for present functioning. If the patient's father died of a heart condition, such a diagnosis may be particularly terrifying to a patient. On the other hand, experience with past hospitalization can prepare a patient for a current one. A hernia patient, for example, may report lower levels of distress at hospitalization when he has gone through the surgery before.

Social workers also explore how patients and families have dealt with illness and other troubles in the past. Does the person tend to resolve problems independently or to turn to others? Have family members been responsive or unresponsive to the patient's need for help in the past?

One other feature of coping has a bearing on present adaptation. When people have gone through several crises or life transitions in the very recent past, their personal and network coping resources may be overstrained or depleted (20,21,46). A women who has lost her mother and separated from her husband within the last few months may be more devastated by a child's illness than is a mother who has had a year of relative tranquility.

Social workers assemble a picture of the patients' cultural backgrounds, past crises, current situations, and the resources or constraints each of them reveals for current problem solving. Each setting requires a somewhat different depth and emphasis in the information gathered for assessment purposes. However, standard formats for assessment are being developed for use by social workers in health care. Figures 4 and 5 are two examples of such assessment formats[1].

FIGURE 4

A CONCEPTUAL MODEL FOR A MEDICAL-SOCIAL DIAGNOSIS

I. Individualization of the Patient: value considerations (considerations of him or her as a whole person, a unique individual)
II. Analysis of the Patient's Illness or Disability
    A. Technical information (diagnosis or prognosis: possible permanent impairment)
    B. Socioethnic cultural influences
    C. Social implications (visibility, criticality, chronicity, predictability)
III. Analysis of the Psychosocial Impact of the Illness on the Patient and His Social Milieu
    A. The patient's or his family's perception of his problems and goals
    B. The social system review
        1. Roles and prior social functioning: life-style (who he or she is: background, capacities, prior performance)
        2. Reactions to illness and life situation: feelings, attitudes, motivation for coping
        3. Relationships within his or her social milieu (who they are; nature of relationships)
        4. Resources for coping with his or her problems
            a. Financial (sources of payment for care; source of support)
            b. Environment (community and housing; physical and emotional security)
            c. Institutional (vocational, educational, religious, and social agencies)
            d. Personal: family, friends, affiliations (that influence behavior or experiences; coping ability)
IV. Medical-Social Diagnosis (Impression and Plan)
    A. Assessment of the problem presented through the four Rs
    B. Medical, personal, interpersonal, practical (Impression)
    C. The range of interventive measures to be instituted and by whom (Plan)

Source: Bertha Doremus. "The Four R's: Social Diagnosis in Health Care," *Health and Social Work* 1, No. 4 (November 1976): 127. Reprinted with permission of the National Association of Social Workers.

[1] It must be stressed that assessment formats are intended *only* to *order* the content gathered during an assessment interview. They should not be used as interview guides.

FIGURE 5

THE SOCIAL STATUS EXAMINATION IN HEALTH CARE

A. *THE EXAMINATION ITEMS*

ITEM 1. Indicate 1) the developmental stage in life to which this client belongs; and 2) the development level the client has achieved.

ITEM 2. Indicate the client's illness. Explore together with the client(s) the impact of the illness or disability on the client's current behavior. Some illnesses directly modify behavior, while in other cases behavior change is an indirect result of illness.

ITEM 3. Illness and disability nearly always influence the quality of membership in family and with other important persons. What are the family and other membership issues linked to the client's illness?

ITEM 4. If the client is a member of a racial or ethnic minority there may be some specific relationship between the illness and such group membership(s). In addition, cultural factors often influence the social management of illness, as may issues of gender and sexual identity.

ITEM 5. Estimate social class membership of the client(s) and its connection with the social management of illness. The class values of social workers and client(s) may differ and this needs to be taken into account in the evaluation of how clients deal with illness or disability.

ITEM 6. How does the client's illness influence his/her occupation? Include here a brief discussion of abiities/disabilities, temporary or permanent, limitations in work functioning, etc.

ITEM 7. How does the client's illness/disability influence his/her financial condition? What income maintenance efforts are being made? Does the client have savings, is he/she supported by others, and by whom?

ITEM 8. Does the client have health, accident, disability, life insurance? Is it being used to pay for the illness/disability? Who pays? Is he/she entitled to Veterans' benefits?

ITEM 9. What transportation is available to the client? To relatives or other visitors?

ITEM 10. What kind of housing is available to this client? What is the impact on illness/disability on housing as well as housing on illness/ disability? Who lives with the client?

ITEM 11. Describe the client's mental functioning. Is he/she aware of time, place, person? Can the client participate knowledgably in decision making in regard to his/her future?

ITEM 12. Does the client understand the nature of his/her illness/disability? How does the client express concern over the illness/disability?

ITEM 13. Can this client follow medication and other self-care instructions?

ITEM 14. How ready or reluctant is the client in asking for help? Or in using it where offered? How well does the client work with the social worker or other health care personnel?

B. Write a summary based on your material from A-14 with a formulation of this client or clients.

C. Write an assessment of this client(s) based on your interview(s) related to Section A 1-14.

Source: Hans Falck, The Social Status Examination in Health Care. Virginia Commonwealth University, 1980. Reprinted with the permission of the author.

The process of social work assessment does not merely comprise the gathering of information and the identification of problems. Rather, this process accomplishes much more to set the stage for service delivery. One task is to introduce the patient (and/or family) to the nature of the work together. The patient and social worker begin their work as strangers. Most patients have only vague or stereotyped expectations of the social worker, limited perhaps to help with financial problems or discharge plans. The completeness of the information patients will share depends on the social worker's ability to communicate effectively his or her function and role, and the purpose of the interview. The social worker must be able to explain these clearly and succinctly, and to seek feedback that the patient has understood. By doing so, the social worker indicates the topics that will be appropriate to discuss and the types of activities he or she is available to carry out. This creates structure for the patient with resultant certainty and direction for his or her communicating. It also informs the patient about what kinds of help he or she can expect from the social worker (23,38,48,52).

Early in their contact, the social worker must also demonstrate the kind of person he/she is. To communicate about difficulties and undertake the work required, patients must feel that the social worker will understand and be able to help. They must sense that the social worker is listening carefully, and understanding the specific way they are experiencing their situation and is appreciating the difficulty and pain they face. With words, gestures, and facial expression, the social worker demonstrates to the patient that he/she is being understood and encourages further communication. The social worker may "reflect back" feelings, or may "reach for" feelings, helping the patient to articulate his emotions and attitudes about a matter under discussion (38,52). During assessment the social workers must also show that he/she commands the resources and expertise to be able to offer effective help.

The social worker also demonstrates the purposefulness of their work together through the focused, well-directed exploration of the patient's situation. Skilled questioning both explores an area and maintains the focus on a particular topic. At the same time, the social worker must listen for and help the patient articulate his/her concerns. Maintaining the balance between being attuned to the patient's feelings and carrying out the tasks of assessment and service planning is a skill acquired through much practice.

Another task accomplished during the process of assessment is the mobilization of the coping resources of the patient or client. By involving the client in the discussion of the situation, by supportive listening and by reflective analysis together, the social worker begins the process of engaging or supporting the patient's problem-solving efforts. Whenever possible social workers make assessments in a way that conveys the mutuality of the process. For example, when appropriate, the social workers help patients or family members express their own ideas about solutions to problems they have identified together.

Social Service Planning

Assessment ends and social service planning begins with "contracting" — an explicit agreement about how the social worker and client will proceed. The agreement or "contract" defines which problems need to be solved, which of them is most urgent, what the priorities will be, what will be done, and who will carry out the specific tasks. For example, a woman facing a mastectomy may agree that her first priorities are a plan for her children's care, their emotional needs and their need for information and her communication with them. The social worker and client will agree on a plan of action for each of these problems (13,48).

As a step linking assessment and social service planning, the social worker reviews and organizes the information s/he has gleaned about the patient, the illness, and the total situation. This will be written down in a form ranging from a brief social summary or evaluation to a detailed history and psychosocial assessment, depending on the nature of the treatment and the requirements of the setting. The summary formulates a view of the patient and situation, including facts gathered and conclusions inferred (clearly distinguished from one another). The written assessment concludes with the statement of the problem identified, the order in which they will be attacked, and the plan of action for each. This may serve merely to organize the social worker's thinking, planning, and subsequent work, but can also be used to communicate to other professionals or agencies information that will help them in their work with the patient. In some settings, written contracts are used with patients, often for the purpose of keeping their work with the social worker well focused.

Depending on who must be involved in problem-solving, social service planning takes place with the patient, with family members and with other health professionals. While planning might be viewed as part of assessment, there are good reasons for emphasizing it as a discrete, distinct step. An explicit planning step focuses the actions of social worker, patient and others involved. It guarantees patient's and family's right of self-determination, in that, when possible, they must be aware of and agree to the steps to be carried out. Plans may, of course, need to be reformulated, but making explicit initial and revised plans prevents drifting into courses of action which may have not been well thought out. Finally, a defined set of goals and methods provides a baseline for later evaluation of the work accomplished.

Service Delivery

There are many facets to the services social workers offer. For heuristic purposes, they are separated for discussion here. We will examine a number of separate facets: counseling and emotional support; resource provision; collaboration and consultation; and group services. (Figure 6 provides an overview.) With the exception of group services, service delivery in medical settings almost always includes all of these. "Counseling" — a way of supporting the patient and relieving painful feelings — permeates all transactions between social workers and patients. The process of problem-solving to find resources and meet needs created by the illness is in fact a counseling process. Only as the social worker is able to attend to and respond to feelings can the patient's energies and capacities be freed for problem-solving. The use of a supportive accepting relationship is essential to all social work help.

Supportive counseling with patient and family is helpful in several ways. An earlier section described the sources and consequences of the painful emotions experienced by patients and families in the face of a serious illness. These strong feelings interfere with taking in new data, and with using the information already at hand, and therefore with the process of problem-solving and adaptation. For example, a man who experiences deep grief over the loss of a limb, but cannot acknowledge or express this feeling, is likely to remain preoccupied with the loss. He may be hindered from progress toward integrating his changed state into his self-image and from seeking substitute activities and gratifications. The social worker may help such a patient to voice his feelings and to talk about the meaning of his situation and his reactions to it. Patients experiencing profound feelings of fear, loss and anger can be helped to feel better just through talking about them, sometimes repeatedly. When such feelings can be expressed and understood, the patient's coping and adaptive abilities are sustained and released.

FIGURE 6

HOW SOCIAL WORKERS HELP

Problems of Patient and Family	*Examples of Interventions*	*Possible Resources*
Painful, overwhelming feelings; fear, isolation, grief	Explore, empathize, listen reflectively	1. Social worker's relationship
	Support patient's ventilation of feelings, mobilize coping abilities	2. Patient's coping and self-healing abilities
	Facilitate opening lines of communication	3. Significant others (family)
	Sensitize other staff to problems, and the need for listening	4. Other staff
		5. Groups for patients and/or family members
Confusion, lack of information	Involve patients and family in peer support groups	1. Veteran patients/groups
	Facilitate communication of questions and answers	2. Professionals
Resistance to getting needed medical care	Facilitate providing information about likely consequences	1. Other professionals
	Ascertain source of resistance and resolve it if possible	
	If a reasoned choice on the part of the patient, support right to self-determination	

FIGURE 6 (continued)

Problems getting to the hospital or clinic	Identify with patient appropriate resource Make referral and/or facilitate patient's use of it Provide funds, if necessary and available Teach patient how to use public transportation	1. Ambulance services 2. Taxis 3. Family or friends 4. Volunteer transport services 5. Public transportation
Problems entering the hospital	Identify problem interfering with hospitalization and promote use of appropriate resource	1. Information for professional staff 2. Family/friends 3. Community agencies 4. Financial resources
Rehabilitation *Patient:* need to adjust to losses of function, regimen *Family:* problems created by changes in patient's functioning	Prepare patient and resource Help facilitate referral and use	1. Rehabilitation centers 2. Vocational rehabilitation 3. Self-help groups 4. Financial resources 5. Home-health care agencies and homemaker services

FIGURE 6 (continued)

Problems of discharge from hospital following serious illness	Assess function and needs of patient, gather information, assess suitability of resources, physical charactieristics of home Identify with patient most appropriate resource. Find and mobilize the necessary resources. Prepare patient for the transition, and for use of the resource. Explore and help patient deal with feelings about helplessness, dependency.	1. Nursing homes, extended care facilities 2. Homemaker and home care agencies 3. Family, friends, neighbors.
Preexisting chronic problems: housing marital legal parent-child mental illness substance abuse	Explore, reinforce and heighten patients' and families' motivation to get help with the problem. Provide information about resources and programs; facilitate referral and successful linkage to programs.	1. Family service agency 2, Child guidance and child welfare 3. Drug and alcohol programs 4. Advocacy groups

People who are seriously ill or who face severe and overwhelming problems also can feel very isolated, for their preoccupying concerns are different from those who do not share their situation. People unable to carry out their responsibiities and cut off from their usual source of rewards often respond with feelings of low self-esteem and worthlessness. The concern and attentiveness conveyed by the social worker breaks down the patient's sense of isolation and restores a sense of worth.

Psychological support of these sorts may suffice to restore coping and problem-solving capacities of patients and family members. More frequently, the social worker continues to participate with the client in analyzing problems and figuring out the ways they can be resolved. Sometimes the social worker must also take on the role of helping clients to question their self-defeating or dysfunctional ways of dealing with the difficulties at hand. If a patient's way of dealing with stress is to retreat, to share his or her feelings with no one, and to ask for help from no one, the social worker may help him or her look at the undesirable consequences of this pattern and to map out other choices of behavior. Thus, the social worker's counseling help about health problems can be directed toward prompting and expanding patients' and families' coping and problem-solving skills.

Help with the relationships between the patient and one or several family members may also be the focus of social work counseling. Patients may need to be helped to ask for more in the way of emotional support from their kin. A spouse may use help in expressing and mastering his grief to become better able to deal helpfully with his dying wife. Marital partners, or parents and children may need to learn new ways of talking together and solving problems. The social worker may help the patient to change some aspect of his/her behavior toward a loved one, may work with the partner, or may counsel them together. This work is required in order to strengthen the capacity of patient and family to adapt to a medical crisis. The helpfulness of family relationships and family support can be of critical importance during illness.

Resource provision and linkage is another feature of service delivery. While supportive counseling will assist patients in solving some problems, many of the needs of patients and families during a health crisis require resources from other systems. As problems to be worked on are identified, patient and social worker consider what resources might be available and acceptable for the solution to each need. Social workers play an important role in facilitating the use by patients and families of the resources and services needed to solve their problems.

What kinds of resources are needed? The catalog of the sorts of problems confronting patients suggests some of the material resources and concrete services that clients might require. Patients need to find transportation to the medical setting or money to pay for costs of getting there. They need help in obtaining the financial resources for paying for their care by applying for Medicaid or managing the "red tape" surrounding their insurance. They need to identify people to take care of those dependent on them, such as children, during the time they must go to the doctor or be in the hospital. They need rehabilitative care or even a totally new living situation after discharge. For each of the material needs discussed in the earlier section, a resource meeting that need must be found by the social worker and client.

Informal resources of the patient's own social world sometimes contain the help sought (16,22,42,46). Patients have families and neighbors; they belong to churches and other organizations and communities. Working with the patients, social workers help them to identify persons and resources in their own informal social network, which might provide the transportation, child care, nursing care, financial aid, or emotional support. The social worker may assist the patients to plan how they themselves can request the needed aid, or when necessary, he or she may intervene on the patients' behalf. This could entail an exploration process in the support network itself or involve requesting the aid from those already identified by the client. For example, the social worker and the mastectomy patient may identify a network of close friends and relatives who will assist with babysitting during the mother's frequent visits for chemotherapy.

While natural supports may often be strong and the request for help may be uncomplicated, relationships and situations may also be complex; patients may have conflicts about asking for aid, and their potential helpers may be ambivalent about providing it. For these reasons, considerable skill is required to ascertain the appropriateness of the proposed help and to obtain the cooperation of the helper. Activating natural supports, however, not only economizes on the formal source of services, but also can strengthen and integrate the patient's social network. This enhances the basis for future cooperation and exchange.

Formal resources are more often drawn on. Because the informal network cannot always provide the help needed, a very large part of social work help in medical care settings consists of helping patients and families find in the system of social and health services the concrete resources they need for resolving their problems (46,48). These include services to solve problems in getting to the health care facility and making use of care. Difficulties with transportation to the hospital, babysitting, or homemaker services and paying for care have already been described.

Social workers link patients with community resources to help resolve problems that will interfere with continued medical care. If family members cannot take care of a woman's children while she comes into the hospital, then she may require a homemaker or foster care service. If financial resources have run out, patients have to apply for medical assistance or other sources of payment for medical care. If no family member or friend can help with transportation, then the patient may need funds for taxis or the help of organized agencies or volunteer groups. Often an illness or health condition creates a host of problems for which patients and families must seek help from community services. Changes in a patient's physical capacities due to chronic ailments such rheumatoid arthritis or end-stage renal disease may require vocational rehabilitation services, home health services or help from local housing resources. To remain at home, a terminally ill patient may need special equipment such as a hospital bed, wheelchair or oxygen, as well as the services of the visiting nurse and homemaker.

Planning for all the continued care needed by patients takes on special significance when discharge following a hospitalization will otherwise not be possible. Older, sicker people require a longer recovery period, and sometimes lack family members who care for them; they make up a large proportion of those needing help with discharge planning. Third party sources of payment (most state and federal programs and private health insurance) restrict their coverage for hospitalization to care that can be provided *only* in a hospital. When the patient no longer receives active treatment, payment for hospital care ceases; a patient needing convalescent care must be transferred to an extended care or skilled nursing facility, or some alternative plan must be found (61). Social workers operate under considerable pressure to find scarce nursing home placements. In some settings, plans are made for care following hospitalization before the person is even admitted (preadmission planning).

While much of social work help goes into finding resources to deal with lingering effects of illness, social workers also help patients and families to locate community resources to solve other complicating problems. Urgent and debilitating problems of living can interfere with attention to health care, and can so depress patients' morale as to undermine their physical health. Some families require referrals for clothing or for financial support for alleviation of serious housing problems. Sometimes they need help from legal services, family services agencies, psychiatric service, foster and adoptive resources, day care, or employment programs. For some families, the medical care setting may be the only community agency with which they have dealt. As critical problems come to light during their contact with the setting, the social worker may represent the first person who has offered help in dealing with some of these emergency situations. To varying degrees medical care programs legitimate and support social service attention to the wide range of needs of patients and families. Renal services, rehabilitation departments and obstetrical care for high risk or teenaged mothers are some examples of programs in which the importance of providing comprehensive help has been recognized.

Learning about resources is a special skill required of social workers. To link patients with these resources outside the health care system, the social worker requires both extensive knowledge of the sources of help in the community and skills in connecting patients to them. Social workers learn of resources through a continuing search process. The workers in a department may develop and share a "resource file," i.e., a listing of resources to meet specific problems. Social workers also know of and use information and referral services of the social welfare system in their community. Health and welfare councils, city agencies and community organizations often provide such "I & R" services. Social workers also cultivate an informal referral network; one may learn that a particular worker at family court or in adult services has special expertise in resources. Finally, social workers may cultivate personal ties with workers in agencies to which they make referrals. Through in-person orientation visits they gain detailed first hand information about services. Often, personal acquaintance may prove useful in paving the way for clients.

Facilitating referrals is another skill required. The first task of the social worker is to know about resources; the second is to help clients use them effectively. For many patients, referrals do not pose many problems. They may be sophisticated about social agencies, able to handle the discomfort of seeking help, and assertive in approaching new situations and making requests. Many clients, however, often experience confusion and are overwhelmed by the complexity of the service network with which they must deal. The unfamiliarity and formality of the setting, the bureaucratic and sometimes discriminatory treatment, the client's lack of facility in explaining his/her situations and needs, the complexity of application forms requiring a high level of literacy all interfere with successful referrals. Many patients experience difficulty in applying for help from community resources, and in following through, i.e., persisting until the needed help is received. Low income clients may be least equipped to manage an application for help from a community agency; at the same time the public agencies on which they depend for help are often the most impersonal and overwhelming. Sometimes, therefore, the social worker has to prepare clients for what to expect and "role-play" with them beforehand; rehearse what will happen when they approach the other agency.

Many patients, however, not just low income groups, require preparation for their transfer to other potentially complex or overwhelming service settings. The social worker must spend considerable time both allowing the patients to air their fears and fantasies and supporting their preparation for a transition. In one hospital, for example, the social work staff uses a photograph album to introduce patients to their extended care facility. Patients being referred for convalescent care can discuss in detail what to expect to prepare for this potentially traumatic transfer. Social workers may also accompany patients to new settings or find someone else to do so.

The social worker also prepares the receiving agency, interpreting the special needs of the client so that the agency can be as welcoming and receptive as possible; the social worker's relationships with staff in that agency may facilitate these activities. Social workers often work out formal ties and procedures for important and frequent referrals, even arranging for workers from community resources to meet clients in the health care setting. Social workers also advocate with community agencies to cut through red tape and gain for clients needed services to which they are entitled.

Collaboration, i.e., cooperative work, with other staff to resolve the problems of patients is one important aspect of service delivery in medical care settings. Any of the patient problems discussed so far may occasion collaborative work. The way social workers collaborate with others varies, depending on how social services are organized and how integrated they are with the medical services. Social workers may operate quite separately from the other staff, or they may be part of a team. Collaborative relationships will differ depending on such factors as how often the collaborators meet, how well they know one another, how close their respective workplaces are and many other factors. Social workers may be on call for duty with a number of different services, or they may be located within one service, such as a renal dialysis or burn unit. The latter situation permits continuous, casual and frequent discussion with all the staff involved in that unit as well as regular formal team meetings (29,49,59).

Collaboration describes several different kinds of activities. It may amount to the mere sharing of information. For example, in order to assist a patient with discharge planning, the social worker must obtain from the physician, the physical therapist and the nurse detailed information about the patient's medical condition and its prognosis, and the patient's capacity for self care. With such information, the social worker can make more adequate judgments about the appropriate setting or supportive services that the patient will need. Social workers also share with other professionals information which assists them to carry out their responsibilities and to give sensitive, personalized care. The more information available about the patient's feelings and reactions to the illness, the better equipped the staff will be to understand the patient's behavior and feelings. Among some black mothers, for example, a slim baby is a sign of poverty, while a fat baby indicates that there is plenty of food and that the mother is adequately nourishing the infant. The social worker can help a pediatrician concerned about the overfed baby to understand and work with this mother. As another illustration, the social worker may interpret to the physician or other staff members the profound fear of a recently retired man about surgery. The mutual exchange of information enables each staff member, social worker and others, to work more intelligently with the patient. They provide one another with information in their areas of expertise, which the others can use to guide their plans, actions, and communications.

Another level of collaboration occurs when two or more professionals coordinate their planning for their activities with a particular patient and family. Such coordination prevents the development of conflicting plans or the duplication of services. In helping arrange the discharge home of a dying patient, the nurse might take the responsibility for referrals to the visiting nurse and the arrangement for the special hospital bed and oxygen that the patient needs; the social worker might speak with the patient's pastor to obtain some needed support from the patient's congregation. It is clear that the planning of the two professionals together results in a more complete and well-coordinated strategy than would result if each planned in isolation. Thus, professionals working with the same patient do well to arrive at a shared understanding of the services required in a situation and have a clear agreement about which of them will perform each task.

Yet another sort of collaboration is occasioned when characteristics of the medical care create difficulties for the patient and some change in the service is required. A common situation of this sort is one in which there is insufficient communication between professionals and patient. To provide an example, a physician concerned that a patient is not taking a prescribed medication may involve the social worker. A careful social work assessment reveals that not only is there no money for the medicine, but also the patient does not understand what the medicine is for and has only the most rudimentary understanding of his/her condition. In addition to finding a way to pay for the drug, the social worker would plan with the physician a joint discussion with the patient to help him/her understand the condition and how the medicine will help. The social worker collaborates with the other professional in mapping out communications strategies — how matters can be described in a way the patient can comprehend. In the discussion with the patient, the social worker checks how well the patient grasps the information and encourages his/her asking the medical staff further questions.

Another frequent problem is the need to alter procedures or regulations when they do not fit a patient's particular circumstances. As an illustration, intensive care nursery staff may become concerned about a mother's failure to visit her infant. The social worker's exploration may reveal that the mother is unable to obtain a ride during visiting hours, but that a neighbor could bring her when he has finished work. Collaboration with nursery or administrative staff would be aimed at obtaining greater flexibility in visiting hours for this or possibly all parents. In addition, the social worker would interpret to nursery staff the mother's motivation to visit her baby and feelings about being hindered from doing so. This kind of collaboration differs from coordination of planning in that the social worker must influence the other professionals, (though influence may be mutual), in order to resolve a problem that has interfered with the successul treatment of the patient.

Collaboration or teamwork is a ubiquitous feature of work. With few exceptions, roles or occupations are pieces of larger, organized patterns, or interlocking tasks. Because they often function in institutions alongside other professionals with varying goals, social workers in particular are conscious of the interdependent nature of their work. Recognizing collaboration as requisite to best meeting the needs of the patients, the profession of social work has applied its knowledge and skill to this problem. A variety of social work skills contributes to good collaboration.

One skill required is the ability to grasp the perspective of the collaborative partner. Social workers bring to collaboration background information about the professional training of physicians and other staff, some understanding of their professional tasks and assignments, and some grasp of how such tasks shape the other professional's way of understanding the patient and reacting to him/her. As a rather exaggerated example, physicians are equipped by their professional training to deal with physiological processes; their task or mission is to cure or to treat. Their focus on disease makes it more difficult for them to attend to the emotional responses of patients. Similarly, other professsionals perspectives on the patient are shaped by their training and by their particular task.

In collaboration as much as in direct service to their clients, social workers draw on their background understanding about the perspective of the other profession and on their skill at eliciting and understanding the particular view of the individual professions with whom they are dealing. Their skill at "role-taking" or seeing the issue from the other's point of view makes successful collaboration possible.

A second type of skill which the social workers bring is their skill in developing relationships, again, a special asset exercised in their work with clients. Developing relationships depends on recognizing the needs of the collaborative partner and an understanding of process, i.e., the natural steps through which two people develop a relationship. The social worker also uses the self, his/her natural warmth, listening capacity, supportiveness or other qualities to facilitate the growth of good collaborative relationships (14).

A third skill applied to collaboration is the social worker's careful interpretation of his/her role to the other professions (46). This is particularly important when social workers must work with the other staff throughout the setting, rather than with a stable set of partners who grow familiar with the tasks social workers perform. The ability of the other staff to interact with and to make constructive use of the social worker depends entirely on their grasp of the abilities and functions of the social worker. The social worker must describe effectively his/her role and perspective, and make sure that the other staff understand it.

Social work consultation is a special form of collaboration. Social workers provide consultation. In this type of work the social worker bases his/her assessment on the information provided by the other professionals. She/he makes an analysis of the situation, assists and supports the other professional in thinking through problems, and offers specific suggestions about resources or solutions to problems. Social workers offer consultation to emergency room staff, to professionals managing discharge planning, to administrators and to others about the range of problems which arise within a medical care setting.

Group services comprise another method of social work service delivery (11,51). While social workers most often provide help to individuals and families they have also found groups a valuable medium for direct services. Social workers use groups for carrying out many tasks in medical care settings. Some programs use groups for giving information or orienting patients (or families) to the particular service; at one hospital, for example, the explanation of abortion procedures is carries out in a group. Groups may also be used as the medium for some of the work with families of patients. A group for parents of children with cancer, for example, might help them to deal with the illness of their child, specifically allowing them to air their anger, mutually consider coping mechanisms, and share resources that members have discovered. Groups are particularly suitable when a number of patients or a number of families require service and are going through the same kind of problem at the same time. The basic requisite is a sufficient degree of shared problems among the members of the group.

There are many ways in which groups can contribute to achieving the goals of social work services in medical care settings. The ventilation and processing of overwhelming and painful feelings may take place more easily when others share the situation and are familiar with the feelings. For those whose illness has made them feel isolated and separate, different from the rest of the world, others who have shared that experience can most effectively help reduce the feelings of isolation.

Those who share and know a particular health situation also bring other kinds of understanding. Fellow sufferers may be best equipped to confront other group members with their defensive or destructive thought and behavior patterns. A fellow-diabetic or fellow-"fat" are all too familiar with the rationalizations by which dieters may excuse cheating in their regimens. Their confrontations may carry more credibility for some patients. In the same way, members of a group can reward and reinforce positive behavior patterns with an appreciation of the difficulty of maintaining them.

Such continuing support can be highly effective in maintaining behavioral changes. Many unhealthful life style patterns, for example, the use of alcohol, smoking or heavy eating, pervade our society and are strongly supported in normal social life. For this reason, strong and continuous group support may be a key factor in helping a person to sustain a needed regimen. This support can be effective not only for persons needing to treat a continuing illness, but can also be important in preventive health education to help people change disease-producing life style patterns.

In groups, members may share information, for each will have devised solutions to common problems that the other members have not thought of. Finally, help offered by those "in the same boat" doesn't bear the same burden of dependence and inferiority often felt in unilateral helping situations. Physical disability and dependence, feeling one's resources being overwhelmed, no longer feeling in control, or finding oneself burdened with problems for which one has no solution, arouse a strong sense of helplessness and dependence. People deal with these feelings in different ways. Fantasies may be projected onto the helping people, who take on attributes of omnipotence. Class and racial differences may exacerbate the sense of difference and of relative incapacity. In contrast, groups offer the opportunity to be helped by those who are like oneself. Moreover, the group members experience themselves not only as needing help but also as being able to give it, with consequent support for self-esteem. There is a growing movement of peer-support or self-help groups addressed to many kinds of problems and ample testimony to their effectiveness (30).

For many reasons, then, groups provide social workers with an extremely useful resource for helping patients and families in medical care settings. They can promote the effective and lasting learning of new behaviors, either to prevent or to deal with illness or disability. They may provide to patients or their kin crucial resources to support the coping and adaptation required by the losses and changes —brought by disease. Other disciplines have also adopted group methods; both nurses and psychotherapists commonly apply group techniques to therapeutic and educational tasks. Groups in health settings can be the arena for creative collaborative efforts, bringing the specific resources of several professionals to bear on the problems at hand. Social workers might use the group to help patients learn of or to use community resources; nurses might lend their medical understanding. Both might be active in facilitating the group process, as increasingly, both professionals strive to develop their competence in using groups.[1]

Evaluation, Termination and Follow-Up

A clear termination process is a common feature of professional social work practice. It is customary and necessary for the involvement of the social worker in a medical setting to be limited to the period in which the patient is using the setting. The provision of service may be even further limited, due to the pressure of the demands within the setting, to the time during which there is an acute problem for which social work help is needed. Since it depends on the relation with the medical setting, social work contact with a patient may therefore be quite short, or it may extend over a long period. For example, one social worker's contact with the family of an abused child was limited to the 10 days that child was hospitalized. She supported the mother, helped her to visit her child and worked with the hospital staff. During that time, the connections with protective services and a special supportive service for abusive and neglectful families were accomplished (19). Another social worker on a renal dialysis unit worked with a patient over a period of several years, addressing family, employment and medical treatment issues through several phases of the patient's illness (2).

Even though the social worker and patient may end their formal work together, the social worker may continue to be a resource to the patient. Patients continuing the use of the medical setting may drop in or run into the social worker. They may call the social worker when new crises erupt. There may be occasions for them to take up new work together. The social worker in the medical setting is often

[1] In the past, the social work profession viewed group work and casework (i.e., work with individuals) as such distinct methods that social workers were trained and prepared for practice in only one method. Group workers like other social workers identified themselves strongly with their method and indeed organized themselves in separate professional organizations (51). Group work was most identified with recreation and the settlement movement. In recent times, social workers in many settings have recognized the usefulness of group methods and have applied them to many kinds of problems. Current social work education actively promotes the inclusion of group skills in master's level curricula. Graduates already practicing seek out additional opportunities for acquiring or improving their competence in group work.

the only continuous, humanizing link for the patient. For many patients, the social worker may be the sole link to community services.

Termination is an important part of the helping process (13,52). When social worker and patient are ending their work together, they must often deal with relationship issues. This may be critical in making the end of their work a positive experience, in reinforcing the progress the patient has made, and in preparing for the patient's continued coping or growth. If the work together has been extremely intense, or taken place over a lengthy period, a strong attachment may have formed between patient and worker. When such strong relationships are ending, patients may experience emotions such as anger, sadness or fear. The social worker watches for signs of these feelings, and helps the patient to become aware of them and to express them. Sometimes the basis for the feelings is examined, such as the sense of abandonment or rejection that gives rise to the anger, or the sense of danger and helplessness about the future that occasions the fear. By bringing the thoughts and feelings connected with the ending into consciousness and by discussing them together, the ending becomes an occasion for growth. A patient who ends a relationship angry, depressed and frightened, will be less equipped for what is to come. If social worker and patient can express their feelings of caring for each other, then the separation from one another can be a positive experience, with the patient taking lasting strength from the relationship.

In ending the relationship, social worker and patient also review their work together. This can be the occasion for giving the patient recognition for what she/he has accomplished, and enhancing his/her self-image and self-esteem. It can be a way of identifying directions for work by the patient independent of the social worker. The social worker can also reinforce the patient's sense of his/her own strength, and of the resources she/he has on which she/he can draw for further problem solving.

Finally, review and reassessment may also provide the opportunity for looking with the patient at what lies ahead. If the patient is dying, or going to a nursing home, this may be the time for the airing of fears and sorrow and for gaining some solace and support from the social worker. All of these activities may be important for consolidating the gains that have been made, and for strengthening the patient for what is to come.

Evaluation is an essential part of termination. At the time of ending the process, the social worker and patient judge the outcome of their work together. This phase of work has a logical relationship to the process of contracting; at that time problems were identified, and a contract was made about which ones would be worked on and what the patient and worker would each do. As each phase of work was completed, the worker will have reassessed with the patient how well the problem was resolved, what factors prevented resolution, and what still needed to be done. In this way, the contract may have been renegotiated several times, with the focus turning to new problems, or new solutions needing to be found for problems. At the ending phase of work, social worker and client carry out the same kind of reassessment and review. This provides an opportunity for eliciting the patient's view of what has been achieved, of his/her satisfaction with the resolution of the problem, and his or her perception of what problems remain to be worked on.

As another step in the ending process, the social worker will follow up to evaluate whether the patient has successfully gained access to the new services to which he/she has been referred. A call to the referral agency may suffice to make sure of this. One or more telephone discussions with the patient may ascertain that solutions are working, that the patient has followed through on referrals. A call also assures the patient of the continued interest and concern of the social worker. It may be necessary, when referrals haven't worked, for the social worker to continue involvement until the connection with needed agencies is effected.

As part of the evaluation process, the social worker may report back to the referring source, the professional within the system, or an agency outside of the setting. The social worker will provide some information to the referring party about the outcome of the work with the patient, what was and was not achieved. The social worker may also evaluate with collaborative partners their view of the outcome of their joint work, and their satisfaction with the processes of their work together.

The process of ending is a particularly important piece of professional work; it is the occasion for criticism and analysis of the process, and provides feedback to the social worker about the quality of his/her work. It can be the time for assessing what might have been done differently, what might have improved the level of service, or in what way the intentions of the worker may not have been actualized. It is a time for checking whether agreed on tasks were carried out, and examining the sources of problems that may be interfering with successful work, either because of the social worker, or because of inadequacies or impediments in the system. It may, of course, be a time for examining with the patient what kept them from carrying out their part of an agreement, with similar potential for growth on the part of the patient. It is also a time for noting where there are gaps in resources and problems in the setting, which may become a focus for action by the social worker in future work.

INDIRECT SERVICE ROLES OF SOCIAL WORKERS

In addition to their central direct service role with patients, with familes and with other systems on behalf of patients, social workers in medical settings have assumed other roles that have followed logically from their service function. This section will discuss three such roles: administrator, educator and researcher. These will be briefly sketched; the discussion of tasks attendant on these roles is then elaborated in the final section on issues shaping the delivery of social services.

Social Workers as Administrators

Social workers occupy positions as administrators of social work staff, and often of other ancillary staff, such as paraprofessionals, volunteers, patient advocates or discharge planning specialists. Administration, it should be noted, is not a role performed solely by the director of the social work department; in units of any considerable size, the director usually delegates administrative tasks to a number of senior staff. Every master's degree professional social worker shares to an extent in the responsibility for the tasks outlined below, and some hold formal administrative positions, such as assistant director or unit supervisor. The discussion will use the term administrator to designate all social workers carrying administrative functions.

Administrators can be viewed as linking the workers reporting to them with the larger organizational system. Within the social work department, social work administrators are responsible for promoting the optimal professional functioning of workers. They accomplish this through such tasks as assigning work and deploying resources, cultivating a well-functioning work group, supervising the workers who report to them, and organizing in-service training to improve the skills of workers and to increase their resources.

Like direct service social workers, social work administrators must interpret and promote the role of social work services to the hospital leadership. Because of its emphasis on disease and the neglect of the psychosocial dimension of the patient's functioning, the medical care system often fails to understand social work's function. Precisely because it attends to these neglected aspects of the patient's needs, social work labors under a special necessity to interpret and advance its role and to educate others about this role. Information systems for accountability, which will be described in a later section, have created new tools for establishing the value of social work services within the organization. The skilled social work administrator uses data from information systems to justify budget requests, identify unmet needs and document and measure the need for service in areas unstaffed by social workers.

As participants in the larger system of the medical care setting itself, social workers also assist in the ongoing work of the larger organization. Senior social work staff and administrators have formal tasks as members of committees dealing with such issues as quality assurance, patient care or personnel. Informally, social work administrators also contribute their special expertise to the functioning of the larger organization. They develop relationships and alliances with other administrative staff. Because of their knowledge base and experience in understanding how people function, they can often advise and aid in resolving conflicts and tensions within and among groups of staff members (9).

Social work administrators also represent the medical setting in the larger community. They may pave the way for ties with community agencies; they may play an important role as advocates with funding agencies, seeking support for services. As administrative-level social workers supply skills and help with the complex problems medical care settings face, they increase their potential influence within the system, and ultimately, therefore, their ability to serve their clients (9).

Social Workers As Educators

Teaching tasks have always been an intrinsic part of the role of social workers in medical settings (3,10). In an ongoing process, by sharing their expertise in collaboration, social workers continuously educate the members of other disciplines with which they are working. They teach about the influence of culture, family dynamics, economic situation and psychosocial issues on the responses of patients to the setting and to illness. They help their colleagues learn to perceive more sensitively the patients' psychosocial needs as they undergo treatment. They also instruct other staff members about the role of social work and the appropriate application of social work services. Social workers even educate their teammates about the community, its resources and its lacks. All of these topics may emerge quite naturally in the course of collaborative teamwork or in case conferences about specific patients. While for some, these tasks remain implicit, other social workers are highly conscious and purposeful about their educational function with colleagues from other disciplines. In some settings, they may even utilize the medium of a formal lecture or colloquium for teaching.

Many medical settings serve as the arena for the clinical education of nurses, physicians and other health professions. Social workers who provide service in these settings often become involved in the instruction of student health professionals (3,4,10). This may occur tacitly through collaboration of the social worker and the student over the needs of patients. In such cooperative work, social workers may model interviewing techniques or other techniques of relating sensitively to patients. In medical rounds or clinical case conferences, social workers instruct student health professionals about psychosocial aspects of the patients' illnesses, use of care, and needs in the medical setting and the community. Social workers also participate in more formal teaching, such as presentations. lectures or courses.

Many social workers in medical settings also supervise social work students. Social work training at both the bachelor's and master's level includes a field practicum in which the student provides social work help to clients for one or more days a week under close supervision by a field instructor. Medical settings are rich sites for social work education.

Often, social workers supervise and/or instruct other hospital personnel. They may oversee the hospital's "indigenous" paraprofessionals, who serve as community outreach workers, and may provide extensive training to this staff. They may contribute to the in-service training of clerks or nurse's aids, especially when such workers are part of a team, to sensitize them to the importance of their role with patients and to cultivate and reinforce their responsiveness and involvement with patients. Social workers may also participate in the in-service training of volunteers working in medical settings.

The success of social workers in clinical teaching roles led naturally to their appointment to medical and other professional faculties. Some clinical social workers have gained adjunct level faculty appointments in recognition of their role in training students. Social workers have moved into full-time faculty appointments as medical schools increasingly incorporated a social model of disease. The more medicine recognizes the influence of emotions, environment and culture on the course and management of illness, the more useful social work's teaching contribution becomes. By 1975, a total of 595 social workers were participating on the faculties of the 116 accredited medical schools, making up 1.5% of the faculty (23A). Social workers have also assisted in the development of various training schools (and programs), for such new occupations as physicians' assistants or "child health associates" (27).

The diversity of subjects taught by social workers on medical school faculties reflects the extent to which social work has moved from its exclusive focus on individual patients and families to engagement with broader issues in health care. Social workers in medical schools teach:

> psychosocial implications of hospitalization; psychosocial aspects of illness and rehabilitation; death and dying; man and his environment; human behavior; human growth and development; sexuality; marriage (marital enrichment, marital dysfunction); family dynamics; interviewing, social study; family therapy; group psychotherapy; social problems; alcoholism; drug abuse; child abuse; gerontology; family health maintenance; health care of minority groups; issues in health care organization; planning of health manpower policy; fundamentals of the health care system; mobilization and utilization of community resources; function of the social workers; medical social work; urban and rural studies; rural medicine; clinical medicine and medical ecology (23A).

It is likely that social workers will find more and more opportunities for applying their special expertise to the teaching of health professionals.

Social Workers as Researchers

Social work education at the master's and doctoral levels prepares students to be competent researchers (46). In the past, however, social workers' participation in research in medical settings has tended to be in secondary roles and has focused, in general, on medical or medical care issues. Two trends will probably lead to more distinctively social work research, testing the nature and outcome of social work help.

Over the past 10-15 years, social work has adopted an increasingly problem-solving, task-centered approach to direct services (13,48). The new models of social work have included the definition of specific objectives of service, with clear contracts with clients about the problems to be addressed, and the goal of social work help. These models lend themselves to empirical tests of outcome.

Demands for accountability within the health field, to be discussed in the next section, have led to the formation of additional "building blocks." As accountability and computerized information systems come into use, social workers have responded to the need for clearly specified, objective categories for describing patients' problems, types of interventions and outcomes of social work help.

With a growing, carefully defined set of data recording the work that has been carried out within a department, and access to computer systems, social workers should find the barriers to research lowered. The next few years should witness increasingly sophisticated studies addressing a broad range of research problems (44,46).

There is, within the profession of social work, including practice in health settings, growing commitment to empirical studies. A casual perusal of recent years of one journal, *Health and Social Work*, reveals that from 15-50% of the articles in each issue report on empirical, quantitative research. Some examples of topics addressed are:

assessing functional abilities of elderly outpatients
attitudes of social workers toward peer review
emergency rooms
knowledge and use of child health services by Chinese Americans
consultation on alcoholism in a general hospital

Social workers are demonstrating their commitment to empirical research. It seems likely that given present trends, an increasing number of empirical tests of practice interventions will establish a more solid base for practice and enhance social work's credibility.

ISSUES SHAPING THE DELIVERY OF SOCIAL WORK SERVICES

Having considered the process of direct social work services, as well as other roles social workers enact, it is useful to examine some features of the relationship between social work and its environment in medical settings. Four issues that shape the delivery of social work services will be addressed:

1) the role of documentation and quality assurance
2) the mandate and funding for social work services in medical settings
3) how social workers identify clients or case-finding
4) professional preparation of social workers in health care

These themes are selected because they recur in the literature on social work in medical settings. Moreover, each has far-reaching implications for the potential of social work to control the development of its services, or to be constrained by the environment from doing so.

Documentation, Quality Assurance and Accountability

Documentation, quality assurance and accountability have assumed growing importance over the last 10 years. Documentation may be defined as "an organized method of keeping clear and concise statements of problems and of courses of action taken toward resolving them" (4). Quality assurance systems determine what social services were provided and whether they met minimum standards of adequacy. These aspects of service delivery have burgeoned in response to financial pressures on the health care system and the need for controlling costs and the consequent need for justifying services, i.e., accountability. The related development of computerized information systems in medical settings has opened new opportunities for social work.

The instituting of the Professional Standards Review Organizations (PSRO's) supplied a critical stimulus to the development of documentation and quality assurance systems. The primary target of PSRO review encompassed physician services and hospital use. The law mandated, however, that PSRO's eventually also review the services of other health care practitioners. By 1977, many hospital departments of social work had set to work developing quality assurance programs (58). These greatly stimulated efforts to define more precisely the nature of social work services and the criteria for judging their quality.

Social workers document their observations and services, usually in either the medical chart or a social work record, or in both. (Currently regulations of the Joint Commission on the Accreditation of Hospitals provide for direct charting of social work progress notes in the patient's medical record) (28). Social workers had always recognized the necessity of recording information about patients and the help that had been provided to them. These records aided administrative monitoring and provided continuity when patients later returned with other needs. Social workers also prepared social summaries or assessment which communicated information about patients to other professionals treating them. The use of social work notes in the medical chart, however, has led to increasingly focused, objective and economical recording systems. As a result, social work documentation in the medical record now serves as a more effective collaborative tool. The social worker's entries inform other professionals about the patient's background, needs and the planned and executed social work interventions. This clear, concise, and brief material is more likely to be read and comprehended than lengthier notes.

Careful documentation facilitates the processes of contracting and evaluation of services with clients. The documentation process promotes the social worker's clear, goal-directed thinking. Later, the documentation furnishes a concise record of contract and service to review with the client. The social worker's review and evaluation with clients of their work together can play a role in overall determination of the effectiveness of service (5).

Quality review builds on careful and systematic documentation. It may also make use of an explicit "protocol" or delineation of the procedures to be included in a particular category of patient problem. In one setting, a committee of qualified staff members assesses closed cases according to a set of guidelines or criteria agreed on by staff. Objective criteria are not easily delineated, and in some departments, the first standards to be applied relate to the completeness of the record and the reflection in it of elements agreed on as essential in social work practice. (See Fig. 7 for an illustrative excerpt from a review form.) Following review of case records, committees share their comments with the workers (4). This process has the potential to stimulate workers to carry out more orderly work and careful documentation and may also identify barriers to their attaining these aims. Collective problems revealed by quality review may point to topics for in-service training.

Social work audits are another response to demands for accountability. In one setting, a systematic sample was drawn of the entire case load number and a set of audit questions was answered using the records. (Fig. 8 shows some examples of audit questions in this department) (4). Audits can also be carried out on a regional basis. Audits monitor the quality of service and generate profiles of client characteristics and of the work of practitioners or of whole departments.

The use of computers to store and analyze the data generated by social workers' documentation, quality reviews and audits expands opportunities for social workers to improve and promote the work of their departments. Analysis of patient characteristics identifies factors predictive of problems and of the need for social work help, i.e., "risk factors" (6). With this information, groups can be designated for early intervention. Computer analysis of data can also be used to identify gaps in services, evaluate outcomes of interventions and answer research questions. Relationships can be shown between early intervention and a reduced length of stay. Relating obstacles to service or the timing of referrals may reveal recurrent problems that require resolution for efficient and adequate service delivery (57). Social workers can use documentation and quality assurance, audits and computerized information systems to demonstrate the value of their work with clients, to improve the quality of their service and to document the unmet needs of clients.

FIGURE 7
EXCERPT FROM QUALITY REVIEW FORM

	Yes	No	N/A
I. INITIAL SOCIAL SERVICE ENTRY			
1. Is date of initial contact noted?			
2. Is reason for initial contact clear?			
3. Is the service clear?			
4. Are there indications for the need for earlier Social Service entry?			
4a. If yes, who caused delay? Patient? physician? social worker?			
II. ASSESSMENT			
1. Psychosocial history a. Is the history in the chart? (date ________)			
b. Is the absence of the history justified?			
2. Is there some assessment?			
3. Does the assessment reflect some understanding of the patient's situation and problem?			
4. Is the assessment adequate in terms of the problems worker identified?			
5. Does the assessment include social and physical functioning of the patient?			
6. Does the assessment show an understanding of the illness, or disability and its implications?			

FIGURE 8
AUDIT QUESTIONS

1. How did the client get into the social service system of care? Who referred him?
2. What did the referrer request?
3. Did the social worker agree with the referrer's assessment of psycho-social problems? Does the social worker perceive any problems differently?
4. What social need "contracts" for social service were made between worker and client?
5. Do social worker "outcomes" vary according to types of psycho-social needs?
6. What interventive activities were utilized? Over what period of time?
7. Can one develop a technique to determine normative ranges of interventive patterns related to number of contracts or disease entities?

Source: Berkman, B.: Innovations for Social Services in Health Care. In *Changing Roles in Social Work Practice*, ed. Francine Sobey, Phila.: Temple Univ. Press, 1977.

The Mandate and Funding for Social Work Services

In a time of financial pressure on the health care system, the mandate and funding for social work in medical settings emerge as critical issues. The Joint Commission on the Accreditation of Hospitals includes among its standards the provision of social work help. Many federal and state programs have also required that social services be furnished. Title XVIII (Medicare) originally specified medical social services as a component of patient care (44), though the requirements of the component was later rescinded. The Maternal and Infant Care Program, which paid for obstetrical and post-partum care for low-income women, required social work evaluation as a condition of its payment for care. Programs that prescribe the availability of social work help usually set standards governing the level of preparation of the workers and criteria for the type of care to be provided. The mandate for provision of social work services in medical settings is a complex subject, with varying standards and degrees of specification of requirements.

Even more complicated is the way social services in medical settings are paid for. A special program funded from a source outside the setting may include payment for social services as a specific item in the planned budget. Examples of such programs are family planning, renal dialysis, learning disabilities, etc. (24). For social services not funded in this way, the administration of the hospital allocates a portion of its budget for the social work department. Although insurance does not technically cover social work services (24,57) and outpatient services in general are neglected in most health insurance programs (4), the costs for social services are recovered through the reimbursement for patient care which the hospital receives from Medicare, Medicaid and private insurance fees, as well as other monies the hospital obtains. What this means, however, is that reimbursement bears no relation to the amount of social work help provided for a particular patient. It also means that the kind of social work help the setting supports depends on the treatment of and payment for these services by funding sources outside the hospital.

One solution might be direct fee-for-service payment to social workers. There are many arguments against the entire fee-for-service system, particularly in the context of runaway costs for health care. In medical settings, however, some professionals (physicians and psychologists for instance) can bill patients or third-party sources for each specific service while others (e.g., almost all social workers) cannot. This system handicaps social work in its ability to obtain funds and to secure its place and standing within the setting, and thus to advocate for patients' needs. If social work could charge third-party payers directly for its services, it would have greater professional discretion over the type of service it provides. In the absence of this feature, the hospital administration dictates to a greater degree the form social work services will take. Therefore, social work must usually justify to administrators the cost-saving advantages of their services. Administrators may emphasize discharge planning, which directly saves hospitals the costs of overstays — patients remaining in the hospital beyond the time covered by third parties — at the expense of social work help justified by other needs of the patient.

State licensure of social workers may carry them one step closer to fee-for-service payments (41). If national health insurance were enacted, it would increase the demand for social work service in medical settings; yet without licensure, direct payment for these services is unlikely (44). The context of rising health costs requires the careful justification of all components of the health care system and the weighing of cost-effectiveness. A completely altered system of payment for care is no doubt desirable. The way the current system, however, pays for social services constrains the professional autonomy of the social worker and limits the degree to which a department can respond to the needs of patients.

The complexity of the funding for social services, however, presents social work with the potential and the responsibility to influence *how much* it receives. By providing careful documentation of patient need, based on thorough assessment, a social work department can strengthen a hospital administration's hand in increasing per diem payments from third-party sources. Strong social work documentation also puts social work in a better position to compete with other departments within the hospital in the hospital budgeting process. Even more important, educating the medical staff and demonstrating the contribution of social work to their effectiveness may win powerful allies in the fight for payment for social work services. Social workers can also obtain funding from outside the setting by developing proposals for special projects and by working with state health officials. At all levels, social work must argue its case and advocate for adequate social work support as part of an effective system of medical care. This effort must be made with individual services, such as oncology and orthopedics, with the hospital administrators, and with legislators and those who implement government-funded programs. By effective collaboration with other professionals in this endeavor, social workers can gain support for provision of their services.

How Social Workers Identify Clients or Case-Finding

Historically, other professionals have had responsibility for identifying patients with social or psychological problems and referring them for social work help. In community hospitals especially, patients have "belonged" to the physicians, who take responsibility for all decisions. It has been estimated that physicians initiate 40 to 71% of all referrals to social work in medical settings, while patients and families account for 14-20% (9). Thus, most referrals depend both on the primary professional's perception of the patient's problem, and on his/her grasp of the social work role. As a result, only patients with certain types of problems may be referred. Some physicians, for example, recognize financial but not family problems affecting medical care. Commonly, patients and families are not referred until there is a full-blown crisis, when the patient signs out against medical advice, or is ready to be discharged with nowhere to go.

As one solution, social workers are striving to educate other professionals and patients about the role of social work. Aggressive involvement in health team conferences is one means of doing this (4); in-service training programs are another method. One social work department developed a written guide to patient and family services for other staff members (24). Problem oriented social work charting in the medical record also begins to educate other professionals about the role of social work.

A second strategy is to institute independent screening mechanisms, so that social workers, not other professionals, define the need for their own intervention (4). These may be based on independent social work review of all charts in a clinic or on a hospital service. Increasingly, social workers are using their improved information systems to identify problem-related patient characteristics and risk factors so that referral of patients in those categories can be automatically carried out (56). Screening criteria grounded in empirical data gain in credibility.

Preparation of Social Workers for Practice in Medical Settings

As Federally funded problems have extended health care coverage to a larger population, the demand for medical social services has increased. An estimated 50% of the social workers meeting this increased demand, however, have no more than a bachelor's degree (44); 17.4% of about a thousand *directors* responding to a survey by the Society of Hospital Social Work Directors held no degree higher than a bachelor's degree (54). These phenomena require some explanation.

Until recently, only a person with a master's degree in social work was considered professional. Many social work positions in medical settings, nevertheless, were occupied by workers with bachelor's degrees, with or without a social work background. This was due to a shortage of trained master's level social workers, when professionally trained social workers would have been preferred for the positions (4).

During the "democratizing" movements of the 60's, two developments complicated this picture. The bachelor's level of social work preparation was redefined as the entry level professional degree. The second development was the movement for the use of paraprofessionals or "indigenous" workers for social work tasks, who could overcome some of the cultural, racial, and class barriers between providers in the health care system and many of its users.

Some departments continue to utilize bachelor's level workers, some employ bachelor's workers with master's level social workers in supervisory and administrative positions, and some employ social workers with at least master's education exclusively. In the face of the fiscal pressures on the health care system, there has been continued impetus for the use of BSW's and other bachelor's level social workers in positions in medical social work. BSW's command a lower salary, and even including the cost of supervision by MSW's, a system using BSW's will be less costly.

Certain tasks can be skillfully performed by an adequately prepared bachelor's level workers: gathering information and assisting in applications for services to meet concrete needs and providing a continuous, warm, supportive relationship linking patients and families to services within the medical setting. To the extent that persons with a bachelor's level of preparation can perform these tasks in a skilled and professional way, economic constraints would dictate that they not be performed by more highly paid professionals with more costly and specialized training (33,47).

At the same time, it is certain that BSW's and even more so, bachelor's workers without social work preparation are less or not at all equipped to carry out many other functions of social workers in medical care settings. Clearly, certain tasks can only be performed by practitioners with a well-developed skill and knowledge base. Some examples are the teaching of students, supervision, in-service training, planning, administration and research. Other tasks more central to the service delivery role, such as collaboration, informal education of other staff, or work with patient groups, can be *adequately* performed by non-MSW's with proper preparation and supervision. The longer and more theoretical training of MSW's, however, tends to produce the intellectual resources and discipline for more sophisticated and complex practice.

Finally, it is an unavoidable fact of life that persuasiveness tends to be linked with prestige. Social workers must be able to present the psychosocial needs of patients and gain recognition for them from other staff and from the system. Unlike other personnel whose tasks are a taken-for-granted part of the delivery of medical services, social workers in most medical settings continually have to interpret both their professional role and the patients' needs. The prestige of professionals is almost directly related to years of education (15); social workers with gaduate degrees will in general command higher prestige than those without, and therefore will have an advantage in influencing other staff. A department staffed by MSW's will therefore tend to carry more authority within the medical care system than will one predominantly made up of bachelor's workers.

A social work department can intelligently use several levels of staff, in one of a number of possible models. Bachelor's level workers can be used for service delivery with MSW's providing their training and supervision. Another model utilizing BSW's assigns to the MSW the assessment of patient and family and design of the treatment plan, which the BSW then carries out. A third model proposes that MSW's and BSW's share cases and work in tandem, each carrying out the tasks appropriate to their level of skill and judgment. Other arrangements would simply assign different categories of cases to the two levels of workers with MSW's or DSW's carrying responsibility for the more complex, indirect practice tasks that have been discussed (4,24,33,44). There is no one correct model for staffing social work departments in medical care settings. What is important is the clear definition of tasks to be performed and of the degree of judgment and responsibility required, the assignment of a person appropriately prepared to carry it out and the proper support with in-service training, continuing education and supervision.

Two factors will shape further developments: standards of professional qualifications for social workers set by accrediting and funding agencies and the potential of the research now being conducted within social work departments. The National Association of Social Workers proposes that directors and supervisory staff hold graduate degrees from schools accredited by the Council on Social Work Education (39A). JCAH (Joint Commission on the Accreditation of Hospitals) and HHS guidelines stipulate that, where there is a hospital social work department, its director must meet this standard (28). Currently, however, the Department of Health and Human Services has proposed removal of this criterion from Medicare/ Medicaid Conditions of Participation. Until social workers can persuade accrediting and funding agencies to set and adhere to standards commensurate with the demands of social work in medical settings, social work will operate at a disadvantage.

The current analyses, using computerized information systems, can begin to address empirically the issue of the level of complexity of social work tasks and the degree of expertise and training required to perform them adequately. Many commentators predict that current research will contribute to the sound and intelligent use of varied levels of staff (59,33).

With increasing professionalization, social workers' consciousness grows of their capacity and responsibility to shape the circumstances of their work. Demands for fiscal stringency and the need for accountability have produced a variety of unanticipated but healthy consequences. As a result, social workers are achieving increased clarity of their role and purpose. Social work in health care has the tools to continue its evolution and to strengthen its capacity to promote the health and well-being of those it serves.

REFERENCES

1 American Hospital Association: *Hospital Statistics*, 1981 Edition, Chicago, 1981. Table 12A p. 192.

2 Bare M: Confronting a Life-Threatening Disease. In, *Social Work in Health Settings*. Toba Kerson, ed., New York: Longman, 1982.

3 Bartlett H: Ida M. Cannon. *Social Service Review* 49:208, 1975.

4 Berkman B: Innovations for Social Services in Health Care. In, *Changing Roles in Social Work Practice*. Francine Sobey, ed., Phila: Temple U. Press, 1977.

5 Berkman BG, Rehr H: Social Needs of the Hospitalized Elderly: A Classification. *Social Work*, *17*:80, 1972.

6 Berkman B, Rehr H, Rosenberg G: A Social Work Department Develops and Tests a Screening Mechanism to Identify High Social Risk Situations. *Social Work in Health Care*, *5*:373, 1980.

7 Boaz R: Health Care Systems. In, *Encyclopedia of Social Work* 17th issue, National Association of Social Workers, Washington, D.C., 1977.

8 Bracht NF: Health Maintenance Organizations. In, *Social Work in Health Care*. N. Bracht, ed., New York: Haworth Press, 1978.

9 Bracht NF: Social Work Practice in Hospitals: Changing Directions and New Opportunities. In, *Social Work in Health Care*, Neil F. Bracht, ed., New York: Haworth Press, 1978.

10 Bracht NF: Social Work Consultation and Teaching in Health Agencies and Medical Schools. In, *Social Work in Health Care*, Neil F. Bracht, ed., New York: Haworth Press, 1978.

11 Carlton TO: Social Work with Groups in Health Settings: A Bibliography of Social Work Books and Articles Published from 1970 to 1980. Virginia Commonwealth University (pamphlet).

12 Chisholm SE, Deniston OL, Igrisan RM, Barbus AJ: Prevalence of Confusion in Elderly Hospitalized Patients. *Journal of Geriatric Nursing*, *8*: 87, 1982.

13 Compton BR, Gallaway B: *Social Work Processes*, Homewood, Ill: Dorsey, 1979.

14 Conway JB: The Why and How of Relationship for the Social Worker in A Health Care Setting. *Journal of Otto Rank Assoc*, *14*:40, 1979.

15 Coser RL, Rokoff G: Women in the Occcupational World. *Social Problems*, *18*:535, 1971.

16 Finlayson A: Social Networks as Coping Resources. *Social Sci and Med*, *10*:97, 1976.

17 Freidson E: *Professional Dominance*. Chicago:Aldine, 1970.

18 Fry J: *Medicine in Three Societies*. American Elsivier Publishing Co, 1970.

19 Fujimoto M: Help for Family with an Abused Child. In, *Social Work in Health Settings*, T. Kerson, ed., New York: Longman, 1982.

20 Fuller S, Larson S: Life Events, Emotional Support and Health of Older People. *Res. on Nurs. and Health, 3*:81, 1980.
21 George L: *Role Transitions in Later Life.* Monterey, Cal: Brooks/Cole, 1980.
22 Germain CB, Gitterman A: *Life Model of Social Work Practice.* New York: Columbia University, 1980.
23 Green JW: *Cultural Awareness in the Human Services.* Englewood Cliffs, NJ: Prentice-Hall, 1982.
23A Grinnell RM, Kyte NS, Hunter S, Larson TA: The Status of Graduate-Level Social Workers Teaching in Medical Schools. *Soc. Work in Health Care, 1*:317, 1976.
24 Grossman L, Harrell, W and Melamed M: Changing Hospital Practice and Social Work Staffing. *Social Work*, 411-415, Sept. 1979.
25 Holmes R, Rahe R: The Social Readjustment Rating Scale. *Journal of Psychosom. Res, 11*:213, 1967.
26 Hookey, P: Social Work in Primary Care in *Social Work in Health Care.* Neil F. Bracht, ed., New York: The Haworth Press, 1978.
27 Hutter MJ, Zakus GE, Dungy CI: Social Work Training of New Health Professionals. *Health and Social Work, 1*:125, 1976.
28 Joint Commission on the Accreditation of Hospitals. *Accreditation Manual for Hospitals* Chicago: Joint Commission on The Accreditation of Hospitals, 1980.
29 Kane R: The Interprofessional Team as a Small Group. *Social Work in Health Care, 1*:19, 1975.
30 Katz A: Self-Help Groups, *Encyclopedia of Social Work* (17th issue) Washington, DC:NASW, 1977.
31 Lubove R: *The Professional Altruist.* Cambridge: Harvard University Press, 1965.
32 Lucente F and Fleck S: A Study of Hospitalization Anxiety in 408 Medical and Surgical Patients. *Psychosom Med, 134*: 304, 1972.
33 Lurie A: Staffing Patterns. *Social Work in Health Care, 2*:85, 1976.
34 McKinley JB: A Case for Refocusing Upstream: The Political Economy of Illness. In, *Patients, Physicians and Illness*, E. Gartly Jaco, ed., New York, Free Press, 1979.
35 McKinlay JB, Dutton, DB: Social Psychological Factors Affecting Health Service Utilization. In, *Consumer Incentives for Health Care.* S.J. Mushkin, ed., New York, Pro-Dist, 1974.
36 Mechanic D: *Medical Sociology*, 2nd ed., New York: Free Press, 1978.
37 Mezey M: Stress, Hospitalization and Aging. In, *ANA Proceedings of Research Sessions.* Kansas City, ANA Publications, 1979.
38 Middleman RR, Goldberg, G: *Social Service Delivery.* New York, Columbia University, 1974.
39 Miller E: The Changing Structure of the Medical Profession in Urban and Suburban Settings. In, *Patients, Physicians and Illness* 3rd edition, E. Gartly Jaco, ed., New York, Free Press, 1979.
39A National Association of Social Workers:NASW Standards for Social Work in Health Care Settings. Washington, DC: NASW, 1981.
40 *New York Times*, Sunday, October 10, 1982, p. 8C. Schweicker's Plan for Fixed Price Hospital Fees.
41 Niemann DA, Hoops A: Can Private Hospitals Afford to Provide Social Services. *Social Work in Health Care, 3*:175, 1977.
42 Nuckolls KB, Cassel J, Kaplan BH: Psychosocial Assets, Life Crisis and the Prognosis of Pregnancy. *American Journal of Epidem, 95*:431, 1972.
43 Palmiere D: Health Services:Health and Hospital Planning. *Encyclopedia of Social Work.* Washington, DC: NASW, 1977.

44 Phillips B: Health Services:Social Workers in *Encyclopedia of Social Work* (17th issue) Washington, DC:NASW, 1977.
45 Pincus A, Minahan A: Social Work Practice: *Model and Method.* Hasca, Ill., F.E.Peacock, 1973.
46 Regensburg J: *Toward Education for Health Professionals.* New York:
47 Rehr. H. ed.: *Medicine and Social Work: An Exploration in Interprofessionalism.* New York, Prodist, 1974.
48 Reid WJ, Epstein L: *Task-Centered Casework* New York, Columbia University Press, 1972.
49 Rubin I, Beckhard R: Factors Influencing the Effectiveness of Health Teams. *Milbank Mem Fund Quart, 50*:317, 1972.
50 Schwartz M: Situation/Transition Groups. *American J. Orthopsychiatry, 45*:744, 1975.
51 Schwartz M:Social Group Work:The Interactionist Approach. *Encyclopedia of Social Work* (17th issue) Washington, DC:NASW, 1977.
52 Shulman L: *The Skills of Helping Individuals and Groups* Itasca, Ill.: Peacock, 1979.
53 Skipper J and Leonard R: Children, Stress, and Hospitalization. *J. of Health and Social Behavior, 9*:273, 1968.
54 Society for Hospital Social Work Directors, Membership Survey Results Reported (mimeographed) 1981.
55 U.S. Department of Health, Education and Welfare. *Health, United States, 1979.* DHEW Publication O. (PHS) 80-1232.
56 U.S.Senate, Special Committee on Aging:Health Care Expenditures for the Elderly: How Much Protection Does Medicare Provide? Washington: U.S. Govt. Printing Office, 1982.
57 Volland P: Social Work Information and Accountability Systems in a Hospital Setting. In, *Social Work in Health Care*, Neil F. Bracht, ed., New York, The Haworth Press, 1978.
58 Wayne MA: PSRO: Issues in Health Care Policy. *Health and Social Work* 2:25, 1977.
59 Wise H: The Primary Health Care Team. *Arch Int Med, 130*:438, 1972.
60 Zborowski M: Cultural Components in Response to Pain. In, *Patients Physicians and Illness.* E. Gartly Jaco, ed., Glencoe, Ill, Free Press, 1958.
61 Zelinka JD: Discharge Planning. In, *Social Work in Health Settings.* T. Kerson ed., New York, Longman, 1982.

Chapter 3

SOCIAL WORK IN MENTAL HEALTH SETTINGS

EDGAR A. PERRETZ*
ARTHUR F. MOFFA, JR.
WILLIAM SILVER
S. REID WARREN, III

INTRODUCTION

This chapter affords the reader a panoramic view of the part that social work plays in a variety of mental health settings, using the wide spectrum of essential services of community mental health centers as a general frame of reference. The main underlying purpose of the chapter is to convey the rationale, the posture, the policies and the thrust of social work as they have been brought to bear upon the field of mental health over this century.

These considerations importantly affect the nature of social work practice and the content of services rendered by social work practitioners. This chapter is confined to the questions that concern social workers in relation to mental health and illness and the tasks which social workers have assumed in addressing those questions in relation to persons across the continuum from the well to the profoundly ill. There is no intention to deal with methods of practice, i.e., "how-to-practice" material; that is beyond the purview of this chapter.

While this chapter does not pretend to offer a history of social work in mental health settings, there is no denial of the historical perspec-

*The collaborators gratefuly acknowledge the scholarly leadership provided by Edgar A. Perretz in organizing and developing this chapter. His recent untimely death leaves a void for his colleagues and students who have worked and studied with him.

tive which has been presented. For example, we span three-quarters of the twentieth century from the first appointment of a social worker in mental health in the year 1905 to the early 1980's, pausing to call attention to the report of the National Institute of Mental Health (30, p. 17) that there were 31,312 social work positions in mental health facilities across the United States in 1976. In that same year, 18% of the professional patient care positions in mental health facilities were held by social workers, 13% by psychiatrists, an additional 3% by non-psychiatric physicians, 12% by psychologists, 26% by registered nurses, 6% by physical health professionals, and the remainder by "other mental health professionals" (30, p. 11).

Within the same three quarters of a century, education for social work in mental health settings — also called psychiatric social work — changed from an in-service training program for those employed in the field, or an apprenticeship program for college seniors during the pre-World War I period, to a graduate professional program, requiring full-time class work and coordinated field practice in an approved mental health setting over a two-year continuum.

In the beginning, social workers were given ad hoc assignments, e.g., to do social histories in a busy out-patient clinic or in the admissions unit of a hospital, for physicians who were positively disposed to their services. As their training and competence evolved, their services spread across the entire spectrum of mental health services. We have used the community mental health center as a model/frame of reference to demonstrate the utilization of social workers in mental health settings, especially over the last quarter of this century. Hence, we have described the activities of social workers in each of the following components or service areas designated as high priorities by the National Institute of Mental Health:

In-patient
Out-patient
Partial hospitalization
Emergency
Consultation and Education
Child Mental Health
Services for the Elderly
Screening Services
After-care
Transitional Services
Social Support Services
Alcoholism
Drug Addiction

Of the 31,312 social work positions in mental health facilities in 1976, there were 7,957 social workers employed in federally funded community mental health centers (28, p. 31). Social workers were most numerous among the four mental health professions, since psychiatrists numbered 3,738, psychologists 4,543, and registered nurses 6,761.

It would be an over-simplification to cite numbers alone to demonstrate the place that social work has carved out for itself in the field of mental health. The preponderance of social workers in the staffing of federally funded community mental health centers is in itself an acknowledgement of the value attached to the services rendered by social workers in a mental health setting. Yet, it is the content of *social care* and the psychosocial rationale of social work that account for the contribution that the profession aims to make. It is that rationale, as it is translated into services across the mental health and illness continuum, that this chapter addresses.

THE COMMUNITY MENTAL HEALTH CENTER: A FRAMEWORK FOR PROVISION OF CARE

The National Mental Health Act of 1946 (P. L. 79-487) established the National Institute of Mental Health (NIMH), which has profoundly affected the development of the mental health professions ever since then. NIMH support for mental health research produced a plethora of literature reporting progress on that research and increasing a public understanding of mental health and illness. It also set in motion a system of support for training of research personnel in the sciences and the professions associated with the field of mental health.

In 1955, the Mental Health Study Act (P. L. 84-182) paved the way for recommendations calling for deinstitutionalization and community-based services. In reality, it was the report in 1961 of the Joint Commission on Mental Illness and Health (29) which furnished a "blueprint" for the framing of specific provisions of the Community Mental Health Act of 1963 (P. L. 88-164). This Act and its amendments have inevitably had a powerful effect upon the organization and delivery of mental health services throughout the U.S.A.

The mid-1960's were years of ferment and optimism, of experimentation and innovation, of yeasty change and excitement in the field of mental health. The National Institute of Mental Health (NIMH) was vibrating with activity, and appropriations from Congress filled its sails with confidence that its mandate could be carried out — with distinction. This high level of aspiration on the part of NIMH meant that only the most meritorious research and training proposals, in the judgment of advisory groups and staff, were supported and that applications for funding of community mental health centers had to meet rigorous standards, that site visits were made to inspect the centers and that monitoring of their ongoing programs became standard operating procedure to insure quality control and compliance with regulations.

The so-called "essential services" of a community mental center will serve rather well as a frame of reference for a review of the spectrum of activities in which social workers are involved in the mental health system of this country. Those indicated as "essential services" were the priorities which emerged from a wide range of programs stretching from pre-care to after care. Among other criteria then by which a community mental health center was defined under the regulations formulated to carry out the intent of the Community Mental Health Act of 1963 were the following services: in-patient, out-patient, transitional, emergency, and consultation/education.

IN-PATIENT SERVICES

The intent of the law was to shift the mentally ill from confinement in state and county mental hospitals to less restrictive community living arrangements. Developments in chemotherapy had already made it possible to set this trend in motion in the 1950's. Concerted effort over 20 years led to a dramatic reduction of inpatient care episodes, which dropped sharply from 77.4% in 1955 to 55.4% in 1965, then to 42.6% in 1971 and next, to 27.9% in 1975. The decline of in-patient services in state and county hospitals was, by design, similarly steep for the same years: 48.9%, 30.5%, 18.5%, and 9.3%. According to the President's Commission on Mental Health (35:93), shorter periods of hospitalization and alternatives to hospitalization have been the twin objectives of mental health planners.

The consequences of this trend for public and voluntary hospitals designated to serve as short-term intensive treatment centers and the implications for social work practice within the context of these in-patient programs are examined in the section on *Inpatient Treatment*.

THE TREATMENT OF MENTAL ILLNESS: A BRIEF HISTORICAL COMMENTARY

During the first half of this century, state hospitals for the mentally ill were jammed. There were many accommodating over 5,000 patients and some in excess of 10,000. There was an acute shortage of psychiatrists during that period, and a large percentage of them were in private practice. Patients who could afford the fee-for-service arrangement were frequently involved in psychotherapy or psychoanalysis. These, and a limited number of patients who had been identified as most amenable to treatment in public clinics, were the "fortunate few" among the mentally ill.

Instead of therapeutic attention, it was mainly custodial care that patients received in the over-crowded, under-staffed state hospitals (16). Many chores were assigned to patients in the name of "work therapy," but the monotony of mopping floors can hardly pass as a substitute for treatment. Besides, the patients who were assigned to work projects were frequently those who had shown signs of improvement.

The ethos of the state mental hospital was characterized by "distancing" the patient from the rest of society. Since a "crazy" person manifests behavior which is often frightening or offensive, this seemed to call for his banishment to a place where he might be "straightened out" or throttled. Custodial attention in the large wards of state hospitals frequently degenerated to the level of subduing the patients. Patients were generally *committed* to the state hospital. They were confined to locked wards. They were obliged to follow hospital rules of conduct, day and night. They were subjected to deprivation of privileges and other punishment, for infraction of rules. They were usually left to the mercy of ward attendants, some of whom were competent, caring, and compassionate and some were not. See Greenblatt *et al.* (16)

The capacity of the patient to conform to hospital rules was frequently used as a criterion for assessing his improvement. In short, compliance was equated with good adjustment; whereas, agressive or resistive behavior was usually regarded negatively. While one can readily understand how defiance on the part of a patient would create management problems for the attendant staff, it is not hard to recognize some unfortunate consequences of this assessment process. The patient who was already confused by the distortions in reality arising from his mental illness might be further disturbed by the inexplicable demands of the hospital. If he had demonstrated what might be regarded as "righteous indignation" outside of the hospital, he could find himself in isolation or bound down in physical restraints.

This leads us to a brief reference to shock treatment. There is little question that the patient who was committed to the state mental hospital was regarded as somehow "uncontrollable" in the community. If he continued to be "uncooperative" and there was no remission of his symptoms, this often led to the conclusion that somatic procedures (sterner measures!) were indicated.

Insulin shock treatment and electric convulsive therapy, which were discovered in 1933 and 1935, respectively, became important new tools in the treatment of schizophrenia and manic-depressive psychosis. Electro-convulsive therapy (ECT) emerged as the far safer and more simply administered of the two. Although there were certain side-effects, including fractures, which occurred during the convulsion, these problems were reduced in time by the use of muscle-relaxant drugs. There was wholesale, if not indiscriminate, use of ECT in state mental hospitals. It occurred as much to solve problems of patient management as to effect therapeutic change.

There was considerable uncertainty among psychiatrists in the 1940's about the therapeutic value of concurrent psychotherapy for patients receiving ECT. This is not entirely surprising since little was known about the etiology and physiology of schizophrenia, and less was known about the effect of ECT on the organism except for the observable and electroencephalographic reactions of the patient to whom it was administered. These factors, combined with the shortage of trained personnel, led to an inordinately heavy reliance upon ECT to roll back symptoms, to bring the psychotic episode under control, to free the patient from his confusion, to pave the way for the patient to benefit from the *milieu* of the hospital, and to prepare the patient for discharge. ECT was no panacea, and patients who were discharged after one series of ECT frequently required readmission for a second, third, or fourth time.

The 1940's were pivotal years in other ways. The large number of young men who were discharged from the military service for neuropsychiatric reasons directed public attention to the urgent need for expanded, improved, and publicly-supported mental health services. Accordingly, legislation was passed in 1946 which established the National Institute of Mental Health, and initially it was mandated to provide support for mental health research and for training of personnel in the mental health professions, including psychiatry, clinical psychology, psychiatric social work, and mental health nursing.

The introduction of psychotropic drugs in the early 1950's added some important new "weapons" to the arsenal of the psychiatrist and the mental health establishment. Although they too had side effects, there was nothing to compare with the profound fatigue, severe memory loss, the extreme "wear-and-tear," and sometimes the fracture, caused by ECT. Insulin shock had been far more forbidding for the patient and far more cumbersome for the staff. These procedures created a hornet's nest of iatrogenic problems and generated responses ranging from terror to anger on the part of the patient who was subjected to them. One can just imagine how this affected the relationship between patient and therapist. One can, likewise, imagine what a vast difference the psychotropic drugs made — with their tranquilizing effect upon the patient. Some nausea, dizziness, headaches, sweating, skin eruptions, even temporary double-vision — to mention but a few complications — were reported. But the effect of the psychotropic drugs was two-fold: *control* over the disturbed patient, who became *subdued* without being "clobbered" by his therapist, and *contract* with the patient who was *rendered more accessible to psychotherapeutic intervention.*

The numbers of trained mental health professionals were increasing noticeably by the late 1950's. Interdisciplinary collaboration in the treatment of mental illness became standard practice in teaching hospitals and most progressive treatment centers. Mental Health education was thriving, and mental health propaganda called for early detection and early intervention for mental illness. Concurrently, there was a popularization of psychiatric concepts and terminology. It had become fashionable to have undergone psychoanalysis, and (in certain social circles) psychopathology and therapy were subjects for lively social conversation.

Community mental health centers, which became the priority of the 1960's, are discussed in considerable detail in this chapter. Suffice it to say, in this context, that they were intended to provide a full spectrum of services (7) within the boundaries of a catchment area (ranging in population from 75,000 to 200,000) to persons of all ages, irrespective of income, psychiatric diagnosis and probable duration of treatment. The emphasis was on *appropriate* care in place of benign neglect. This meant continuity of care, integration of services, and community involvement. This was a tall order because it was linked with the inexorible trend toward deinstitutionalization and community-based care for the mentally ill.

The patients' right movement of the 1970's profoundly affected the delivery of services to the mentally ill. Simply stated, it had the net effect of reducing the patient's vulnerability to decisions made by mental health professionals which could have major implications for his mind and body as well as life and liberty. In the case of Wyatt V. Stickney (49), a landmark decision was rendered that a patient, whether voluntary or involuntary, has the right to treatment and can not be detained unless there is evidence of benefit to the patient or improvement of his condition as a result of the treatment process. The court had ruled that deficits in ratio of staff to patients, content of the treatment program, and physical facilities had not been conducive to the patients' welfare and that the rights of the plaintiff had been violated.

This landmark decision set off a chain reaction across the land. State after state passed legislation addressing the rights of mental patients which had the effect of limiting the activities of professionals and imposed new obligations upon them, which significantly affected hospital administration and the treatment transaction. A major example is the patient's right to know what the treatment plan is, to be kept apprised of his progress, and to have access to professional staff in the dynamics of reformulating treatment over time in order to be an integral part of and to benefit from the therapeutic process. The same right is guaranteed to the family. What may be expressed as a single *right* becomes a cluster of factors, which have powerful impact on the delivery of services. The right of access to a lawyer, as one might expect, has resulted in the contesting of many decisions which have been perceived as violations of patient rights. This has greatly complicated the provision of appropriate in-patient care, in particular, for the mentally ill. Yet the protection of rights has been a giant step forward in the annals of health care.

Professional Standards Review Organizations (PSRO's) were established in the 1970's to develop guidelines for practice in the field of mental health, in particular. Other sectors of the health care enterprise were confronted with the need to do likewise. The recommendations for specific conditions to obtain or procedures to be followed in order to maintain specified standards of practice were formulated by national standard-setting organizations which have jurisdiction over hospitals and mental health centers for accreditation purposes. PSRO's were, then, an important response to a mounting public concern regarding the *efficiency* and *quality* of care for the mentally ill. This thrust should yield benefits to the provider as well as the consumer of mental health services, although the negotiations which lead to these protective "compacts" are long and tortuous.

Community care has been the intention, the hope and the plan for the 1960's, 70's, and '80's. It was expected to achieve the objective of deinstitutionalization of all patients who were not a clear and unmistakable danger to society or to themselves. The community mental health center was intended to have central role in this plan. That is why we have assigned so much space to the community mental health center as a concept, as a policy, as a plan, as a therapeutic program, and finally, as an organizational structure for the delivery of mental health services.

THERAPEUTIC ENDEAVOR VS. SOCIAL REFORM

The first ten years of psychiatric social work (1905-1914) were part of the "progressive period" in American history. It was an era in which *social reform* was the preoccupation of the profession, when the priorities of social workers were regulation of child labor, maternal and child health, protection of women in industry, housing conditions and tenants' rights, the humane assimilation of millions of European immigrants, etc. These themes involved social workers in political and social action, and in social reform.

The investment of social work energies in *social reform* was quite different from that of social workers who were attracted to *psychiatric* social work, with its emphasis on therapeutic considerations. One fixed its attention on environmental and societal phenomena; the other fixed its attention upon the individual, the family, and groups of people regarded as most vulnerable to mental illness.

These two contending themes are emphasized in social work education and social work literature to this day, and each has waxed and waned, but both have exerted powerful influence upon the direction of the profession throughout the past three-quarters of this century. Yet, these seemingly contending elements are likely to complement each other. Reform is essentially concerned with "repairing the damage" or the pathology, which is partially attributable to injustice.

EARLY DEVELOPMENTS: 1905-1929

Social work services were established in the "neurological clinics" of the Massachusetts General Hospital, at Bellevue Hospital and at Cornell Clinic, both in New York City, during the year 1905.

Dr. James Putnam, in charge of the neurological clinic at the Massachesetts General, appointed a full-time social worker for the first time in 1907. French (12) extracted the following from the annual reports for the years 1907-1910:

> Of special significance are the close working relationships with the physicians in charge of the clinic and the responsibility carried by the workers for treatment as well as for social investigation. They shared in the supervision of patients in their homes and communities and aided in the arrangements for employment, recreation, and better adjustment in family relationships. . . . The workers also maintained a close relationship with the social agencies in the community (p. 36-7).

Boston Psychopathic Hospital was opened in 1912 under the direction of Dr. E. E. Southard. Miss Mary C. Jarrett was appointed to take charge of the social service program in 1913 with a mandate to assist in the study and treatment of mental disease. Southard and Jarrett were avant-garde in their thinking as well as their collaboration in practice. French (12) illustrates this point by quoting them as follows:

> The medical and social aspects of out-patient treatment for nervous and mental disorders are so closely interwoven that they can hardly be discussed separately. . . . In most cases, medical treatment is supplemented and reinforced by social care (p. 38-9).

Mary Jarrett assumed leadership in involving social workers in contributing to the research function of the hospital and participating in public health education regarding mental illness. She advocated and conducted in-service training courses for social workers. In 1914, she initiated an apprenticeship training program at Boston Psychopathic Hospital for students enrolled at the Smith College. The sequel to this venture was an important project in the history of social work education: the first formal program in *psychiatric* social work, combining classroom instruction in psychiatry and social work theory and clinical experience. This project was undertaken at Smith College in the summer of 1918 as an accelerated training program to prepare a cadre of 60 students for the war-time emergency, which had already called attention to mental illness and the high rate of casualties attributable to "nervous breakdown" and to anxiety states and other disorders associated with the carnage of war.

This project together with the inauguration of a regular curriculum in *psychiatric social work* at Smith College in the ensuing year represented the launching of a specialized field of practice within social work. In 1922, a petition was submitted to the American Association of Hospital Social Workers for the formation of a Section on Psychiatric Social Work. This was only an interim arrangement until, in 1926, the American Association of Psychiatric Social Workers was established. In addition to its promotion of *psychiatric* social work as a specialization, it became the standard-setting body for curriculum development and the national certification agency for practitioners in psychiatric social work.

These developments in psychiatric social work were occurring during the era of the "mental health movement," which began in 1908 with the publication of Clifford Beers' book, *The Mind That Found Itself*, followed in the same year by the founding of the Connecticut Society for Mental Hygiene through the effort of Clifford Beers. Next came the founding of the National Committee for Mental Hygiene whose first secretary was Clifford Beers. When in 1917, the National Committee directed its attention to the psychiatric problems of men in the armed forces, public and professional interest coalesced around concrete steps that could be taken to treat those with symptoms of mental illness *and* to prevent the onset of mental illness within the general (civilian) population.

A prime example of this new awareness is to be found in the child guidance movement, in which psychiatric social work began to play a significant part in the 1920's. Children, referred to the child guidance clinic because they had been disruptive in school or by the juvenile court, most often for theft, property damage, or sex offenses, were examined in depth for the *psychosocial* and *developmenal* etiology that might offer clues to the resolution of their problems. Another factor which explains the "climate" of thinking during that period was the emergence of *orthopsychiatry* with its emphasis upon 1. the process of development in all its dimensions (physiological, psychological, interpersonal, sociocultural, and spiritual); 2. etiology and the concept of multiple causation; 3. borderline emotional problems of childhood and adolescence; 4. interdisciplinary or interprofessional approach to the diagnosis and treatment of emotional and mental disorders; and 5. preventive efforts, involving mental health education and reaching out to the lay community.

Social workers found congenial colleagueship within the context of the *team* which developed among those in psychiatry, psychology, education and others who subscribed to this philosophy of helping children and their parents. Social work earned a respected place for itself in the child guidance clinic for two reasons. It had become axiomatic that a troubled child could not be helped — indeed, was not treatable! — unless a parent (preferably both parents) or surrogate parents were involved in the process. Since the parents are inevitably locked in a psychosocial relationship of utmost intimacy with their own child and provide the models (whatever the quality!) along with the "power" to enhance or inhibit many aspects of development, the axiom has withstood the tests of time. Because of the psychosocial content of the transaction with the parent(s) and the case management aspects of affording continuity of service to the family by linking up with school and other community resources potentially supportive to the child, it has become traditional for the psychiatric social worker to engage the family throughout the entire treatment process.

SOCIAL WORK IN THE 1930's

At the beginning of the century, and again during the economic depression of the 1930's, the social reformers were in the ascendancy. The prime example is Jane Addams, a renowned social worker, best known to readers of her books, *Twenty Years at Hull House* (1910) and *Second Twenty Years at Hull House* (1930), and as the recipient of the Nobel Prize in Peace in 1931. Then there were social workers in positions of leadership, such as Harry Hopkins and Frances Perkins, to mention only the "celebrities" of that era, who were involved in social policy formulation anf social reform.

However, the influence of orthopsychiatry (23) on the one hand, and psychoanalytic theory on the other, had stimulated *psychiatric* social workers to map out an area of expertise and of specialization in mental hygiene, as it was then called. There was debate over the question: was it the mental health *setting* which signified that the person was a specialist in *psychiatric* social work, or was it the acquisition of special knowledge of psychiatry that conferred status on the practitioner? A partial answer to this question can be found in the efforts throughout the decade of the 1930's to establish standards for practice beginning with the Report of the Milford Conference (24, pp. 37-38) which stressed competence based on knowledge. There was a preoccupation throughout the 1930's regarding the need to revise standards of membership in the American Association of Psychiatric Social Workers (AAPSW) and to reformulate standards of education and practice.

PSYCHIATRIC SOCIAL WORK, 1940-1980

The mental health professions were profoundly affected by World War II. The uprooting of millions of civilians on the home front and the deployment of millions of military personnel to combat and related duties around the world posed staggering mental health problems in themselves. However, during the war emergency, Selective Service had found it necessary to reject over one million draft-age conscripts for neuropsychiatric reasons and during the course of the war *more* men received medical discharges from the Army, Navy and other services for neuropsychiatric disorders than for any other reason.

There was a severe shortage of mental health personnel on the home-front during the war years; however, the same could be said for the Armed Forces as evidenced by the fact that there were fewer than 3,000 qualified psychiatrists in all in 1945, an estimated 71% shortage of psychiatric social workers, and a 92% shortage of psychologists (NIMH).

In the meantime, psychiatric social workers had gained recognition in the Army and the Air Force in 1943 when ASN 263 was assigned to personnel who qualified by reason of professional education, and by 1946 qualifications in social work were recognized as a basis for commissioning officers.

The high incidence of neuropsychiatric casualties during the war and the alarming realization that mental illness was the No. 1 health problem in the nation paved the way for the passage of the National Mental Health Act of 1946, with federal support for training, research, and services.

These developments, combined with benefits to ex-servicemen, and traineeships made available by the National Institute of Mental Health, the Veterans Administration, the Office of Vocational Rehabilitation, Children's Bureau, *et al.*, attracted a large number of applicants to schools of social work. The post-war bulge in enrollment in schools of social work was marked by a large influx of men into the profession. In addition to social case work, group work, community organization, social administration, and research received heavier emphasis and opened new career options to students in psychiatric (and other) areas of social work.

The 1950's were characterized by consolidation of the specialty organizations, including the American Association of Psychiatric Social Workers, under one umbrella. The National Association of

Social Workers (NASW), established in 1954, had the effect of unifying the profession in this new era of expansion and opportunity. The same could be said for the founding of the Council on Social Work Education (CSWE), which replaced the American Association of Schools of Social Work as the standard-setting and accrediting body.

The Council invested itself in an ambitious Curriculum Study, in which it did *not*, however, undertake to examine education for the profession *by specialization*, but by methods and curriculum areas, instead. (*Social Work Curriculum Study*: W.W. Boehm, director, 13 volumes; New York: Council on Social Work Education, 1969). It is our opinion that specialization had been viewed as a devisive force within the profession. While specialization was undeniably a continuing force, changes in terminology from "psychiatric social work" to "social work in mental health" are to be found in the literature. Others would contend that this occurred in order to emphasize the unique contribution of social work in the field of mental health instead of using the adjective, which describes another profession, as the modifier. Nevertheless, the National Institute of Mental Health continued to use the term "psychiatric social work".

Since this was the decade in which psychotropic drugs made their debut and social policy called for reducing dependency on the mental hospital as the locus for care, social work had begun to turn its attention to community care and to the new challenge of short-term intensive treatment.

The 1960's were turbulent, to say the least — "the best of times and the worst of times"! They were full of promise for the mental health field, full of hope for the poor and the disadvantaged, yet riddled with alienation, disenchantment, polarization, confrontation, and disdain for authority. As a consequence, psychiatric social workers were largely preoccupied with the service demands of the evolving community mental health programs, while social workers in other sectors were equally preoccupied with the social change (or social reform) imperatives that were inherent in programs spawned by the "war on poverty."

The National Institute of Mental Health was authorized to provide grant support for training, research, and service (as well as funds for construction) to achieve the objectives of the Community Mental Health Act of 1963, and in the campaign to bury the old mental hospital mold, they offered special incentives for experimentation and innovation in community mental health, including the day hospital, the half-way house, the socialization center, the store-front crisis center, the walk-in service, the employment of non-professionals and persons indigenous to an area whose population was comprised of any particular ethnic or racial group.

Students (trainees) in psychiatry, clinical psychology, psychiatric social work, and mental health nursing were engaged in their respective educational programs in ever-increasing numbers.

The following data are indicative of the increases in social work trainees, in particular:

Master's Degrees Awarded to Graduates* of Schools of Social Work in the United States, by Sex, Selected Years, 1944-45 to 1978-79.

Academic Year	*Total*	*Men*	*Women*
1944 - 45	839	43	796
1947 - 48	1,765	496	1,269
1950 - 51	1,923	744	1,179
1962 - 63	2,505	1,025	1,480
1968 - 69	5,060	2,029	3,031
1974 - 75	8,824	3,037	5,730
1977 - 78	9,476	2,644	6,832
1978 - 79	10,080	2,772	7,308

* In all areas, i.e., not limited to psychiatric.

Excerpted from the Supplement to the *Encyclopedia of Social Work*, 11, (p. 51, updating p. 1669)

It is also worth noting the increase in the number of schools offering post-master's and doctoral education in social work over a forty year period and the increase in the number of doctorates actually awarded.

Schools Offering Post-Master's Programs and Doctoral Degrees Awarded in Social Work in the U.S.A., Selected Years, 1949 to 1979*

Year	*Number of Schools*	*Number of Doctoral Degrees Awarded*
1949	9	6
1959	15	26
1969	20	89
1976	33	179
1977	34	179
1979	38	174

Excerpted from the Supplement to the *Encyclopedia of Social Work*, 11, (p. 51).

The clinical experience was more than ever before *interdisciplinary* and for social work it was geared to: short-term-treatment, intervention with the family, group therapy, developing community resources, promoting citizen awareness of mental health and illness, and sponsoring education, recreation, employment and community living alternatives for the rehabilitation of the mentally and emotionally ill. Federal funds for training had increased from the level of $1.1 million in 1948 to $73.2 million in 1965, with the peak year being 1971, when the level had risen to $110 million for training in all the mental health professions (11, p. 888).

There was an inexorible tendency toward employment in community mental health centers (CMHC's). They had become the centerpiece of social policy in mental health and the long-awaited haven for persons at any point on the health-to-illness continuum. This was the place where there was "action": innovation in treatment modalities, flexibility in administration, easy access and continuity of care for the patient, commitment to the catchment area (the community) served by the CMHC, training, research, opportunity for professional growth, and a positive esprit-de-corps across the professions — as never before. Last, but not least, they were favored with funds from federal, state, and local sources. Thus, mental health professionals, including social workers, gravitated to them in the 1960's.

In the late sixties and early seventies, social work succumbed to the same convulsions that racked the other mental health professions. In a period of extreme social upheaval, overriding concern for the human condition can cause a partial eclipse: it can cause the clinical worker to doubt the value of what he/she is doing with the individual client, patient, or family. Overt expression of mistrust came from those sectors of the community that the mental health services were intended to reach: the poor and the minorities. In addition, the non-professionals, who had been employed to assist in reaching out to those previously deprived of access to service, had begun to assert themselves, politically, by claiming that they were more effective with their "brethren" among the poor and minorities than the professionals and as far as they were concerned, the professionals could move over or move out — if their jobs were at stake.

Since these were the years when high priority was assigned to "maximum feasible participation" of consumers as board members of community mental health centers, it is *not* hard to imagine how much potential there was for explosive confrontations and power struggles — especially in certain inner city catchment areas. Then, there was the contention that Black patients had to be treated by

Black professionals, Latinos by Latinos, etc. These issues are illustrative of the volatile state of minority politics in many urban communities during the period spanning the civil rights movement and the Vietnam war.

In the seventies, more than ever before, advocacy became a major acknowledged role of the social worker, whether in mental health or elsewhere. Civil rights, minority rights, patients' rights, women's rights, consumers' rights, *et al.*, reinforce each other, and those who are disabled, poor, undereducated, inarticulate, powerless, and lacking access to legal and other forms of protection need someone to intercede for them. For the confused patient and the beleaguered family, the social worker was/is a logical person to protect them from the hazards of "bureaucracy" — within the mental health system or in the community.

One of the major problems in American society, which the profession addressed seriously, was that of institutional racism, i.e., the systematic exclusion for racial reasons of any person from his/her right to education, employment, housing, health and welfare benefits, etc. Discrimination against citizens based on color of skin or religious preference or ethnic origin is both a violation of the law and an act that is ultimately damaging to the person's security, and as such, it is a danger to his mental health. Thus, it became necessary for social workers to deal with this pervasive social pathology in our midst at the level of individual therapy, in administrative decisions, and at the level of policy formulation, i.e., across the entire spectrum.

Perhaps more than ever before, social work has committed its energies to evaluation of its activities. Questions raised by nonprofessionals had undoubtedly caused them to adopt a somewhat defensive posture. The pressure for fiscal accountability in the early seventies placed an additional obligation upon social work (along with the other mental health professions) to design some measurements of effectiveness of their services. Certainly as funding began to taper off, the competition for fewer dollars created even greater demand for accountability, efficiency, effectiveness, and economy — which led to Professional Standards Review Organizations (PSRO's). Briefly stated, PSRO is a system of checking on patient care by peers within a profession by measuring the nature and duration of treatment and response to that treatment for a particular patient with a specified diagnosis against consensually validated standards as set forth by the mental health facility in accordance with the guidelines of the Joint Commission on Accreditation of Hospitals (JCAH).

There has been a concerted effort since the Academy of Certified Social Workers (ACSW) was established in the early sixties to achieve two objectives: to assume proper responsibility for the competence of practitioners by testing them in practice under supervision and subjecting them to examination to test their knowledge base *and* to secure legislation, state by state, for purposes of establishing certification, registration, or licensing procedures. Given the nature of the health arena, it is quite important for social work to take this route, along with the other professions.

THE PSYCHOSOCIAL AND BIOMEDICAL MODELS IN MENTAL HEALTH

Early in this century, social work adopted a bio-psychosocial view of the person who needed or received professional service (37). It is accurate to assert that the profession has been most concerned with the *social functioning* of individuals, groups, or larger collectivities. The centrality of this concern manifests itself in the historical roots of the profession, in the goals and the tasks that it set for itself, in the competencies that the profession sought to develop, in the role that has been staked out for social work among the mental health professions, and in the social philosophy and ideology of the profession.

The contribution of social work is based upon premises which differ in many respects from those of the biomedical model (22). Traditionally, the social worker has referred to the person as a *client* rather than a patient. This difference is not as subtle as it seems, since *client* is a more egalitarian term than *patient*. Associated with this difference is the basic concept of helping the client to help himself (6) as contrasted with that of administering treatment to a "passive sufferer," described in medical parlance as the patient (9). Social workers have been inclined to provide *services*, which have contributed to therapeutic objectives, but they tended to engage in what they have generally called a "helping process" in which the client was expected to be as active as possible. This point is substantiated by the reference to "working *with* the client," which is heard over and over again in social work practice (6). This approach is much preferred over doing things *to* or *for* the client. In fact, the latter is sometimes questioned and described disparagingly as "superimposing" on the client.

The *biomedical model* focuses on the disease process (22) or the pathology; whereas, the *social model* emphasizes *social functioning* (or dysfunction), which calls into question the entire social milieu as an integral part of any assessment of the client. That is not all: it means that the members of the family are more than "resources" to the client; they inevitably affect the client and are affected by the client. They are, therefore, included in the helping process. Under the influence of the social model, there is an emphasis upon *capacity* rather than disability, upon elements and evidence of wellness as opposed to illness, upon helping the client to resolve his own problem, upon prevention of further loss of footing or status, and upon effecting change (improvement) in circumstances external to the client.

Thus, the helping process places ultimate responsibility upon the client. The social worker is expected to be a catalyst who enables the client to sort out and define his/her problem, to examine the alternatives available, to act upon them in relation to a particular aspect of the problem, and to regain his equilibrium and his capacity to cope with the realities of living (40).

The psychosocial dimension of mental illness is probably the paramount factor in determining the course of treatment for the patient. Since social behavior looms so large as a factor in the *perception* of the mental health patient by his family, his friends, fellow workers, his employer, his neighbors, and the rest of society, that in itself imposes a weighty responsibility upon the profession which claims this sector as its major focus. In a ground-breaking tome called *Social Diagnosis* Richmond (37) began staking out the various kinds of evidence the social worker needs for a fuller understanding of complex human problems and the elaboration of the biopsychosocial model that has become the terra firma of social work education.

The tolerance for the behavior of an individual importantly affects the point at which he will be regarded as deviant or abnormal; whether behavior is controllable or threatening to others, amusing or disruptive, and whether the person is too confused and out of touch with reality to face the daily tasks of a spouse, parent, an employee, neighbor, and law-abiding member of a community.

Servan (40) reminds us that "several factors are of particular importance in the rehabilitation of the schizophrenic patient in the community," and he includes:

1. "support of and the quality of interaction with family members in whose care many of the patients are released . . ."
2. "the attitudinal expectations of the family regarding the patient's social functioning, specifically his ability to fulfill social roles as a productive member of the community . . ."

3. "the continuation of treatment on an outpatient basis and following through on the recommended medication program . . ."
4. "the patient's level of awareness of his difficulties in coping with community demands and of his deviant behavior which affects his willingness and motivation to seek help voluntarily before the stress is experienced in extramural living culminate in another enforced hospitalization" (pp. 205-206).

It can be seen from the foregoing that the formerly hospitalized patient is "judged" by those who are most closely associated with him on a daily basis in terms of his *social functioning* and that psychosocial criteria are crucially important in determining what becomes of the patient. Item 3 above, continuation of treatment, is frequently construed as complying with the rules of the game, although it means adhering to a prescribed treatment regimen, when taken literally. In addition, since psychotropic drugs are involved, patient's compliance is as reassuring to the "care-taker" as the medication is stabilizing to the patient. Contrariwise, the patient's failure to continue creates anxiety for the "care-taker," who may attribute the slightest "misbehavior" to withdrawal from chemotherapy.

The centrality and pivotal significance of *social functioning* in the study, diagnosis, treatment, and prognosis of mental illness is observable in the giant stride that the American Psychiatric Association (4) took in a recent major revision of its *Diagnostic and Statistical Manual* (DSM III). In the past, attention had been focused on personality, developmental, and physical disorders, and these factors (with important modifications) continue to constitute the three "axes" or criteria for assessment of the patient. But, in addition, Axis IV fixes upon a range of psychosocial stressors from minimal to catastrophic, which are regarded by the clinician or clinical team as having "contributed to the initiation or exacerbation of an individual's mental disorder".

Axis V fastens attention upon a scale for rating the highest level of adaptive functioning in the past year for adults in various circumstances and children of different ages. Effectiveness of social functioning includes social relationships, occupational functioning (or school for children) and use of leisure time. Williams (46) has this to say about Axis V:

> "It has long been recognized that one of the most accurate indicators of clinical outcome is the level of premorbid functioning that an individual is able to sustain" (p. 104).

Hence, the social component of mental illness has been officially recognized as being intimately interrelated with assessment criteria which had come out of a biomedical tradition. This brings together a more comprehensive approach to the understanding of mental illness and to the treatment and rehabilitation of the patient.

GRADATIONS OF CARE WITHIN THE FIELD OF MENTAL ILLNESS: WITH PARTICULAR REFERENCE TO PRIMARY CARE AND PREVENTION

It is useful for our purposes to conceptualize the delivery of mental health services in somewhat the way Garfield (13) did in 1970 in relation to health services in general. A large proportion of time is devoted in the general practice of medicine to emotional problems of living and various gradations of mental illness. This is called *primary care*. Earlier in the century, when we were still ravaged by communicable diseases, for which there was no known immunization, acute, life-threatening sickness required most of the attention and time that the primary care physician had to offer. Since the life-threatening communicable diseases have been brought under control, life expectancy has increased and far more time is now required to help patients cope with symptoms, discomforts, and disabilities associated with chronic disorders, which, however, are *not* confined exclusively to the later years of life.

In the 1980's, information about health and illness is widely disseminated across the population. There is a growing awareness of life-style factors which affect the maintenance of health. This has stimulated demand for primary care on the part of *well* persons at the same time that it has raised an awareness among them of their own responsibility for keeping fit. This gets expressed in terms of revised diet, exercise, concern about smoking, use of alcohol, stress management, accident prevention and highway safety . . . on the part of an increasingly health-conscious, sophisticated population. The *well* person may range from the infant to the adult who is seen for a periodic check-up. In the case of the adult, he/she seeks personal assurance from this contact that "all systems" are functioning normally. If this is the case, the visit affords the person "peace of mind" and can be construed in that sense as a mental health service. The mother who takes the infant to the family doctor or well-baby clinic and finds that at three months or six months the baby is developing normally, receives both guidance and reassurance which ought predictably to reduce anxiety for her. It is no doubt clear that the *well* person is an active seeker of health education. The physician may do some of this important task, and he/she may delegate some to nurse or social worker, who may decide to see the person individually or as part of a group with similar needs — all classifiable as *primary prevention.*

The *worried well* are an increasingly large segment of the population who demand time, sometimes out of proportion to their needs, and indeed, far beyond their *medical* needs. A holistic approach to the patient *does*, in any event, take us beyond his/her needs. The person who has sustained the loss of a loved one, someone who has recently been divorced, a third person who has just received notice of termination of employment — all three of these are candidates for conditions which may lead them to seek medical attention. Backaches and headaches, sleepless nights and daytime fatigue, feelings of rejection and inferiority, isolation, anxiety and depression may cause these *worried well* to suspect that they are succumbing to illness. Teen-agers who are worried about their grades in school or feel unpopular with their peers react to these exogenous factors by *somatizing* their complaints; they too experience episodes of headaches, flatulence, nausea, cramps, skin irritations, constipation, diarrhea, backaches, and many other discomforts. Some of these may be classified as the *early sick* or incipiently ill, if you please. But the act of seeking medical attention justifies a temporary absence from school or withdrawal from the peer group and may relieve the person of some tension associated with the life situation.

On the continuum, then, from *well* to *worried well* to *early sick*, we do not claim air-tight compartments, since we are trying to conceptualize human behavior in flux, with the result that the status of a case may change drastically from one time frame to another.

In both of these cases, the following belong to the category of worried well: the young woman (age 30) who is emotionally distressed because she can't conceive and another young woman (age 16) who is even more upset because she is pregnant and unmarried, a sophomore in high school, and utterly unprepared to be a mother. They require considerable help, some aspects of which are "psychobiological" in nature, but the rest are psychosocial, involving a husband in the first instance and putative father and the teen-ager's parent(s), in the second.

Then, there are the worried (but well) parents of the diabetic child, who required guidance and emotional support in parenting because of the chronicity of the condition with its implications for all members of the family. These are but a few of the examples of the worried well, whose problems are multi-dimensional and call for psychosocial intervention and social services. However, there is another sub-type who brings vague complaints to the inner office of the primary care provider: anxieties, self-doubt, self-blame, self-depreciation, compulsivity, obsessions, impulsivity, etc. — all "piggy-backing" ill-defined somatic complaints. These are worried well patients who want and need someone to care about them enough to *listen* to them and to *pay attention* to them.

Some of these early warning signals may be detected by the vigilant teacher, school nurse, or school social worker in the case of the child or adolescent. The child, whose parents are at war with each other, may blame himself for their unhappiness and their conflict. The child who is disruptive because he is starved for attention may go to any length to attract attention — *even negative* attention, and needs help. The same applies to the child who lies, steals, or bullies others. Early intervention in these situations is of utmost importance because the opportunities for *prevention* of much more serious pathology may be available. There is no doubt about the saying, trite as it may seem: "an ounce of prevention *is* worth a pound of cure".

As we consider the spectrum of care, we observe that some of the early sick find their way to specialists, but those exhibiting bizarre social behavior, who are classifiables as *moderately* to *severely sick* will naturally be referred to psychiatrists and other mental health professionals. Those who threaten to bring harm to themselves or others tend to be obvious candidates for emergency attention. Others with a more insidious onset of symptoms, including confusion, disorganization, delusions, hallucinations, etc., may "get by" within the family until the patient is no longer able to conceal the symptoms. Then, the symptoms arouse anxiety and may lead the family to involve their general practitioner or the CMHC or the police, depending upon the resources of the family, in order to secure hospitalization for the patient. The hospitalization may be short-term followed by day care and transitional services with regularly scheduled visits to an after-care clinic — or whatever seems appropriate.

For those with chronic and recurrent episodes of mental illness, a plan of *social care* must be laid out — in the patient's own home or in some substitute. For those who do not have families, there are boarding homes, convalescent homes, and domiciliary facilities, but it is sometimes necessary for patients with families to be placed in

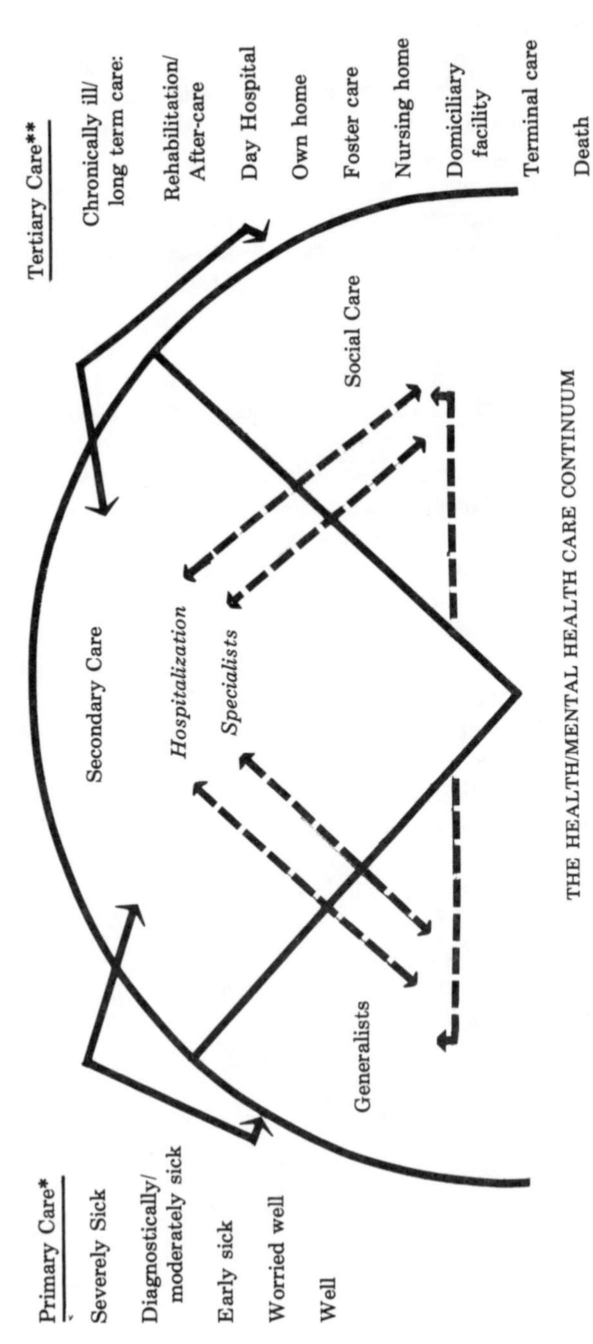

THE HEALTH/MENTAL HEALTH CARE CONTINUUM

* Items listed clock-wise under *Primary Care* may or may not represent a continuum; this will depend on the condition of the patient(s).

** Items listed clock-wise under *Tertiary Care* do *not* represent a continuum; they are merely *examples* of settings where care is provided.

substitute care facilities to avoid the pre-existing incompatibility, which *may* have contributed to the episode of illness and may impede recovery.

Contacts with specialists in mental health and periods of hospitalization for mental illness are characterized as *secondary care.* The various stages of rehabilitation, which run the gamut from home care across many types of substitute social care arrangements, constitute *tertiary care.* For the chronically ill, tertiary care may be long-term and even life-long care.

While this conceptualization of mental health services uses the Garfield model as a point of departure, it is far more than an elaboration upon the original model. It is a reformulation of it, with particular relevance to primary care and prevention in the field of mental health and to psychosocial content and social care in all three stages of the continuum.

SOCIAL DIAGNOSIS

The rationale that undergirds the taking of a social history must be clear to the social worker who does the interview(s) and to all of his/her professional colleagues. Every question and each interview in its entirety should have a purpose, and that purpose should be made clear to the interviewee, whether that person is the client/patient, relative, or a resource outside the family. The general purpose of the social history is to provide evidence which leads to a social diagnosis of the patient *within the context of his social situation,* since the person does not exist within a vacuum, but is keenly affected by members of family, friends, neighbors, employer (or other functionaries, if unemployed), to say nothing of creditors, landlord, storekeepers, and hundreds of others.

Let us assume for present purposes that the psychiatrist has "examined" the candidate for admission to a short-term (intensive care) in-patient unit. Since there is a presumption of mental illness, which *may* affect the credibility of the examinee's responses or interfere with his capacity to respond appropriately, the contact made by the social worker with the "nearest-of-kin" should afford clarity in many respects. More importantly, the spouse, parent, adult child (as interviewee) provides a view of the candidate-for-admission (hereafter called the patient), which yields the evidence from which a social diagnosis is derived. The social diagnosis combined with psychological testing and the psychiatric examination of the patient point the way for the *formulation of the treatment plan.* Our position is that this composite or holistic assessment is far more likely to be accurate than any unidimensional review. Let us see why.

The social worker as interviewer seeks to elicit information about the pre-morbid personality of the patient, a then-and-now comparison of his behavior with concrete examples and selected direct quotations from the interviewee, if they are especially sharp and illuminating. A longitudinal history of the person as a member of his family *of origin* and his relationships with parents and siblings, together with stressful or traumatic experience within that context and whatever is known about his methods of coping, provides important impressions regarding early *patterns of behavior*. Whether he was part of an intact family, whether he was part of a solo-parent family, whether he felt loved and supported or rejected and exploited, whether he felt approval, indifference, or disapproval at home and at school, how he as an adolescent fared with his peer group and his contemporaries of both sexes, how he worked through the emancipation process in his youth — these and other lines of inquiry yield a *developmental history*, which must be pursued into the stage of development where he is today, for example, in young adulthood.

If this person is married, the social worker will need to examine every facet of the marital relationship, including the interdependency, division of labor, sexual satisfaction, financial responsibility, social compatibility, etc. If there are children, the patient's involvement and his/her track record as a parent, his relationships with each of the children, his satisfaction or frustration with them, etc., are highly pertinent to the life situation. A careful review of his experience in the world of work, his vocational aspirations, his frustrations and disappointments, his attitudes toward work as something ranging from a challenge (affording satisfaction) to a drudgery (causing boredom), along with impressions of relationships with superordinates, peers, and subordinates, add another dimension to this social history. Needless to say, periods of unemployment and expressions of cynicism, self-depreciation, anger, depression, hopelessness, alienation, etc., are important findings. These are illustrative areas of inquiry for social history-taking — for purposes of social diagnosis — and must be regarded as such, mainly because of the uniqueness of each life situation and the wide diversity across any population.

Another, but by no means secondary, purpose of the interview with the nearest-of-kin is to assess this person's attitudes toward the patient, his/her perceptions of the onset of the illness and connections between events in the life of the family and the recognition of "early warning signals." As the closest relative interacting with the patient, the interviewee has probably played an integral part in his day-to-day life situation, perhaps facilitating, maybe impeding. Although the *relative must not be interrogated as if he/she were "another patient,"* the social worker must be alert for indications of constructive/destructive attitudes toward the patient, expressions of remorse or guilt for past behavior toward the patient, tolerance/intolerance, readiness/unreadiness to cooperate with the hospital, etc. Evidence of this kind is not given spontaneously in many cases; it requires skill at eliciting painful revelations — self-revealing material of which the inverviewee is ashamed — by exploring "areas of privacy" with a merciful purposefulness. It requires an acumen on the part of the social worker to probe many responses containing objective facts for feelings about them. Feelings are subjective facts, and they are important *findings* when one's purpose is to assess the dynamics of a relationship in order to understand the influence that *B* has had upon *A* and then to "get a reading" on the kind of tender-loving-care and support (or benign avoidance) of the patient that is predictable — in the treatment process that lies ahead. Ultimately, the purpose that we are staking out is two-fold: to ascertain where the relative "stands" in relation to the patient and how the relative can be involved as an ally in helping the patient to regain his equilibrium. Related to both is the question: how amenable is the relative to taking guidance in nurturing the patient through a period of hospitalization and convalescence toward the achievement of positive social functioning?

The uses of social diagnosis up to this point have been confined to direct service modalities, i.e., in treatment directly administered by one or more members of the multi-disciplinary team. However, treatment planning, especially in a short-term treatment program, should anticipate discharge planning. While this obviously includes the closest relative as a major resource, it goes beyond this person. In the event that the closest relative is unavailable by reason of physical or mental illness, overwhelming anxiety over the patient's condition, or absence from the home for other reasons, substitute care may have to be arranged. Social workers provide linkage — a liaison role — to an entire network of community resources (34). Contact with public health nursing, homemaker/home health aide, employment, public assistance, family service, child protection, elder-care, veterans', Social Security (OASDHI), and many other services are possible resources which may be tapped selectively, in keeping with the patient's particular needs and those of the family.

Where the family becomes totally unavailable, for whatever the reason, it may be necessary to develop living arrangements in the community that most nearly meet the patient's needs, if the patient can not fend for himself. This is intended to reduce the time and cost of hospitalization by expediting discharge procedures, and that depends upon early, methodical, team-planning for the patient's discharge.

DIAGNOSTIC EVALUATION OF THE PATIENT

Any diagnostic evaluation of the patient which claims to be comprehensive and holistic will include content that reflects the social functioning of the individual. The most cursory perusal of the outline that follows, which is included mainly for *illustrative* purposes — and *not* necessarily to be regarded as a recommended outline for interviewing — supports this point.

It must be remembered that *diagnosis* is not a static factor. Diagnostic evaluations are undertaken at various stages in an episode of illness to serve as a basis for: initial treatment, changes in course of treatment, progress toward discharge, program of after-care, readmission, and many aspects of psychosocial, economic, environmental, and situational planning. Therefore, there is *no form* that will satisfy all phases, stages, and places of treatment. This is where professional education, training, and experience dictate the use of a wide repertoire of considerations and a judicious line of inquiry in keeping with the needs of the patient, family, or clientele.

OUTLINE FOR SOCIAL SERVICES HISTORY

(Headings are to be used for clarity and quick retrieval of information. Other headings specific to a particular case may be used).

I. *Identifying or General Data*

Should include admission #, age, sex, religion, marital status, occupation, referral source, nature of legal commitment, informant's name, reliability and relationship to patient.

II. *Presenting Problem* (main complaint)

1. Onset of difficulties, *description* of illness in chronological order of the illness from the earliest time at which a change was noticed until admission to the hospital. Indicate the reason for hospitalization.

2. If relevant, describe the patient's *mental state*, particularly if history is obtained shortly after admission and if the patient acts as his own informant. This could include *general behavior* exhibited, especially anything abnormal, *talk, mood,* delusion or *misinterpretations, compulsive* phenomena, *orientation, memory, insight,* judgment, etc.

III. *Past Psychiatric History*

Dates of past hospitalization, duration, precipitating symptoms and factors, and an indication of what hospital or mental health center was attended, including private treatment.

IV. *Patient Precautions*

Inquire in depth from the patient, family, and referral agency what precautions about the patient's present or previous behavior we should know about: i.e., 1) history of violent or aggressive behavior including homocidal behavior — handling of guns, knives, etc.; 2) history of fire setting or other significant destructive behavior; 3) history of suicidal thinking or behavior or other self-destructive behavior.

If you elicit no significant behavior under this heading this should be so stated. All patient precautions behavior information should be conveyed to the head nurse, the unit director and the attending physician immediately. List in progress notes, also.

V. *Social History*

A. Early Childhood Development

1. Childhood behaviors — tantrums, stammering, phobias, night terrors, bedwetting.

2. School experience — standard reached, evidence of ability of backwardness, special abilities or disabiities, hobbies, interests.

3. Early development — delicate or healthy, precocious or retarded.

4. Health during childhood.

B. Family relationships, interactions

1. Father — health, age or age at time of death, personality, occupation, ethnic or national origin, religion, type of relationship with patient.

2. Mother — health, age or age at time of death, and cause of death, personality, occupation, ethnic or national origin, religion, type of relationship with patient.

3. Siblings — enumerated in order at birth, personality, occupation, health or illness, marital status, relationship with patient.

4. Social position of the family — any familial diseases, alcoholism, abnormal pesonalities, mental disorder, etc.

C. Marital history

Spouse's age, occupation, personality, compatibility. Children — list chronologically given names, ages, personality, any significant events, emotional relationship to parents. Dating and social relationships if not married.

D. Educational experience including academic and vocational.

E. Occupation, including military service.

Job satisfaction, present economic circumstances, ambition, satisfaction or reasons of dissatisfaction.

F. Patterns of social relationships.

Includes friends (group clubs), work relationships, (leader, follower, aggressive, submissive, adjustable), history of drug or alcohol use.

VI. *Medical History and Medications*

Illnesses, operations, accidents, allergies, review of systems if known. Habits of alcohol, tobacco, marijuana, injectables. ECT. List medication of current use and past psychotropic medications.

VII. *Impressions and Current Psycho-Social Resources*

Specific mention should be made of patient's strengths, limitations, including family, community, employment interaction. Also intellectual activities and interests.

VIII. *Social Service Treatment Plan and Goals*

(Special attention and mention of continuity of care and relationship to CMH/MR center)

Work of family
Work with other social, legal, mental health, medical or rehabilitative agencies
Preliminary plans
Follow-up plans, goals

SOME CHARACTERISTICS OF SOCIAL WORK INTERVENTION IN RELATION TO CLIENT/PATIENT INTERRELATED NEEDS

			Social-Environmental		
Social Work Intervention	*Bio-*	*Psycho-*	*Intra-Family*	*Inter-Personal*	*Community*
Advocacy					
Brokerage					
Case Management					
Clarification					
Coordination					
Expediting/Implementing					
Facilitating					
Helping/Enabling					
Informing/teaching					
Improvising/Developing					
Mediating					
Organizing/Initiating					
Provision "concrete" service					
Psychosocial Therapy					
Planning/ Police formulation					
Social Administration/ Consultation					
Supportiveness (social-psychological)					

OUT-PATIENT SERVICES

Data from the National Institute of Mental Health indicates the significant change in the locus of care from the institution to the community. The inpatient services in state hospitals in 1955 accounted for 818,832 patient care episodes or 505 per 100,000 population. The number of inpatient care episodes, by 1973, decreased to 651,057 or a rate of 313 per 100,000. Ten years after the passage of The Community Mental Health Centers Act of 1963, the total episodes provided by federal community mental health centers was 1,175,498, almost twice the inpatient episodes (651,857) the state mental hospitals provided. (Kramer, 21)

Battle cries for deinstitutionalization included: a) the work of Wolfensberger (48) calling for individuals with mental retardation to be treated as normally as possible; b) that of Maxwell Jones (20) which describes the impact that the larger community exerts upon institutions and individuals; and c) the pressures from the civil rights movement for treatment to follow due process and take place in the least restrictive setting possible.

In retrospect, the degree to which the previous institutionally based services were challenged to protect civil liberties and to provide additional community-based services, ranging from prevention to aftercare, is indeed commendable. In the 1960's, some social workers predicted that our community-based services would "put state hospitals out of business" and further, that "progress" would be assessed by noting how many chronic cases were *closed.*

One can only explain such naivete or miscalculation by recalling that the strong desire is to reduce the hopelessness of patients with long-term mental illness. It is, however, a sign of the growing maturity of social work as a profession that we read one definition of its mission by Robert Morris (25) "as caring for a chronically dependent population." Social work practice has come full-circle, then, from deploring to advocating quality chronic care. For example, social workers in acute and chronic outpatient services are recommending the easy re-entry of chronic patients into state hospitals, thus recognizing the different needs of acute and chronically disabled individuals. Social workers also have become less concerned over the charge of "elitism" in using the word "chronic" and become more concerned with social justice in seeing to it that each individual receives the treatment or care he or she needs.

Difficult questions remain to be resolved, however. For example, with the passage of Medicare and Medicaid in 1965, many city hospitals, where indigent psychiatric patients had received care, were closed. It was thought that these individuals could now be treated in the psychiatric units of private community-based general hospitals and outpatient programs. The pressures on these facilities were further accentuated in many states by the mandate of the Community Mental Center Act of 1963, requiring all individuals to be evaluated and/or treated in the community before entering the state hospital. This is referred to as "a single point of entry" to preclude what in 1976 the Joint Commission on Accreditation of Hospitals (17) called unnecessary consumerism. Social workers and other mental health professionals were thus forced to thoroughly evaluate and treat every individual in the community, if at all possible.

As the community-based services became established, they not only began finding new individuals who needed acute care, e.g., marital therapy, but also numerous chronic conditions, many of whom had spent years in state hospitals. Members of this category were required to spend 30 days in a community hospital with acute patients before readmission to state hospital for intense treatment. This was a problem for the community because in some cases it ruined the therapeutic environment in small community-based psychiatric units within general hospitals. This is because the treatment plan for an individual with chronic schizophrenia who has few resources (health, financial, social, etc.) is very different from an individual who has an acute depression, but reliable, strong family and interpersonal resources in his community.

Such frustration led many states to pass legislation that allowed individuals to enter the mental health delivery system at any point through community or institutional services. The multiple entry delivery system has more flexibility (e.g., direct admission and readmission to state hospitals), but this model can be abused if too many individuals are treated in the community system. The key to understanding this dilemma seems to be the careful evaluation of all bio-psycho-social factors. The social work profession is uniquely prepared to focus on this level of analysis. Specific diagnostic/assessment frameworks and their use in mental health outpatient services will be addressed in the pages that follow.

It is interesting to note that once the mental health services were reorganized and changed, our practice also changed. When we undertook to treat more individuals in their communities, we had to rely more on family therapy and less on individual therapy. Social workers, like Virginia Satir, (39) developed many of the basic theoretical underpinnings for family theory and family therapy techniques. General systems theory contributed to this work, as well, by developing the interrelatedness and interdependencies of all individuals and their environments.

In 1981, *Social Work*, the official journal of National Association of Social Workers, devoted an entire issue to conceptual frameworks. The 26 authors who contributed articles to that issue concluded that, "the purpose of social work is to promote or restore a mutually beneficial interaction between individuals and society in order to improve the quality of life for every one and that social workers . . . focus on person-and-environment in interaction" (41).

This conceptual model explains why social workers have found such compatibility with community mental health centers, which is essentially an epidemiological model. That is to say, it concerns itself with the health of a given population. It also focuses on primary prevention, addressing question which lead to mental illness, e.g., through outpatient consultation to schools; secondary prevention (early identification and treatment, e.g., through outpatient therapy); and tertiary prevention, preventing further breakdown, e.g., with aftercare services. Before discussing the clinical applications of the psycho-social framework (i.e., person and environment interacting), one broader subject should be noted. All social workers study social welfare policy. This understanding enables them to appreciate the economic, social, political and historical forces that shape mental health legislation and the delivery systems that it creates. This knowledge has prepared many social workers to administer community mental health centers and to link them to the broader social welfare structure, ranging from child welfare to geriatric services. In fact, one could view the significant case management function (detailed later) that social workers perform, as a concrete interpretation of this social welfare perspective.

When we look at what social workers in outpatient mental health do, we gain some fresh insight into what they are all about. Although they share many common functional duties, such as individual psychotherapy, crisis intervention, group therapy, family therapy and case management, with other mental health disciplines, the social worker brings a unique perspective. Social workers have an understanding of the poor, ethnic and class differences, racism, oppression, and a broad-based view of the life cycle. This provides many tools to assess not only an individual but the psycho-social context. Social workers fully appreciate that disorganized individuals frequently have disorganized environments and that one needs to assess the point of intervention where the maximum benefits can be realized. This perspective allows social workers to move freely back and forth from looking at an individual and individual interventions to intervening with the environment. Further, it allows a social worker to conceptualize and appreciate an individual within a social context without actively intervening in that context except through the individual (i.e., psychotherapy).

The import of psycho-social factors is highlighted by the publication in 1980 of the *Diagnostic and Statistical Manual of Mental Disorders* (DSM-III) by the American Psychiatric Association (4). This innovative manual is based on a multiaxial system for evaluation. The system has five axes: Axis I covers clinical syndromes, conditions not attributable to a mental disorder that is a focus of attention or treatment and additional codes; Axis II covers personality disorders and specific development disorders; Axis III, physical disorders and conditions; Axis IV, the severity of psycho-social stressors; and Axis V, the highest level of adaptive functioning in the past year. In short, this provides a bio-psycho-social framework for evaluating individuals. This is quite different from the previous edition (1968) of this manual, *DSM-II* (3), which addressed only the content in Axes I and II. Janet B.W. Williams, the social worker who was Text Editor, Project Coordinator and Co-principal Investigator in DSM-III field trials, and a member of several committees that advised the task force responsible for the development of DSM-III, states that, "In extensive teaching of DSM-III all over the country, this author has found that clinicians . . . find Axes IV and V clinically useful . . ." (4).

In outpatient mental health clinics, social workers traditionally conduct the first session with a client to serve as a broker and to provide a "bridge" between the client and the clinic. Since social workers are also trained in many settings (e.g., child welfare, prisons, housing projects), they are uniquely qualified to handle the case management responsibilities with other agencies in coordinating the care for a client. In certain areas such as mental retardation, the social work staff spends the majority of its time mainly coordinating care and serving as an advocate for clients.

Social workers in adult outpatient mental health services treat individuals, couples and families who have a complete range of mental health problems. They also do preventive work with employers and community groups, e.g., outreach.

Other social workers focus on the special needs of children and use art, play therapy, family therapy and other techniques to help children and their families. Extensive coordination must also take place between these social workers in outpatient mental health and the school systems.

Occasionally, there are clients who have severe psychosocial problems, but these individuals are not so dysfunctional as to require full inpatient service. Conversely, an hour of outpatient treatment each week would never meet their needs. These clients are referred to partial hospital programs which treat clients from 9-5 daily or in some cases, every evening, if the client attends school or works. These programs offer many of the services found on an inpatient setting but save the cost of 24-hour care and intrude less into a person's life.

Social workers in outpatient mental health are facing many challenges. The increasing role of consumerism and pressure from the legal system have required social workers to offer even higher quality services. Mental health professionals, including social workers have responded by incorporating various technologies, e.g., psychotropic drugs in psychiatry, family therapy, electronic media in recordkeeping and supervision in training, etc., to advance their skills in assessment and treatment.

At the time of this writing, it is not clear whether the United States is truly committed to offering a broad-based continuum of services for all economic classes. It should be noted that upper income clients never really used publicly funded community mental health centers (CMHC's). Middle income clients have frequently paid on a sliding scale system that allowed the lower income and indigent clients to pay little or nothing through the use of Medicaid. It appears the middle class has vented its frustration by demanding that services to indigent clients be curtailed. The attitude appears to be, "Why should they have care for free that I can not really afford to purchase?" The political alternative of increasing the tax burden on wealthier individuals and business does not appear to be viable at this time.

Finally, whether a further restriction on limiting care to the most profoundly impaired, such as chronically psychotic clients, will be imposed, remains to be seen. If this care is limited finally to institutional settings, then we will have come full circle.

PARTIAL HOSPITALIZATION

Day hospital is sometimes used as a substitute for full hospitalization. It affords the patient the full array of treatment modalities available in a hospital on a 9:00 A.M. - 5:00 P.M. basis, yet it relies heavily upon the cooperation of the family to whom the patient returns each evening (and weekends) for emotional support to the patient and cooperation with the treatment program.

The social worker is centrally involved in eliciting from nearest of kin not only the history of the situation but the dynamics of this person's relationship to the patient. The social worker provides interpretation to the family of the treatment program and solicits their investment in it through their regular contacts with the patient. The intervention on the part of the social worker may seek to sponsor some modification of behavior on the part of the relative(s). Or, it may call upon some resource in the community that will help the patient and/or the family to cope more effectively.

The adjective which best describes a day hospital or free-standing-day care program — aside from therapeutic — is *social* since it is the social milieu of day care which is consciously used by the social worker and the rest of the staff to help each patient to achieve improvement in his *social functioning* in relation to his/her self-care, interpersonal contacts, the world of work, etc. Social workers engage patients in groups, involving them in thinking about tasks for the day, which may range from preparing the noon meal to making a given number of items for a contract work project, and carrying out the plans which the group had agreed upon — under the guidance of the professional person functioning as facilitator.

Day care, then, serves variously as an alternative to hospitalization, as a first step following hospitalization on the way to complete discharge, or as an assessment center for the patient moving in either direction.

EMERGENCY SERVICE

How do we define a "psychiatric emergency"? The following is an arresting and — for our purposes — a cogent commentary on the subject, Glasscote, *et al.* (15).

> "Only a few kinds of behavior seem to be consistently accepted as constituting or implying a psychiatric emergency, namely, suicidal behavior, whether seriously meant or a gesture, assaultiveness, property destruction, extreme anxiety, panic, and bizarre behavior. The first three are almost invariably considered by everyone to constitute an emergency. . . .
>
> Classification as a psychiatric emergency seems largely contingent on one's being conceived of as a *social* emergency. Of course, many social emergencies are not psychiatric emergencies, but virtually all psychiatric emergencies are simultaneously social emergencies." p. 11

The social worker can be importantly involved in sorting out (assessing) which is one and which is the other or, in helping the family deal with the social emergency associated with the psychiatric episode and helping to defuse the social emergency which is misperceived, sometimes by the friends, family, or the police as a psychiatric episode.

Another way of stating the case is that the mental health staff are bombarded by "urgencies" which are not emergencies. In the scheme of things, these may be lower priority episodes which require attention, but not immediately and not in the E.R. or emergency unit, which, in most hospitals is inundated by vast numbers of human agonies. The urgency which arises out of the anxiety and fear that relatives experience — as contrasted with the symptoms presented by the patient — deserves attention, but it may be the function of the social worker to address this factor, in cases where a psychiatric emergency is ruled out, to prevent the turbulence from creating chaos in the E.R. and at the same time responding humanely and appropriately to the needs of an anxious, frightened family.

CONSULTATION AND EDUCATION

These services are of a different order from those already described. C and E services had two global objectives: to compensate for severe shortages in professional personnel in the field of mental health and to upgrade the knowledge of the public about mental illness in order to improve attitudes toward the mentally ill and the wide spectrum of treatment modalities. After all, it was "only yesterday" in the early 1950's that half of all the hospital beds in the United States were occupied by patients with a psychiatric diagnosis. The intent of the Congress in passing the Community Mental Health Act was to reduce institutional care drastically in favor of community-based care (7,11,14). Such a major shift, predictably, required a reorientation of the professions involved, of the prospective patient population (clientele) and their families, of the health and social welfare agencies in the community, and the citizenry whose lives would be affected and whose moral support — to say nothing of tax dollars — would count immensely.

By the mid-1970's, the intent of Congress had been achieved, as indicated by the following: The U.S. Department of Health, Education and Welfare (43)

> In 1955, only one-fourth of the treatment episodes were in outpatient settings; by 1975, outpatient episodes account for three-fourths of the total. p. 70.

The management of this volume of mental illness *in the community*, of conditions ranging from incipient to recurrent, acute to chronic, mild to severe, required consultation to and further education for physicians in general practice. The same was true for nurses and the allied medical professions.

This was certainly true for social workers employed in agencies providing services to families and children and doubly important for public assistance workers regularly in contact with multitudes of poor under-served families who were (and are) particularly vulnerable to mental and physical illness and disability. Social workers acting as consultants may offer *case consultation* on assessing an individual or family situation and means of intervention that may enable the client(s) to resolve their difficulties, no matter how complex — and, alas! these interpersonal conflicts are seldom simple. Another form is *administrative consultation*, which might involve the reorganization of a staff of a social agency to assume responsibility for new functions, such as, providing emergency shelter, temporary care, and counseling services for children and adolescents for example, who have run away from home. The child may be confused and emotionally ill or may have tried to escape from abusive, punitive, psychiatrically sick parents — or otherwise threatening conditions at home. In this instance, the child protection agency will require considerable advice and consultation in designing a program to meet the particular needs of its locality. Once committed to the new program, the staff might benefit immeasurably from *group consultation* on mounting the program, protecting the rights of the children, interacting adroitly and sensitively with the parents, sorting out the crux of the problem without seeking legal adjudication, etc.

Another phase of C and E service involves the training of non-professional personnel, often indigenous to the neighborhood where there is a heavy concentration of high risk families, of formerly hospitalized, and of those presently in treatment. The so-called "indigenous worker" can be instrumental in helping the patient gain access to treatment or to receive a particular service which is critical to his recovery. Sometimes they can "run interference" for the client by demanding repairs to the housing where the client lives — when the client, hampered by his low income, unemployment, loss of credit, illiteracy, his position of powerlessness, to say nothing of his psychopathology — can not speak for himself. They may act as agents (or brokers) for minorities who, by reason of ethnic, racial, religious, or linguistic differences, experience oppression and more limited access to various services than other segments of society. Poor people tend to trust these indigenous workers, who represent a bridge to a strange and forbidding zone of operations, the Mental Health Center. In spite of great effort to dispel misconceptions, the very place is too heavily equated with insanity or lunacy — for which banishment had for centuries been the answer. Banishment by institutionalization is a danger to which minorities have been subjected in our society and others.

SCREENING SERVICES

The child, adolescent, youth, or adult who displays deviant or disturbed behavior may be detained by the police. He may then come to the attention of the courts. If the offense is serious or if it is the second or third in a series of offenses against the law, mental illness as a factor in the commission of the offense may or may not come to light in the process of adjudication. There is greater likelihood that the young "offender" who lives in a poor inner city area will come to the attention of the police and the court system than his counterpart in a middle-class suburb. In the suburban community the parents are more likely: a) to intercede for the young "offender," b) to cover up for him and for the reputation of the family, and c) to "bail him out" of trouble by taking the advice of the school, the family doctor, or their lawyer to seek help for the young "deviant." Desparation, exasperation, or anxiety on the part of the parents may lead them to the mental health center or to psychiatric attention on a private basis, if they or their advisors have recognized symptoms of mental illness. The injustice of leaving it to chance, whether the young *deviant* is an offender who is punishable or a sick person who requires treatment under the aegis of a mental health program, is obvious.

Hence, screening services were made available to the court system by the community mental health centers as another "essential" service, in accordance with the 1975 amendments. These services were designed to provide assessment planning for the cases referred by the court, access to treatment considered most appropriate and (at the same time) least restrictive, and to the extent possible to afford an alternative to inpatient treatment for those channeled into the mental health system, irrespective of age.

The social worker is frequently the liaison between the two systems: the court and the mental health center. He/she is most frequently the intake worker or initial contact in the latter setting and the professional person who carries out the coordination and implementation of the planning that eventuates in the mental health center. This function is often called *case management*. It is at the same time an administrative function and an element of direct service to the person who has been "transferred" from one system to another and requires *help over time* in extracting benefit from the mental health treatment program.

AFTER-CARE

Every professional person assigned to this unit in the mental health system (as well as the system itself) is caught between Scylla and Charybdis on the problem of after-care. There are patients who come regularly and faithfully for after-care, i.e., following discharge from the hospital. They are generally seen by the physician or the nurse regarding the therapeutic effect, side effects (if any), and dosage of prescribed drugs.

The social worker sees the patients for purposes of affording them *social support* and a sense that *someone cares* about them, about their progress, and about their frustrations in adapting to the community and the adversities for them as "*convalescents.*" If the convalescent is "growing stronger" — and this is what the term denotes — this progress must be reflected in his *social functioning* as well as mind and body. The social worker, as a specialist in this area, is, therefore, concerned with a host of related questions. If the patient has returned to his own home, how is he getting along with his family? If he has returned to or been referred to a job, how productive is he? How does he regard his fellow workers? His supervisors? If he had lost his job and had none upon discharge, what progress was he making at securing employment? How was he managing on limited finances during the interim period? If living in a transitional care arrangement, how comfortable is he in the temporary residence? How does he spend his leisure time? Has he regular contact with friends or family? How does he spend his evenings? Alone or with congenial companions? Is he feeling lonely, depressed, anxiety-ridden, unusually paranoid? What is worrying him? Keeping him awake? Interfering with his appetite? Causing him "head-aches"? The foregoing are simply indicative of the line of inquiry that the social worker might pursue in assessing the social functioning domain. Compare Serban (40:205). Helping the patient to focus on one factor at a time, as he defines problems, and to target in on that piece of behavior or need for change may help him (as a convalescent) to feel *less* anxious and somewhat more as if he can keep afloat until he feels "dry land" under him and some traction on it — at least until his next visit or until something external to the treatment situation propels him toward health (adaptive) behavior.

Then there are the *no-shows*, the patients who do not keep their appointments at the mental health center. Some may forget the appointment. More often than not, there is lack of hope and of motivation — lingering sickness — which causes the patient to dismiss the after-care program as pointless. It may be an endogenous depression which destroys confidence in himself or the indifference of the community or the cruel, relentless, and insurmountable pressure of the "real world" which convinces him that there is no use. Or, it may be that the patient is so fragile and incapacitated by his psychosis (if so diagnosed) that he can not mobilize himself or extricate himself from the cocoon of bedclothes in which he has been hiding — perhaps for days and nights on end.

The clinic may pursue the patient by telephone, if there is one where he lives. It may be necessary however, to "deputize" someone, a catchment area (sometimes indigenous) worker or social worker to visit the patient to persuade him to come to the clinic or to report on his condition so that appropriate action can be taken. It may be found that the patient requires emergency care or hospitalization.

For those who do attend and avail themselves of after-care, the social worker may use group therapy as the modality of choice. This is not simply to provide service to ten or twelve within the same time-slot. It is because some patients are more responsive to the group experience and that they benefit from interacting with other patients, learning about the means used by others to resolve their difficulties and deriving moral support from a human group, all of whom are in the same predicament.

We began by saying that the staff, psychiatrist, psychologist, social worker, mental health nurse and others, feel as if caught between Scylla and Charybdis in after-care unit. It may be the volume of work. It may be the weightiness of the mandate for after-care as an *essential* service. Patients are entitled to continuing care, irrespective of diagnosis, duration of previous hospitalization, age, current treatment regimen, presence or absence of family and critical social support in the community, and income — to say nothing of prognosis. Reference has been made repeatedly to the frustration factor for the *patient(s)*, but it is altogether fitting and proper to acknowledge the frustration experienced by the therapist(s) in after-care.

If the regulations call for twelve months of after-care following discharge from hospital, this sets boundaries within which continuity of care is provided toward achieving the objective of full discharge for the patient. Because communities are ill-prepared to receive former mental hospital patients and because these patients are too often discharged before they are ready to manage themselves and cope with the complexities of life with their famiies or in some alternative environment, the pressure on the after-care unit is enormous. Since much of the mental illness, schizophrenia, for example, is chronic illness, with sustained periods of *stability* followed by episodes of "symptomatic behavior" and *instability*, some patients are faced with the "revolving door" syndrome: the wear-and-tear of in-and-out-of-hospital experience, and in their way some after-care staff members experience this phenomenon — at least, vicariously — *with* their patients.

TRANSITIONAL SERVICES

By definition, the term *transitional* refers to a number of programs which are designed to assist the patient *in transit* toward his place back in the mainstream of community life. Half-way houses have been developed to receive the patient in transit. Some have been called three-quarter-way houses to convey the idea of advanced progress en route. They are frequently operated as co-operative residences, with the patients being expected to pitch in and do their share of the chores associated with maintenance. In addition, they are often run by a house committee, consisting of patients, under general rules of conduct that are staked out by the sponsor, which may be the mental health center or another community agency that has contracted to provide the service. It is not uncommon to find a social worker, with previous experience or special skill in social group work, taking charge of this type of program. The program is designed to improve social, vocational, and self-care skills and to promote the constructive use of leisure time.

For persons living in their own homes, in groups homes, boarding (often called "foster") homes, which are somewhat like those described under Services for the Elderly, there are socialization centers. They combine the characteristics of a social club, a hobby house, a recreation program, and a rehabilitation center for former mental hospital patients. Staff provide enough structure to help new "members" make a connection with the center and to help them to use the resources of the center, including their membership as a stepping-stone to human relationship. Membership also represents the reality of *belonging* to a group, which is an encompassable part of the community. The group affords newly referred persons the opportunity to make contact with a wide spectrum of their *peers*, who have lived through similar experiences, some of whom may have kindred interests. *Belonging* to the socialization center is symbolically important since it provides a *place* where the member is, by definition, entitled to all the rights and privileges attached to membership. Indeed, there may be "conditions" associated with membership, e.g., approval and rewards for behavior which contribute to harmony and positive interpersonal relationships and "penalties" or disapproval for behavior which is disruptive or destructive. Members themselves frequently exercise responsibility for enforcing the "rules of the club." The rationale for the rules rests upon the purpose of the center: to promote healthy coping behavior on the premises — with a view toward helping the members to achieve self-mastery which carries over to human relationships beyond the center.

The reality of *belonging* to the center, where members are truly *welcome*, instead of being received condescendingly by "superordinates," is intended to have a therapeutic impact upon them. It is regrettably true that these former patients may be rejected in many places if they are known to have been released from a mental hospital. It is likely that they will arouse anxiety and hostility if their behavior is conspicuously uncustomary. The socialization center is not really intended to be a place of refuge from the community or the laws of the community; it is much more a foothold in and a "proving ground" to help the former patient to establish contact with the rest of the community. Yet, there is little doubt that the friendly, non-threatening atmosphere of this social support center must afford the members the feeling that it *is* a place of refuge from the impersonal, uncaring rush of pedestrian and vehicular traffic of the city streets.

SOCIAL SUPPORT SYSTEMS

For persons who return to their families and their own homes after hospitalization or those who seek and find help without resource to hospitalization for mental illness, social support systems of various kinds are essential (5,11,26).

The social system of a religious group or a congregation can be very valuable. Let us cite a case where the patient had "strayed away" from his church and had become involved in activities which, by the standards of his church and the ethics of the community, were offensive and immoral. This person had begun to think, even to assume, that his sins were so unforgivable that there was no room for his "redemption." Worse yet, he was so full of guilt that he assumed that he was not worthy of returning to his church (or the faith of his youth) and not worthy of communion with his Maker. Irrespective of his therapist's religious orientation, the psychiatrist, psychologist, or social worker is guided by the needs of the patient, who, in this instance, was searching for help in making a new connection with an institution he had previously known. The value system of the church had afforded *structure* which he missed; the doctrine of the church had furnished *moorings* which he had lost; membership in the church had conferred *status* upon him; and above all, it had also given him a *connection* with co-religionists that was socially supportive in nature. The church had, of course, provided him access to clergymen, whose overtures he had regarded as *oppressive* during his illness; yet, they might be valuable human resources in a period of recovery.

The social support system of a peer group who constitute themselves as a *mutual aid group* can serve as a powerful catalyst in the treatment process (38). There is mounting evidence of the wide-spread use of so-called mutual aid and self-help groups in the field of mental health. The best-known and the largest of these is Alcoholics Anonymous, which has earned a great deal of public attention and respect for its activities and its accomplishments. It operates on the principle that recovering alcoholics can help those who have not yet acknowledged their addiction — i.e., that they too are alcoholics — to take that first quintessential step. This then carries the helper along a path of assisting the beginner/helpee to find the strength within himself through a faith in his Higher Power (as he/she defines the Creator) to maintain sobriety from one day to another. This statement does not pretend to do justice to a system, whose work has undergone testing and refinement over the half century since AA was founded.

AA has also developed Al-Anon for the families of alcoholics and for the immeasurable support that mutual aid can afford them in coping with the alcoholic member of the family and the hardships imposed upon the family by his/her addiction/illness. AA went on to develop Al-Ateen for the teenage children of alcoholics who are faced with the psychosocial problem of living with an alcoholic parent, having that parent for a model and needing to rely upon a person who is rendered unreliable by the destructive forces of his addiction.

Some alcoholics benefit from mental health services. Those who do not may find the mutual aid approach of AA quite beneficial because of the "dogged determination" — the supreme commitment

— of the helper to the task of "reaching" another. However, it should be emphasized that the "rescuing" transaction involves mutual investment. The helper can not "rescue" the helpee unless the latter wants the help, wants to cooperate, wants to give up and abuse of alcohol — in spite of the agony that it will cause him — in order to gain the serenity of a new-found freedom.

Still others may find some combination of mental health care and AA support, used adjunctively, meeting their needs. In any event, it is essential for the mental health professional to understand the dynamics of mutual aid inherent in the AA approach and to be receptive to tapping this extremely important resource in the community for patients/clients who are inclined to use it and for those who are not amenable to standard therapeutic interventions for alcoholism.

The factor which emerges concomitantly is the remarkable benefit that the helper derives from finding that he/she has strength enough to help someone else (38). It confirms other indications that he/she is recovering by maintaining sobriety through a first, second, or third and perhaps a later anniversary of that achievement. This self-control is, in turn, associated with a restored psychosocial and spiritual balance which the recovering alcoholic tries to maintain "one day at a time" — as they say in AA. The idea behind this terminology is that alcoholism is regarded as an illness that is not amenable to a "cure," nor is the alcoholic *cured*. Instead, he/she strives to achieve abstinence and in the course of doing so, tries to make amends for the pain or injury that he has caused his family and others.

Since mutual aid and self-help organizations represent an almost unlimited potential array of resources in the community, mental health professionals, including social workers, are and should be interacting with them in a variety of ways: 1) by making referrals to them for the unique help that they have to offer, which, as we have observed, is quite different from that of professionals; 2) by assisting in the establishment of new groups and judiciously withdrawing when the organizations can proceed under their own power in order not to interfere with the self-help concept; 3) by providing consultation and support, if invited; 4) by serving on advisory committees, perhaps related to questions of health education or continuity of the organization.

In addition to Alcoholics Anonymous in the wide field of mental health, there are Gamblers Anonymous, Narcotics Anonymous, Neurotics Anonymous, Overeaters Anonymous, Parents (for abusing) Anonymous, Schizophrenics Anonymous — to mention only a few organizations, whose efforts rely heavily upon the philosophy, program, materials, and the structure of AA.

ALCOHOLISM AND ALCOHOL ABUSE/DRUG ADDICTION AND DRUG ABUSE

By 1970 alcoholism and drug addiction had captured the attention of the American public to such an extent that the organizational framework in which the National Institute of Mental Health was "lodged" became known as the Alcohol, Drug Abuse, and Mental Health Administration (ADAMHA), of which the National Institute of Alcohol Abuse and Alcoholism (NIAAA) and the National Institute on Drug Abuse (NIDA) were major components. Community mental health centers were required to provide alcohol and drug abuse services, since the definition of "essential services" had, not surprisingly, been expanded to include them.

Because of the complexity of these subjects, which deserve far more space than we have within a single chapter, it seems prudent to acknowledge their importance without addressing them more fully in this chapter. Instead, we refer the reader to the chapter by Joanne E. Mantell elsewhere in this volume.

INPATIENT TREATMENT

The United States has, at various periods in history, taken either a humane or custodial approach in inpatient treatment of the emotionally disturbed. A study of this history reveals an almost cyclical development over the years as philanthropy, various levels of government and crusaders in human rights have responded to the placing of the emotionally disturbed in jails, almshouses, or large governmental psychiatric facilities. In Philadelphia, the Pennsylvania Hospital, founded by Benjamin Franklin in 1750, and Friends Hospital, founded in 1812 and modeled by the Quakers after the Retreat at York in England, set fine precedents for the treatment of the emotionally disturbed (47). Humane approaches and the concepts of protection and asylum were put into practice.

Initially, county and state hospitals, fashioned after the private hospitals, were small and stressed quality care. However, from about 1850 as the emotionally disturbed were moved from jails and almshouses to government facilities, larger and larger hospitals were built to accommodate increasing numbers of disturbed individuals. Often, the mentally retarded, palsied, socially outcast and others were also placed in these larger facilities. The hospitals became large Victorian edifices: walls were built around them; wards housed up to 100 individuals; locks were prevalent; and the costs to county and state governments became staggering. This trend prevailed for about a hundred years — well into the mid-20th century. Individual humane treatment gave way to custodial care in the majority of these hospitals, although there were exceptions in both the public and private sectors.

During the second half of the 20th century, substantial changes began to take place in therapeutic approaches toward the emotionally disturbed. One example, Embreeville State Hospital in Chester County, Pennsylvania, developed an "open door" policy in 1956. Doors were unlocked and both staff and patients expected that community placement would become one of the major rehabilitative efforts used to interrupt institutionalization and chronic mental illness. It is interesting to note that this hospital, which once had 1,130 patients, closed in 1980.

By the mid-sixties, after the passage of the Community Mental Health Centers Act of 1963 and its amendments, the states passed mental health and mental retardation legislation designed to complement the Federal Act. Encouraged by the Federal Act and Federal "seed money," the states began to develop community-based inpatient services, rather than county or state mental hospital-based inpatient services, featuring short-term intensive treatment programs. About two-thirds of these services of short duration were provided in psychiatric inpatient units of general hospitals. In some states where there were high quality private psychiatric hospitals, the short-term inpatient services were provided there.

A prototype of the Community Mental Health Center, Penn Foundation (14) in Sellersville, Pennsylvania, operated in cooperation with another local facility, Grandview General Hospital, with partial funding from the State Office of Mental Health and Mental Retardation. The Foundation's approach to inpatient treatment was to have patients occupy general hospital beds at night, interspersed among the medical and surgical patients. During the day, they received milieu and other psychiatric therapy across the street from the hospital at the day treatment program. These newer approaches represent a significant contrast to long-term custodial care. Inpatient units serve "catchment areas" where the individuals work and live. They are close to relatives and friends who can visit and carry less stigma than the state hospital. In addition, there is the expectation that the patient will move to outpatient treatment and discharge within a few weeks. Inpatient care is measured in days and weeks rather than months, years or decades.

In addition, for the first time, it usually meant that the low-income, emotionally disturbed would receive care in normal community resources instead of being relegated to governmental inpatient facilities located miles from home. The care of all of the emotionally disturbed came under the scrutiny of the board of the general hospital, the Joint Commission on Accreditation of Hospitals, Professional Service Review Organizations, Quality Assurance committees and the review of insurance companies. All of these safe-guards were designed to insure that the inpatient treatment of the emotionally disturbed was appropriate to the diagnosis, time-limited, cost-effective and for acute conditions. Simultaneously, it was dovetailed with outpatient services, such as 24-hour emergency services, partial hospitalization, and aftercare services instead of being a remote non-integrated modality (29).

In contrast with previous inpatient approaches, the new treatment philosophy called for short-term crisis intervention designed to support the individual's strengths, maintain contact with family and work, and other facets of the patient's community support system. In contrast to long-term treatment originally designed to "cure," to provide asylum or custodial care, the newer approaches were designed to reduce the stigma of mental illness, to return the individual to neighborhood and family and to control the costs of the most expensive component of the total treatment regimen. The emphasis, therefore, was to help the individual to feel more comfortable quickly and provide a reduction in symptoms so that the person could function at optimal or near optimal level as soon as possible.

Team approach is not particularly new, but it is not always given full implementation. The full impact of the team approach is often thwarted by professional "turfdom," absence from team meetings by one or more disciplines, acting as solo therapist and thereby thwarting coordination and team efforts.

Inpatient treatment teams are comprised of psychiatrists, nurses, social workers, therapeutic activities workers (e.g., occupation and recreation therapists), psychologists, and internists. Other specialists sometimes find a place on the team and can include behavioral therapists, family therapists, dieticians, and neurologists.

The *psychiatrist* is usually the team leader for medical and legal reasons. The psychiatrist, with the input of other disciplines provides the evaluation, diagnosis, prescription and regulation of medication, and requests medical consults. S/he may be the primary therapist or designate another team member to provide the majority of treatment. S/he is responsible for reading and evaluating the results of medical consults and lab reports and acting upon any abnormal findings 1. on his own, 2. through the team, 3. by referral to a general hospital service, or 4. in aftercare treatment.

Nurses, in addition to following through on medical orders regarding regulation of medication and specific patient care approaches, may also provide therapy or function as the patient's "contact" person, a person with whom the patient discusses problems, feelings and grievances. Nurses, on duty twenty-four hours a day, provide continuity of patient care and report reactions and observations to the treatment team.

Social workers carry the main responsibility for maintaining contact between the patient and the family, outpatient treatment resources, and other community agencies and services. In addition to obtaining a social and family history, providing concrete social services, discharge planning and assuring continuity of care, the social worker may also provide family therapy and other therapeutic interventions.

Psychiatry, more than any other branch of medicine, has a major social component to it. In fact many of the stresses which cause anxiety or depression or contribute to the severity of more serious psychiatric disturbances are social in nature. These stresses include family disequilibrium, inadequate housing, insufficient income or public welfare payments, and the helplessness and hopelessness born of poverty. Many of these social problems are long standing and not easily dealt with during a short-term inpatient stay. Some of the problems may have no immediate solution. These social problems will probably continue to plague the individual and limit the family after discharge.

It is apparent that the best medical and pharmacological treatment will provide little lasting amelioration of symptoms if the already emotionally distressed individual must return to a hostile or indifferent family, to inadequate welfare payments or to boarding homes which are too often crowded, poorly supervised and sometimes exploitative.

The in-patient social worker, in cooperation with outpatient therapists or case managers has the responsibility to dovetail the treatment, housing, income and social agency supports to the special needs of the patient. The social worker is a broker, if you will, between the patient and the best boarding home available, the proper outpatient treatment sources, the necessary leisure time activities, the welfare office to obtain a cash grant, and sometimes the services of several social agencies, such as the court, child welfare office, visiting nurses and various rehabilitation and vocational resources.

Discharge planning, which requires family involvement, is often a very difficult and taxing aspect of the total treatment regimen in that emotions run high, and patients may remain quite symptomatic. Moreover, post-discharge social, treatment, living adjustment and welfare services are frequently difficult to obtain, and the process brings out the worst in bureaucracy.

Psychologists, in addition to offering various forms of therapy, are also called on to provide psychological testing to discern I.Q., level of functioning, vocational aptitude, and diagnosis. Some psychologists also provide programs designed to modify or reshape behavior.

Psychiatric units, in whatever type of larger facility, still struggle with the policy question: whether to have open or locked units. The trend is definitely toward open units. Advances in psychotropic medications, attitudes of professionals toward the emotionally disturbed and patients attitudes about themselves and their rights have definitely improved the treatment approaches toward individuals with mental disabilities.

At this writer's hospital, three 22-bed units were unlocked in 1976. Despite staff concern that the patients would leave, very few did. Staff found that they had to rely on verbal persuasion and enabling the patient to ally himself with the healthier aspects of his personality to make mature decisions about remaining in treatment until therapeutic goals had been reached. There was also less of a "we-they" relationship between staff and patients when the units were unlocked.

New emphasis on full patient rights guarantees that individuals who are not overtly suicidal or assaultive may sign into and out of a psychiatric facility whenever they want to, providing that they require inpatient treatment. Even the involuntarily admitted individual has a court hearing within a few days and now has the right to periodic progress review by clinical and quality assurance staff. His/her initial admission, if subsequently extended, must be through the court system with legal counsel present. Contrary to popular thought, the majority of admissions to psychiatric facilities are voluntary. This is in sharp contrast to previous practices where many individuals were involuntarily committed for long or indefinite periods of time.

Present day inpatient psychiatric treatment emphasizes the therapeutic milieu of the unit. Instead of relying heavily on individual psychotherapy, the unit stresses patient-staff government, clinical programs, various therapeutic modalities and activities which highlight the short-term nature of inpatient care, and result in quick reintegration with family, work, and neighborhood. This concept of the therapeutic community or milieu relies on the health, stability, and support of the community to provide a major component of the total treatment provided to the individual (Wilmar, 47).

Individual psychotherapy is provided by skilled clinicians representing a number of professions: psychiatry, psychology, social work and nursing. It is usually focused on helping the patient to gain insight, to grow emotionally and to handle social situations. There is a large educational component in all therapies — helping the patient to learn to use different ways of handling stress, anxiety, depressive symptoms, uncomfortable social situations, and problem solving. Although psychoanalytic treatment, including non-directive approaches, has been used in the past and still finds favor with some therapists, more directive and directly educational approaches are now used. Because of the short-term nature of community treatment, individual therapy is often time-limited, goal-directed, and frequently contractual in nature with jointly agreed upon treatment objectives within a specific number of therapeutic sessions to attain those objectives.

Like individual therapy, *group therapy* can be run by most professionals who are trained and skilled in group therapy, group process or social group work. Participants receive help, treatment, insight, support or complete therapeutic group task assignments, depending on the nature and objectives of the design of the group approach. Short-term inpatient groups must, of necessity, focus on the areas of reality orientation, social adjustment, discharge planning, group support to group participant and similar issues.

Family therapy is designed to focus on family interaction — within the nuclear family, extended family and between generations of families. No one person (primary patient) is seen exclusively as the family member with emotional problems or symptoms. Rather, the family is seen as dysfunctional or emotionally unhealthy. Family therapy helps to bring about family equilibrium, define family issues which the family as a whole need to work on and place responsibility for improvement on the family rather than on any one member. Various other forms of family intervention are also employed, utilizing family therapy techniques or other family approaches.

All therapeutic approaches are, of necessity, short-term in keeping with the philosophy of crisis intervention, cost-containment and quick return to a less restrictive setting. The approaches stress reality-oriented issues, family re-integration, social and interpersonal adjustment and amelioration of symptoms with the expectation that longer term treatment will be on an outpatient basis.

One of the major treatment approaches in a short-term inpatient unit is the titrating and prescription of medication. In modern psychiatric practice medication is employed to reduce symptoms quickly, to help the individual feel emotionally comfortable, to become verbal and responsible for making decisions about his/her treatment and to return to a regular life situation. Symptom relief is achieved as quickly as possible to help the individual become stabilized and to keep the length of treatment on an inpatient basis as short as possible. Brief inpatient psychiatric treatment, as with brief medical or surgical treatment, is the preferred course so that dependency on the hospital does not occur and so that cost containment is maintained.

Patients on psychiatric units sometimes require additional medical care, neurological evaluation, surgery or treatment for medical or sensory disabilities. In addition, in the case of intractable or life-threatening depressions which have not responded to therapy or a course of anti-depressant medication, electro-convulsive therapy may be prescribed. General hospital psychiatric units refer patients within their particular facility, while free-standing psychiatric hospitals have transfer agreements with various specialty hospitals in the community.

Larger general hospital psychiatric services and free-standing psychiatric hospitals usually have special units devoted to particular age ranges or psychiatric problems. There could be a forensic unit for the short-term evaluation and treatment of offenders, a crisis intervention or locked unit for individuals who are overtly suicidal or assaultive; an adolescent unit, older adult or geriatric unit, children's unit, and a unit to treat individuals who are substance abusers. Each of these special units has a particular treatment philosophy, goals and objectives, treatment programs to match philosophy and goals and treatment modalities best designed to treat these particular age ranges and disabilities.

Northwestern Institute of Psychiatry is a 146-bed modern hospital located in the Philadelphia suburbs on 11 wooded acres. It has nine specialized units. All patients have semi-private accommodations in motel-like rooms. Staff do not wear uniforms, and the interior designers have minimized hospital-like surroundings in order to create a relaxed atmosphere. In 1969, the Board was awarded a staffing grant to develop a community mental health center to serve three neighborhoods in Northwest Philadelphia. In 1975, the Board completed building a new psychiatric hospital; in 1976, they opened a day treatment program nearby; in 1980, they affiliated with an alcoholism treatment facility; and in 1981, they built a new community mental health center bulding.

At its inception, the Board dedicated itself to serve the community sector. Northwestern Institute treats the largest number of Medicare and Medicaid patients of any private psychiatric hospital in Pennsylvania and receives a majority of referrals from community mental health center and 24-hour emergency services.

Many of the patients have formerly been treated in state psychiatric hospitals for a duration ranging from several years to several decades. They have chronic illnesses and institutionalized behaviors and approaches to life adjustment incompatible with those outside of the state hospital. Other patients are representative of those who would have gone to state hospitals in the past, but no longer do, as the state phases down the institutions. Many of the patients are characterized as having few family, housing, financial, social and community supports. Some have no families. If there are families, they are often overwhelmed and beleagured by their own problems or the intensity of the family's emotional difficulties.

Other patients treated at the hospital do come from a more supportive environment, have private insurance, have illnesses which are less chronic, and have families who are invested in their welfare.

Northwestern treats the full range of psychiatric disabilities in individuals from 13 years through old age. The disorders are severe anxiety and depression, schizophrenia, manic depression, character disorders, adjustment reaction to adolescence, adulthood, or situational stress, explosive personality and the emotional problems of the mentally retarded.

The hospital has a well staffed quality assurance program for monitoring and evaluating medical records, clinical practices, length of stay and conducting clinical audits on a regular basis. The hospital is a member of the local Professional Services Review Organization

(PSRO), the first private psychiatric hospital in the state to achieve this status.

The average length of stay is 26 days. This number is elevated somewhat by the sometimes higher utilization rate of adolescents and the elderly who sometimes stay for several months. The majorty of patients leave in three or four weeks.

Long term institutionalization has ended for most chronically mentally ill individuals. For example, in 1967, Philadelphia State Hospital had a population of over 6,700 patients. By 1980, the population was under 1,000. Similar circumstances prevail in other public institutions nationwide. While many of these persons have made a fairly adequate adjustment and life for themselves outside the confines of a large facility, others require regular readmission to short-term inpatient units. This is attributable in part to the nature and severity of their illness. In far too many instances, however, they require readmission because of a dearth of outpatient services, halfway houses, supervised boarding homes, and adequate public welfare services. Unfortunately, this situation will, in all probability, become worse due to inflation, tight money and the demand for cost-effective health care.

From a social worker's standpoint, "cost effectiveness" calls for more adequate funding of outpatient and aftercare services, partial hospitalization programs, least restrictive treatment alternatives, better quality supervised living arrangements and additional public welfare cash grants and services. Unfortunately, the emphasis for the 1980's seems to be on inpatient treatment, the only modality which is adequately reimbursed by governmental and private insurance plans.

Only half of the 1,700 originally planned community mental health centers were funded. Those which remain face severe cutbacks in funding from all three levels of government, federal, state and local. These trends appear to place an even grater reliance on the provision of *inpatient* treatment. In addition to the cost factor, it is questionable whether an over-reliance on inpatient care is the best treatment approach to individuals with psychiatric disorders.

This shift from the social psychiatry and community mental health of the 60's and 70's places a greater emphasis on the medical model in inpatient facilities. The term *"medical model"* has been used pejoratively in the past, but we do not view it negatively as long as the emphasis does not diminish the team treatment approach or the importance of the contributions made by each team member on behalf of the patient.

The promise of a "bold new approach" has been only partially fulfilled. Institutionalization of patients for years or for decades is becoming a practice of the past. Short-term crisis interventive treatment and an emphasis on quality have helped remove some of the stigma of mental illness.

COMPARATIVE CIRCUMSTANCES, BY RACE

The tendency for minorities to suffer a disadvantage in the movement toward deinstitutionalization was reported by the President's Commission on Mental Health (35, p. 831) as follows: that the rate of institutionalization has decreased for blacks as well as whites; however, the decrease for white men has been 46% as compared with 25% for black men, and the decrease for white women, 53% as compared with 42% for black women.

Another view of their comparative circumstances may bring these realities into sharper focus and shed some light on the resistance that blacks and other minorities express in various ways to the intrusion (as they see it) of psychiatric personnel, irrespective of the profession. Again, the President's Commission (35, p. 832) reported that in 1975 whites of both sexes were admitted to State and County Mental Hospitals at the rate of 161 per 100,000 population as contrasted with 344 per 100,000 for blacks. The most striking contrast was to be found among males, 25 to 44 years of age, where the rate for white was 349 and for blacks, 1033. For the age group 18 to 24, the rate for white males was 344 and for black males, 892. The evidence shows that the anxiety felt by black citizens toward the mental health establishment and those who run it was not without foundation; there was clear and present danger for them of being institutionalized, and the danger was far greater for them than for whites.

SPECIAL NEEDS OF CHILDREN

The report in 1970 of the Joint Commission on Mental Health of Children (18) called particular attention to the unmet mental health needs of children and adolescents in our society. Special concern was expressed for children of the poor and those of designated minorities, among whom the rate of mental illness was significantly higher. Particular attention was directed to the need for preventive service *in addition to* systematic and comprehensive health and mental health services. In the interest of brevity, we do not intend to review the whole litany of complaints against the deficiencies in our health, education, and welfare systems, to say nothing about those of the public employment services of our society, as staked out by the commission. Yet, we do regard a major recommendation for a child advocacy system to guarantee mental health services as being highly compatible with the posture of social work and a role which the profession has undertaken since its inception.

Some social workers have focused on "clinical" practice, as discussed elsewhere in this chapter, but others have focused upon community organization and social planning with the protection of children from abuse, neglect, and exploitation as the major motif of practice. A well-remembered example would be the indefatigable efforts of the most prominent social workers for the prohibition of child labor during the first decade or so of this century — to say nothing of the establishment of the U.S. Children's Bureau in 1912. In a like manner, their concerted effort as part of a coalition of advocates for comprehensive maternal and child health services led to the first federal legislation which provided support to the states under the Sheppard-Towner Act of 1921.

Some social workers have chosen the child guidance clinic or mental health clinic as the focus for their activities; some have chosen the family service agency; others have worked in child protection agencies; still others have been employed in the schools or the juvenile courts; and, of course, some in residential facilities for children. The perfect tense used here is intended merely to indicate a commitment to children's services over time, since social workers are widely and similarly distributed to this day. Finally, the point at issue is that a certain percentage of the parents receiving social casework or counseling services in Family Service agencies are quite similar to some of those encountered in the mental health center or child guidance clinic (31); therapeutic objectives with them are similar; and in both instances, a social worker has probably rendered the service.

MENTAL HEALTH OF CHILDREN

The question of the etiology of emotional and behavioral problems in children and in adults is as old as thinking man himself. Whether deviant behavior is internally motivated by demons, heredity or unconscious drives, or externally maintained by fate, social injustices or family inconsistencies, is a dialectic that has permeated the evolution of mental health practice through the ages. Different time periods have emphasized different aspects of causation and of accountability. These factors are dependent on the social, cultural and economic conditions of the time. Social work in the mental health field reflects this dialectic, particularly in the treatment of children.

Social work's involvement in social and psychological treatment emerges at the turn of the century from two traditions: social change and rehabilitation. A focus on social change may be found in the lack of environmental supports toward normal functioning, and that given these supports, individuals will naturally adapt to healthy and productive patterns of behavior. For example, the settlement house movement was an attempt to address the stresses and alienation of urban life through a reorganization of the community. Pumphrey (36) says:

> The settlement movement saw (the individual) as a member of a group through which joint activity could be conducted. It did not overlook the need for broad social and economic reforms but it saw these as growing out of the experience, thinking an action of the whole population of a neighborhood cooperating with similar groups in other neighborhoods. (p. 71)

As such, the scope of social work involvement was at all levels of organizational reform, from affecting national policy through legislation, to the settlement houses which led to community organization as a specialized area of social work practice.

The development of social case work from a tradition of almsgiving to an approach toward rehabilitation is represented in the emergence of the Charity Organization Society in 1901. In an effort to coordinate diversified philanthropic activities, the COS introduced the concept of "treating" the recipients of charity. The assumption was that poverty was a reflection of a lack of personal esteem and that the locus of change was in the individual's adopting a more prudent and respectable lifestyle. Treatment entailed education and encouragement in a relationship that emphasized kindness and caring.

Freudian psychoanalysis further influenced the development of social case work, not only in providing a more complex theoretical basis for supporting individual growth, but in emphasizing the active participation of the client in achieving the goals of treatment. Allen (2) says:

> Social work in its growing sensitivity to the living human being and the part he could take in his own adjustment developed its interest in case work when the individual was regarded less as a recipient of help, but more as a participant in a process designed to help him deal with realities of his living (p 233).

The beginning of an integrated approach to treatment, finds its ultimate expression in the orthopsychiatric movement and the child guidance clinics. Prior to that, there is little differentiation in the theoretical and practical approaches between the emotional problems of children and those of adults. According to Warner (43):

> Child Guidance arose as a preventive measure to remedy the situation evidenced by the increasing numbers (of children) admitted to psychopathic hospitals and brought before the courts (p. 318).

Orthopsychiatry provided an alternative to conceptual models of treatment which emphasized interventions aimed at controlling deviant behavior in a multifaceted way. In 1909, when William Healy began his work with delinquents in Chicago, there were limited theoretical or practical approaches to their rehabilitation. Lowery (23) tell us that:

> The notion, then fairly prevalent among neurologists and psychiatrists, was that serious antisocial behavior betokened something pathological in the offender (p. 16).

Healy provided a comprehensive medical, social and psychological assessment as part of his diagnostic evaluation that preceded treatment, according to Lowery (23):

> When we took into account these as important environmental influences upon the child who became delinquent any proof of heredity or of criminalism was not forthcoming (p. 21).

A multidisciplinary team approach to the evaluation and treatment of the social and emotional problems of children, became the model for child guidance clinic treatment, bringing about a marriage of individual and contextual approaches to treatment in the collaboration of psychiatry and social work. Allen (2) had this to say:

> Psychiatry with its medical background was rooted in a concern for the biological forces operating in a man, creating the conditions cared for in our mental hospitals, and in the earlier period the main preoccupations were the hereditary and constitutional factors and the relation of somatic disturbances to the etiology of mental aberration. . . .

> Social work, on the other hand, grew out of the community and was largely concerned with the social forces which made for difficult living. With a sociological orientation, social work functioning was more concerned with the environment adjustments and with the individual as a participant in this process (p. 232).

The Philadelphia Child Guidance Clinic, established in 1925, provided a prototypical model for the evaluation and tratment of children. Treatment was founded on the basic assumption that the problems of children were caused and maintained by a combination of intrapsychic conflicts internalized by the child, that prevented optimal utilization of his own intellectual and emotional resources, and by social influences, primarily the family, peer groups and the school, that had not adequately supported the child's normal social adaptation.

This multilevel approach to a problem required the specialized skills of multiple disciplines. The psychiatrist, trained in his medical specialty, but with additional training in psychotherapeutic interventions with children, would assess the child in terms of his physical, neurological, and his emotional functioning. The social worker concomitantly, initiates an assessment of the social conditions in which the child operates. This begins by taking a detailed social history of the child's development from the parents. The worker then elicits from the parents their response to the child and his problems as they evolved over the years.

This social assessment also traces the change of responses between husband and wife over this time period, giving a fuller appreciation of the many social and emotional factors influencing the child's adjustment in his family.

Similarly, the worker focuses on the effect of the school environment, and its influence on the child's adaptability both socially and academically. It is in the interplay of social forces effecting a child and family's development that provides the social worker with a context for understanding current problems.

The social worker deals closely with the parents, initially in helping them appreciate the struggles the child is having, helping them support the child in finding healthier ways of coping. Attention is also paid to parents as adults, with stresses of their own which impinge on their functioning as parents, and as spouses. The focus on parental influence on the development of the child is a significant step in the elaboration of a more coherent approach to treatment. Similarly, with the shift of the locus of behavior from within the individual, to a combination of individual and contextual factors, the burden of responsibility for changes shifts from the child himself, to the child and his parents. To quote Allen (2) again:

> The chief difficulty in working directly with a child is that frequently helps the parents to avoid the major issues involved by giving them the feeling that the psychiatrist, because he is doing a lot of direct work with the child also feels that the changing of the child in some manner really is the most important thing (p. 20).

The orthopsychiatric movement broadened the approach to the psychological needs of children. The focus on the social context of the child was particularly relevant in families afflicted by the disorganizing stresses of divorce and single parenthood, of poverty and of illness. These situations highlighted the interdependence of the emotional needs of the child, with the support required of the child's social structures. With the increase of divorce and breakdown of the traditional two parent family, the need for social work intervention became more prominent. Societal concern over the extent of mental and emotional problems, aroused after military involvement in the Second World War, led to the Mental Health and Study Act of 1955, financing community mental health centers to treat the causes of emotional distress. Conceptual models for the treatment of children proliferated, each based on different assumptions on which causes, maintains, and solves the problems children encounter in their daily living. Three major treatment approaches will be discussed, providing some framework for understanding the implications of these differences: a psychodynamic approach, a child guidance approach, and a family therapy approach.

Psychodynamic Approach

Freudian psychoanalysis provided the major orientation to psychodynamic theory and treatment. It assumes that powerful unconscious forces operate within the individual and often come into conflict with the individual's conscious wishes, or society's expectations for the individual. Serious conflicts lie at the root of most problems, which can result in pathological symptomatology. Since these conflicts are often unconscious, that is, not in the patient's awareness, treatment entails the free expression of thoughts and emotions in a therapeutic relationship, to elicit the basic conflict. With this new insight, the patient can be relieved of distress and make new choices in his life that will allow a healthier adaptation. The therapist serves as the nonjudgmental recipient of the patient's free associations, interpreting its meaning and relevance to the patient. With this insight, the patient gains a greater sense of control in his life.

Adaptations of analytic approaches have evolved over the years, but all share a basic philosophy and orientation that the root of emotional difficulty is in the internal dynamics of the patient/client's psyche. The application of analytic approaches to children developed in conjunction with the interest in the cause and treatment of delinquency. Non-verbal techniques for communication, for example play therapy, facilitated the therapeutic process with children who are unprepared for the heavy emphasis on verbalization. The internal conflicts of the child emerge in play and it is through the therapist's acute awareness of the child's "unconscious" communications that a resolution can be found.

Child Guidance Approach

Intrapsychic approaches were extremely long term, requiring significant resources in the availability of trained child analysts, and there was no assurance of significant change, particularly with more difficult and chronic problems. As Healy noted in 1932, according to Lowery (23):

> The material obtained bearing upon unconscious motivations is extremely illuminating; the curative results in the face of long-standing internal conditioning and external vicissitudes were meager (p. 40).

Social work's contribution in the understanding and respect for the social manifestations of psychological stresses, became a perfect complement to the newly developing area of child psychiatry. It is in the collaboration between the social worker and the child psychiatrist in the child guidance model of treatment that the integration of the internal experiences of the child and its external manifestations of behavior, found its most lucid expression. To quote Allen (2) again:

> Here psychiatry with its therapeutic emphasis and social work with a case work emphasis together provide a clinic service that include parent and child but where the core of the service is around the child (p. 236).

A child guidance approach both appreciates that the child can make his needs manifest only in a relationship of trust. It, however, recognizes that parental influences play a crucial role in the child's ability to establish a trusting relationship. In treatment, the social worker carefully joins with the parents in their concerns for their child and in that process establishes a relationship with the parents that not only enables them to support further autonomy for their child, but allows the social worker to explore problems which they are experiencing as marital partners, and as adults. Allen (2) states it as follows:

> The child within the framework of his biological equipment is undergong constant change . . . at the same time he is discovering himself in relation to his parental figures. They provide a living framework within which the child awakens, where he gains a feeling of his separateness and independence while, at the same time, utilizing his feeling of his dependence to gain a livable sense of values as a member of society (p. 37).

The problems in this process of separation become manifest in the course of treatment and form the basis of ongoing casework with the parents and psychotherapy with the child.

Family Therapy Approach

While a classical child guidance approach significantly shifted the locus of causation and of treatment from the child's intrapsychic structure to the problems in growth and autonomy that involved the parents and child, the development of family therapy approach further generalized the model to the patterns of interaction among family members. A "systems" approach to family treatment in the 1950's coincided with a trend toward the deinstitutionalization of severely disturbed patients who could be managed within their communities. The problems these patients presented often defied traditional forms of treatment, psychodynamic as well as child guidance approaches. Both relied on the resources of the individual and the nuclear family to deal with the problems. However, in more severe cases, mental or social breakdown, such as schizophrenia, or juvenile delinquency, these structures are often themselves limited in their ability to effectively deal with the problems. A new more dynamic form of conceptualizing these problems was found in a family systems approach to treatment. In it, a problem in an individual is viewed as a symptom of stress within a larger system, whether it be nuclear family, extended family, or the family's relationship to the commmunity. A family systems conceptualization focuses on how a problem is maintained, rather than searching for the ultimate causes of the problem.

The family systems model is an adaptation of concepts borrowed from the hard sciences, and applied to the field of social interaction by the anthropologist, Gregory Bateson, in his revolutionary study of the families of schizophrenics. With the help of Don Jackson, Jay Haley, Virginia Satir and others, Bateson evolved a strategy to treating a population resistant to other treatment approaches. Similar approaches were being developed by Murray Bowen in his multigenerational approach to families with a psychotic member, Salvador Minuchin in his structural approach to families with a delinquent child, and a number of other innovators in the family field. What these theorist practitioners have in common is a means of conceptualizing a problem of individual behavior as symptomatic of disfunction within a larger system. The resolution of the problem can only be achieved within the context of that larger system. Separating out the "identified patient" was seen as scapegoating one member. The family then became the "patient" and treatment entailed intervening in a way that would change family patterns of interactions, to allow normal growth on the part of the identified patient. The social worker in a family approach becomes something of a system strategist. Though mindful of the individual perceptions and feelings of each of the family members, his major focus is to support changes in the way family members communicate and relate to one another.

Where the boundaries between the function of the psychotherapist and that of the social worker were extremely clear, in the child guidance model, the former dealing with the inner world of the child and the latter specializing in the social contexts of the child, a family systems approach collapses these functions, so that there is considerably less differentiation in how a social worker would operate as contrasted with a psychiatrist or psychologist. Certainly, each of the professions has its specific set of skills and social accountabilities. The physician trained in the biological assessment of the individual is most competent and legally licensed to prescribe medication, while the psychologist may use psychometric assessments to measure certain functioning. The social worker's training is based on the assessment of social interaction on individual functioning. In the opinion of Napier and Whiteker (27), "It is possible that the social worker's training is the most appropriate education of all for family therapy since social systems are the direct focus of the (family therapy) field" (p. 289).

In some respects, social work has gone "full circle" in the area of child mental health, from a focus on the contextual circumstances that make for high levels of individual stress and personal suffering to a focus on the internal operations and management of that stress, back to the way in which adaptive styles become manifest in behavior and affect the individual's social context. The fact is that the dialectic of internal versus external realities is an ongoing one. Each new approach offers a new perspective, but the dialectic always remains the same. Social work has always distinguished itself in its consistent emphasis on the social realities in which people live, whether the focus is on the individual, the family, the community or on the national policy. Though the coming years will be a test of that commitment, particularly as it affects the delivery of mental health services, the dialectic will always remain.

SERVICES FOR THE ELDERLY

Another "essential element" of community mental health was the provision of services to the elderly. In 1965, the resident patient rate per 100,000 population for those over 65 in state and county hospitals was 773, and by 1975 it had been reduced to 245. Not surprisingly, those over 65 were hospitalized at a rate higher than any other age group. The rate for *all age* groups hospitalized in 1965 was 248 as contrasted with the above mentioned 773 per 100,000 for those *over 65*, and in 1975, the rate was 91 for *all age groups* as contrasted with 242 for those *over 65* (35:95).

Althouth deinstitutionalization was occurring for all age groups, the principle has been harder to implement among the elderly, some of whom have spent many years within the walls of a hospital. Hence, the rate of residence, inflated by the rate of *retention*, has been highest for the elderly. At the same time, in-patient *admissions* of those over 65 in 1975 were lower by far than for any age group except for those under 18 years of age. This probably reflected a disinclination to admit new patients from this age group and an even stronger bias against readmissions.

What, then, were the alternatives? In fact, the shortage of alternatives where quality of care could be assured had become an alarming problem. Yet, policy had decreed that patients should be discharged to the community. Thus, there was an irreversible exodus from the hospitals to communities which were often unready and unable to cope with the numbers referred. Benign neglect was too frequently reported because domiciliary facilities were overcrowded or understaffed. These ranged from private homes to large "intermediate facilities." The private home provided room and board along with some privileges in the home, some assurance of human contact for and limited surveillance over the *resident*, as ex-patients are sometimes called.

The term "resident" may seem like a mere euphemism, but there *are* good reasons for substituting it for "patient." They are: 1) that it signifies a change of status; 2) that it implies that the rights of a citizen are restored in keeping with that status; 3) that more can be expected of a *resident* in terms of self-care; 4) that there is greater freedom accorded a *resident* with respect to leaving the home for outside contacts, entertainment, and shopping; 5) that decisions about the use of money or the way a *resident* spends his time are largely left to that person, and 6) that the persons in whose home a *resident* lives must assume the role of host or hostess — not "Keeper."

The social worker serves as consultant-liaison to the host or hostess, whose home is intended to afford the *resident* a quality of life which is *less restrictive* than the hospital from which he/she has been discharged or, stated more positively, an optimum experience within the context of a family constellation. Whether the *resident* is clutched to the bosom of the family or remains peripheral to it depends on many factors. A person may feel safer on the fringes of the family because he can not risk a greater emotional investment. He may be relatively happy and secure on the fringes of the family, with access to its members but limited involvement in the social complexities of their lives. The stance of the family and the personalities involved will importantly affect the "contract" that is worked out for the resident. For instance, do *residents* eat with the family? watch TV with the family? "pitch in" and help with chores? attend religious services with the family? The *contract* has to be reviewed periodically, not exclusively for purposes of monitoring the quality of "care," but as much for the sake of providing encouragement, flexibility, and support to the host and/or hostess — toward the achievement of realistic goals.

The social worker may have to intercede around lack of initiative on the part of the ex-patient/resident, his/her over-dependency, demandingness, passivity or whatever the behavior may be. The intent of the periodic visit is to assess the patient's progress and to explore with the host/hostess ways and means of their assisting the resident in maintaining habits of daily living and doing what is (for him) most "fruitful." When the resident is failing to thrive in the environment, appropriate intervention may entail consultation with other members of the treatment team, changes in medication, etc. If the resident is acutely unhappy in the home and negotiations with the host/hostess do not suffice, he may have to be moved to another home — if there is a vacancy available. On the other hand, if the complaints seem to be a product of the complainant's illness — and this must be assessed more carefully — there is the possibility of using a re-admission to hospital for a limited period of time for therapeutic purposes.

Caring about the well-being of the resident is a cardinal expectation of the host/hostess. Yet, the very nature of the "contract" between the resident (who *is a former patient*) and the host/hostess *does* confer some "authority" upon the latter. Although the resident has all the rights of a citizen, he/she is vulnerable in a variety of ways. The host/hostess is presumed to be the *well* person and therefore, capable of making some "judgments" about the resident's behavior. If the host/hostess does not exceed the authority attached to the position held, all is well. The social worker visiting the premises must be alert and vigilant about this type of "bind" for the resident.

Worse yet is the unscrupulous administrator of a home — often the larger and more impersonal place — who intentionally exploits the resident. This takes the form of neglect, sometimes to the point of cruelty — even criminal neglect. Another form of exploitation is seizure by the administrator of the funds which come from various sources to support the *resident*. Variations on this theme range from petty "gouging" of the person (a former patient) to defrauding the person. Intervention on the part of the social worker may require his/her resorting to legal means and other forms of advocacy for the protection of the resident who is being victimized.

STAFFING THE MENTAL HEALTH SERVICES

With the passage of the Community Mental Health Act, which was signed by John F. Kennedy on October 31, 1963, all the professions associated with mental health were destined to expand. Social work was no exception. By 1976 the National Institute of Mental Health (30, p. 26) reported the number of positions in mental health facilities in the United States, as follows:

NUMBER OF POSITIONS IN MENTAL HEALTH FACILITIES, BY PROFESSION, IN THE UNITED STATES IN 1976

Profession	*Total*	*Full-time*	*Part-time*	*Trainee*	*Full-time Equivalent*
Psychiatrists	23,390	7,549	9,210	6,631	15,339
Psychologists	20,536	11,973	4,661	3,902	15,251
Social Workers	31,212	22,474	4,717	4,021	25,887
Registered Nurses	45,163	35,147	6,013	4,003	39,392

At a glance, one observes that there were almost three times as many social workers as psychiatrists and about twice as many social workers as psychologists employed *full-time* in mental health facilities in the United States. It may be somewhat more useful to examine *full-time* equivalent staffing hereafter to achieve greater clarity in comparing the professional personnel assigned to various components of the mental health system in the United States.

For example, full-time equivalent positions, by discipline, in *psychiatric hospitals* in the U.S. in 1976, were reported by NIMH (30, p. 30) as follows:

NUMBER OF POSITIONS, BY PROFESSION, IN PUBLIC AND PRIVATE PSYCHIATRIC HOSPITALS IN THE U.S. IN 1976

Profession	*Total*	*State & County Mental Hospitals*	*Private Mental Hospitals*
Psychiatrists	5,702	4,333	1,369
Psychologists	3,598	3,039	559
Social Workers	6,732	5,948	784
Registered Nurses	18,493	15,098	3,395

With the mandate for deinstitutionalization occurring in the mid-1970's and continuing to the present, there has been heavy pressure on social service departments and social workers in public mental hospitals in particular to develop alternative arrangements in the community. Planning for patients to return to their own homes frequently entails the repair of relationships that have been damaged as a consequence of the mental illness. Preparation of patients for the intracacies of interpersonal relationships outside the hospital is frequently undertaken in group "therapy" sessions. Alternatives may include a foster care plan, a boarding home, a group home, a half-way house, a convalescent center, a hostel or hotel, one's own home — any of these combined with an aftercare plan which links the patient up with out-patient attention for the ensuing year. It is the responsibility of the social worker to develop this linkage with the family or substitute care-providers in the community.

General hospitals, which are characterized by their responsibility for providing short-term in-patient care for acute conditions, whether medical, surgical or psychiatric, present a different set of priorities for medical, nursing, and all other staff, including social work. The escalating cost of hospitalization has led to the development of utilization review and professional standards review organizations

(PSRO's) as methods of monitoring and limiting the patient's stay in hospital. The psychosocial nature of mental illness is such that the social worker's contribution to the study, diagnosis, treatment, prognosis, discharge, and after-care plan for the patient (as a continuum) has proven to be essential. The presence and the input of the social worker on the *team* of professionals who make decisions affecting the patient and family (involving both to the extent possible) confer a coordinating-expediting role upon the social worker.

In the out-patient clinic, the social worker is expected to help the patient with the realities that may have triggered the episode of illness that had led to hospitalization: failure or insecurity in marriage, parenting, employment, homemaking, making ends meet, sexual behavior, school performance, self-discipline and living according to the law. The social worker is also operating at the apex of a program to prevent hospitalization when dealing with the here-and-now realities that affect the social functioning of the patient who is overwhelmed by a combination of his own vulnerability and external stress factors in his life situation.

The numbers of full-time equivalent positions in general hospitals providing psychiatric services in the U.S. in 1976 were reported by NIMH (30, p. 31) as follows:

NUMBER OF POSITIONS BY PROFESSION, IN GENERAL HOSPITALS PROVIDING PSYCHIATRIC SERVICES IN THE U.S. IN 1976

	*General Hospitals**	
Profession	*Psych. In-Patient*	*Psych. Out-Patient*
Psychiatrists	1,935	1,998
Psychologists	528	828
Social Workers	1,095	1,420
Registered Nurses	9,083	360

*Exclusive of federal hospitals

In free-standing out-patient clinics and community mental health centers, social workers have moved beyond their earlier and more traditional "job specifications." Because of their demonstrated competence in policy formulation and planning, in community organization and development of resources, and in the implementation and administration of services, social workers have been employed in considerable numbers for assignments in the middle and upper echelons of administration in free-standing out-patient clinics and community mental health centers. The numbers of full-time equivalent positions in these settings, as reported again by NIMH in 1976, (30, p. 31) were as follows:

NUMBER OF POSITIONS, BY PROFESSION, IN MENTAL HEALTH CLINICS IN THE U.S. IN 1976

Profession	*Free-standing Out-patient Clinics*	*Community Mental Health Clinics*
Psychiatrists	1,449	2,292
Psychologists	3,704	4,543
Social Workers	5,755	6,752
Registered Nurses	830	4,588

The expansion of the mandate under amendments to the Community Mental Health Centers Act in 1975 increased the pressures being exerted upon out-patient facilities. This was *precisely* the time when *revenue-sharing* legislation mandated the disbursement of large sums of federally collected dollars by local government in accordance with local priorities. Expenditures for mental health were not trump cards in the hands of local politicians who live by rules of political and fiscal expediency. Health services were almost predictably destined to suffer. For example, Philadelphia General Hospital, one of the oldest municipal hospitals in the United States, which had accounted for approximately 250,000 out-patient visits per annum through its medical, surgical, psychiatric and other clinics, was *closed*, forever, in 1977 and has been demolished since then.

As a consequence of the strain upon professional personnel responsible for patient care in out-patient settings was the re-alignment of staff and some re-allocation of duties. Far more responsibility for crisis intervention, with new patients and supportive therapy with after-care patients was assigned to social workers than ever before in free-standing out-patient clinics and in those under the aegis of community mental health centers. Many have become active as group therapists and co-therapists with groups ranging widely in age, diagnosis, duration of illness, social situation, etc.

NIMH (30, p. 83) reports a preponderance of social workers as compared with other professionals employed in residential treatment centers for emotionally disturbed children. The actual number of positions, by discipline, is psychiatrists, 460; psychologists, 634; social workers, 2,091; registered nurses, 399. Ever since the establishment of the American Orthopsychiatric Association, which has been committed from its inception to multidisciplinary membership and a multi-dimensional approach to the assessment and treatment of mental illness, social workers have been prominent in its ranks *and* in the special area of child mental health. See Lowery (23).

EMERGING ISSUES IN PSYCHOSOCIAL CARE OF THE MENTALLY ILL

It is hardly our intention to indulge in prophecy in this final commentary; it is more nearly an effort to recognize the direction in which immediate past and current trends are taking us. The ethos of the early 1980's seems light years apart from that of the early '60's. There was a buoyancy, a fervor, and an optimism — maybe a false sense of limitless possibilities — in the early '60's, the Camelot years! Those were the years when the community mental health movement gained momentum. The idea that community care was bound to be positive and that hospitalization was, ipso facto, bound to be negative was patently falacious, as sweeping generalizations often are. The assumption that public funding would be forthcoming in ever-increasing amounts for ever-expanding programs in mental health was obviously unrealistic.

Things have not been the same since that war in Vietnam. It taught us many bitter lessons, and it cast a pall of gloom over the land. We could not feel proud of our part in the war; it had left us feeling corrupted and guilt-ridden. And that was hardly conducive to the morale — or the mental health — of our whole society! This was followed by a severe slippage in industry, by inflation, recession, unemployment, and the vexing realization that big government was unable to curb inflation and all the rest. Of course, the closing months of the Nixon years did very little to inspire confidence in government. As more and more Americans have felt their purchasing power reduced by double-digit inflation and as they have found their jobs jeopardized by widespread failures in small business and huge cut-backs in major industry, they have withdrawn support for *social programs*. Besides, it is somehow easy to use social programs as a scapegoat for ugly fiscal problems that refuse to go away.

THE PRIVATE VERSUS THE PUBLIC SECTOR

With cut-backs in support for community mental health centers, there is ample evidence that psychiatrists have been reverting to private practice. This trend has been hastened by the increased numbers of Americans whose insurance policies include some coverage for mental illness or those whose HMO membership includes some provision for limited psychiatric attention. Psychiatrists find the bureaucracy of the community menntal health center, the volume of patients, the perennial struggle to maintain fiscal support, and the lack of autonomy — all rather frustrating.

Although coverage for psychiatric attention has become more widespread as part of a larger package of fringe benefits which employees have received, usually through the collective bargaining process, the percentage of the population thus protected is small. When almost 10% of the labor force are unemployed, these millions of adults are more vulnerable to mental breakdown from situation stress, but they and their dependents are woefully underprotected.

Quality assurances has been a preoccupation of consumer groups, of the professions, of standard-setting and accrediting bodies like the Joint Commission on Accreditation of Hospitals (JCAH), the federal monitors within the National Institute of Mental Health (NIMH), *et al.* These forms of surveillance are necessary and valuable. However, if third-party payments continue to be diverted from the community mental health centers to practitioners in private practice, such a trend could spell trouble for the centers and their clientele.

A high percentage of subscribers to Health Maintenance Organizations (HMO's) are salaried persons or wage-earners with some job security, to say nothing of the self-employed who elect to join. Those who are covered by health insurance policies which include psychiatric attention are similarly "low risk" families. That is, viewed from an actuarial point of view, regularly employed persons and their dependents are *less* likely to require frequent and costly attention for mental and physical illness. Moreover, they are less likely to require *very* costly attention for *chronic* illness than poor people, the aging/aged, the *ir*regularly employed, the *un*employed, the unemploy*able*, i.e., those with disabilities and severe deficits, including mental illness.

The concern here is that the pendulum could swing in the direction of funding psychiatric services outside of the community mental health center and divert revenues away from these centers. High-income families are and have always been able to afford psychiatric attention. However, with any continuing realignment of psychiatric personnel in the private practice sector, this could create the twin problems of *siphoning off third-party payments* and "diluting" the services available at the community mental health centers. Concommitantly, it might mean that the poor and other high risk patients (cited above) might continue to use the centers, but those with other options may prefer to consult psychiatrists, to say nothing of psychologists and social workers, in private practice. This eventuality is fraught with some dangers for the mental health system, as we have known it since the implementation of the Community Mental Health Centers Act of 1963. If there is further attrition among professional staff, the CMHC's will no doubt do their best to maintain a program. But, if the CMHC's are rejected by one segment of the population because there are doubts about quality of care *or* there is stronger confidence in the quality of care elsewhere, the danger of a "two-track" system raises its ugly head. That danger is that one is for the "haves" and the other, for the "have-nots" of our society; that one is good, caring, and competent and that the other is not even a close second.

RENEWAL OF THE BIOMEDICAL APPROACH

Another danger on the horizon arises from the new orientation of some segments of psychiatry. For decades, there has been a closing of the gap between the biomedical and the bio-psychosocial models of practice. A new allegiance to a biomedical, psychopharmacological approach has some implications for the way psychiatrists interact with social workers, clinical psychologists, and nurses in the treatment of mentally ill patients and transactions with their families. The biopsychosocial orientation, which led to an emphasis upon social stress and adaptation as significant diagnostic criteria and variables in therapy, opened the door to considerable interdisciplinaqry collaboration. In the course of time, the collaboration led to some remarkable blurring of roles among members of the team, and the "captain" of the team was frequently challenged by the clinical psychologist, the social worker, and the nurse — probably in that order. The psychiatrist who acknowledges the importance of the contributions made by the other professions to the treatment process and respects his/her colleagues may, nonetheless, miss the autonomy that other M.D.'s and psychiatrists in private practice enjoy — and "jealously protect"! Whether the psychiatrist finds the variations on "team approach" exciting or irksome, it must be conceded that a multi-disciplinary setting is complicated by time, turf, and treatment considerations, to say nothing of personal idiosyncracies, temperaments and philosophical differences.

One result of the fiscal constraints upon CMHC's and the complexity of practice, cited above, has been that a division of labor has developed in some CMHC out-patient clinics, where vast numbers of patients are maintained on psychotropic drugs administered by psychiatrists, while supportive attention, counseling, and psychotherapy are left to the social worker. Some might contend that the social worker is the logical choice to provide this type of supportive help, while others would argue that it is simply more economical for the social worker to carry this responsibility in CMHC's because the dollar amount for the time of the psychiatrist is much higher than for that of the social worker. Besides, there are more social workers on staff; hence, there are far more patient-contact-hours with social workers than with other professional staff (30, p. 80) excepting for registered nurses vis-a-vis patients who are hospitalized.

THE ISSUE OF PRIVATE PRACTICE IN SOCIAL WORK

Social workers have been employed within a social agency context from the beginning. Psychiatric social work took root in mental hospitals, out-patient clinics, and child guidance centers. Social casework, social group work, and community organization were recognized as major helping methods in social work which were intended, *over time*, to enable clients or a clientele to work out solutions to their problems. It has been traditional for social workers to involve the family in the treatment of the patient in relation to the mental or physical illness and to *lean upon* and *extract from* the community those resources that might be beneficial to the individual. Hence, the service rendered by the social worker in the mental health setting is a *process* which aims to be supportive and problem-solving over a continuum. In the parlance of social work, practice became "agency-based" from the outset, and social workers did not strive to embark upon private practice.

Medicine, on the other hand, started with a focus on the episode of illness as the unit of attention, and solo, fee-for-service, private practice developed across the American landscape. As psychiatrists moved into mental health programs under public auspices and social workers were associated with them in ever-increasing numbers, the potential of private practice began to appeal to some social workers. It must be remembered that psychiatrists often devoted a major portion of their time to private practice and the remainder, to a public clinic. Occasionally, a psychiatrist might invite a social worker with whom he had been associated to join him in private practice, or the social worker may have begun seeing parents/patients on a private basis from those attended at the public clinic. In the early period of private practice the social worker's position was ancilliary to that of the psychiatrist because: 1. he was a licensed doctor of medicine and therefore, had legal authority in the field of mental health; 2. he had an already-established private practice; 3. the social worker was probably dependent upon him for referrals; 4, the social worker may also have depended upon him for consultation; 5. collaboration may have been based on a division of labor which required the social worker to see the parent, the spouse or the adult child (i.e., care-provider for the patient, but not the patient as such); and 6. fees were often collected by the psychiatrist and then shared on some mutually agreed upon basis with the social worker.

The number of social workers engaged in private practice was quite limited. Most of them were part-time. However, there was some evidence of their having striven for greater independence in private practice. By the 1950's, there was considerable controversy within the profession, as reflected in the literature of that decade, on the issue of private practice in social work. There were those who contended that the social worker in private practice could not offer the full range of services usually associated with the repertoire of the "agency-based" social worker. Thus, whether the social worker was seeing the patient or the nearest-of-kin, the service rendered was limited to "therapy" or "psychotherapy." It was necessary, however, for social workers in private practice to portray the services they offered in terms which appealed to the *market*, and most potential clients knew what *psychotherapy* or *marital counseling* meant. Paradoxically, clients were quite willing to consult a social worker on a private basis, but they were more uncertain about the meaning of *social casework* than they were about *psychotherapy*.

Ambivalence over private practice and the controversy already mentioned during the 1950's culminated in a series of decisions by the Commission on Social Work Practice in 1959, the Board of Directors in 1961, and the Delegate Assembly of the National Association of Social Workers (NASW) in 1962, which accorded official recognition of and sanction to the private practice of social work (44). This led to the development of the Academy of Certified Social Work (ACSW), whose purpose is to certify to the profession and to the public that, in addition to completion of requirements for a Master's degree in social work (M.S.W.), a person is found to be fully qualified to practice by reason of having completed two years of full-time professional practice in social work under the supervi sion of an ACSW member and having passed the ACSW-administered certification examination.

By 1976, there were still "no more than 2,189 . . . in private practice in this country and of these, no more than 1,270 practiced privately full-time" (44). By 1980, however, ACSW membership seems to have been an accepted qualification for private practice of social work across the U.S.A., particularly in states which had not yet passed legislation addressing the question. By 1982, the legislatures in 23 states, Puerto Rico, and 5 provinces of Canada had enacted laws according licensure, certification, registration or other official testimony of qualifications.

By 1982, the membership of NASW was about 90,000. The first edition of the *NASW Register of Clinical Social Workers* was published in 1976 and the third edition, in 1982. This annotated directory, together with the *Registry of Health Care Providers in Clinical Social Work* in 1981, are major reference guides to thousands of social workers across the nation whose credentials have been examined by the standard-setting bodies of the profession and to determine whether they were qualified for independent practice — both agency and privately-based.

PREVENTION

Ultimately, it is the prevention of mental illness — as contrasted with the treatment of it — that will yield the greatest dividends. Social workers have taken their rightful place among the professions involved in the treatment of the mentally ill, and recent developments in the domain of primary health care may hold promise. The deployment of social workers to district and neighborhood health centers to provide counseling and guidance aimed at the promotion of *wellness* among family members might yield positive results.

Likewise, deployment of social work personnel in industry, labor unions, and places of employment, where they can intervene around critical issues that pose hazards to the mental health of the individual and potential hazards to the stability of his/her family, holds additional promise. By the same token, outreach problems to the beleaguered solo parent on public assistance (AFDC) and to the recently unemployed worker, helping him to cope with the financial crunch, family crisis, and his own panic might help to reduce vulnerability to breakdown.

Health education and preventive intervention around incipient every-day problems of living can be offered — and is being provided — by radio, on TV, by syndicated columns in newspapers, *et al.* Social workers and other mental hygienists must use these media too.

However, the greatest *demand* on the part of the well person who consults his family doctor (i.e., for primary care) is for advice and guidance on life-style problems, which have enormous implications for the mental health of the individual and his/her family. Social workers are natural candidates to fulfill this need in primary care settings, whether in HMO's, district or neighborhood health centers, private group practice, or wherever possible.

HOME CARE

A majority of those recovering from mental illness or experiencing a remission of symptoms, which may be regarded as satisfactory improvement following an episode of illness, may be best served by home care (32) i.e., care in one's own home. The most obvious reason for this is that the patient very frequently prefers to be at home, where he/she is close to family and familiar surroundings. This pre-supposes that the patient has a home and an in-tact family situation. If both of these elements are accounted for, there are many factors affecting the feasibility of home care: 1. the patient's condition and therapeutic needs; 2. compatibility between the patient and the potential care-giver within the family; 3. the availability of that person (which depends upon his/her mental and physical health, whether employed outside the home, and willingness to assume responsibility for whatever care-giving entails); 4. the predictable effect upon other members of the family if the patient returns; 5. planning for substitute care (by a home health aide) when the care-giver requires relief or must be away from the home; 6. anticipating any emergencies which may arise and how they might be handled, and 7. planning social support services to obviate emergencies and to insure continuity of care to the patient *without jeopardizing the health and well-being of the care-giver and the rest of the family*. This is a very short review of considerations and omits reference to such logistical factors as access to after-care facilities, transportation, physical lay-out of the home, *et al.*

The most obvious omission is that of *cost*. Home care is probably *least* costly of all *if* the home is conducive to the maintenance of the patient's "equilibrium" and, again, *if* the patient's care is not destructive to the family. Yet, it is important to offer this caveat: that the complications and recurrent, episodic nature of certain types of mental illness place great strain upon the care-giver and family, who, without access to supportive professionals, may be unable to carry the complexities of the assignment, in spite of their best efforts.

Social services are being curtailed — in the name of economy, just now — and that could be the straw that breaks the camel's back, whether the social service is delivered by a public health nurse, a social worker, or a health education specialist. In the final analysis, care of the patient in his/her own home may be forced upon us for the sake of economy — true economy or false economy!

MENTAL HEALTH LAW

During the early 1970's legal safeguards were enacted at all levels of government to protect the patient from unwarranted deprivation of his/her rights, as we have seen. These laws have reflected social policy in the field of mental health which has stressed the importance of deinstitutionalization or "decarceration." The implementation of this policy has led to the rejection of the concept of *asylum*, which was represented by a place of "retreat" and a form of "refuge" from the maelstrom of competitive urban life, in particular.

With the mass exodus of patients from the large state hospitals in various stages of partial recovery, city and county facilities, including the community mental health centers, have been taxed beyond their capacity to provide continuing care. This results in a disservice to the discharged patient, increased anxiety and sometimes great hardship for the family of the patient, and finally exasperation and intolerance on the part of citizens who encounter the patient. These encounters may be casual, i.e., occasional passerby observations of the pathetic "bag lady" or "vent man," hallucinating over something arising out of her/his schizophrenic frame of reference. Or, worse yet, the encounter may involve an attack upon a man, woman, or child by a mentally ill person who is "at large" in town or in the countryside.

In many jurisdictions, the law has been written so painstakingly to protect the patient — which in itself is laudable — and has been so rigidly interpreted by the judges that: 1. many persons who really need hospitalization, because they represent a "clear and present danger" to themselves or others, are not committed; 2. some profoundly ill persons suffer from benign neglect because *mere* confusion, dilapidation, and malnutrition, though extreme, are not justification for commitment; and 3. mental health *professionals have been extremely hampered in carrying out treatment deemed essential to the patient* and in justifying further detention of the patient.

As a result, there is some indication that public concern may be mounting to the level of indignation. Disenchantment with government in general and anxiety over personal safety because of the escalation of violence only serve to magnify legitimate concern about the flaws in mental health law. It is, therefore, predictable that major revisions will be proposed — and probably adopted — to correct these flaws and to achieve "a happy medium." Although the verdict has not been rendered, there *are* indications that public opinion is arrayed against the current policy of "over-protection" for the mentally ill because this operates to their detriment by depriving them of sorely needed care. This is a very controversial issue and there will be fierce opposition to any revision in the law that will affect the right to "due process."

FULL CIRCLE

There are those who claim that we may have come full circle in the quest for alternatives to the state mental hospital. The chronicly ill — especially those in the two "umbrella categories" of schizoprenia and cerebral arteriosclerosis — have been moved, perhaps over a rather zig-zag route, from one institution to another, i.e., from the mental hospital to a nursing home or some other long-term care facility. The "zig-zag route" refers to various unproductive efforts on the part of the mental health professionals to involve the community in *reclaiming* these patients when the community, out of frustration, anxiety, inertia, impatience, or for whatever the reason, is actively/tacitly engaged in *disclaiming* them. Since proprietary nursing home beds far outnumber those available under public or non-profit auspices, public funds for the chronically mentally ill, e.g., Supplemental Security Income (SSI) for the permanently and totally disabled or old age assistance, are being funneled into the private sector, where social services are least likely to be available. The notable exceptions would include certain sectarian homes which are administered by or affiliated with a network of community resources.

There is growing concern that the person with an acute short-term episode may be getting short-shift in out-patient clinics because of the volume of work (size of caseloads) and curtailment of staff in tax-supported centers. The concern is focused upon a widespread over-reliance on the psychotropic drugs, which have the effect of rolling back the symptoms (anxiety, confusion, depression, etc.) without touching the complex factors which have given rise to the symptoms. In short, professional time for psychotherapy and the resolution of intricate interpersonal problems is sacrificed for the sake of economy.

This may turn out to be false economy if one considers the potential value of early intervention and early treatment, in particular, as a form of secondary prevention.

AN INVENTORY OF TWENTIETH CENTURY EVENTS RELEVANT TO SOCIAL WORK IN MEDICAL HEALTH

1898 — First training courses in social work, New York Charity Organization Society precursor to the New York School of Philanthropy

1899 — First juvenile court in the U.S., established in Chicago

1901 — Courses in social work offered by Extension Department, University of Chicago

1904 — New York School of Philanthropy (now Columbia University School of Social Work), founded by Charity Organization Society

— Boston School of Social Work (now Simmons College), founded

1905 — First medical social worker employed by Richard L. Cabot, M.D., at Massachusetts General Hospital

— First psychiatric social worker employed by James J. Putman, M.D., at Massachusetts General Hospital

1906 — First after-care agent (social worker) employed by New York State Charities Aid Association at Manhattan State Hospital, N.Y.C.

1908 — *A Mind That Found Itself* by Clifford Beers, published

— First state-wide mental hygiene society (Connecticut), founded by Clifford Beers; beginning of the mental health movement

— Chicago School of Civics and Philanthropy (now the University of Chicago School of Social Service Administration), established

1909 — National Committee for Mental Hygiene, established

— First White House Conference on Children held

— First mental hygiene clinic for children established, Juvennile Psychopathic Institute in Chicago

— Philadelphia Training School of Social Workers (now the University of Pennsylvania School of Social Work), established

1911 — Social workers employed by New York mental hospitals, after-care

1912 — U.S. Children's Bureau established

— Dr. Richard C. Cabot argued that social worker and doctor constituted a team of peers in the treatment of the patient

1913 — First social service department in a mental institution, Boston Psychopathic Hospital, under Mary C. Jarrett

1913 — Social worker employed at Phipps Clinic, Johns Hopkins Hospital

1915 — *Social Service and the Art of Healing* by Richard C. Cabot, M.D.

1917 — *Social Diagnosis* by Mary Richmond, eminent social worker

— National Conference on Social Work emerged; founded in 1873 as the National Conference of Charities and Corrections

1918 — American Association of Medical Social Workers, established

— First formal training program for psychiatric social workers, offered by Smith College Training School of Social Work

— American Association of Hospital Social Workers, organized

1919 — National Association of School Social Workers, organized

— Association of Training Schools for Professional Social Workers, established

1920 — Child Welfare League of America founded

— First Ph.D. in Social Work granted by Bryn Mawr; University of Chicago followed suit in 1924

— *Social Casework* (journal), first known as *The Family*, initiated

1921 — American Association of Social Workers (later reorganized as National Association of Social Workers), established

1924 — American Orthopsychiatric Association, founded

1926 — American Association of Psychiatric Social Workers, established

1927 — American Association of Schools of Social Work, established

— *Social Service Review* (journal) initially published by University of Chicago Press

1929 — Milford Conference, report published as *Social Casework: Generic and Specific*

— *Mental Hygiene and Social Work*: by Porter R. Lee and Marion Kenworthy (of the New York School of Social Work)

1930 — *A Changing Psychology in Social Casework* by Virginia P. Robinson (of the Pennsylvania School of Social Work)

1931 — Nobel Peace Prize awarded to Jane Addams, eminent social worker

1934 — First licensing law for social workers enacted in Puerto Rico; precursor to laws passed in the states

1935 — Social Security Act passed as P.L. 74-241

— WPA (Works Progress Administration) established; placed under direction of Harry Hopkins, social worker

1943 — Psychiatric social work designated as a military occupational specialization for non-commissioned officers who qualified

1944 — Psychiatric content required as one of the "basic eight" courses for all social workers (in accredited schools of social work)

1945 — First state law for registration of social workers passed in California

— *Common Human Needs* by Charolotte Towle (of the University of Chicago School of Social Service Administration), published

1946 — National Mental Health Act (P.L. 79-487)

— First person commissioned as a social work officer in the U.S. Army with social work education as the qualifying factor

1947 — First NIMH grants awarded to schools of social work for training in psychiatric social work

1949 — Dartmouth Conference on *Education for Psychiatric Social Work* in graduate schools of social work

— *A Comparison of the Diagostic and Functional Casework Concepts* by Cora Kasius

1951 — *Social Work Education in the United States* by Ernest Hollis and Alice Taylor

1952 — Council on Social Work Education, established; replaced American Association of Schools of Social Work (established, 1927)

1954 — Institute on Social Work in Psychiatric Hospitals, Lake Forest, Ill.

1955 — National Association for Social Work; superseded the general association founded in 1921 and the medical and psychiatric, founded in 1918 and 1926; incorporated four other specialist groups

— National Mental Health Study Act passed (P.L. 84-182)

1961 — Academy of Certified Social Workers (ACSW qualifications), established

— *Action for Mental Health*: Final Report of the Joint Commission on Mental Illness and Health

1962 — Conference on Public Health Concepts in Social Work, Princeton, NJ

1963 — Community Mental Health Centers Act (P.L. 88-164)

1965 — Medicare and Medicaid established as Titles XVIII and XIX of the Social Security Act

— New York passed state law for certification of social workers

1970 — National Institute on Alcohol Abuse and Alcoholism established (P.L. 91-616)

— Joint Commission on Accreditation of Hospitals requires that social service must be provided to patients and families

1971 — Wyatt V. Stickney decision: establishing the right to treatment for the mentally ill

1972 — Supplementary Security Income (SSI) enacted (P.L. 92-603)

1974 — Title XX of the Social Security Act, providing social services to the mentally ill (inter alia) in receipt of public assistance

1975 — O'Connor v. Donaldson decision: establishing mental patient's right to release, if not dangerous to himself and not receiving treatment

— Special Health Revenue Sharing Act (P.L. 96-398)

1978 — Report of the President's Commission on Mental Health

1980 — Mental Health Systems Act (P.L. 96-398)

— DSM III (Diagnostic and Statistical Manual of the American Psychiatric Association), accorded explicit recognition to social stress and social functioning factors in 2 of the 5 axes delineated; edited by J.B. Williams, social worker

1981 — Doctoral programs, leading to DSW or Ph.D. degree, offered in 38 of the 85 graduate schools of social work which, in 1979, graduated 10,080 with Master's degrees and 174 with Doctorates

---

Compiled by Edgar A. Perretz, using (among others) the following references: Alexander and Weber, 1977 (1); L.M. French, 1940 (12).

REFERENCES

1. Alexander, C.A. and Weber, D.N.; Social Welfare: Historical Dates. *Encyclopedia of Social Work*, 2 Vols., II: 1497-1503. Washington, National Association of Social Workers, 1977.
2. Allen, F: *Positive Aspects of Child Psychiatry*. New York: W.W. Norton, 1963.
3. American Psychiatric Association: *Diagnostic and Statistical Manual of Mental Disorders*, DSM II. Washington, D.C., 1968.
4. American Psychiatric Association: *Diagnostic and Statistical Manual of Mental Disorders* (Third Education), *DSM III*, Janet B.W. Williams, Text Editor, Washington, D.C., 1980.
5. Berkman, T: *The Practice of Social Workers in Psychiatric Hospitals and Clinics*. New York: American Association of Psychiatric Social Workes, 1953.
6. Biestek, F. and Gehrig, C: *Client Self-Determination in Social Work*. Chicago: Loyola University Press, 1978.
7. Brown, B.S. and Cain, H.P. II: Many Meanings of "Comprehensive": Underlying Issues in Implementing the Community Mental Health Center Program. *American Journal of Orthopsychiatry*, XXXIV: 834-839, 1964.
8. Butler, R.N. and Lewis, M.L.: *Aging and Mental Health: Positive Psychosocial Approaches*. St. Louis: V.V. Mosby, 1977.
9. Committee on Psychiatry and Social Work: The Relationship between Psychiatry and Social Work. *Group for the Advancement of Psychiatry*, (GAP), VII:71, 21-24, 1969.
10. Dartmouth Conference: *Education for Psychiatric Social Work*. New York: American Association of Psychiatric Social Workers, 1949.
11. *Encyclopedia of Social Work*. 17th Edition. 2 vols. "Mental Health," 849-904. Washington, D.C.: National Association of Social Workers, 1977.

12. French, L.M.: *Psychiatric Social Work*. New York: Commonwealth Fund, 1940.
13. Garfield, Sidney R.: "The Delivery of Medical Care," *Scientific American*, 222:15-23, 1970.
14. Glasscote, R., Sanders, D. *et al: The Community Mental Health Center: An Analysis of Existing Models*. Washington: Joint Information Service, American Psychiatric Association and National Association for Mental Health, 1964.
15. Glasscote, R., Cumming, E., *et al: The Psychiatric Emergency*. Washington: JIS, American Psychiatric Association and National Association for Mental Health, 1966.
16. Greenblatt, M., York, R., Brown, E: *From Custodial to Therapeutic Patient Care in Mental Hospitals*. New York: Russell Sage Foundation, 1955.
17. Joint Commission on the Accreditation of Hospitals: *Principles of Accreditation*. Chicago: 1976.
18. Joint Commission on Mental Health of Children: *Crisis in Child Mental Health: Challenge for the 1970's*. New York: Harper and Row, 1970.
19. Joint Commission on Mental Illness and Health: *Action for Mental Health*. New York: Basic Books, 1961.
20. Jones, M.: *Beyond the Therapeutic Community*. New Haven, Yale University Press, 1968.
21. Kramer, M.: *Psychiatric Services and the Changing Institutional Scene*, 1950-1975. Rockville, MD.: National Institute of Mental Health, 1977, 4-5.
22. Leifer, R., *et al.*: The Medical Model as Ideology. *International Journal of Psychiatry*, IX:13-35, 1970.
23. Lowery, L.: *Orthopsychiatry, 1923-1948*. Nw York: American Orthopsychiatric Association, 1948.
24. Milford Conference: *Social Case Work: Generic and Specific*. New York: American Association of Social Workers, 1929.
25. Morris, R.: Caring for vs. Caring about People. *Social Work*, 22:353-9, 1977.
26. Nacman, M.: Social Workers in Mental Health Services. *Encyclopedia of Social Work*, (17th Edition). Vol. II, 1977, pp. 897-904.
27. Napier, A. and Whitaker, C.: *The Family Crucible*. New York: Harper and Row, 1980, 289.
28. National Institute of Mental Health: *(CMHC) Community Mental Health Center Staffing: Who Minds the Store?* Series B, No. 16, DHEW Pub. No. (ADM) 78-686. Washington: U.S. Government Printing Office, 1978.
29. National Institute of Mental Health: *Inpatient Services*. Chevy Chase, MD: 1969.
30. National Institute of Mental Health: *Staffing of Mental Health Facilities, United States, 1976*. DHEW Pub. No. (ADM) 78-522, Superintendent of Documents, U.S. Government Printing Office, Washington, D.C.: 1978.
31. Osberg, J.W.: *Cooperation Toward Mental Health: Conference of Community Psychiatric Clinics and Family Service Agencies*. Trenton, New Jersey: Department of Institutions and Agencies, 1962.
32. Pasamanick, B.: *Schizophrenia in the Community*. New York: Appleton-Century-Crofts, 1967.
33. Pennsylvania Department of Public Welfare: *Toward Complete Systems Integration*. Harrisburg: 1976, p. 4.
34. Perretz, E.A.: Comprehensive Mental Health Centers: Some Implications for Social Work Practice. Conference paper (lithographed) Bethesda, MD., National Institute of Mental Health, April, 1964.

35. President's Commission on Mental Health: *Task Panel Reports Submitted to the President's Commission on Mental Health.* Vol. 2, Washington: U.S. Government Printing Office, 1978.
36. Pumphrey, R., (ed.): *The Heritage of American Social Work.* New York: Columbia University Press, 1961.
37. Richmond, M.: *Social Diagnosis.* New York: Russell Sage Foundation, 1917.
38. Riessman, F.: The "Helper-Therapy" Principle. *Social Work,* 10:27-32.
39. Satir, V.: *Conjoint Family Therapy.* Palo Alto, CA: Science and Behavior Books, 1964.
40. Serban, George: *Adjustment of Schizophrenics in the Community.* New York: Spectrum, p. 205-6.
41. *Social Work*: Special Issue: Conceptual Frameworks, 26:1-93, 1981.
42. U.S. Department of Health, Education and Welfare: *Health in America: 1776-1976.* Washington: DHEW, Pub. No. 76-616, 1976.
43. U.S. Department of Health, Education and Welfare: *Health: United States, 1978.* DHEW Pub. No. (PHS) 78-1232. Hyattsville, MD.: National Center for Health Statistics, 1978.
44. Wallace, M.E.: Private Practice: A Nationwide Study. *Social Work,* 27:262-267.
45. Warner, A.: *American Charities and Social Work.* New York: Crowell, 1930, p. 318.
46. Williams, J.B.W.: DSM-III: A Comprehensive Approach to Diagnosis, *Social Work,* 26:101-106, 1981.
47. Wilmar, H.A.: Defining and Understanding the Therapeutic Community. *Hospital and Community Psychiatry,* 32:95, 1981.
48. Wolfensberger, W. and Nirje, B.: *Normalization: The Principle of Normalization in Human Services.* Toronto: National Institute of Mental Retardation, 1972.
49. Wyatt, J. Stickney: 344 F. Supp. 373/387 *M.D.* Ala., 1972.

Chapter 4

SOCIAL WORK IN PHYSICAL REHABILITATION

JUDITH HIRSCHWALD

"Healing is a matter of time but it is also sometimes a matter of opportunity"

— Hippocrates: Precepts (1)

INTRODUCTION

Physical rehabilitation is a process, a philosophy, and a concept, as well as an institutionalized form of specialized health care practice. As such, evolution and change have been evident throughout this century. The opportunities afforded to the individual with a severe disability are greater today than in 1960, but more restrictive than hopefully will be seen in the year 2000. With the designation of 1981 as the International Year of Disabled Persons, there is an added impetus and potential avenue for consciousness raising which may lead to increased research, legislation, and programmatic opportunities.

This chapter will first address the history and philosophy of physical rehabilitation, including recent legislative mandates. The changing role of social work as the main focus of the chapter will reflect and parallel the historical evolution of rehabilitation as a concept and philosophy. Finally, the chapter will address the scope and influence of various regulatory bodies on the practice of social work in physical rehabilitation.

HISTORY

The roots of physical rehabilitation as a sphere of concern to society in general and to the medical professional in particular can be directly traced to the two major wars of this century. Following World War I, recognition was given to the potential waste both in human and economic resources, of the disabled veteran. Consequently, the Federal Vocational Rehabilitation Act of 1920 was passed to attempt to, in part, repay the nation's debt to disabled servicemen and to afford them the opportunity to return to the work force. The majority of the returning servicemen were amputees, and the major thrust of the rehabilitation efforts at that time was vocational retraining and job placement.

Following World War I, general interest in rehabilitation declined, but, in addition to the legislative beginnings, several pioneer institutions for rehabilitation services emerged: The Institute for the Crippled and Disabled in New York, the Cleveland Rehabilitation Center, and the Milwaukee Curative Workshop. However, the major emphasis remained with the veteran and with the provision of vocational, not medical, services.

In the early days of World War II (1943), the Barden-Follette Amendment extended the provisions of the Vocational Rehabilitation Act to include civilians as one potential solution to the existing manpower shortage (2). The years following World War II again saw a renewed interest and concern in the provision of services for the individual with severe disability. The Vocational Rehabilitation Act of 1954 made additional provision for physical restoration services (medical, psychiatric, and psychological examinations, surgery, therapy, prosthetic appliances, hospitalization, and convalescent care) as well as funds for increasing the supply of trained personnel and expanding facilities (3). As a consequence of this legislation, there was a significant expansion of specialized facilities to meet the specific needs of the physically disabled population. By 1971, more than 2,600 provider facilities (4) and over 76,000 (5) rehabilitation personnel were involved in rendering services to an estimated 13,438,000 persons in the United States felt to be limited in their activities by one or more disabling conditions (6). The major expansion of facilities and services was toward serving the needs of the civilian population, while the veteran continued to receive rehabilitation services through the network of Veteran's Administration facilities. This dual tract of services, one for civilians and one for veterans, which continues to the present time, has obvious roots in the history of the field.

The next significant legislative landmark in the provision of services for the physically disabled was the Rehabilitation Act of 1973. The 1973 Act was also crucial as a mandate for the civil rights of the individual with a disability. Among the most innovative provisions of this Act are the following stated purposes:

- Evaluate the rehabilitation potential of handicapped individuals.
- Conduct a study to develop methods of providing rehabilitation services to meet the current and future needs of handicapped individuals for whom a vocational goal is not possible or feasible, so that they may improve their ability to live with greater independence and self-sufficiency.
- Evaluate existing approaches to architectural and transportation barriers confronting handicapped individuals, develop new approaches, enforce statutory and regulatory standards and requirements regarding barrier-free construction of public facilities, and study and develop solutions to existing architectural and transportation barriers impeding handicapped individuals (7).

For the first time, legislative consideration was given to the provision of services to those individuals who might not have an immediately definable vocational goal, but whose "quality of life" might be enhanced through rehabilitation services. The act also mandated client participation in the definition of his rehabilitation goals and plan, with the requirement for an "individualized written rehabilitation program" to be developed jointly by the vocational counselor or coordinator and the handicapped individual. In the area of civil rights for the disabled, Sections 503 and 504 of the Act were most significant. Section 503 essentially states that:

> Any contract in excess of $2500 entered into by any Federal department or agency . . . shall contain a provision requiring that, in employing persons to carry out such a contract the party . . . shall take affirmative action to employ and advance in employment qualified handicapped individuals.

Section 504 states that:

> No otherwise qualified handicapped individual in the United States, shall, solely by reason of his handicap, be excluded from the participation in, be denied the benefits of, or be subjected to discrimination under any program or activity receiving Federal financial assistance (7).

For the first time in our history, the individual with a disability was protected against the violation of his civil rights; a mandate was established to end discrimination; and an attempt was made to bring the individual with a disability into the mainstream of life.

The 1978 Amendments to the 1973 Rehabilitation Act furthered some of the concepts mentioned above. Section 504 was expanded to cover Federal executive agencies. A client appeal procedure was established for the adjudication of alleged unfair practices in the "individualized written rehabilitation program." A community service pilot program entitled Projects with Industry was designed to enhance the potential of employment inroads into private industry. Title VII of the 1978 Amendments legislated "independent living centers" and enumerated services to enhance the ability of a disabled individual to live independently and function within his family and community. Such crucial new services as appear in this list are transportation, recreation and attendant care (8).

The history of legislation over the past 60 years is crucial to the understanding of society's changing view of the individual with a disability. The legislative changes can be traced in the following brief summary. The first and early concerns were for the disabled veteran to whom society perceived an implicit obligation. Disabled civilians were then recognized as an important manpower source, and services were extended to cover them. Early efforts focused primarily on the return of the individual to a position of economic self-sufficiency, but, as advances were made in the health care field, services were extended to include medical and psychological treatment for the disability prior to the eventual goal of employment. However, continuing throughout this period, the legislation reflected a "take care of" attitude toward the disabled person. Finally, the most recent legislation begins to address the issues of civil rights, equality, nondiscrimination and to recognize the right of the disabled person to participate in the same benefits of society as the able-bodied person. Quality of life issues thus surface, even though the ultimate goal of eventual gainful employment is retained. As institutional programs and services tend to reflect these prevailing attitudes of society, the impact of legislation on physical rehabilitation services will be apparent in the remainder of this chapter.

DEFINITION AND PHILOSOPHY OF REHABILITATION

In the preface to his textbook on *Physical Medicine and Rehabilitation,* published in 1958, Dr. Howard Rusk writes:

> The first objective of rehabilitation medicine is to eliminate the physical disability if this is possible; the second, to reduce or alleviate the disability to the greatest extent possible; and the third, to retrain the person with a residual physical disability to live and to work within the limits of the disability but to the hilt of his capabilities (9).

In the preface to a book entitled *Psychological Practices with the Physically Disabled*, published in 1962, Dr. Rusk writes:

> The more experience we have the more we recognize that it is frequently not the physical disability *per se* that limits the disabled person functionally, but rather his psychological reaction to his disability (10).

The field of physical rehabilitation, virtually from its inception, has recognized the critical importance of an interdisciplinary team approach to meet the multifaceted needs of the individual with a disability. If the overall goal was to maximize the potential of the individual physically, emotionally, socially and vocationally, then the skills of the physician had to be augmented by the skills of the physical, occupational and speech therapists, social workers, psychologists and vocational counselors. Thus, the early approach to physical rehabilitation was a team model — a model which persists to the present time.

While the team approach to the rehabilitation of the individual with a physical disability has remained consistent, significant changes in definition and philosophy have occurred. Rehabilitation is increasingly being viewed as a long-term process which will continue throughout the life of the individual with a disability. Rehabilitation centers are beginning to define their role and function according to this more long-term view. Twenty years ago, rehabilitation services were focused primarily on the span of time immediately following onset of disability or immediately after the recognition that such services could improve the individual's functional capabilities. Comprehensive services were rendered to the individual until his maximum functional potential was reached, and then discharge to his home and community was accomplished. Follow-up services or readmission might occur, but, in general, the rehabilitation centers were uncomfortable with readmissions and tended to view this need as a failure on their part to accomplish the stated goals on the initial admission. Rehabilitation centers are now changing. They are beginning to view their services as appropriate life-long resources for the individual with a physical disability and to anticipate and even encourage the return of the individual for periodic re-evaluations or readmissions.

As an outgrowth, in part, of the legislation earlier described, the rehabilitation center has also broadened its concept of the individual who can benefit from physical rehabilitation services. While vocational goals continue to assume importance for many individuals, the issues of improving "quality of life" and enhancing independence are more frequently than before viewed as legitimate and critical reasons for admission. Rehabilitation centers are also becoming involved in the complex rehabilitation and long-term management of extremely severely disabled individuals who are more frequently surviving the acute care phase. New challenges are being presented to enhance the quality of life for the individual who has suffered severe brain trauma or the respirator-dependent quadriplegic individual. Vocational goals, if they exist for these individuals in today's society, are very difficult to define and may only be possible many years down the road. However, the individual has the right and the rehabilitation center the responsibility to assist the individual in resuming the maximum role possible within the mainstream of his family and community.

A more subtle philosophical change may be evident within the field of physical rehabilitation which has yet to more fully emerge: that is the role of the patient. The individual who is a patient within the rehabilitation process has always been able to exercise greater control over his treatment than, for instance, the surgical or orthopedic patient. However, control and manipulation by the patient was not generally viewed by rehabilitation personnel as positive, desired or encouraged. Rehabilitation services, as embodied within a physical rehabilitation center, are beginning to be viewed as only one small phase in the overall rehabilitation process for a given individual. Control is being delegated to the patient as the legitimate decision-maker concerning what services will be received and when.

In the last ten years, we have seen a reorganization within the service delivery system which is an outgrowth of a philosophical stance at the Federal level. The major reorganization in service delivery has been the designation by the Federal government of regional centers of expertise in the treatment of the most complicated and catastrophic disabling conditions — namely, to date, spinal cord injury and traumatic brain injury. At the time of this writing, seventeen centers have received Federal designation as Regional Spinal Cord Injury Centers and approximately ten as Regional Brain Trauma Centers. Statistics show that the admission of individuals with these disabling conditions to a regional center reduces the length of stay, minimizes the number of complications and enhances the rehabilitation of the individual. However, the designation of these centers also means that some individuals will receive rehabilitation services in centers geographically distant from their families and communities, thus raising some dilemmas and challenges to their reintegration into their home communities. The Veteran's Administration has also designated regional centers of expertise within their system, and, therefore, the dual tract of care, seen in the historical background, persists to the present time.

To summarize, the basic philosophy of physical rehabilitation as a team endeavor has not changed markedly over the years. However, the view of the rehabilitation center and its services as a lifetime resource for the individual with a disability is new. "Quality of life" issues, while always significant in rehabilitation, are intensified by the admission of more severely disabled individuals, many of whom do not have easily definable vocational or avocational goals. The role of the disabled individual as a significant determiner of his own program is beginning to emerge. Changes in the organization of service have occurred and will probably continue to occur at the national level. However, the major thrust of physical rehabilitation, to enable the individual with the disability to maximize his potential for living physically, emotionally, socially and vocationally, has not basically altered, even though the philosophical stance and the attitudes toward disability and the disabled individual may have shifted. In fact, this shift in attitude has begun to afford to the individual with a disability greater opportunity to make choices and to enter into the mainstream of life.

CONSUMER MOVEMENT

An introduction to a chapter on social work in physical rehabilitation would not be complete without a discussion of the disabled consumer movement. The disabled consumer movement, primarily a product of the 1970's, can claim a major responsibility for the legislative advances and philosophical shifts, described above, and has had significant impact on the role of social work in a rehabilitation setting. Most simply, the disabled rights movement, built on the experiences of the civil rights movement of the 1960's, demands equal rights and equal access.

> A new generation of groups for the disabled was born, such as the American Coalition of Citizens with Disabilities and Mainstream, Inc. Like older and more established groups, they lobbied for better social service, and protested the endless catch-22 provisions in the welfare laws that hurt the severely disabled. But they also demanded something more: they called for significant structural changes in housing,

> public buildings, and transportation that have long posed barriers to their mobility; and they began working for an end to the prejudice and job discrimination that had proved far more obstructive to an active life than such handicaps as blindness, deafness, or paraplegia (11).

Architectural barriers are the result of attitudinal barriers, and, in essence, the disabled population was negating the stereotyped, paternalistic view of them by the able-bodied world. The able-bodied world has generally viewed the individual with a disability as "a perennial patient," "someone needing lifetime institutional care," "dependent," "passive," and "unable to participate fully in the social and vocational spheres of life." The disabled rights movement is essentially an effort to afford the individual with a disability the same life choices as are afforded to the non-disabled person, such basic choices as where to live, where to work, how to travel (or to travel at all), and what recreational or social activities to pursue.

The militancy of the disabled population, as well as a more enlightened attitude among some legislators, has brought about changes. The 1973 Rehabilitation Act and the subsequent 1978 Amendments are one specific example. Debates in many major cities regarding the provision of accessible mass transportation is another example. Some breakthroughs have occurred in housing. Independent living centers, managed by individuals with disabilities to provide a range of services for disabled individuals, are emerging and receiving some Federal funding. However, attitudes change slowly. The individual with a disability will continue to struggle to be viewed as a "competent, mature, adult" by rehabilitation personnel and by the able-bodied world in general.

ROLE OF SOCIAL WORK

The role of social work within physical rehabilitation has paralleled and mirrored the changes in the entire field.

The necessity to include social work as an integral component of the rehabilitation team was recognized early by the administrators and managing physicians of rehabilitation centers. Dr. Rusk, writing in 1958, defines the role of a social worker as follows:

> Direct services to patients is only one aspect of the social worker's function. Of equal importance is her work with the families and the sharing of her findings with the other team members so that the best possible service can be given the individual patient (12).

Thus, the role of the social worker as offering direct service to patients and families and as a consultant to the rest of the team was legitimized and accepted early in the history of physical rehabilitation. In my opinion, the opportunity to expand and redefine the social work role is greater in this field of health care than in any other. The dilemma for social work has been to clearly define its role, its philosophical stance, and the treatment modalities which meet the needs of the population served.

In general, the social worker in a physical rehabilitation setting confronts a population of individuals and families who are newly experiencing the impact of severe permanent disability. The "typical" individual admitted to a physical rehabilitation setting has been judged "medically stable" by his acute care physician following the initial insult or injury, and ready to begin an intensive program of physical restoration. Neither the individual nor his family are aware, at this time, of the tremendous impact which the disability will have on the individual's life, that of his family, and the changes which will be required.

The dilemma for social work has been to choose the strategies for intervention which afford the greatest opportunity for the individual and his family to meet and deal with the physical crisis which confronts them and to eventually resume the ability to make their own life choices as individuals and as a family unit. These life choices will probably be significantly altered due to the physical disability, and new roles, responsibilities and relationships will emerge. Obviously, the strategies for intervention chosen by the social worker will derive from his/her philosophical stance regarding the impact of disability on an individual and family unit and his/her view of the process of coping with the disability. A review of the literature, highlighting attitudes and strategies toward treatment interventions with the individual who has suffered a severe disability, sheds some light on the struggles and dilemmas which have been prevalent over the past twenty years. These differing approaches will be highlighted under the specific modalities described below. In general, the shift which occurred is from the traditional "psychotherapeutic models" which tended to focus on a definable almost universal "adjustment process" for the individual to a model which views the entire rehabilitation process in a "learning framework." In this framework the primary focus is on helping the individual acquire the skills, physical and emotional, to live with a disability. While the choice of treatment modalities is not, in reality, as clear-cut as presented above, the emphasis has shifted from focusing primarily on the depression and anxiety exhibited by the disabled individual in a one-to-one psychotherapeutic model to devising strategies and programs for learning the skills which will be crucial to the individual's resuming his role as a competent adult in the outside world. In short, the shift has come in viewing the newly disabled individual not as someone who has a severe emotional problem secondary to his disability, but as one who primarily needs to learn to deal with his social reality and social relationships as a competent adult, even though his physical capacity to perform certain activities may be significantly altered.

Prior to addressing the varying roles of social work, both current and anticipated, some theoretical considerations will be addressed. These considerations reflect the biases and philosophical framework of the author, and are thus important to understand as the construct within which roles are defined.

THEORETICAL CONSIDERATIONS

For many individuals within a rehabilitation setting, the onset of their disability can be pinpointed as "one moment in time" (i.e., an accident, a stroke, an amputation). The impact of that "one moment in time" will eventually be felt in every aspect of the person's life, from self-esteem, body image, interpersonal relationships, to sexuality, vocational opportunities, housing, and recreation. Therefore, the rehabilitation process, in its broadest sense, will involve a relearning, touching on every aspect of life. The individual will need to relearn to function as a total human being, working, playing and finding satisfaction in relationships in an environment designed for able-bodied people.

One of the more common misconceptions of many professionals in the field of rehabilitation is that there also exists "one moment in time" when the individual suddenly "accepts" or "adjusts" to the disability, even though there is no clear-cut definition as to what "accept or "adjust" means. Learning to live with a disability is a process which will continue throughout the person's lifetime. In fact, the experience of this author suggests that a disabled person never relinquishes that last spark of hope that "someday, sometime" the disability "will go away." This hope may in fact be the core that enables him to continue to rebuild his life, in whatever way is satisfying and productive to him.

Nonetheless, the literature of rehabilitation is filled with articles and theories on the so-called adjustment process, describing stages of shock, denial, depression, anger, and "acceptance." The inference is that an individual must pass through these various stages to suddenly reach the magical point of "adjustment." Shontz, as one proponent of the stage theory of adjustment, describes the stages of response in the following phases:

(1) *Pre-lude* — beginning at the first sign of disturbance (i.e., "something is wrong").
(2) *Warning* — beginning at the first sign that existing patterns of adjustment and coping are inadequate.
(3) *Impact* — beginning at the point at which the diagnosis or severity of the situation is confirmed.
(4) *Shock* — characterized by the feeling that the individual is observing events in which he is not an active participant.
(5) *Retreat* — that period of time when the shock is too great to be borne for long, and the individual will retreat or, in extreme situations, totally deny the existence or implications of the critical situation; and
(6) *Acknowledgment* — consisting of a "succession of limited re-encounters with a crisis," each re-encounter producing a gain in reorganization and ending with a renewed retreat (13).

Most proponents of the various stage theories do not postulate an orderly step by step progression, but do imply that some recognition of the stages are a crucial prerequisite to the attainment of the goal of acceptance, adaptation or adjustment.

Although these concepts are useful when viewing the rehabilitation process in general, on an individual basis they are often misleading. The disabled individual is as unique in his coping mechanism as any of the able-bodied population, bringing to this traumatic situation the personality characteristics and coping devices which worked effectively prior to the injury.

Depressive reactions, observed particularly in the early phases post-onset, are often ascribed to mourning over loss of body functions. This reaction may actually be due in part to sensory deprivation, often a component of the disability, and restricted environmental stimulation (14). In other words, the problems encountered may be the result of sensory and social isolation and not necessarily the product of psychological adaptations. Although mourning is obviously a normal and adaptive response to a catastrophic loss, it is important, to recognize other significant factors involved, and, most important to recognize that a traumatic disability does not necessarily create pernicious psychological effects on the injured person. In fact, in the words of George Hohmann, himself a paraplegic:

> The "normal" individual appears to experience a sequence of predominant feelings and attitudes as he attempts to cope with his injury. These reactions are considered to be the normal sequelae of any severe loss, and might be described as "the normal reaction to an abnormal situation" since the loss of function of a major portion of one's body is certainly an abnormal situation (15).

However, three theories related to depression may be useful constructs in viewing the reaction of the newly disabled individual and in formulating strategies for social work intervention. First, Fordyce (16) discusses depression in terms of the loss of positive reinforcers; that is, when a significant reinforcer, such as the tremendous change in lifestyle secondary to loss of physical ability, is withdrawn, the person enters a state of grief which can be dissipated when other reinforcers are at his disposal (17). Fordyce suggests that the effectiveness of any rehabilitation program depends on the extent to which relevant reinforcers are available to the disabled person. Seligman expands this concept in his theory of "learned helplessness" such that depression is not the result of the loss of reinforcers but rather the loss of control over reinforcers (18).

The issues of control and helplessness are extremely significant for the individual with a disability. These issues surface early in the acute care environment, and persist, with varying intensity, through the rehabilitation phase and through life in the home and community environment. For some, the issues of control and helplessness are critical factors relative to their physical functioning. If an individual is unable to achieve physical independence at a wheelchair or ambulatory level through rehabilitation services, then he/she will need to learn to cope with needing and accepting help, often with the most personal aspects of self-care. This individual may no longer have control over when he gets up in the morning or when he goes to bed, since the meeting of his needs must be scheduled around the other responsibilities of his caretakers. Even for the individual who is independent at a wheelchair or ambulatory level, his degree of control and level of independence will be limited by the architectural and attitudinal barriers erected by society.

One additional view from the literature of the rehabilitation process seems critical before discussing the role of the social worker in rehabilitation. Roberta Trieschmann, in the publication which grew out of her study of the state of the art of psychological, social and vocational adjustment to spinal cord injury, states:

> A major premise of this book is that rehabilitation is the process of learning to live with one's own environment (19).

With this brief theoretical background, one can begin to formulate the role of the social worker in physical rehabilitation from the philosophical stance of this author. Stage theories of adjustment offer only minimal benefit in understanding an individual's process of coping with disability. The process of coping with a disability is a lifelong endeavor and parallels, in many ways, the process by which an able-bodied person learns to deal with his/her life in more satisfying and productive ways. However, for the individual with a disability, especially in early stages following onset, the issues of control and the opportunity to reassert oneself as a capable responsible human being are critical.

SOCIAL WORK INTERVENTION WITH THE INDIVIDUAL

Severe physical disability does not respect social, economic, cultural or age barriers. Thus, the social worker in the rehabilitation environment is confronted with a representative crosssection of the population of the geographic area in which the center is located. The older population will tend to reflect the disabilities generally associated with aging and chronic disease. Among the older population, amputations (secondary to diabetes or circulatory disease), hemiplegia (secondary to stroke), and the residuals of fractures (commonly the hip) occur with the greatest frequency. Among the younger population, the most commonly occurring disabilities are a result of trauma or of those diseases whose onset is typically at a young age. Spinal cord injury (paraplegia and quadriplegia), traumatic brain injury, and traumatic amputations are frequently occurring diagnoses, as well as residual disability secondary to such disease entities as multiple sclerosis.

However, in spite of the origin of the disability and the uniqueness of each individual, some powerful common denominators are identifiable. The majority of individuals who enter a physical rehabilitation center will be discharged to their homes and communities with significant residual permanent disability, unable to be "cured" with current medical knowledge. The presence of the disability will impact on every aspect of their life, and, in the words of many persons who have had the experience, "Life will never be exactly the same as before." Not only has their ability to function physically been altered significantly, but also their concept of themselves and their capabilities and limitations in all spheres of life has been altered. They are now physically disabled and will be viewed by the able-bodied world as "different," with the various stereotypes and prejudices ascribed by the able-bodied world to those individuals whom they perceive as "different." The ability of each individual to ultimately face and cope with this "difference" varies tremendously, but some common approaches and intervention strategies can be identified as critical to the social work role in enabling the now-disabled individual to begin to cope. The approaches and interventions, common to this role in physical rehabilitation, will be described under the following headings: (1) initial assessment; (2) goals; (3) intervention strategies; and (4) re-assessment.

Initial Assessment — The first and perhaps most critical component to the definition of a viable social work intervention strategy with a particular individual is the initial assessment. The social worker must develop a comprehensive knowledge base of the individual's life style prior to the onset of the disability. Knowledge concerning "what was important in life" to this individual prior to the onset of his disability will serve not only as a good predictor of the anticipated impact of the disability, but also as a critical data base in making choices regarding potentially helpful intervention strategies. To know that the individual got out of bed each morning is not enough.

The social worker must understand in as much depth as possible for each individual, "why" he/she got out of bed each morning. What was the life style and life pattern of the individual prior to onset, and what positive reinforcers existed in his/her life as motivating factors? For some individuals, the accomplishment of personal goals and objectives in the vocational realm was critical and may have been the key motivating force in their life. Work may also have provided significant rewards in the relationships formed and in companionship for avocational pursuits. For another individual, primary "meaning" in life may have derived from his/her relationship with a spouse and children.

Obviously, the answer to this question will vary tremendously and will rarely be singular in nature. However, the social worker must understand in depth the positive reinforcers and rewards in life for the individual prior to onset, for this knowledge will now provide valuable input in helping the individual to restructure his life around his previously existing system. If work was not an activity which produced rewards and satisfaction for the individual pre-disability, the setting of vocational goals as a high priority in the physical rehabilitation process would not provide sufficient reason for the individual to put forth the tremendous additional physical effort to now get out of bed in the morning.

As part of an initial assessment, the social worker must also gain knowledge regarding the previous coping patterns of the individual in a crisis or stressful situation. Some individuals, especially among the younger age group, have not had significant prior experience with severe life crisis, but they have still begun to develop patterns of coping with stress and frustration. Again, previously existing patterns will vary tremendously, both in terms of their form of expression and in terms of their effectiveness. Some individuals when under stress find an outlet in verbalizing their frustrations and concerns. Others find relief in physical activity, such as slamming a tennis ball, running or playing basketball. Some people find comfort in the presence of others; some people want to be alone. Whatever the previous patterns of coping may have been, the social worker needs to develop an understanding of these patterns and their prior effectiveness for the individual.

Rotter has postulated that all individuals can be generally grouped in one of two ways in terms of the perception of the ability to control life situations. Those individuals with an "external locus of control" will perceive environmental factors (factors outside themselves) as having the primary control over their behavior and their life choices. An individual with an "internal locus of control" will perceive his own actions and behaviors as key determinants in the outcome of a given situation (20). As the issue of control over his body and his environment is obviously critical to the newly disabled individual, Rotter's theory has considerable relevance in evaluating an individual's perception of both his ability to exert control and the manner in which he will attempt to exert it. As the social worker assesses with the individual his/her previous life style and pattern of coping with stress, the individual's perception of his ability or inability to control the circumstances of his life will emerge. Again, this information is crucial to the social worker in helping to define effective intervention strategies.

The final critical assessment of the social worker is in the examination of the support systems of the individual and his/her ability to effectively use these systems. Obviously, an evaluation of these systems must be more comprehensive than simply a listing of family members and "significant others." An individual with a large family and numerous friends may in reality not have a support system, either because the system does not know how to support or the individual does not know how to elicit support. In addition, in this author's experience, even a potentially effective support system may, in fact, become ineffective in the presence of severe physical disability. Frequently, the tremendously physical status of the individual with a disability significantly alters the ability of family members and friends to offer support according to previously existing patterns. A family member or friend may be reluctant to touch or hold the newly disabled person, for fear of somehow causing further injury or discomfort. Friends and family may be reluctant to discuss their current activities, recognizing that the disabled individual may no longer be capable of participating with them in these activities now or in the future. Therefore, even an initial assessment of the existing support system must also evaluate the immediate functional capability of this system for the individual.

In addition to the broad areas mentioned above, many more specific aspects of the previous and current life situation of the individual are important in an initial assessment. Within the context of the anticipated physical limitations, a detailed description of the architectural barriers within the home, school or work place, and community are important. Existent and potential financial resources are critical, due to the tremendous economic burden of disability to the individual and family. The costs of prolonged hospitalization, specialized equipment, and initial and ongoing medical-surgical supplies are staggering. Added to the expense of disability, the income of the individual and family may be altered temporarily or permanently, particularly if the disabled individual was a wage earner within the family unit.

The availability of transportation, actual and potential, also is a key determiner of the degree of eventual mobility which will be possible for the disabled person. The ownership of a car suitable for adaptation or the existence of a resource to secure a specially equipped van can make the difference between a homebound existence and the freedom to travel. A detailed exploration of avocational/recreational pursuits is important as an end in itself, as well as frequently opening up avenues to eventual vocational pursuits. A sexual history is important, as the physical disability may have altered the individual's physical capability. Even if it has not altered physical functioning, it will certainly have altered his/her view of himself/herself as a sexual person.

Finally, life goals and life dreams play a role for all of us, no matter how unrealistic they may be. To know the previous goals and dreams of the individual who is now confronted with restricted physical function is critical to a further understanding of how to help the individual to restructure his life.

Obviously, the assessment as envisioned is extremely comprehensive and will gradually emerge only through a sustained relationship. One's real understanding of the deeper goals and motivations of another human being is limited at best. However limited may be the eventual assessment, the critical intent is to gain as much understanding as possible of the individual pre-disability, for the major goal is to enable him/her to regain as much as possible his previous sense of self-worth, self-direction and satisfaction from life. Without the knowledge of those motivating factors prior to onset, the strategies for intervention set during the physical rehabilitation process will be meaningful to the social worker and/or the rehabilitation team but will not be meaningful to the individual. The next section will attempt to define the goals of physical rehabilitation which are especially relevant to the knowledge base, value system and skills of the social worker.

Goals — The single most critical goal of the social worker in the physical rehabilitation process is to enable the individual with a disability to regain a sense of his own self-worth and the capability to re-exert control over his life and environment. Following a severe physical insult with resultant physical limitations, feelings of dependency, helplessness and impotence are natural. As an outgrowth of the initial assessment, the social worker has the knowledge of the spheres of the individual's life which are critical to him/her and can therefore assist him/her to focus the beginning efforts at re-asserting capabilities in the areas of anticipated highest motivation. The choice of the area, however, is not simple, must take into account many factors, and carry a high probability for success. The social worker must have an awareness of the individual's internal process and, therefore, a sensitivity to the timing of any efforts. The social worker must also be aware of the physical limitations of the disability so that the strategies developed are compatible with the individual's physical capabilities at any given point in time.

One of the initial steps in the achievement of the goal is to begin to help the individual exert control and sense influence over his environment. The environment chosen may appropriately be an aspect of his rehabilitation program or may be a piece of his interaction with family and friends. For example, in many acute care hospitals, especially when an injury or insult is catastrophic, the major lines of communication are established between hospital personnel and family. The patient may not be totally ignored, but his opportunity and his perception of his right to question in detail his injury and treatment is often limited. Thus, depending on the social worker's perception of the individual's need and readiness and the individual's perception of the same issues, a beginning task could be set as simple as requesting an appointment with the physician. The individual can arrange the appointment and raise whatever issues may be critical for him.

In general, it is important that the family not be present at such a meeting, at least initially, for the intent is to provide the opportunity for the individual to assess with the physician his particular situation. The intent is also to establish the direct lines of communication between the individual and the physician and to give the individual the opportunity to communicate his goals for his rehabilitation. The above is perhaps a simplistic example, but the messages given to the individual are critical. First, at least two important individuals, the social worker and the physician, have communicated their belief that he is capable of assuming a direct role in his management. Second, the previous lines of communication are changed and, potentially, the individual will become the source of information regarding his goals and progress to his family. The beginning message to the individual is that he is worthwhile and still capable of direct input into his plan of care.

As the individual is emotionally able to assume more responsibility for planning and decisions, the social worker needs to encourage and support the assumption of that responsibility. Since the rehabilitation setting often functions as a testing ground, particularly for the newly disabled individual, the issue of patient control over his own treatment is critical. He may not have a realistic choice as to whether or not his bowel program is accomplished on Tuesday night, but he can have a choice as to the timing of the program and, within limits, the exact nature of the program.

As the individual is able to assume more control over his life within the rehabilitation setting, the issues of control over his life in the family and community become more crucial. For those individuals for whom employment in the same or a different setting is realistic, the expectation of return to work is introduced early, often within weeks and certainly within several months following onset. Many barriers to this goal may exist, and the individual may not yet recognize his anticipated physical limitations, but the introduction of work as a goal, if realistic, reinforces the concept of "normalcy," at least functionally if not physically. The expectation of the resumption of the "normal" role within the family is also introduced, even though realistic physical limitations may alter the exact nature of the role. A father who is now quadriplegic may not be able to actually play baseball with his sons, but he can manage a team, attend baseball games with them, or instruct them in batting or pitching. In summary, the belief and demonstrated attitude of the rehabilitation staff in the individual's continued self-worth and capability of functioning as a competent person with control over the decisions in his life is crucial to the individual's eventual ability to believe in himself.

A corollary of the above, of course, is the ability of the social worker to allow the individual to make choices which the social worker may not perceive as "correct" decisions at a given point. While the social worker has the responsibility to explore the consequences of the choices, the individual has the "right to fail" or to make choices which may not be in his best interest at that point.

Another issue which often arises in a rehabilitation environment is the setting of limits on behaviors, especially when the population includes a large percentage of adolescents. Obviously, limits on behaviors need to be set for the newly disabled adolescent, in the same manner as limits would have been set prior to onset. Acceptable and unacceptable behaviors need to be defined, the reasons for the limits explained, and the potential consequences of the continuance of unacceptable behaviors spelled out clearly. Excusing unacceptable behavior on the basis of the disability would only reinforce the individual's feeling that somehow he is not now responsible for his behavior and is not perceived as retaining the same emotional controls as before.

While certain behaviors are not tolerated, one behavior potentially viewed as difficult and not encouraged by other health care personnel is actually encouraged and taught as a skill in the rehabilitation setting. This skill is the ability to manipulate. For an individual with a severe physical disability, the ability to manipulate the environment and those individuals within it is often necessary for survival. Manipulation can, of course, be manifested through many different behaviors, some of which can produce the reverse effect of that which is desired. Manipulative behavior which tends to alienate others is not productive. However, the goal would be to continue to encourage the manipulative behavior, but attempt to teach the individual to use the skills in a different manner to still ensure that basic needs are met.

Critical to the accomplishment of the above listed goals is the cooperation, support and consistency of philosophy between the rehabilitation staff and the defined support system. If mixed messages are being communicated by these two systems, the process of redefinition by the individual of his own self-worth and value is much more difficult.

Intervention Strategies — Within the social work role in the rehabilitation setting, the basic strategies used remain relatively traditional. The two major modalities employed are individual and group services. However, in both areas, though more markedly in group services, the focus and purpose of the interventions has shifted with changing philosophies and values.

Individual Services — Individual services remain a consistent treatment modality within a physical rehabilitation setting. Interviews are scheduled, unscheduled, highly structured or not, dependent upon the prevailing philosophy of the social worker and the perceived needs of the individual. The major focus remains support, the therapeutic intervention dependent upon the needs of the individual and the contract between the individual and the social worker.

The feelings aroused by and the implications of the disability for the individual and for his/her family are certainly the central focus for every individual. Relationships with parents, spouse and children universally need reevaluation and reassessment due to the increased stresses the disability imposes on these relationships. Individual and family concerns and problems which may have predated the disability are frequently exacerbated by the disability and may reach a crisis point. Considerable effort is also directed toward the numerous and varied specific plans and choices which must be made. Can the current house or apartment be modified to accommodate a wheelchair, or is moving to a new location the only alternative? Is returning to a former job feasible, or should schooling or retraining be considered? What are the implications of these choices for me as an individual and for my family? Many individuals have said that the experience of learning to cope with a disability has caused them to totally reevaluate their lives and often to reorder the importance of previously existing priorities. The social worker has a clear role with the individual in helping with his/her feelings regarding the disability and in assisting in the process of learning to cope with the changes which have been imposed on his/her life.

Group Services — Service to individual in groups has been a modality within a rehabilitation setting virtually since the inception of rehabilitation. Traditional and existing models have tended to form groups by disability diagnosis based on the existence of some common natural concerns arising from the nature of the disability. Groups have usually set as their primary focus mutual support, sharing and problem-solving regarding common feelings and concerns. Some rehabilitation settings have formulated groups on a psychotherapeutic model. In general, the leadership for the group work component of the program has been social work, although, in many settings, such groups are co-led by social work and psychology.

As the rehabilitation process is being increasingly viewed as a learning process, new purposes and dimensions are being conceptualized and actualized within the framework of a group. Regularly scheduled groups, often with mandatory attendance, are serving a crucial teaching function. Physicians, nurses, occupational and physical therapists and speech therapists are using a group model to impart certain basic universal information, such as maintenance of wheelchairs, intermittent catheterization philosophy and program, or the definition and consequences of a stroke. These teaching sessions are frequently organized for patients or may include patients and families. Often a social worker has assumed the responsibility for the organization of the program and may also be the consistent leader. At times, such teaching sessions evoke feelings as well as specific questions, and the presence of the social worker is critical to the expression and discussion of these feelings.

Within the past ten years, sex and sexuality have emerged as open subjects for research and discussion, in society at large as well as for the population who have physical disabilities. In addition to the availability of individual counseling for specific family concerns, seminars, meetings, conferences and group counseling sessions are consistently scheduled within most rehabilitation settings. Excellent audio-visual materials as well as numerous publications are now available. They not only cover specific questions, recommendations and common areas of concern, but also discuss feelings, attitudes and experiences of other disabled persons in affirming or re-affirming their own sexuality.

Groups have also been organized around specific identified areas of concern or around events in the rehabilitation process which are viewed as times of increased anxiety. Some examples of such groups include an admissions group, a discharge group or a vocational group. Depending upon the expressed and perceived needs of the population, a vocational group could also consider the learning of specific information or skills, such as job interviewing, completing resumes or the rights of the disabled in employment. Social work frequently has a role in the leadership or co-leadership of these groups.

Assertiveness training groups are also emerging in physical rehabilitation, as awareness increases of the need for the individual with a disability to possess certain interpersonal skills in dealing with an often hostile able-bodied world. These groups may begin within the initial rehabilitation phase, and, through role-playing and role rehearsal, assist the patient to deal more effectively with the rehabilitation environment and personnel.

Leisure counseling as a discrete entity is being introduced into the physical rehabilitation process primarily by specialists in therapeutic recreation but often by or in conjunction with social workers.

The potential for group work intervention within the rehabilitation setting is obviously significant and is only beginning to be fully recognized and expanded. In my opinion, the social work role within these various group structures can be as broadly or as narrowly defined as the individual social worker defines his/her role. The basic skills required are social work skills, although additional knowledge and a working understanding of the models used may be needed in some areas.

Reassessment — Within the framework of the relationship, the social worker and the individual must provide opportunity for assessment of progress toward mutually defined goals. Since the ultimate goal has been defined as the individual's resumption, to the extent possible, of his pre-disability life style, criteria for evaluating progress must exist. In a previous section, concepts of stage theories of adjustment have been rejected by this author, and, therefore, the attainment of these stages cannot provide a conceptual framework for evaluating the individual's progress toward the stated goals.

To this author, the most valid measures for the social worker and for the individual lie in his/her ability to resume pre-disability patterns of behavior and to envision satisfying goals and objectives for the future, realistic to the limitations imposed by the disability. Simply stated, the assessment of the individual's progress toward effectively coping with his disability lies in the evaluation of behaviors.

Some rehabilitation professionals are concerned with the individual's ability to acknowledge his disability as permanent and basically unchangeable for the future. For them, one goal is for the individual to eventually be able to acknowledge that "he knows he will never walk again" or "will never be able to use his arms normally." In fact, many, maybe even most, individuals will never relinquish the "hope" that their physical status may some day drastically change. In my opinion, their feelings regarding the permanency of their disability is basically irrelevant to their ability to effectively cope with their physical limitations on a day-to-day basis. Therefore, in order to assess the individual's progress, it is critical to evaluate present and immediate behaviors and stated goals rather than stated or anticipated future achievements. For instance, an individual may adamantly cling to the belief that his/her disability is not permanent and that he/she will walk again, in spite of what the physicians and staff say. Yet, this same individual, in planning toward discharge from the rehabilitation center, is discussing the building of ramps, rearranging the home for first-floor living and participating in driving instruction in a car with hand controls. How then does one evaluate the progress of this individual toward learning to effectively cope with a disability? In the opinion of this author, one evaluates the current behaviors as realistic to the situation and respects the need of the individual to "hope that life will be different in the future."

In addition to the verbalized goals of the individual, the rehabilitation setting and process provide many opportunities to observe and evaluate behaviors which evidence the individual's beginning abilities to cope with his changed physical status. The degree of appropriate control which he/she exerts, or attempts to exert, over his/her rehabiitation program is one indicator. The amount of responsibility which he/she assumes for his/her own care, either directly or in the teaching of others, is another factor. His/her use of free time within the center can also provide additional clues to initial coping mechanisms. A rehabilitation setting also affords the opportunity for the individual to request passes during the evenings and on weekends to pursue activities with family and friends. The individual's use of these passes provides another critical area for the evaluation of his/her ability to cope with a disability. The passes also obviously provide the individual the opportunity to "test out" himself and his abilities and skills in the home and community environment. His/her evaluation of the outcome of these encounters with family and friends and in the community are critical to a general assessment of progress.

As one observes and evaluates the defined behaviors, however, one must always maintain an awareness that no "universal yardstick" exists. A specific individual's behaviors can only be evaluated within the context of his pre-disability behaviors and life style. Only within the context of the initial assessment and of his total functioning do these behaviors assume meaning. For an individual who engaged in few social activities outside the home pre-disability, a weekend pass spent entirely within the home environment can be evaluated as "normal" and expected for him/her. For an individual who, pre-disability, participated in numerous activities outside the home, repeated weekends spent within the confines of the home assume an entirely different meaning.

In addition to concern with observable behaviors, additional input can be gained through an evaluation of the individual's life goals for himself and his anticipated satisfaction from the attainment of these goals. Again, any evaluation must obviously be within the context of existing knowledge concerning that individual's previously defined life goals. If school or work were important to the individual pre-disability, can he/she identify these goals as retaining their importance and ability to be accomplished and provide satisfaction within the limitations of the disability? When alterations in these goals are dictated by the physical constraints imposed by the disability, can the individual begin to identify new goals which retain a high degree of anticipated satisfaction?

In addition to the above described goals and observable behaviors, the individual's beginning ability to restructure and re-form previously existing relationships or to form new relationships reveals important information regarding his/her ability to cope with a disability. In general, the able-bodied person does not know how to relate to an individual with a disability. If the able-bodied person had a relationship with the disabled person pre-disability, the re-establishing and re-working of this relationship is even more difficult. Many individuals with a disability feel that the initiative and major responsibility for the redevelopment and restructuring of the relationship lies with the individual who is disabled. Whether or not this statement is valid is irrelevant, since experience shows that the able-bodied person is usually unable to handle his/her own feelings of self-consciousness, guilt or pity, and the responsibility falls to the individual with the disability. Thus, the individual with the disability needs to learn the skills and has to develop a sufficient comfort level with his/her own physical limitations to "reach out" to the able-bodied person. The degree to which the newly disabled person recognizes and accepts this responsibility and develops the skills needed to restructure important relationships provides valuable input as to his/her beginning ability to survive and gain satisfaction.

This section on reassessment has focused primarily on an evaluation of the individual's own process in learning the internal skills to deal with a disability. Obviously, the internal process of the individual is critical, and an assessment in this area will lead to the formulation of new goals and different intervention strategies for the future social work relationship.

However, in addition to an assessment of the individual with the disability, the social worker must continually assess and attempt to influence the outside reality as well. The outside reality for the individual with a disability can be generally defined in three areas: (1) the rehabilitation environment; (2) the family; and (3) the objective physical environment in the home and community. The responsibility of the social worker in influencing the rehabilitation environment and the family will be addressed in more detail in a later section. The social worker has a key responsibility in trying to assist the individual to utilize all the resources possible to provide a physical environment within which he/she can function with maximum independence. Architectural barriers in the home must be eliminated to the extent possible. If the individual will function primarily from a wheelchair level and seven stairs provide access from his home to the outside, his motivation and ability to resume activities in the community is irrelevant.

The social worker and the individual must exhaust all possible resources to secure adequate ramping, an outside elevator lift or more accessible housing. The social worker must also be thoroughly familiar with the rights of the disabled and insure that the individual knows these rights. The individual may set the return to work as an important attainable goal, but discrimination may prevent the individual from actually returning to work. The social worker must be aware of when the individual's rights have been violated, insure that the individual is aware of his/her rights, and assist as needed in the appropriate procedures to secure these rights. Thus, the external barriers erected by society which limit the individual's return to a productive life style are of as critical concern to the social worker as the internal barriers erected by the individual. Both the internal and external factors must be continually reassessed, so that new goals can be set by the individual and the social worker for their ongoing work together.

SOCIAL WORK INTERVENTION WITH FAMILIES

The individual does not exist in isolation, either pre-disability or post-disability. Therefore, a critical concern of the social worker must be the identification of and intervention with the closest social unit with which the individual identifies. Usually, this unit will be identified as the "family." The primary areas identified as important under the section "Social Work Intervention with the Individual" apply also to the family.

Initial Assessment — The first task of the social worker must be a comprehensive and thorough assessment of the family and of the previously existing family structure. The first goal is to identify the family, both in the perceptions of the family and in the perceptions of the individual. Although these two perceptions may be identical, the social worker must insure that the persons whom the individual with the disability perceives as his/her "major supports" are compatible with the family's perceptions of the key support structures.

Once the key support structure has been identified, the social worker must evaluate the efficacy of this structure. The strengths and weaknesses, both existent and potential, are critical to the selection of appropriate intervention strategies. It is critical to evaluate previously existing patterns of expressing and giving support within the family in terms of their current ability to meet the needs of both the individual and family members. Knowledge of the prior roles and responsibilities assumed by each member of the family, including the individual who is now disabled, is critical.

In addition to the above historical data regarding the family unit and its pre-disability structure, the social worker needs to carefully assess current concerns and project into the future. The often sudden and catastrophic onset of a disability of one family member causes significant stress on the family unit and has probably already necessitated role changes. The social worker needs to be especially sensitive to the current stresses on individual family members and on the family unit as a whole. However, realistic or unrealistic, the family or one member may be feeling guilt regarding the onset of the disability. A father may feel his son would not have broken his neck diving into a quarry if he had warned him more often of the dangers of the quarry. A wife may feel her husband would not have had a stroke if she had not argued with him the previous evening. Thus, the family's perception of its responsibility for the cause of the disability is critical to an initial assessment.

When the individual is transferred to a rehabilitation setting, the family is frequently exhausted and functioning at a high level of stress. Hours have been spent waiting outside and inside intensive care units and hospital rooms in the acute care setting. The transfer of the individual to another institution generates anxiety and evokes very different emotions, from "hope that now he will get better" to "despair that his condition is so serious that the general hospital has given up on him." Families may already be arguing over the perceived unequal burden and responsibility being borne by different family members. Certain previously defined responsibilities and roles of the individual who is now disabled have been assumed in this interim period by other family members, sometimes easily but sometimes with difficulty and even anger. A wife who never handled the financial affairs of the family may be struggling to manage monthly bills. A father may have been the chief disciplinarian of adolescent children, and the mother feels helpless to maintain the previously existing rules and regulations. Thus, the family is coping with a dual stress from which the patient has often been protected. They are balancing their perceived responsibilities to the "sick" family member with their normal or increased responsibilities for the smooth operation of the rest of the family unit. The social worker needs to evaluate these immediate stresses and perhaps intervene immediately in helping the family to structure or restructure the roles they are assuming in the present. In addition, the ability of the family to respond to this immediate crisis needs to be assessed as a potential predictor of the family's ability to respond to long-term crisis. The family of an individual who is now disabled will need to make both long- and short-term adjustments in their structure.

The social worker also needs to assess the family's current understanding of the medical and physical implications of the disability. Is their perception of the etiology and nature of the disability accurate, and have they been apprised of the anticipated goals and length of time in the rehabilitation phase. The social worker needs to evaluate their current knowledge and also assess their ability to assimilate additional specific information immediately and at periodic intervals.

Finally, the social worker needs to assess the learning potential of the family unit and each of the family members. If the individual with the disability will have ongoing need for physical assistance, in all probability, a family member or members will need to assume responsibility for this care. The only exception would be if personal financial resources, community resources or insurance benefits are adequate to purchase such service in the community.

Thus, the initial family assessment provides the social worker with the knowledge needed to set social work intervention strategies and to provide consultation to the rehabilitation team regarding appropriate structuring for their interaction with the family.

Goals — The major goal in working with the family of an individual with a disability can be simply stated in two dimensions. First, the family resources need to be mobilized to provide the physical and environmental supports to allow the individual to eventually function at a maximum level of independence. Second, the family needs help in assisting in the reintegration of the disabled person into as functional a role as possible within the family unit. Impinging upon their ability to accomplish these goals will be their feeling regarding the disability and their eventual ability to view the disabled family member as a functioning capable adult.

Intervention Strategies — Since the family is a critical component of the rehabilitation process, frequent, consistent and varied interventions, both on an individual and group basis, are essential.

The social worker offers individual services to families, focused in several key areas, dependent upon the needs as perceived by the family and social worker. For some families, problems which pre-existed the disability become the key barriers to the provision of adequate supports to the individual and prevent effective family functioning. Therefore, at times, primary concern must be directed toward the alleviation of these problems before the major focus can shift to the present and into the future. The most commonly encountered previously existing problems fall into the areas of marital difficulties and parent-child relationships. Family members, individually and collectively, must have opportunity to express their feelings regarding the disability, both as a legitimate concern for the individual and for its impact on them. In addition to expressing feelings about the disability *per se* they also need an opportunity to examine and express feelings regarding the new roles and responsibilities which may be imposed on them and the changes in their life goals and objectives. Thus, individual counseling with family members, as well as counseling within a dynamic family unit model, are primary intervention strategies within a physical rehabilitation process.

A physical rehabilitation setting provides significant opportunity for families to share with other families common concerns, feelings and plans. Therefore, family groups are a common treatment modality. Such groups vary tremendously in focus and content. Some groups have as a basic purpose the mutual support of families. Others also incorporate or offer separately didactic material organized around a specific disability diagnosis. Groups offering family members or significant others an opportunity to discuss specific information regarding sex and sexuality are also important.

Some groups are structured around only families, and others include both families and the disabled individual. At times, the decision as to the openness of the group is structured by the rehabilitation staff, and, at other times, the decision is open to the individual and his family.

As in the previous discussion regarding the use of groups as an intervention strategy, social work is significantly involved in the planning and organization of such groups, as well as in a leadership or co-leadership capacity.

In addition to the strategies described primarily as psychological/emotional supports, the social worker has a key role with the family in helping them to plan with the individual for the physical changes and specific equipment which will be required in the home. The intent is not only to provide the maximum functional independence for the individual, but also to maximally reduce the responsibilities which the family needs to assume. A team of specialists from the center, often including a social worker, may visit the home to make recommendations regarding necessary structural changes which are commensurate with the family's financial resources. The social worker then can assist the family, as needed, in the implementation of these suggestions. Equipment, such as wheelchairs, beds and patient lifters, are not of course prescribed by the social worker, but the responsibility for insuring that the proper equipment is in the home at discharge does rest with the social worker. Numerous teaching sessions with the family must be scheduled and interpreted, as well as an evaluation made of the family's feelings regarding the variety of activities, often involving very personal care, which they are required to learn. The social worker assumes responsibility to insure that the structured teaching process is meeting the needs of the family.

Reassessment — The reassessment tools available to the social worker with a family do not differ significantly from those described for the individual. The key measure remains the observation and knowledge of family behaviors and the extent to which the family unit contributes attitudinally and physically to the individual's ability to resume as much of his/her previous lifestyle as possible. While the primary goal remains the greatest possible reintegration of the disabled person into the family unit, the social worker must also assess the emotional and physical costs to family members in supporting this reintegration, as the greater goal is to maintain a functional family unit. Thus, a balance must be maintained which does not produce excessive stress to the individual or to the family unit. The results of this process provide the social worker with the opportunity to reassess the working relationship with the family and to set new goals and objectives.

SOCIAL WORK INTERVENTION WITH THE REHABILITATION STAFF

As previously stated, early responsibility was delegated to social work, by physicians and administrators, to share their knowledge of the individual and his family with the rehabilitation team, so that periodic evaluation of progress and goals could be achieved. Within a rehabilitation setting, numerous structures exist, both formal and informal, for this collaboration to occur. Traditionally, structured team staffings occur on a regular basis to assess each individual's progress and the attainment of mutually agreed upon goals. Such staffings usually occur weekly. In addition, team meetings with patients and/or families are held at frequent intervals. Since rehabilitation centers are usually small institutions, the opportunity for collaboration on an informal basis is quite prevalent.

Social work can assume different roles during these collaborative contacts, dependent upon the purpose of the contact and the perception of the social worker as to the most effective intervention strategy. One consistent role is as the "informer/interpreter" regarding the individual's and family's reaction to the disability and the implications of the disability to them and their life style. A second common role is that of coordinator or case manager. The social worker is the professional who must often assume the role of insuring that the staff, individual and family are consistently together in the planning and completion of all the tasks essential to discharge. Thirdly, the social worker most often assumes primary responsibility for resource development and referral. Individuals and families, especially when confronted with discharge home, frequently need at least initially as comprehensive a support system in the home as is available in the community. The social worker's knowledge of and ability to mobilize these community resources provide critical support especially in the first weeks following discharge.

In addition to the social worker's ability to interpret individual and family behaviors, additional skills are frequently utilized to help the team to develop common, consistent and more effective strategies in dealing with behaviors and attitudes. In this role, the social worker functions primarily as a consultant to the team. Another role, frequently assumed by social workers in rehabilitation settings, is as an "advocate" or perhaps more appropriately "facilitator" or "mediator." Due to the nature of the setting and the goals of rehabilitation, conflicts frequently arise between staff and patients regarding goals, acceptable behaviors and the granting of certain privileges, such as passes. The issue of control between staff and the individual is a common and anticipated area of conflict. The social worker may choose to assume a strong advocacy role, but may also function more as a mediator or facilitator of communication between patient and staff in the problem-solving process.

The roles described are not consistently or exclusively limited to social work, and some may, at times, be more effectively handled by a member of another profession. However, these roles are consistent with the skills and knowledge base of social work, and, when assumed by another professional person, consultation with social work frequently occurs.

SOCIAL WORK INTERVENTION IN THE COMMUNITY

Social work education has traditionally defined areas of skill and expertise in three practice modalities: (1) casework or work with individuals; (2) group work or work with individuals in groups; and, (3) community organization. Within the health care field, social workers have not generally assumed a major role in community organization. However, social work does have a legitimate responsibility, knowledge base and skill in facilitating a creative working relationship between a health care institution and the community served. In fact, the assumption of this responsibility can, and in the opinion of this author, should be a critical intervention strategy. The purpose of such intervention is to enable the health care delivery system to become more responsive to the needs of the consumers and potential consumers. The facilitation of a dynamic relationship between the institution and the community can result in more accessible relevant health care services and in a more responsive, involved community.

A search of the social work literature in the area of community organization from a health care base is generally non-productive.

Therefore, the following description of possible methodologies and strategies for such intervention is derived from the author's own experience in an acute care setting and physical rehabilitation environment. Prior to attempting to assume a role in facilitating such a relationship between an institution and the community, certain key elements must be evaluated.

Perhaps the first critical question to be addressed is "who or what is the community?" For some institutions the answer can be derived by an examination of the geographic area within which the majority of consumers reside. If the primary thrust for the development of a consumer-institutional relationship lies in the delivery of emergency medical care, the social worker can easily examine the most frequently occurring geographic boundaries for the use of the emergency service. From the base of a physical rehabilitation setting, the social worker can assume that the primary consumer thrust is toward individuals with a physical disability within a given geographic area.

Once these broad areas are defined, the next critical step is to identify existant, viable community or consumer groups within the target population or population area. Church groups, resident associations, or consumer activists groups may provide the beginning linkages with the broader community.

Concurrent with the definition and examination of the community target groups, the social worker must carefully assess the internal structure of the health care institution relative to the potential feasibility of the assumption of a community organization role. The first and perhaps most key element to assess internally is the power of the social worker within the organization. Power is both implicit and explicit, deriving from the skill and expertise of the social worker, as well as from the formal delegation of power from the administration. In order to carry this role, the social worker must have the delegated power and authority to carry the values and goals of the institution to the consumer group. If such power is to be delegated, the administration and social worker must share a similar value base in developing goals for the organization. Simply stated, the administration must strongly support and believe in the concept of consumer involvement in the design of a health care delivery system and support the competence of the social worker in faciitating the institution's relationship with the community.

Initially, the administration may not totally comprehend all the potential implications and consequences to the institution of such a relationship. In this author's opinion, a total awareness of the potential consequences is not critical for the administration to know in the early stages. The critical elements are the social worker's assessment of the motivations, value base, and flexibility of the administration in the decision to develop a working relationship with a consumer group or community.

Another primary element is the social worker's assessment of the ability of the institution (administration) to respond quickly to the request of a consumer group. The response may be directly from administration to the group or the decision may be carried by the social worker. However, the critical concern is whether or not the social worker has access to the organizational decision makers, and whether or not the organizational structure and personalities are conducive to making rapid programmatic decisions when indicated.

The ability of the social worker to establish credibility with the consumer groups is another key element. The social worker must be viewed by the consumer as an individual who has a power base within the organization and hence, the ability to "get things done." The social worker must also demonstrate that he/she has the position within the institution to "speak for that institution" in the areas of consumer concern. In order to establish this trust, the social worker must be clear when he/she has the ability to speak definitively for the institution, and when further administrative decision making is essential. If further administrative action is needed, the social worker must be clear as to why a higher authority is needed and within what time framework a decision can be made.

The social worker must be able to precisely define and re-define for himself/herself and, at times, for the organization or the consumer group the goals which initially brought them together. The social worker must be aware of both the "open and hidden agendas" of the institution and the consumer group and insure that both remain compatible and encompassible within the relationship. The social worker must understand the frustrations, personalities and organizational problems of both groups and help each of them to understand the capabilities and limitations of the other. The social worker must be able to assist both groups to refocus and redefine overall goals when smaller less important concerns seem to jeopardize the relationship. The social worker must maintain a finely tuned sense of timing to the past and present history of both organizations so that the process between them does not threaten their own growth and development. Finally, the social worker must maintain a clear perception and role definition of the organization he/she represents, even while carrying at times an advocacy role for the consumer to the institution.

The knowledge base, values and skills described above are certainly not peculiar to community organization, but are generic to all social work practice. Social workers in health care settings must continue a strong commitment to the development of a health care delivery system which is accessible and relevant to the needs of consumers and potential consumers. The assumption of a legitimate social work role as a facilitator in community/institutional relationships is one potential intervention strategy to achieve this goal. The benefits which can be derived from the existance of such a relationship are considerable. New programs may be developed, such as hypertension screening clinics, services for alcohol and substance abuse or transitional living services for the physically disabled. Consumers may become partners with professional staff in the delivery of emergency care or in peer counseling with newly disabled persons. Strong community support for new programming can result in joint fund raising efforts and in joint applications for private or governmental grants. The role of social work within the community as a facilitator of consumer/institutional relationships seems a natural outgrowth of the role of social work in health care.

EMERGING SOCIAL WORK ROLES

The changing nature of the philosophies of rehabilitation and of social work have blended to create an opportunity for expanding roles for social work within the field of physical rehabilitation. Role redefinition and re-structuring have also been dictated by the emergence of the consumer movement. The new roles which social workers are assuming will vary tremendously dependent upon the philosophical base of the social worker, the individual institution and the climate of the community within which both are located. However, some potential emerging roles, familiar to this author, will be described.

As the traditional physical rehabilitation setting (the rehabilitation center) begins to broaden the concept of its role as a legitimate life-time resource to the individual with a disability, the potential opportunities for social work programming expand. Following discharge from the protected environment of a rehabilitation center, the on-going goals for the individual can be defined in three spheres: (1) prevention of medical complications; (2) maintenance of functional skills; and, (3) the assumption of a life style which is satisfying to the individual. The first two goals are easily definable and measurable. The third goal includes virtually all aspects of the individual's life functioning; work, leisure time activities, relationships and a feeling of self-worth. Obviously these major concerns and remaining goals following discharge focus in the psychosocial arena. Thus, the potential need exists long-term and periodically for all the intervention strategies earlier described. Individual and family counseling is a service potentially available to an individual and his family following discharge. Recognizing the finite resources of the rehabilitation center, but also knowing the general inaccessibility and lack of awareness of community resources to meet the needs of the disabled, many social workers have been forced to assume an educational and resource development role within the community. Group services are frequently offered to discharged patients and their families both with a structured teaching approach and within a counseling framework.

As increasing numbers of more severely disabled individuals are surviving acute care to enter the rehabilitation process, "quality vs. quantity of life" issues surface more frequently. The issues and conflict often seen are portrayed with some sensitivity in the recent Broadway production of *Whose Life Is It Anyway*. While obviously dramatized somewhat for the theater, the issues are concisely raised by the individual who makes a clear rational choice to die rather than "exist" with a degree of disability unacceptable to him. The strong reactions of the staff to his choice are vividly portrayed, as well as the need for a forum in which to express and work through their feelings. In centers which recognize the stresses on staff, especially among nursing personnel, in dealing with such individual choices, support groups are being organized for staff. Social workers, often in conjunction with psychology or psychiatry, are defining new roles in leading these groups.

In many areas, social work is struggling to define a legitimate role within or as a partner with the consumer movement. Perhaps as many different approaches and models exist as the number of social workers and consumers. However, the emergence of the disabled consumer movement is critical for the social worker to consider and to assume a major leadership role within the institution in developing a mutually beneficial relationship. Centers for Independent Living, as one outgrowth of the disabled consumer movement, are coming into existence in many communities. These centers are developed and administered by individuals who are themselves disabled, and provide a rich resource for the individual with a disability. Social workers can view the independent living center as simply another community referral resource or develop ways of creating a partnership between the "professionally staffed rehabilitation center" and the "consumer staffed" independent living center. One example of a creative partnership could be the provision of attendant care services by the independent living center and the training of the attendants, as appropriate, by the physical rehabilitation center. Another example lies within the collaboration and close working together of the social worker and the peer counselor to more effectively meet the needs of a particular individual and his family.

Social workers are assuming roles with Centers for Independent Living with groups of disabled consumers in building "transitional living centers", facilities where an individual with a disability can learn the skills needed to live independently in the community. The teaching staff in these facilities must include both professionals and consumers, for the knowledge and skills of each are critical to the intent of the program. Social workers are increasingly joining with disabled consumer groups in the fight for equal opportunity and equal access in employment, in recreational activities, in housing and in transportation. Recognition is finally being given by the physical rehabilitation field to the knowledge and expertise of the consumer group in the areas of equipment adaptations, resource identification, accessibility evaluation and advocacy. Social workers are increasingly assuming a community organization responsibility for developing and sustaining the linkages between the institution and the disabled consumer movement.

As social work is beginning to expand and create some of these roles, the opportunity to impact upon institutional programming, philosophy and policy is clear. Increasingly, social work is impacting not only upon the programming which occurs within the walls of the institution, but is helping the institution to reach out into the community and to create a new physical rehabilitation concept — a "center without walls".

REGULATORY BODIES

The decade of the 70's has witnessed an outpouring of Federal and State regulations regarding all aspects of service offered in health care settings. In general, the intent of the legislation has been to increase the accountability of health care providers, especially in the context of the spiraling costs of health care. The effects on health care institutions have been overwhelming, particularly as one views the geometrically increasing number of man hours delegated to the assurance of compliance with regulations. While an evaluation of outcomes and strict accountability were, perhaps, inevitable and overdue in the health care field, the volume of documentation now required creates some dilemmas for providers. While many of these concerns are generic to the entire health care field, several unique challenges are presented to rehabilitation settings. The primary focus of this section will be to define those concerns which are especially relevant to the field of physical rehabilitation.

A physical rehabilitation center is usually accredited as a "speciality hospital", and is, therefore, accredited and regulated by the same regulatory bodies as an acute care hospital. Thus, the identical state standards and standards of the Joint Commission on Accreditation of Hospitals apply. Physical rehabilitation settings are also subject to the same regulations under Utilization Review, Quality Assurance and PSRO as the acute care setting. Several problems arise in applying these uniform standards to acute care and specialty hospitals.

The first problem lies in the obvious divergent purpose and thus, population of the acute care hospital and the physical rehabilitation setting. Average lengths of stay are extremely different, and criteria used to measure progress are not the same. In fact, the development of uniform criteria and standards of care for various disability diagnoses has been extremely difficult. Developing standards of care for a provisional diagnosis of appendicitis can and has been accomplished. Certain objective findings must be documented, a standardized diagnostic work-up can be developed and an appropriate time interval established. If the diagnosis is confirmed, an appendectomy will be performed and an expected length of stay post-surgery can be established. The standardization of care for the quadraplegic patient in a physical rehabilitation setting is not impossible, but is certainly much more difficult. Goals are established on admission and progress toward those goals can be monitored. However, significant progress for this severe disability cannot be measured in days or weeks, but often only in months. Family teaching and discharge planning are complicated, and inevitably are influenced by many factors outside the control of the institution, patient and family. Such factors are supplier delays in securing complex special equipment and contractor delays in completing minimally needed home renovations as well as the psychological status of the patient and family are frequently occurring examples of such delays. In fact, lengths of stay have been considerably reduced over the past ten years but uniform standards of care have not really been established.

Additionally, the staff of a typical physical rehabilitation center is quite small in number, even when compared to the staff of a community hospital. Therefore, the division of labor to meet the myriad of standards for documentation, committee meetings and audits is difficult. In general, the entire burden falls to a "handful of people". A medical staff of five to ten physicians may have to assume the same monitoring responsibilities as a medical staff of thirty or forty.

In addition to the accrediting bodies familiar to the acute care hospital, most rehabilitation facilities will also choose to be accredited by the Commission on Accreditation of Rehabilitation Facilities (CARF). CARF has recently initiated a standard for program evaluation. The principle states:

> The facility shall have an evaluation system to identify the results of facility services and the effect of the program on individuals served in such a way that program performance can be improved and community support can be enhanced (21).

The obvious intent of a program evaluation system is to define desired outcomes which are measurable and which can be compared to a set of standardized expectations of outcome. Universal standards do not exist relative to an acceptable or expected level of medical complication or decrease in functional ability. Even more difficult is the task of setting expected outcomes or standards in the psycho-social-vocational aspects of an individual's life. An individual outcome can be measured only in terms of the goals and objectives set for that particular individual. Group outcomes, while retrievable, have little value unless compared against each individual's predisability level of functioning.

In addition to the inherent difficulties in defining anticipated, measurable outcomes, program evaluation mandates post-discharge contact with each individual who has received rehabilitation services. While the mandate from program evaluation is limited to data collection, ethical and moral considerations dictate the provision of services to deal with the problems encountered in such follow-up contacts. Therefore, the impact of program evaluation on the staff of a rehabilitation center is two-fold. First, staff must be available to collect follow-up data regarding the individual's post-discharge performance related to expected criteria. This data can be collected through direct contact, telephone contact or through the individual's completion of a form mailed to his home. Secondarily, staff must be available to attempt to intervene with service at least in situations identified as crisis or high risk. Since such outpatient and/or outreach services are minimally, if at all, reimbursable by third party payers, the financial drain on the institution is also significant.

Thus, while the mandates and requirements of regulatory bodies have the potential to allow for valuable program evaluation and the subsequent development of more effective programming, the rehabilitation staff experiences a considerable burden in complying with these mandates.

CONCLUSION

Social work in physical rehabilitation has emerged from a traditional focus on the psychological process of the disabled individual and his family to an expanded role within the larger social and political areas. This expanded role has developed from both internal and external forces.

Internally, the profession has increasingly recognized that an individual with a disability may in fact be more "handicapped" by the attitudinal and architectural barriers of society than by the original disability. Consequently, treatment modalities have increased the emphasis on the teaching of skills and focus less routinely on the inter-psychic processes.

The independent living movement has afforded the physical rehabilitation center the opportunity to "hear the voice of the consumer" and to join forces in the attainment of mutual goals. Essentially the consumer movement exists to eliminate those barriers which prevent the individual with a disability from having the same life choices as the able-bodied person.

In response to these internal and external forces, social workers in physical rehabilitation settings have increasingly assumed roles with the individual, with the physical rehabilitation center and with consumer groups in the assurance of accessible housing, affordable attendant care, equal employment, available transportation and the elimination of social barriers. Social work has a unique opportunity to evaluate and to access inequities and scarcity of community resources and to join forces with appropriate groups to insure increased opportunities for the individual with a disability. This broadly defined role as an initiator and catalyst for system change is assumed with an individual and his/her family, with the physical rehabilitation setting, with the larger community environment and within the political environment.

For an individual and his/her family, the role may be to enable them to secure an apartment which provides the accessibility for their continued functioning as a family unit. Within the physical rehabilitation setting, the social worker may act as a catalyst in initiating a program in assertiveness training to enable the newly disabled individual to better negotiate with an uncooperative landlord. The social worker may work closely with a consumer group in securing resources for independent living within the larger community. In the political arena, social work has unique knowledge and experience in the need for regulation and mandates for accessibile housing. These defined roles are all a natural progression of the unique set of knowledge, values and skill of the social work profession. The roles as described can and must be assumed by the social worker on all levels of practice: on-line staff, supervisor and administrator. The role of the social worker within physical rehabiitation is only as limited as the creative capabilities of the individual social worker. In essence, the social worker can best serve as the dynamic force between the institution and community, thus increasing the responsiveness of each to the needs of the other. Only in this way can the institution and the community assure that the individual with a disability will have the same opportunities in our society as the able-bodied person.

REFERENCES

1. Cited by: Rusk, Howard A.: *Rehabilitation Medicine.* C.V. Mosby Company, St. Louis: 1958. Front Piece.
2. Rusk, Howard A., M.D., and Taylor, Eugene J.: *New Hope for the Handicapped,* Harper and Brothers Publishers. New York, 1949, pp. 63-64.
3. Rusk, Howard A., M.D.: *Op. Cit.,* p. 20.
4. U.S. Department of HEW: *Rehabilitation Facilities Needs in '70's.* National Summary of Need for Rehabilitation Facilities, Monograph No. 1. Washington, D.C., Social and Rehabilitation Service, Rehabilitation Services Administration, 1971.
5. Riley, E., and Saad, A. Nazi (Eds.): *Disability in the United States: Compendium of Data on Prevalence and Programs.* Columbus, Ohio, The Ohio State University, 1970.
6. U.S. Dept. of HEW: *Chronic Conditions Causing Activity Limitations,* U.S., 1965-1967. U.S. Public Health Service Publication No. 1000, Series 10, No. 61.
7. Rehabilitation Act of 1973.
8. 1978 Amendments to the 1973 Rehabilitation Act.
9. Rusk, Howard A., M.D.: *Op. Cit.,* p. 7.
10. Rusk, Howard A., M.D.: In, *Psychological Practices with the Physically Disabled,* edited by Garrett, James F. and Levine, Edna S. Columbia University Press, New York. 1961 Preface, p. VII.
11. Gliedman, John: The Wheelchair Rebellion, *Psychology Today,* August 1979, p. 59.
12. Rusk, Howard A., M.D.: *Op. Cit.,* p. 256.

13. Shontz, Franklin D.: *The Psychological Aspects of Physical Illness and Disability*. Macmillan Publishing Company, Inc.: New York, 1975, pp. 160-166.
14. Eisenberg, M.G. and Faconer, J.A.: *Treatment of the Spinal Cord Injured*. Springfield, Illinois. Charles C. Thomas. 1978.
15. Hohmann, George W., Ph.D.: Psychological Aspects of Treatment and Rehabilitation of the Spinal Cord Injured Person. *Clinical Orthopedics and Related Research*, #112, October 1975, pp. 81-88.
16. Fordyce, W.: Behavior Methods in Rehabilitation. In W. Neff (Ed.), *Rehabilitation Psychology*. Washington, D.C.: American Psychological Association, 1971.
17. Lazarus, A.: A Learning Theory and the Treatment of Depression. *Behavior Research and Therapy*. 1968, 6, pp. 83-89.
18. Seligman, M. Helplessness: *On Depression, Development and Death*. San Francisco. W.H. Freeman and Co., 1975.
19. Trieschmann, Roberta B.: *Spinal Cord Injuries. Psychological, Social and Vocational Adjustment*. Pergamon Press: New York, 1980, p. 20.
20. Rotter, J.: Generalized Expectancies for Internal versus External Control of Reinforcement. *Psychological Monographs: General and Applied*, 1966, 80, 1-28.
21. Commission on Accreditation of Rehabilitation Facilities. *Standards Manual for Rehabilitation Facilities*. Copyright 1980 by the Commission on Accreditation of Facilities, 2500 North Pantano Road, Tucson, Arizona, 85715.

Chapter 5

SOCIAL WORK AND PUBLIC HEALTH

JOANNE E. MANTELL

Public health is concerned with the community's organized efforts to protect, promote, and restore people's health. Public health policy is directed toward formulating broad, long-term health goals and strategies and projecting health trends (94).

Public health is historically rooted in environmental sanitation and communicable disease control. Under its auspices, sanitary measures were devised to protect community, food and water supplies; surveillance systems were designed for the reporting of infectious diseases; and clinics were operated for the detection and treatment of tuberculosis (TB), venereal disease and maternal-and-child-health problems. Public health is, therefore, pathology-oriented. Public health officials were initially drawn from medical, nursing and sanitary engineering disciplines. Identification of specific organisms as pathogenic agents and the introduction of immunization to control bacterial infections reduced morbidity and mortality of most infectious diseases. Consequently, public health concerns shifted to chronic disease prevention.

Today, the scope of public health has been broadened to include such problems as self-imposed life-style risks, the psychosocial aspects of disease, mental health, dental health and occupational health hazards. Equity of access to medical care, health problems of special populations, health education, health planning, and health policy are also addressed by public health practitioners and planners.

The author wishes to thank Thomas E. Fuszard, Rosalie Kane, D.S.W., and Alfred H. Katz, D.S.W. for their constructive suggestions.

Responsibility for public health is dispersed among all members of a community. With the expansion of public health activities, such professionals as nutritionists, dentists, health educators and social workers have become integral to public health programs. The public health workforce currently comprises more than half a million persons. The membership of the American Public Health Association (APHA), this country's national professional association, reflects the diversity of disciplines and specialties within the field of public health. APHA is divided into numerous sections, including public health nursing, maternal and child health, environmental health, mental health, gerontological health, dental health and veterinary public health to name a few. In 1970, the social work section, now about 500 strong, was formed.

Public health reflects a commitment toward enhancing healthy standards of living through its development of needed social machinery. Preventive and treatment services for the public are generally provided by federal, state or local public health authorities, which act in the public's interest to protect the health of the community.

Public health differs from clinical medicine in that its focus is preventive rather than curative or palliative. Its emphasis is on the needs of population groups rather than on individuals. Whereas a physician diagnoses an individual's illness based on objective and subjective symptoms, public health practitioners investigate the causes and distribution of disease in the community and attempt to control its spread through observation and empirical and inferential methods.

Whenever promotion and advancement of health of the community are at stake, there usually exists concern as to which level of government should provide support for their costs. Often, when programmatic and policy decisions are made at a local or state level, it is possible that the health interest of the public will not be adequately protected.

Government agencies typically have planning and regulatory responsibilities for health programs. The United States Public Health Service (PHS) is the primary federal agency charged with developing health protection and maintenance programs and formulating public policy and goals to improve people's health. The PHS employs personnel through its Commissioned Corps and the Federal Civil Service. The responsibiities of the PHS are broad and include such diverse functions as 1) prevention and control of communicable and preventable diseases; 2) surveillance and monitoring the safety and efficacy of food, drugs and other health products; 3) recruitment and training of a health workforce; 4) provision of different levels of care (emergency medical services, primary medical services and prevention and treatment of mental and substance abuse disorders), and 5) delivery of health services to defined populations (Native Americans, seamen and prisoners). Other federal agencies, such as the Environmental Protection Agency, Veteran's Administration, Bureau of Mines, Federal Aviation Agency and the Department of Energy also perform public health functions. State and local governmental agencies have also been involved in planning, delivery and evaluating community-based preventive, environmental and personal health services and in inspecting and licensing health care facilities. The PHS and state and local health departments, however, should not be confused with public health as a discipline or field of practice.

A FOCUS ON PREVENTION

Within the last decade, there has developed a growing consciousness about the importance of preventive interventions as compared to acute-oriented curative care for problems that jeopardize the health of the public — such problems as TB, influenza and rubella, for example. Prevention, as defined within a public health framework, incorporates not only control of disease but rehabilitation of its victims. Prevention is usually divided into primary, secondary and tertiary levels. Primary prevention interventions are prophylactic health actions — immunization, water fluoridation, smoking control, seat belt usage and others — designed to prevent the occurrence of disease or injury through eradication of pathogenic agents in the environment or of reduced exposure to them. The efficacy of primary prevention is measured by the number of new cases of the disease within a specified period. Secondary prevention activities refer to screening procedures, such as those used to detect glaucoma, hypertension or cervical cancer, which aim to detect disease in asymptomatic individuals or diagnose disease in the symptomatic. The mission of these activities is to preclude unidentified or incipient disease from progressing into an advanced state. Secondary prevention activities are frequently directed toward populations believed to be at risk, that is, groups of vulnerable individuals who have a higher probability of developing a disease or disability than the general population. The efficacy of secondary prevention techniques is measured by the number of cases of the disease identified in an early stage.

A distinction between primary and secondary levels of prevention relates to knowledge of outcome. With respect to primary prevention, the effectiveness of an intervention cannot be discerned without a long-term controlled experiment at the population level. The benefits of primary prevention activities are almost impossible to establish at the individual level. At the time of a swine flu immunization, an individual who takes the vaccine does not know whether he would have developed the flu. With a secondary activity such as genetic screening, the outcome is discernible — the presence or absence of the genetic disorder is identified in the screened individual. The individual can be made aware promptly of whether he/she has the disorder.

Tertiary prevention activities are directed toward delaying the progression of disease, as well as ameliorating, palliating and rehabilitating its side effects; and thus prolonging and improving life. Examples include insulin administration, physical therapy to the spinal cord-injured, and limb amputations of patients with osteogenic sarcoma.

Federal legislation, government executive decisions, allocation of monies and numerous large-scale public opinion surveys (31) reflect emerging interest in disease prevention. The 1974 National Health Planning and Resource Development Act charged health systems agencies — federally-supported health planning organizations in communities — with responsibility for providing disease prevention programs. In 1979, an Office of Health Information, Health Promotion, Physical Fitness and Sports Medicine was created to plan, coordinate and develop policy options regarding federal prevention activities in such areas as immunizations, family plannning, hypertension control, sexually-transmitted diseases, anti-smoking campaigns, infant and adolescent health, occupational safety and health, substance abuse, fluoridation and toxic agent control (35).

This interest in prevention has not been limited to the Federal government; most states have implemented health promotion programs with assistance from the Public Health Service. In addition, there has been considerable interest in screening, risk-reduction and health education on the part of a number of non-government groups such as Blue Cross and Blue Shield, health maintenance organizations, and voluntary health agencies. In times of fiscal austerity, these preventive programs are in great jeopardy of losing funds. To counteract the step-child status that has traditionally been accorded prevention in our health care system, the Department of Health and Human Services has recently launched an extensive media campaign and proposed a $242 million block grant directed toward prevention programs, including fluoridation, high blood pressure, and adolescent pregnancy (93).

There is widespread, though not universal, belief that the expansion of disease prevention activities is cost-effective. Health costs are escalating more rapidly than the general rate of inflation, and traditional cost-containment measures have largely been unsuccessful. Changing demographics and illness profiles challenge the skills of preventive medical practitioners. Decreasing infant mortality and gradual aging of the population structure have resulted in a preponderance of chronic, degenerative disease problems. By preventing disease or impeding its progression, the need for more expensive care at a later, more acute stage of illness is reduced. Preventive efforts have been largely equated with routine, periodic health examinations. Recently completed studies raise questions as to the efficacy of general medical examinations in reducing the incidence of health problems for the asymptomatic and especially on their cost-effectiveness (83, 97).

Recognition that the health of an individual is linked to the social as well as the physical environment led to public health's concern with social pathology. In particular, public health and medical officials are considering the ways in which social, cultural and psychological factors increase one's predisposition to disease, cause disease, and influence its progression.

AN HISTORICAL OVERVIEW OF PUBLIC HEALTH SOCIAL WORK

Public health social work has had different emphases during its evolution, encompassing a broad array of activities and functions. During the social reform period in the late nineteenth and early twentieth centuries, social workers became involved in prevention, casefinding and treatment of tuberculosis, venereal disease, maternal and child health problems and handicapping conditions. The utility of such social work practice in public health was described by Barnett (5) in 1967:

> If health is perceived to include more than medical or biological entities, and is a by-product of social systems, then social work is intimately related to public health. Family planning, alcoholism, suicide and drug addiction are public health and social problems. The major social problems of today — juvenile delinquency, racial discrimination and violence, poverty, crime, child neglect, marital incompati-

> bility and divorce, deterioration of the inner city and expanding suburbia relate to health and to welfare . . . medicine, education, and social work are concerned with the individual, the family, and the community. They all have a concern for prevention, early casefinding and early mobilization of high quality care provided through a network of specialized services.

Casefinding, program planning, community outreach, policy formulation, coordination of services, program and staff consultation and training and education of other health professionals in the community have long been considered essential features of social workers' roles in public health as has disease prevention. Specifically, social workers intervened in patients' lives by helping them modify unfavorable conditions and by influencing physicians' attitudes about medical care (77). Social workers were expected to be knowledgeable about disease, interpreting the impact of patients' illness and hospitalization to the patients' families and to doctors and nurses. Arming patients with medical information was intended to increase awareness of preventive measures and facilitate use of community medical resources.

TB management was the passport for social work's entry into the hospital because the contribution of social services could be readily demonstrated by showing bacillus disease to be propagated by poor social conditions (16). Casework services were offered to patients in hospitals, sanitariums and in the community (9, 53) to help them manage their illness, cope with separation from family and effectively use community resources. Social workers were expected to encourage patient adherence to medical regimens. Social workers in local health departments strongly identified with TB control. Although their role was not clearly defined, public health social workers participated in community-wide casefinding surveys by reporting conditions under which TB patients lived and facilitating referrals to medical and social agencies. During the era when TB was rampant, school health programs, slum clearance, clean housing and improved street sanitation were promoted, and legislation limiting factory sweat shop conditions and mandating tenement house inspections was passed (17). In 1944, Public Law 410 created the Division of Tuberculosis Control under the aegis of the Public Health Service and was financed by federal-state matching funds for surveillance, prevention and detection of TB (81).

Federal matching fund programs for TB services were largely responsible for the expansion of social work services in local health departments. In local communities, while social workers continued to engage in counseling patients and families and in casefinding, a program-centered and administrative consultation role emerged. Social workers planned health programs, educated the public, helped patients accept treatment, and interpreted laws and regulations to patients for medical care and public assistance eligibility. Social workers employed by the Public Health Service served as staff consultants and liaisons to state and local health departments, assisting them in the collection of sociodemographic data, mobilizing community resources and developing needed social services. Unfortunately, as consultants, they were often isolated and lacked the collegiality and support of fellow professionals.

There were other pressing sociomedical needs besides TB to which social work responded. During and after World War I, there were epidemics of venereal disease, influenza and polio. Partly because venereal diseases were laden with social taboos and moral evaluations, pressures to control venereal disease culminated in Federal legislation, the Chamberlain-Kahn Act, which created the Division of Venereal Disease within the Public Health Service. Subsequently, the National Venereal Disease Control Act was passed. It provided Federal financial assistance to state and local health departments for the development of clinics for surveillance, early diagnosis and treatment of venereal disease. Social work interventions centered on three tasks: educating the victims and families about the causes and dissemination of syphilis so as to prevent further spread of infection; tracing the syphilitic's sexual contacts; and encouraging patient compliance with treatment (43, 72). During the influenza epidemic of 1918-19, social workers functioned as epidemiologists, tracking children in the community who were at high risk because their parents had died of the flu (30).

Social work also entered the field of maternal and child health, through public health departments and public assistance medical care programs. The launching of the Federal Children's Bureau in 1912 marked the beginning of public awareness of government responsibility in promoting the physical, social and emotional health of mothers and children. The Bureau initially investigated the causes of infant mortality and, subsequently, maternal mortality. Social and economic factors, e.g., marital status and income, were found to be negatively associated with the death rates of mothers and children. A medical social work section was established within the Children's Bureau and regional offices of the Department of Health, Education, and Welfare (78). Bureau staff provided program and case consultation to states to stimulate the development of child welfare programs in communities. In 1927, the Shepard-Towner or Maternity and Infancy Act mandated the first grant-in-aid program to improve maternal and child health services and provided the foundation for the development of a national network of the state-administered programs that currently exist. The grant-in-aid was contingent upon the state formulating and developing maternal and child health plans. Medical care was provided during pregnancy, delivery and in the post-partum period, and health education concerning the need for proper hygiene, nutrition and pelvic exams was emphasized. Title V of the Social Security Act of 1935 provided federal grants-in-aid to the states to extend and improve health services for mothers and children, including crippled children's and child welfare services.

Maternal and child health programs emphasized prevention rather than treatment. Programs embraced a range of diverse problems, including prenatal care, dental health, accident prevention, nutrition, school health examinations, sex education, health education, poison control, accident prevention, teenage pregnancy, substance abuse, child abuse, and immunizations (34). State departments of health developed medical care programs for mothers and their newborn. Special demonstration projects were implemented in some states for high-risk populations, e.g., premature and low-birth-weight newborns and unmmarried pregnant adolescents.

Social workers concentrated their efforts in integrating health and social services, coordinating and expanding community resources and acting as liaison between hospitals and community agencies (29). This entailed identifying barriers that impeded mothers' effective use of health services as well as increasing patient awareness and utilization of these maternal and child health services. Setting standards for services and educating the public about maternal- and child-health concerns fell within the domain of state public health social work consultants. In addition, social workers became involved in professional education. For example, the American Association of Medical Social Workers joined with the National League for Nursing to help patients deal with the psychosocial concomitants of illness (17). Social workers worked closely with nurses and other health professionals in genetic counseling, family planning, adolescent pregnancy and care of the newborn. The deployment of social workers as consultants was significant in that it indicated that direct service was not the only method to deal with the social needs of patients and their families.

The Crippled Children's program provided preventive medical services to children from birth to 21 years of age. Detection and diagnostic services of handicapping conditions became mandatory, regardless of financial eligibility, although states were able to impose eligibility requirements for treatment and usually did so on a sliding-scale basis. There have been widespread variations in patterns of service delivery and interpretation of handicapping conditions. Although multi-disciplinary programs, which are frequently collaborative endeavors between crippled children's services, hospital clinics and local health departments, have usually delivered such services in most states, a few programs have developed through contractual arrangements with private physicians (34). Definitions of the variety of conditions considered to be handicapping generally depend on a state's financial resources, personnel and administration interest in a particular disorder.

In 1944, the Children's Bureau Advisory Committee on Services for Crippled Children recommended that comprehensive medical care be extended to children with all types of handicapping conditions such as asthma, epilepsy, polio, tuberculosis, congenital syphilis, heart disease and diabetes (81). Today, most states have interpreted broadly the meaning of "handicapped." As many infectious diseases are controlled through immunization, most recent efforts have been directed toward children's chronic disease problems. In 1976, Title XVI of the Social Security Act was amended to provide Supplemental Security Income benefits for the purchase of medical, social and educational services for disabled children from birth to sixteen years of age (Public Law 94-566).

These last two pieces of maternal- and child-health legislation directed attention to the vast social and psychological costs associated with health problems of mothers and children. Federal guidelines required social-work participation in state-administered maternal and child health programs. Consequently, after 1935, state health departments began to expand their social work staff. In many cases, the legislation resulted in the inception of social work services in state health departments. Under the leadership of Dr. Martha Eliot and Ms. Edith Baker, social work was introduced into Army, Navy and state programs for crippled children (17, 80). Social workers served as staff members in Crippled Children's Programs and the Bureau of Public Assistance of the Social Security Board.

The Emergency Maternity and Infant program, authorized by Congress in 1943, extended maternal and child health services to dependents of the military through the end of World War II. This program provided Federal funds to state health departments. Once again, Federal regulations mandated social services, contributing to expanding the number of social workers involved in maternal and child public health programs.

Federal grants-in-aid were also given to states to set up multidisciplinary clinics for the diagnosis and treatment of mental retardation. In addition, scientific advances in knowledge about genetic and metabolic diseases led to the development of screening programs for the early detection of mental retardation. Social workers initially served as consultants in state health departments, but as community retardation clinics evolved, they assumed positions with local health departments and hospitals. Social work was gradually extended in state health department clinics for other diseases such as cancer and those causing blindness and hearing impairments. Despite this public health activity, it was not until nearly 1950 that a public health specialty within social work gained professional recognition. In 1949, the American Association of Medical Social Workers (AAMSW) in collaboration with the American Public Health Association's (APHA) Committee on Professional Education (1) issued a statement concerning the functions and processes of public health social work. Stated functions of social work in public health programs include identification of community health needs; program planning and implementation; policy formulation; liaison and coordination of services in the community; consultation, staff development and in-service education; research; and direct casework services to individuals and families (2, 6). Boehm (10) considered social restoration, social provision and prevention as the three core concepts in his description of the functions of social work, and ultimately was influential in infusing preventive content into the social work curriculum and practice (95). Again, the importance of social, emotional, physical and environmental factors in illness and health service utilization was stressed.

Rice (69) identified five common concerns that social work shared with clinical medicine and public health:

1) Understanding the individual and his illness, and particularly factors which facilitate or impede the likelihood of his engaging in preventive health behaviors,
2) Understanding the individual within the context of family and community,
3) Knowledge and coordination of community resources,
4) Comprehensive problem assessment and the need for a multidisciplinary approach to treatment, and
5) Prevention of illness and disability as well as rehabilitation.

In 1959, the National Association of Social Workers (NASW) issued a document that affirmed the need for a clear conceptualization of prevention. The NASW Statement of the Commission on Social Work Practice defined prevention to include facilitation of social change in relation to communities as well as individuals, families and groups. The document, however, did not limit the scope of prevention as dealing with "populations-at-risk," but encompassed all social work activities, including detection and treatment of pathology; therefore, secondary and tertiary levels of prevention, as within its domain. Rapoport (63) considered the focus of social work to be broader than treatment. She delineated three types of social work activities in primary prevention:

1) Early intervention with people in acute need,
2) Coordination of comprehensive health and welfare services so as to minimize fragmentation, and
3) Involvement in social reform and legislative activities oriented toward maximizing family integration.

Later, social workers had varied conceptions of their profession's role in public health. Some were strongly influenced by crisis-intervention theory and preventive-psychiatry principles. Caplan (18) considered direct, preventive mental health services to families as in the domain of social work practice, even in multidisciplinary outpatient settings, and differentiated social work from other health professions by its grater concern with environmental factors. Insley (34) viewed casework practice as requisite for social workers to consult in public health settings, whereas Rice (70) assigned casework to be a lower priority than consultation. Generally, the impact of environmental conditions and structural contraints (e.g., radiation, scarce energy resources and inaccessibility of care) on the context in which medical care was provided was inadequately addressed in the earlier literature. Not until the social-action era of the 1960's, with its emphasis on community organization and planning for the disenfranchised, did social work adopt a more catholic stance toward the public's needs and population accountability.

Wittman (96), building on earlier preventive social work, articulated the most realistic appraisal of the field to date. He proposed that such practice is "an organized and systematic effort to apply knowledge about social health and pathology in such manner as to enhance and preserve the social and mental health of the community". Thus, his definition implies a professional desire for intervention at both individual and community levels.

PUBLIC HEALTH SOCIAL WORK TODAY

Public health social workers practice in a variety of settings, including health departments, maternal and child and youth projects, neighborhood health centers, visiting nurse associations and home health agencies. Public health social work, however, is more than the practice of social work in public health settings. Social workers who address the preventive health needs of groups are practicing public health social work. In a series of papers, Reichert (66, 67, 68) lists the characteristics of the public-health approach in social work practice as orientation to prevention; population accountability; specification of health and disease determinants and dynamics in populations; and orientation to long-range strategies. His description captures the community and prevention foci of public health.

Social workers with a public health orientation perform a number of roles, including casefinding; consultation and education about the psychosocial impact of diseases to other disciplines; coordination of health service resources; participation in policy formulation; program planning and implementation; developing, monitoring and evaluating treatment services; and serving as project officers and program analysts for federally-funded grants and demonstration projects. These tasks are often performed in relation to such special populations as persons with genetic disorders, pregnant adolescents and high-risk newborns. Community-oriented functions are included in this perspective, but direct patient-care services are often peripheral benefits of programs in public health settings.

Public health principles have spread into areas of social work practice other than those in traditional public health settings (11). Public health as a field of study has become increasingly attractive to social workers. Today, several schools of social work offer joint social work/public health degrees. Social work as a whole strongly emphasizes individual-centered preventive techniques. These social work interventions have not been geared toward healthy persons' avoidance of or protection from health hazards; rather, intervention is with symptomatic and disabled populations (secondary and tertiary levels of prevention). A population focus is requisite only in that interventions may be directed toward a small group of individuals experiencing similar problems in a clinical setting. High-risk screening systems have been adopted in many hospitals to differentiate patients who do not have pressing needs for social work services from those in acute need of such services (65). In such instances, the screening is to prevent or impede the progression of psychosocial dysfunction among individuals or groups of people with some common attribute who are already patients.

Many preventive social work interventions emphasize Rapoport's conception of intervention at the beginning of acute need to promote optimal physical, psychological and social well-being. Thus, vulnerability is determined early to prevent or decrease problems. Cyr and Wattenberg (23) and Caplan (18) describe the preventive role of social work in a family-health clinic. Shaw and Shaw (76) have developed workshops for new parents and expectant parents with an educational, experiential, and preventive orientation to enhance parental self-esteem, facilitate communication, and implement mutual problem-solving. Preventive mental health services which focused on promoting good mental health in the mother-child relationship were offered to pregnant women with no known psychopathology or socioemotional problems. Clinic interviews and home visits focused on pregnancy and parenting on achieving life goals, stresses of labor and delivery and potential for sibling rivalry. Social workers used basic casework techniques — ego support clarification, anticipatory guidance and environmental modification — but tailored them specifically to prevention goals. Breslin (15) discusses the role and function of the social worker as manager of a preventive intervention service in a newborn care unit, working on family stresses precipitated by infant illness. Support and education began as soon as the infant entered the unit to preclude or mitigate the effects of major crises. Preventive social work counseling with families of epileptic children has centered on alleviation of parental fears and fantasies about the causes and sequelae of epilepsy; health education about epilepsy; treatment, medical management and control of seizures; and advice regarding behavioral management of the child (4).

Social workers have used practice and organizational and research skills in these preventive interventions. They have been nominally involved, however, in assessment of community health needs, program planning and service delivery for large groups of people, structural reforms, legislative lobbying and health policy development. Even in classical public health settings, social workers have been inattentive to improving environmental conditions, such as protection from occupational hazards, air pollution, radiation and accidents.

Current conceptions of public health social work are confounded by lack of discrimination and specificity as to definition and scope. A tendency to categorize diverse helping activities under the umbrella of public health social work has impeded refinement of the conceptual framework. The recently developed Standards for Social Work Programs in Public Health Settings (3) illustrate the breadth of the field. In addition to the standards for all health social work, the following three specific standards for social work in public health were added:

1. The social work component of a public health program shall participate in planning for the protection of communities from health hazards, the promotion of improved personal care and the prevention of ill health.
2. The social work component of a public health program shall participate in planning to assure that all persons-at-risk, in the target area have access to health services.
3. The social work component of a public health program shall collaborate with other disciplines in the provision for consumer participation in the planning and delivery of health services.

Thus, the key concepts emphasized as unique to social work in public health compared to social workers in other health settings are: prevention; accountability to an entire group at risk rather than to those who present themselves for service; and activities to promote consumer involvement in health planning and service delivery.

THE EPIDEMIOLOGIC FRAMEWORK

What is Epidemiology?

The basic method for measuring the health of a community is epidemiology. Epidemiology has been defined, among other ways, as the study of the distribution and determinants of disease in relation to characteristics of groups in which it occurs (47, 48). Thus, epidemiology examines patterns of disease in relation to a defined population.[(1)] The basic unit of analysis is a group of people, rather than an individual.

Epidemiology has both descriptive and analytic purposes. Descriptive epidemiology delineates characteristics such as demographic features (age, sex and race), biological markers (blood phenotype, antibody titres and hormonal status), socioeconomic attributes (education, occupation and income), and health habits (dietary intake

[(1)] For further discussion of patterns of disease occurrence, see Fox J, Hall C, Elveback L: *Epidemiology: Man and Disease*. New York, MacMillan, 1970.

and alcohol and tobacco consumption) of persons in a given locale. Analytic epidemiology seeks to understand etiologic factors and causal processes of a disease and control major health hazards in communities, for example, outbreaks of food poisoning and Legionnaire's Disease.

Another major contribution of epidemiology is its identification of groups at high risk for particular diseass and health problems. Risk implies the degree of probability of acquiring a disease. In considering a population-at-risk, one needs to take into account the sociodemographic characteristics and exposure to noxious stimuli of persons in the group. Risk assessment refers to the chance of adverse health consequences under a specific set of circumstances occurring at a later time. Behavioral risks of ill health have increasingly become a focus of attention. In particular, there is emphasis on firmly-entrenched, deleterious health habits such as smoking, excessive drinking, consumption of polysaturated fats, overworking and sedentary lifestyle. For example, cigarette smoking has been associated with increased likelihood of lung cancer. Risk factors are being pursued to increase understanding of the development of disease. This approach should facilitate design of risk-reducing behavioral strategies targeted to achieve individual lifestyle changes and, consequently, modify the risk of disease.

Epidemiologists analyze the transmission of infectious diseases in an agent-host-environment triad. Agent refers to a factor which is requisite for inducing a particular disease, disability or pathological state in a susceptible host. The agent may be physical (asbestos, ionizing radiation, lead), chemical (polyvinyl chloride, carbon monoxide), biological (influenza virus, tubercle bacillus), nutritional (enzyme and vitamin deficiencies), or social (low socioeconomic status, poor education, inadequate housing and sanitation). A susceptible host refers to a person who lacks sufficient resistance to a particular pathogenic agent and is, therefore, incapable of protecting himself/herself from contracting a disease. Environment refers to physical, biological, social, economic and climatic conditions, independent of the agent and host factors (e.g., the relationship between seat belt usage and auto accidents) which facilitate or deter the transmission of a disease. With increasing application of epidemiologic techniques to the study of diseases with non-specific etiologic agents (e.g., mental disorders), and recognition of the multifactorial origins of many chronic diseases (e.g., coronary heart disease), the traditional epidemiologic triangle has become polygonal. Although epidemiology developed by isolating communicable diseases, such as plague and cholera in the twentieth century, it is now being applied to the study of chronic diseases. In the 1970's, the scope of epidemiology was broadened to include social, psychological, and behavioral determinants of disease (e.g., social or familial disorganization, inadequate social supports, crowding, and stress) as well as diseases which do not necessarily have a known biological etiology (e.g., alcoholism, drug addiction, and various types of mental disorders). Hence, the terms social and psychosocial epidemiology emerged.[2]

Measurement of Morbidity and Mortality

Some states have mandatory reporting systems to facilitate disease control. Systematic reporting permits surveillance and monitoring of disease trends over time, such as seasonal variations as well as disease distribution according to population characteristics of age, sex, race, socioeconomic status and location. Because of factors such as social propriety, such reporting systems are frequently incomplete, as in the case of venereal diseases. Incidence and prevalence rates are used to describe morbidity (disease) patterns.

Certain concepts are essential to understanding and measuring the morbidity patterns of a target population or community. The term "incidence" refers to the risk of acquiring a disease in a defined population during a specified time interval. It is a rate that is calculated by the following formula:

$$\frac{\text{Number of new cases or events}}{\text{Population at risk during given time period}} \times 1{,}000 = \text{X cases per thousand}$$

Incidence measures the rate of development of a disease by providing information as to how many people become sick during a period of time. The value of incidence statistics lies in their providing information about the probability of disease, i.e., identifying factors that affect the likelihood of a group developing a disease.

[2] For detailed discussion of the scope of social epidemiology, see: Bahnson C: "Epistemological Perspectives of Physical Disease from the Psychodynamic Point of View." *American Journal of Public Health* 64:1034, 1974; Cassel J: "An Epidemiological Perspective of Psychosocial Factors in Disease Etiology." *American Journal of Public Health* 64:1040, 1974; Graham S: "The Sociological Approach to Epidemiology." *American Journal of Public Health* 64:1046, 1974; Syme L: "Behavioral Factors Associated with the Etiology of Physical Disease: A Social Epidemiological Approach." *American Journal of Public Health* 64:1043, 1974.

The term "prevalence" refers to a measure of the total number of living cases of a specified disease in a defined population at a given point in time. The prevalence rate is computed by the following formula:

$$\frac{\text{Number of cases of a disease}}{\text{Total population during given time period}} \times 1{,}000 = \text{X cases per thousand}$$

It is a snapshot of a community at a point in time and measures the amount of disease existing in a population. Thus, prevalence tell us how many people are sick during a period of time, and reflects both old and new cases of disease. No statements can be made about what factors may have caused the disease. Prevalence is a function of the number of people who have become ill in the past and the duration of their illness. Prevalence rates of chronic illnesses are higher than incidence rates since patients often present a long course of disability before cure or death occur. Since prevalence data reveal the extent of a problem, they are particularly useful for planning health services, facilities, and personnel, as well as providing on-going monitoring and surveillance of a health hazard such as venereal disease. Therefore, prevalence rates are essential for needs-assessment studies.

As there are obviously differences in the frequency with which people die during given time periods, mortality is a death rate that measures the risk of dying. The crude mortality rate is the number of deaths in a defined population and is computed by the following formula:

$$\frac{\text{Number of persons dying from a particular cause or all causes of death}}{\text{Total population during given time period}} \times 1{,}000 = \text{X cases per thousand}$$

Since the crude death rate often gives a distorted picture of the mortality experience, specific death rates can be calculated for particular population subgroups according to sociodemographic characteristics, such as among the aged, males, married and non-whites. Infant mortality measures the risk of dying during the first year of life among infants born alive. It is measured by the following rate:

$$\frac{\text{Number of infant deaths from birth to 365 days}}{\text{Total number of live births during given time period}} \times 1{,}000 = \text{X cases per thousand}$$

Infant mortality measures can be further subdivided into neonatal mortality, which is the number of infant deaths in the first 28 days of life per 1,000 live births and postneonatal mortality, those occurring between one month to one year of life. Infant mortality is an important measure because it is a sensitive indicator of a population's health and often a crude measure of its economic status.

Screening is the major public health method that has been used to prevent a morbid event or initiate early treatment. Screening aims to reduce morbidity and mortality in a population by detecting disease in asymptomatic individuals, and through early diagnosis or case-finding in those with presenting symptoms. Thus, the pap smear is a screening technique to detect cervical-uterine cancer in healthy women as well as to diagnose this disease in women with suspicious or abnormal smears. In the latter case, the outcome of the screening procedure may be confirmation rather than identification so that the individual can seek early treatment.

Several criteria are used to evaluate the efficacy of a screening program. The validity of a test indicates how well the procedure discriminates between individuals in whom disease is present and those in whom it is not. Validity has two dimensions, sensitivity and specificity. Sensitivity refers to the ability of the test to give a positive finding when the person truly has the disease under study (a true positive), while specificity is the ability of the test to give a negative finding when the person tested does not have the disease (a true negative). The reliability of a test refers to the ability of the test to give reproducible, repeatable, consistent results.

It would be best for a screening test to be both 100 percent sensitive and specific, but in reality, this does not occur. Rather, high sensitivity of a test is usually at the expense of its specificity, i.e., there is an inverse association between the two dimensions. Since the demarcation line between health and disease is often not clear, e.g., blood pressure readings, a decision must be made, independent of the outcome of the screen, regarding a cutoff point that will differentiate the healthy from the unhealthy. Ideally one would want to choose a cutoff point that gives the lowest number of false positives and false negatives. Decisions about such classifications, which determine diagnosis, depend on a number of considerations, including the cost in terms of identifying false positives, likelihood of not identifying people with the disease, likelihood of the population undergoing a subsequent screening in a reasonable period of time, and the prevalence of the disease (49).

In addition, when considering a test for screening a mass population, its cost-benefit value should be considered in relation to its economic feasibility (it almost has to be inexpensive), seriousness of the health problem in the community (a deadly disease like plague should be given top priority), acceptability (proctosigmoidoscopy to detect colon-rectal cancer has not gained widespread popularity because of discomforts associated with the test), acceptability of treatment for a disease (drugs to treat hypertension often have psychologically-devastating side effects such as sexual impotence), and availability of and access to diagnostic and treatment facilities (geographic proximity, time of the day the test is offered).

The Application of Epidemiology to Social Work Practice

The 1962 Council on Social Work Education Seminar on Public Health Concepts and Social Work Education (22), echoing the earlier work of Rice (70) and Buell (13), indicated that social work should apply epidemiological principles more often and more effectively. Howell (33) suggested the potential of epidemiology as a problem-oriented approach in which social workers can examine an array of factors influencing social problems (such as adoption, illegitimate births, alcoholism, child abuse and delinquency), formulate interventions to reduce the incidence of a disorder, find cases early and remedy disability. To Hamovitch (28) and Katz (40), social work could readily adopt the tools of epidemiology, particularly hypothesis development and testing, examination of associations between adverse health conditions and health behaviors, risk-assessment techniques, measurement of the effectiveness of treatment interventions, and support of rationales for policy recommendations.

How will epidemiology affect social work in the future? Recently Meyer (52) proposed that an epidemiological orientation could help unify the fragmented approach to social work, characterized by diverse practice settings and treatment modalities, and contribute to delineating professional activity with greater precision. She suggests that because specialization lends itself to the delimitation of boundaries, the scope of critical variables affecting a population can be narrowed, and thus make workers' tasks less unwieldy and easier to specify. Her application of epidemiology to social work is problem-oriented — concerned as it is with the incidence and prevalence of psychosocial adaptation — and is framed within an ecological or ecosystems perspective.

Epidemiology is a wonderful tool for addressing community health problems. The community is an object of study in its own right, but also exerts a powerful influence on individuals and subgroups within it. In addition, there is an interaction between health-related behaviors or individuals and the characteristics of the community. Analysis of community structure and processes provides information about the health status and attitudes of residents, organization of health and social services, including their accessibility, acceptability, continuity, and quality, and patterns of health service use. Such data are essential to planning for the provision and adoption of new health services, casefinding, and policy formation, development and advocacy.

In conducting a community health assessment, epidemiologic principles applied to the study of disease are broadened to describe the signs and symptoms of community pathology or malfunctioning, i.e., surveying the pulse of the community. A community health analysis entails information about the sociodemographic characteristics of residents, manpower capabilities, individual and community health practices, degree of disability and work loss, population density and values.

Supplemental data can be gathered from a number of sources to aid in identifying key problems in a community. Census reports provide information about the composition of the community and population density. Nationwide morbidity statistics can be obtained from the National Center for Health Statistics, which engages in continuous health interviews, psychological and physical health examinations and nutritional status surveys on selected population groups. The Center for Disease Control and the World Health Organization maintain nationwide and worldwide reporting systems on many communicable diseases, while the National Institute of Mental Health provides updated epidemiologic data about selected mental disorders. On the local level, many communities maintain registries for the surveillance and monitoring of chronic diseases. Other valuable sources of data include the Department of Public Social Services, Veterans Administration, insurance companies, hospitals and clinics.

Community health planning and assessment in relation to hospitals, prisons, schools, mental health facilities and board and care homes can be problem-focused or goal-oriented. When planning is based on a problem-oriented approach, problem identification becomes the first step in the planning process, such as in needs-assessment studies. With a goal approach, outcome is first considered. In either case, though the ordering is different, the planning process should include goal-setting, problem identification, design plan, implementation, and evaluation of results. For example, in the case of alcohol-related problems among the elderly, it is important to identify: 1) the incidence and prevalence of the problem, 2) number of agencies that potentially serve the elderly alcoholic and the type and level of services provided, 3) drinking patterns and their developmental onset, 4) needs of the client population (physical impairments, stress, financial problems, housing difficulties), 5) priorities for service, 6) personnel resources, 7) cost of funding new programs, 8) agency competence in service delivery, and 9) education and prevention programs as well as treatment services. By creating a profile of this population, social workers can target their interventions toward those in greatest need, engage in community outreach and develop service protocols.

Rape prevention and treatment provide an excellent illustration of how epidemiologic principles can be applied to social work practice. A social worker attached to a health maintenance organization may be assigned the task of finding out whether rape is a common problem in the community. To learn about the incidence of this problem, a needs-assessment study must be conducted in the community. Using a problem-oriented approach to health planning, the social worker will first need to interact with judicial, law-enforcement, hospital and school officials to ascertain the magnitude of the rape problem. Data from these organizations will provide information about patterns of rape incidents — sociodemographic characteristics relating to those most likely to be raped (person), where rapes have occurred (place) and time of occurrence (time). If rape is identified as a major threat to a community, the social worker, along with consumers and other professionals, can then begin to plan, develop, implement, and evaluate prevention and treatment strategies. Many avenues could be pursued, including development and coordination of services by a network of institutions; community education about what to do if approached, the physical and psychological effects on victims, and the need to report incidents of rape; sensitizing police, hospital, mental health and law enforcement personnel to treat victims in a non-punitive manner; and establishment of standardized hospital protocols for the care of sexual assault victims.[3]

MAJOR PUBLIC HEALTH PROBLEMS AND A PUBLIC HEALTH APPROACH TO SOCIAL WORK PRACTICE

This section discusses how social workers use a public health approach to solving selected public health problems. Two health program areas — maternal/child health and substance abuse — illustrate the interplay between public health and social work in the community. Each problem is considered in relation to: 1) definition and etiology, 2) descriptive epidemiology and scope, 3) legislative, policy and program developments, 4) treatment and service trends, and 5) current and potential social work roles.

Maternal and Child Health

Maternal and child health concerns have been a traditional area of interest for public health social work. Public health efforts have been directed toward immunizations and well-baby care, nutritional improvement, dental hygiene, identification of orthopedic, neurologic, visual and hearing impairments, communicable disease control and prenatal care. The creation of the Children's Bureau in 1912 was the first attempt by the Federal government to organize services for the welfare of children in a systematic fashion. As previously noted, the 1921 Shepard-Towner Act and subsequent Social Security Act of 1935 broadened governmental interest in child health to include the health of mothers as well.

At the beginning of the twentieth century, infant and maternal mortality were major causes of deaths in the United States. As a result of improved access to medical care, expanded maternal and child health services, communicable disease control, better living conditions and sanitary measures, family planning education and improved technology for the care of high-risk mothers and infants, there has been a sharp decline in maternal, fetal, perinatal and infant mortal-

[3] For example, see Abarbanel A: "The Roles of the Clinical Social Worker: Hospital-Based Management." *In Rape and Sexual Assault*, C. Warner (ed.) Germantown, Maryland, Aspen Systems, 1980, pp. 141-165, for discussion of a model hospital protocol.

ity rates. For example, the infant death rate though stable between the mid-1950's to mid-1960's fell to 11.2 per 1,000 live births in 1982 (85).

In 1980, a U.S. Surgeon General's Workshop on Maternal and Infant Health was held to consider the current status of maternal and child health services as well as to develop policy recommendations for a national social strategy to reduce infant mortality and morbidity and improve pregnancy outcome in the United States, particularly for populations-at-risk (90). High priority areas in maternal and infant care were outlined, including:

1. Implementation of a national policy that guarantees care to pregnant women in the first trimester of pregnancy, especially prenatal evaluation and counseling regarding the risks of smoking, alcohol consumption and other drugs and environmental hazards.
2. Maintenance of an adequate set of standards of prenatal and infant care, including services for nonpregnant women relating to the occurrence and course of future pregnancy, e.g., infertility, sexually-transmitted diseases, nutrition, genetic screening, substance abuse problems, comprehensive family planning; services in the prenatal period, e.g., pregnancy continuation counseling, childbirth preparation and nutritional assessment; services in the perinatal and postpartum periods, e.g., counseling regarding infant development and behavior, parenting skills; health education; and access to medical services; and infant and family health services in the first year of life, e.g., complete physical examinations, immunizations, and maternal nutritional needs-assessment.
3. Provision of a regionalized system of maternal and child health services that include primary care, educational activities and an evaluation component.
4. Provision of adequate financial support for services, especially increased state funding for perinatal services.
5. Expansion of payment mechanisms for prenatal care, delivery and ongoing child health care for the uninsured through public financing and private insurance.
6. Carrying out of research programs on the causes of Sudden Infant Death Syndrome, initiation of labor, congenital defects and nutrition.
7. Establishment of state and/or local perinatal surveillance systems and training for such personnel.

Thus, the three major themes that emerged for maternal and child health policy include: improvement of service delivery to the underserved, expansion of health promotion and prevention services, and knowledge development.

Major maternal and child health care efforts are directed toward: identification of maternal risk factors for poor obstetrical outcome, reaching high-risk newborn, delivery of prenatal care and provision of services for children with developmental disabilities and congenital anomalies. Prenatal care ideally begins in the first trimester of pregnancy, but unfortunately, about one-quarter of pregnant women receive less than adequate care. Since the early 1970's a regionalized concept of perinatal care delivery, which includes newborn intensive care units and neonatal transport systems, has been implemented by all states to ensure availability of and access to all levels of care for pregnant women and their newborn.[4] To date, however, use and type of perinatal services have not had a significant impact on reducing perinatal mortality.

Increasing attention is centered on genetic screening and counseling so that couples can make informed choices about whether to undertake or sustain pregnancy. An armamentarium of modern technology has been developed to reduce a woman's likelihood of giving birth to an abnormal baby. Amniocentesis is used for women at risk for genetic abnormalities and recommended for those aged 35 and over because of their increased risk for Down's Syndrome. Fetal monitoring with ultra-sound techniques can be instituted to assess intrauterine fetal development and distress.

Accidents, sexually-transmitted diseases, pregnancy among adolescents and child abuse have emerged as a result of changing social practices and behaviors in modern civilization. Family planning has become an issue as couples increasingly choose to defer childbearing or not to have children.

Sudden Infant Death Syndrome (SIDS), or crib death, occurs in about 7,500 to 10,000 babies per year. Death occurs suddenly, usually when an infant is asleep. The rapidity of mortality often results in guilt and sustained grief among the victim's survivors. The etiology and prevention of SIDS have remained a mystery, but there is some evidence to suggest that the syndrome is related to intrauterine

---

[4] For example, see Gluck, L: "Perspectives in Perinatology, Present and Future". In Proceedings of *The First National Workshop on the Delivery of Hospital Social Work Services in Obstetrics/Gynecology and Services to the Newborn*, R. Breslin (ed.), Yale-New Haven Medical Center, 1974, pp. 67-76; Johnson K: "The Promise of Regional Perinatal Care." In *The Surgeon General's Workshop on Maternal and Infant Health*, DHHS Publication No. (PHS) 81-50161, U.S. Departmment of Health and Human Services, Public Health Service, 1981; McCormick M: "The Regionalization of Perinatal Care". *American Journal Public Health*, 71:571, 1981.

irregularities, perinatal hypoxia, mother's age at first pregnancy and high parity (42, 79).

SIDS provides an excellent opportunity for social workers to use primary prevention techniques to preclude daily living problems or mental disorders among survivors and help them deal with their bereavement and loss. For example, development of groups for surviving parents and siblings, community organization to improve existing community resources and develop effective service delivery networks, professional and public education about the emotional dimensions of SIDS, and promotion of early prenatal care are responsibilities that social workers can assume. Hawkins (32) discusses the special needs of the surviving siblings since parents often treat them as if they were dead or are overprotective and overindulgent.

Accidents present a serious health threat to children and account for almost 40 percent of the mortality rate for children between the ages of one and five. Accidents, including poisonings as a result of ingesting common household items, can also cause severe nonfatal injuries. Over the past fifteen years there has been a significant decline in the mortality rate for poisoning in preschool children, largely due to the establishment of local poison control crisis centers and improved child-safe packaging of drugs (50).

Social workers in primary care settings, well-baby clinics, family planning centers and pediatric and obstetrical clinics can educate parents about the risks of accidental childhood poisoning. Parents need to be made aware of the importance of purchasing and using safety closures on all bottles of medicine, putting toxic household substances out of children's reach, keeping ipecac syrup and other first-aid materials at home, and stripping lead-based paints from older dwellings. In addition, parents should be made familiar with the poison information telephone service should they need to call when faced with an emergency. Because the child or mother visits one of these ambulatory care centers for another reason, education for prevention of accidents is rarely offered.

Sexually-transmitted diseases are becoming an increasing threat to newborns and pregnant women. Many sexually-transmitted diseases cause infections in infants as well as sterility and tubal pregnancies in young women. Women infected at the time of delivery may spread the infection during passage of the babv through the birth canal. Some bacterial and viral infections are so mild that they are difficult to diagnose. In particular, herpes simplex infections have a high likelihood of causing infant mortality or severe neurological defects. Fortunately, screening for the presence of the virus in pregnant women can prevent such tragedies. Women with positive test results can undergo a Caesarean section delivery so that the fetus will not be exposed to the virus in the birth canal.

Gonorrhea has reached epidemic proportions, victimizing more than two and one-half million people in the United States each year (46). It is likely that changing patterns of sexual behavior, e.g., early sexual activity of adolescents and multiple sex partners, have increased the incidence of gonorrhea. Gonococcal bacteria are transmitted during sexual contact and can cause infection, temporary pain and discomfort. If untreated for a significant period of time, however, gonorrhea can lead to serious and chronic health complications, including infertility, arthritis, pelvic inflammatory disease, blindness, tubal pregnancy, and among newborn offspring, eye damage. With prompt treatment, however, gonorrhea can be easily controlled with antibiotics.

Preventive efforts to control gonorrhea center on public education. The need for early treatment, availability of diagnostic screening, and the asymptomatic nature of the disease, and its causes are stressed. Social workers provide community health education to high-risk groups, e.g., school programs for adolescents and their parents and health education for the gay and lesbian communities (37). In terms of detection and treatment, they are involved in casefinding and tracking identified disease carriers and contacts, developing hotlines to provide information and referral services, and advocating the need for treatment in a context sensitive to the stigmatizing connotation of sexually-transmitted diseases.

Teenage childbearing in the United States is of vital concern to public health officials. Although the adolescent birth rate has been on the decrease, the pregnancy rate is on the rise. The population of women aged 15-19 years of age has increased as a result of the high birth rate in the late 1950's, as has the number of teenage marriages. From 1960 through 1976, the number of women in this age group increased by 57 percent, from 6.6 million to 10.4 million, but the birth rate decreased from 89.1 to 53.5 births per 1,000 women aged 15-19 (87). In 1976, births to teenage mothers accounted for 18 percent of all births and has remained at this level. There are 1.3 million children living with teenage mothers, about half of whom are unmarried. The out-of-wedlock birth rate for women in this age group increased 57 percent between 1960 and 1976, from 15.3 to 24.0 per 1,000 unmarried women 15-19 years of age (87). There are more black than white single teenage women, reflecting differential outcomes of out-of-wedlock pregnancies and a higher percent of black sexually-active young women.

Increased sexual activity at an earlier age is largely responsible for the high number of adolescent pregnancies. Restricting teenagers' accessibility to contraceptive and abortion information and services does not appear to decrease their activity. Media glorification of youth and sexuality reinforces sexual activity as an everyday occurrence in life.

Unmarried adolescent girls may opt for childbearing rather than terminate a pregnancy because childbearing maintains their culture of poverty and dependency (25). Adolescent females raised in an economically and socially-deprived environment may realize their limited potential for educational, economic and career advancement, and therefore view motherhood as a way of achieving personal status, enhancing self-concept and attaining emotional gratification. Thus, there may be little incentive to break the cycle of marginal existence.

Teenage pregnancy is costly in terms of its health, social and economic consequences.[5] Infant mortality during the first year of life is highest among babies of teenaged mothers, and maternal mortality and the risk of having a low-birth-weight baby are greater. Non-fatal maternal complications, such as toxemia and anemia, are also higher for teenage mothers. Low birth weight can contribute to not only infant mortality, but birth injuries and developmental disabilities. Early childbearing is a major impediment to completing a school career, as about one-half of teenage mothers under 18 years of age never complete high school. Future career opportunities and earnings potential are limited, and result in low-status jobs because of skill deficits.

Ignorance about pregnancy and contraception is high among teens. The out-of-wedlock birthrate has continued to rise in most groups of teenagers, especially among fifteen- to seventeen-year-old whites. Although the proportion of teenagers using contraceptives has increased in the last decade, use of the pill and intrauterine devices (IUD) has declined recently. Teenagers prefer foam, condoms, diaphragms, and withdrawal as methods of contraception.

Only a few states require schools to provide family life and sex education. Generally, the decision is left to the discretion of local

[5] For a lengthy discussion of the problems of adolescent childbearing, see *Teenage Pregnancy: The Problem That Hasn't Gone Away*. New York, The Alan Guttmacher Institute, 1981.

school boards, and many states have not set policies regarding such instruction. Family planning education alone, however, is not sufficient to prevent teenage pregnancies. Fear that their family will find out they are using birth control often leads teenagers to delay obtaining contraceptives, Between 1968-1978, the number of abortions among teenagers nearly doubled. Teens, however, are also likely to delay seeking abortions because of parental consent requirements, cost and psychological factors.

Early prenatal care can aid in averting or reducing the likelihood of health problems as a result of early childbearing for both mother and child. Unfortunately, most teens do not receive prenatal care in the first trimester of pregnancy. Since day care for infants is often limited, it is difficult for teenage mothers to complete their high school education or pursue employment. Foster care, legal assistance, pregnancy counseling and child abuse prevention services are often inadequate. The 1978 Adolescent Health Services, Pregnancy Prevention and Care Act was designed to provide supportive services to pregnant girls, teenage parents and infants and to coordinate the network of existing medical, social, vocational and child-care services. Unfortunately, budget appropriations for such programs have been inadequate. The 1980 Supreme Court decision which declared the Hyde Amendment constitutional blocked Federal abortion funding, upon which so many teenage women are dependent.

Social workers in school settings can play a key role in educating parents about the need for sex education of their children. This may entail encouraging parents to preview the curricula, books and films intended for presentation to their children. Having reviewed the materials, parents may be better able to talk about sex with their children and reinforce the information presented in school. Some social workers in pediatric and maternal and child health clinics engage in extensive primary prevention community outreach efforts to educate teenagers before they become sexually active. Pregnancy counseling is an area in which social workers have been traditionally involved. Teens need to be counseled in a nonjudgmental fashion about the options and risks and benefits that are open to them — prenatal care, legal abortion, and adoption — so that they can make an informed choice. Follow-up social services are also needed to help acclamate pregnant teens to their situation and heighten their awareness of the need for contraception.

Family planning is integral to improving the health of mothers and children — for optimal quality of life, economic independence and security and effective parenting. It includes pregnancy counseling, birth control information, abortion counseling, sex education, and venereal disease screening. Prior to 1965, family planning assistance was primarily geared to the middle class; it was not widely available to lower-income groups as governmental-funded agencies generally did not offer fiscal support for contraceptive advice.

In 1970, Federal legislation, the Family Planning Services and Population Research Act, paved the way for organized family planning services by providing fiscal support for the initiation of programs; two years later, additional legislation made family planning services available to welfare recipients. On the local level, government-supported family planning services were provided by hospitals, health departments and planned parenthood centers.

With the legalization of abortion in 1973, abortion services were recognized as essential to family planning. Growing awareness of the socioeconomic necessity of family planning and the tendency for some Catholics to deviate from official church ideology have served to loosen some of the existing barriers to limiting family size and avoiding unwanted pregnancies. Nevertheless, abortion still remains a controversial, politically-charged issue for both consumers and health professionals. Among some cultural minorities, there has been opposition on ideological grounds. Some people have equated abortion and sterilization with social control of reproduction; a few have characterized it as genocide. Today, there is a resurgence in anti-abortion sentiment among the public. In a number of states, legislation to restrict or prohibit abortions, except in cases of endangerment to a mother's life, rape, incest or fetal abnormality has been introduced, while other states have eliminated coverage of abortions for Medicaid recipients. On the Federal level, the Helms-Hyde anti-abortion bill introduced before a judiciary subcommittee declares that human life "shall be deemed to exist from conception." The intent of this bill is to allow states to prosecute abortion as murder. If this legislation is constitutional, it will reverse the landmark 1973 Supreme Court decision that a woman as a right to terminate her pregnancy.

Direct social work services, such as evaluation of psychosocial needs and referral to community resources, are integral to family planning. Abortion counseling programs focus on helping women understand the consequences of their decision to terminate pregnancy or realize alternatives, plan for effective contraceptive methods, and increase knowledge of reproduction in a supportive environment.[6] Social workers provide pre-operative counseling to women requesting sterilization to insure that their reproductive rights are not violated, informed consent is secured, and irreversible elimination of reproductive capacity is understood. In many hospitals, social workers are members of the committee that approves patients' requests for sterilization. At one metropolitan hospital (75), social workers screen women at high risk for psychosocial problems (secondary prevention) and provide group counseling to help them explore their reasons for undergoing sterilization and cope with the aftermath of surgery (tertiary prevention). Although professional counselors may face personal moral dilemmas about abortion (38), they should not lose objectivity and permit their values to interfere with the needs of their clients.

A public health social work approach to family planning includes consultation with and training of other professional and paraprofessional staff as well as consumer education and advocacy. Skills in epidemiologic methods are useful to identify populations requiring family planning information, e.g., teenagers, the retarded, and older women of childbearing age. Stimulation of consumer/community participation in family planning is essential. Social workers have traditionally been involved in program planning, service delivery, and training of community workers in casefinding, referrals and follow-up. They need to become more active in educational and advocacy measures.

Social workers can educate consumers how to work effectively with community agencies so that family planning services are routinely incorporated into such social and health programs as Aid to Families with Dependent Children, maternity homes and community mental health centers. At the same time, social work planners can explore whether services are geographically accessible, available at convenient times and provided in a supportive environmental milieu. Sex education about the costs and benefits of different contraceptive methods and the reproductive process is particularly critical for groups at high risk for pregnancy.

The entry of social workers into the Federal, state or local political arena is a necessary professional role. Not only must social workers devote themselves to securing funding for family planning programs, but they should insure that family planning is integrated into a com-

---

[6] An excellent discussion of abortion counseling can be found in Kaminsky B. Sheckter L. "Abortion Counseling in a General Hospital." *Health and Social Work* 4:93, May, 1979.

prehensive system of maternal and child health care service delivery (51). Social workers need to examine family planning policies at the state and local levels to determine whether there are restrictive barriers and discriminatory practices, as in the case of abortion funding practices for Medicaid recipients (27). This may entail organizing a coalition of local, state and Federal professional, paraprofessional and lay organizations to lobby for the enactment of desired or repeal of oppressive legislation.

Genetic disorders of parents, such as Tay-Sachs, Huntington's Chorea, sickle cell anemia, hemophilia, Down's Syndrome, phenylketonuria (PKU) and polycystic kidney disease, can cause painful and prolonged illness, profound retardation and premature death among their offspring. For example, severe brain damage occurs in approximately one out of every 15,000 live newborns with PKU. Fortunately, PKU can be detected immediately after birth through routine screening which is compulsory in many states, and is treatable by means of a dietary regimen. There are large social, psychological and economic costs to both victims of genetic disorders and their families. Many other birth defects are potentially preventable if couples desiring children undergo genetic screening.

It is estimated that the costs of mass genetic screening are about one-tenth of those that would be incurred for the care required by a child's handicap. Screening efforts attempt to identify adults who are carrying abnormal genes, detect fetal abnormalities and identify newborns with treatable genetic disorders so as to initiate therapy at an early stage (61). The resulting information is used to help couples make informed decisions about childbearing and abortion. Governmental intervention in genetic screening and counseling is a particularly emotional issue because of its involvement in reproductive decision-making, setting priorities for medical care, and financing such care for individuals at risk for genetic diseases (45).

The management and treatment of genetic disorders require a multi-disciplinary team approach. The conventional genetic counseling team consists of a physician, cytogeneticist, and biochemist, but recently there has been increasing attention to the role of a social worker. Genetic counseling consists of: 1) diagnosis of the genetic disorder, including identification of the genetic mechanism involved; 2) prognosis, 3) identification of risk of recurrence for parents and victim, and the probable risk among the latter's siblings; 4) treatment plan; 5) family counseling around prognosis and reproductive alternatives, and 6) continuous follow-up (14).

Social workers traditionally function in the area of tertiary prevention, e.g., helping families cope with the medical and social impact of their child's defect — regimens imposed as part of treatment, behavioral and developmental problems, anxieties about future pregnancies, financial problems and integrating genetic information (12, 19, 73). They have seldom given genetic information and advice.

There is some controversy as to whether social workers should provide and interpret genetic information to couples. Burns (14) and Katz (41) believe that non-physician professionals as well as lay people can provide such counseling if given adequate education and training about basic genetic information and probabilities for reproductive outcomes. Kiely *et al.* (44) suggest that in addition to their role in intervention, social workers need to adopt a "monitoring-in-anticipation" (anticipatory guidance) approach with families at risk for genetic disorders, i.e., secondary prevention. Differences with respect to whether a directive or non-directive technique is the best approach to genetic counseling have contributed to role tensions among the various professional disciplines (64).

Motivation of social workers to participate in genetic counseling appears to be high, as demonstrated by some of the articles in recent social work literature.[8] In 1976, the Health Research and Health Service Amendments (Public Law 94-278) established a national genetic disease program for basic and applied research, detection, counseling and education, but this legislation did not specify which professional disciplines should be involved. As Katz (41) notes, California has been a pioneer in the training of non-medical genetics counselors under a program sponsored by its state health department. If the evaluation of this program proves such counselors to be effective, then it should ease the way for social workers to participate in areas broader than psychosocial counseling of couples at high risk for genetic disorders.

The provision of genetic counseling per se, i.e., informing parents of the statistical risks of abnormalities in the progeny, requires that social workers be equipped with the knowledge base, practice skills and research capabilities needed for this task. Peterson and Nevin (61) suggest that genetic training be included in the social work curriculum. For example, social workers would need to be aware of the known and unknown etiologies of specific hereditary disorders, the probabilities of a woman giving birth to a defective child in subsequent pregnancies, and the risk that a couple's normal child may be a carrier of the gene defect. The resistance of traditional service providers to accept social workers as genetic counselors will undoubtedly be a barrier to expanding the parameters of social work in this field.

Social workers need to increase their visibility in advocating for people afflicted with genetically-inherited diseases, especially for policy and program development. These activities include: lobbying for catastrophic insurance coverage, ensuring adequate community support for programs, encouraging school systems to develop adequate educational resources for impaired children, and organizing community-wide screening for genetic diseases.

Developmental disabilities occur in about 7 percent of all babies born in the United States each year. One-fifth of all deaths of children aged four or less are a result of congenital physical or mental defects. Congenital defects are structural, functional, or biochemical anomalies that develop in the human organism both before and after birth and cause abnormal developmental mechanisms. These defects may stem from genetic aberrations, i.e., gene mutations or chromosomal abnormalities (Down's Syndrome), prenatal infection transmitted to the developing fetus (rubella and syphilis), gestational disorders (prematurity and low birth weight), insufficient supply of oxygen at birth (anoxia), toxic poisoning, ionizing radiation, chemotherapeutic agents, maternal substance abuse, and metabolic disorders (phenylketonuria). A number of developmental problems are associated with diseases and conditions occurring in early childhood (measles, meningitis, encephalitis, polio and lead poisoning). The causes of approximately two-thirds to three-quarters of all congenital disorders, however, are of unknown origin but are thought to result from an interplay of adverse environmental and genetic factors.

Prevention efforts are concentrated on mass immunizations for infectious diseases, screening for pre- and post-natal disorders, and community-based differential diagnostic centers for evaluation, treatment and follow-up. Prior to the 1960's, institutional care was the predominant type of "rehabilitation" offered to the developmentally disabled with extensive mental retardation. Since the 1960's, there has been a marked trend toward deinstitutionalization of the developmentally disabled, housing the severely impaired in smaller residences, home maintenance, and offering therapeutic and educational services. The disabled were mainstreamed into the community on the assumption that adequate resources, e.g., family support, counseling, training in activities of daily living, vocational rehabilitation, sheltered workshops and halfway houses, would be provided. The Education for All Handicapped Children Act of 1975 was established to ensure special education and services for all handicapped children.

Social workers traditionally work in tertiary prevention programs for the congenitally and developmentally disabled, helping families adjust to their child's impaired intellectual and social deficits and disruptive behavioral disorders. There is a need, however, for social workers to be concerned with how developmental disabilities impact the community. The aftermath of the 1964-65 Rubella epidemic that resulted in some 30,000 congenitally impaired infants illustrates the importance of community planning, long-range strategies and a multi-disciplinary health team to control and manage a disease in which there is residual disability. Impairments ranged from single-organ sites such as hearing loss, cardiac lesions, glaucoma and cataracts, to multiple-organ sites (any combination of the aforementioned and often mild to severe psychomotor retardation).

The consequences of this devastating epidemic called for development of a network of coordinated services to meet the social, psychological and educational needs of these handicapped children and their families.[(7)] A social worker and public health nurses engaged in casefinding, surveillance, identification of children's learning and social deficits and coordination of community planning efforts. Existing community facilities were surveyed to ascertain the need for supplemental services. The social workers, assuming the primary role as service coordinators, served as change agents to facilitate program planning, revision and expansion. Mediation among community agencies was essential to help them realize their limits and obligations. Liaison between families and agencies, through which children's needs were matched with available resources, was also carried out. When the project initiated its own experimental preschool for multihandicapped children, the social worker provided individual and group counseling to the parents of the children (20). Thus, the project became a prototype for a public health approach to meet the complex needs of a specialized population with the use of community organization and planning skills for the early identification, diagnosis and management of the multihandicapped.

Rubella has been virtually controlled since the development of a vaccine, and childhood immunizations and antibody titre screening

---

[(7)] A Rubella Birth Defect Evaluation Project was established in 1965 at New York University — Bellevue Hospital Medical Center by means of an emergency grant from the National Foundation — March of Dimes.

of pregnant women have become routine medical practices. Unfortunately, many communities lacked the foresight to anticipate long-term needs of this multihandicapped population. Today, the project has become a developmental disabilities center (DDC)[(8)] and is funded by monies from the Deaf-Blind Centers Act (an amendment to Title VI), Public Law 94-142, Medicaid, consumers, and various local agencies.

Despite some role overlap between social work and nursing staff, the social workers tend to be primary service providers in the areas of counseling around children's socio-emotional adjustment and residential treatment, parent education, brokerage for parents and community agencies, and parental and legislative advocacy, while the nursing staff performs similar functions as they relate to health status, e.g., counseling parents who seemingly misunderstand their child's diagnosis, as well as intake coordination, physical diagnosis and health maintenance. The social workers provide consultation and in-service education to social workers and other non-social work professional staff in developmental disabilities units. A great deal of social work time is expended not only on needs-assessment, but assisting agencies to build, expand and strengthen their service repertoire and coordinating services among those agencies who have maintained their vested interests in treating children with single-site impairments. One result of planned community endeavors has been the development of group homes with twenty-four hour staff coverage and pre-vocational and vocational training of the multihandicapped with low social and intellectual functioning (24). Social workers provide guidance to parents whose children attend the DDC's experimental preschool and serve on the local school districts' Committee on the Handicapped which evaluates and recommends educational placement for children. Thus, social work practice in developmental disabilities has strong public health components, and focuses on population, community, health planning, and primary and secondary prevention.

Child abuse and neglect traverse all classes and ethnic groups in the United States. It has been estimated that some six hundred thousand to one million children are abused each year, of whom two to five thousand will die. Although child abuse cases have traditionally appeared in the caseloads of protective agencies, hospital

[(8)] The DDC is located at St. Luke's-Roosevelt Hospital Medical Center in New York City and sees more than 100 new children per year; the ongoing population has reached 1,500.

emergency room personnel are increasingly seeing abused children with fractures, malnutrition and extensive bruises.

Child abuse refers to nonaccidental physical injury and neglect, emotional abuse and deprivation, sexual abuse, verbal abuse and other forms of exploitation of children. Child abuse is not a new phenomenon, but victimized children were not brought to the attention of protective service organizations until the last quarter of the nineteenth century.

In 1962, the Children's Bureau formulated a model child abuse reporting law, and by 1970, all fifty states, the District of Columbia, Puerto Rico, and the Virgin Islands enacted mandatory reporting statutes. Reporting systems are essential for identifying suspected cases of abuse and neglect, but they do not ensure that legal action will be taken since many acts of child violence are not reported. Cases of physical injury are often not diagnosed as abuse because health professionals have tended to minimize the seriousness of the injury or are reluctant to question suspected abusers (26). Reporting systems and sensational press publicity, however, have served to heighten recognition of its seriousness and widespread threat to children's well-being. It is difficult to say, however, whether the incidence of child abuse has reached epidemic proportions or merely reflects greater frequency of reporting suspect cases to human service personnel. In addition, reliable estimates of child abuse and neglect are difficult to ascertain because of differential definitions and reporting systems among the states (36).

From an historical perspective, child abuse problems were assumed to be related to the incident itself and therefore mitigated once the abusive or neglectful behavior was extinguished. Recently it has been recognized that conditions of poor hygiene, malnutrition, poverty, and inadequate housing often accompany child abuse. Deficits in physical growth and development, socialization, interpersonal relations, and cognitive, language and motor skills development may occur (54).

The National Committee for Prevention of Child Abuse was established in 1972 to increase public awareness of child abuse and promote policy and programs. Public Law 93-247, the Child Abuse Prevention and Treatment Act of 1974, established a National Center on Child Abuse and Neglect (NCCAN). The goals of NCCAN include: 1) determining the incidence and severity of child abuse in the United States; 2) coordinating the activities of the network of agencies dealing with prevention and treatment of child abuse and neglect;

3) establishing an information clearinghouse for the dissemination of training materials; 4) providing technical assistance to public and non-profit organizations, and 5) ascertaining prevention and treatment interventions. Demonstration projects were set up to provide parent education about child-rearing practices, information and referral services, prenatal and perinatal parent support programs and home health visitor programs. In addition, these projects trained people in the community about the dynamics of child abuse and established community surveillance systems for reporting suspected cases.

Increased public awareness of the incidence and severity of the problem of child abuse and neglect has resulted in the development of a number of community-based prevention and treatment services for child abuse. The Salvation Army, Big Brothers/Big Sisters of America and the Child Welfare League of America provide care and services for deprived, neglected children and their families. In addition, hot lines, self-help groups such as Parents Anonymous, emergency parent services, remediation centers and Suspected Child Abuse and Neglect (SCAN) programs have emerged in response to the pressing needs of abused children. Many hospitals for children have multidisciplinary child abuse teams to coordinate medical, social and psychological services for abused children and their families and educational services for the community.

Social workers have identified with the medical model of child welfare and protection, and consequently, are often more concerned with the physical and psychological aspects of treatment than prevention of child abuse (7). The social worker's primary point of entry in the area of child abuse has been in the arena of individually-focused treatment. They have been active in counseling families identified as abusers or neglectors as well as with victims of abuse.[9] Overcoming parental inadequacy is often the theme of family counseling. Other direct services offered to parents and children include: medical care, legal services, homemaker services, case management,

---

[9] For detailed discussion of the social work counseling role, see Johnson B, Morse H: "Injured Children and Parents". *Children* 15:4, 1967; Lewis J: "Parental and Community Neglect: Twin Responsibilities of Protective Services". *Children* 14:114, 1969; Davoren E: "The Role of the Social Worker", In *The Battered Child*, R. Helfer and C. Kempe (eds.), Chicago, The University of Chicago Press, 1968; and Bean S: "The Parent's Center Abuse Project: A Multiservice Approach to the Prevention of Child Abuse". *Child Welfare* 50:277, 1971; and Tracy J, Ballard C, and Clark E: "Child Abuse Project: A Follow-up". *Social Work*, 20:398, 1975.

case consultation, technical assistance to community agencies, and child advocacy.

Remediation and amelioration of child abuse problems are called for in order to reduce rates of recividism, promote the physical, psychological and social well-being of children and safeguard their rights. Awareness of factors that place children at high risk for abuse and neglect, such as marital strain, mental illness, covert familial disorganization, extensive social isolation and unplanned pregnancy (21) can assist social workers in planning interventions for individuals and/or families that have an increased likelihood of victimizing children. Screening and diagnostic assessment of the family situation can be used to plan services for persons-at-risk who may not be likely to seek professional assistance. Epidemiological data, particularly with respect to incidence of child abuse in a community, will, it is hoped, draw attention to the magnitude of the problem.

Community support is essential to the success of protective services for children. Social workers can promote the development of a comprehensive array of preventive, diagnostic, treatment and protective services as well as assume responsibility for coordinating and improving accessibility to such services. Weinbach (92) cites the need for social workers to educate other professionals about the injuries, conditions and behaviors associated with child abuse so as to ensure referrals and treatment. By adopting an advocacy role, social workers can attempt to influence public policy regarding prevention of child abuse. Community outreach is essential to enhance a community's potential for identifying cases of child abuse and referring children and their families for service. A case registry is one means of maintaining an identification system, but agencies and individuals must be encouraged to report suspected cases of child abuse and neglect.

Substance Abuse

Both alcohol- and other drug-related disorders are serious problems confronting our society today. Both have adverse effects on physical, social, psychological and economic functioning. Drug habituation entails psychological dependence as a result of repeated use of drugs while addiction refers to a physiologic dependency produced by the compulsive need for consumption.

The National Institute on Alcohol Abuse and Alcoholism (89) estimated that in 1975, expenditures for alcohol-related health and medical services were nearly $14 billion; the overall economic cost of alcohol misuse approximated $43 billion; and alcohol-related mortality approached 205,000. Alcoholism afflicted nearly 10 million adult Americans in 1975. Aproximately two-thirds of the adult population drinks, and an estimated 6-10 percent have been defined as problem drinkers (74, 89). Heavy drinking is most frequent among male adults to the ratio of 3.5 men to 1 woman, although the number of female alcoholics has increased (86). In 1975, approximately 3.3 million teenagers aged 13-17 were considered to be problem drinkers (89). The frequency and consumption of alcohol by adolescents do not appear to have changed dramatically since 1974, but the proportion of high school students who drink has increased. Some data indicate that alcoholism has been increasingly on the rise among the aged (50).

It is difficult to estimate the total number of Americans who are functionally disabled as a result of non-alcohol-related drug abuse. Abusers of barbituates, tranquilizers, amphetamines, marijuana and hallucinogens are seldom enumerated unless arrested for criminal activities or undergoing psychiatric treatment.

Drug abuse appears to be rising again after declining for almost a decade. Heroin accounts for the majority of drug addiction problems in the United States. Although the number of heroin addicts declined about 18 percent between 1975 and 1977 (from 550,000 to 450,000), there has still been a two-fold increase since the mid-1960's (59). In the three-year period between 1972-1975, use of cocaine by young adults aged 18-25 more than doubled despite its high costs. There has also been an increase in the non-medical use of prescription drugs such as sedatives among adults over age 25. Frequently prescribed transquilizers, such as valium and librium, accounted for 24 percent of the drug-connected deaths reported by hospital emergency rooms to the Drug Abuse Warning Network. Widespread use of tranquilizers to relieve tension and anxiety is particularly common among women. According to the National Institute on Drug Abuse (NIDA), an estimated one to two million women are dependent on drugs prescribed by physicians.

Use of amphetamines and other stimulants has been on the increase. Between 1972-1977, there was a 75 percent increase (from 12% to 21%) among young adults reporting ingestion of these drugs. Although the use of lysergic acid diethylamide (LSD) has declined since the 1960's, the reported annual prevalence of phencyclidine (PCP or "Angel Dust"), one of the most potent mind-altering substances, has increased among both youth and young adults.

Marijuana is one of the most popular and frequently used drugs in the United States. By the end of the 1970's, more than 42 million people reported that they had tried smoking a "joint", and over 16 million indicated they were currently using the drug.

The health consequences of drug use vary according to the particular substance. Alcohol is a depressant which alters mood and behavior, affects memory and perception and impairs psychomotor coordination. It contributes to fatal traffic accidents, homicide, suicide, cirrhosis of the liver, deaths from fires, certain types of cardiac diseases and irregularities, hypertension, stroke, cancer of the larynx, pharynx, mouth and esophagus, loss of brain cells, brain atrophy, male sexual impotence, spouse abuse, work absenteeism and diminished work productivity. When alcohol is taken in combination with another psychoactive drug, an alcohol-drug interaction can lead to accidental overdose. Heavy amphetamine use can produce rapid mood changes, development of paranoid symptoms, compulsive activity, excessive talking, anxiety, irritability and auditory hallucinations. Valium is generally considered a safe drug, but can be life-threatening when taken in conjunction with other drugs, especially alcohol. Viral hepatitis, skin abscesses, inflammation of the veins and lung congestion may occur as a result of excessive use of heroin. Most research suggests that marijuana is not addictive, although there may be physiologic and psychologic consequences, such as increased heart rate, perceptual deficits and impaired psychomotor functioning. Evidence concerning its long-term hazardous effects, e.g., on the immunological system and social consequences, has not been firmly established.

Drugs can also have deleterious effects on unborn children, there is mounting evidence that heavy drinking during pregnancy may cause defects in fetal development, ranging from mild neurological and behavioral disorders in infants to the severe fetal alcohol syndrome. The fetal alcohol syndrome is characterized by mental retardation, poor motor development, retarded developmental growth and an array of facial abnormalities. Children born to addictive mothers may experience severe drug withdrawal symptoms if their mothers cease taking heroin since the drug is transmitted via the placenta. In addition, there is an increased risk of mortality and low birth weight or gestational prematurity among infants of untreated addicts.

While seemingly paradoxical, alcohol consumption may be beneficial to health maintenance. Recent data from the National

Heart, Lung and Blood Institute have indicated that a moderate amount of drinking (1-2 drinks daily) is linked to higher levels of lipoproteins and may protect against coronary heart disease (55).

Government has assumed a substantial role in the control, rehabilitation and treatment of substance abuse. The Research Council on Problems of Alcohol (1937) stimulated involvement of many national, state and local agencies in the treatment of alcoholism. The establishment of the National Center for Prevention and Control of Alcoholism in 1966, which provided consultation and grants-in-aid to states for alcohol-related research and treatment programs, marked the beginning of explicit Federal interest in alcoholism. In the same year, the Narcotic Addict Rehabilitation Act was passed and represented an effort to provide addicts with an opportunity for treatment and continuous community afterdare. The National Institute on Alcohol Abuse and Alcoholism (NIAAA) was created in 1971 to administer and coordinate federally-assisted alcoholism prevention, treatment, and rehabilitation programs, while a Special Action Office for Drug Abuse Prevention was established to coordinate Federally-sponsored drug abuse prevention activities. Finally, the National Institute on Drug Abuse (NIDA) was created in 1973 for the prevention, treatment and research of drug abuse problems.

Federal support for substance abuse has continued through the channeling of funds for improved quality of care, training and education of personnel, a national clearinghouse for information and education, and basic and supplemental health services for addictive disorders in community mental health centers and health maintenance organizations (HMOs).[10] Under conditions of limited funds for the support of alcohol abuse programs, there will be deference to treatment (short-run approach) rather than preventive activities (long-run approach).

In recent decades there has been a growing controversy over how to deal with the problems of substance abuse. Historically, addictive disorders have been and still are subject to moral evaluation, with victims sent to jails, hospitals, and private sanatoriums or left to wander along "skid-row" areas. Current conceptions of substance abuse consider these disorders as diseases that warrant therapy and rehabilitation rather than punishment.

The number of treatment centers for substance abuse has increased in the last decade. In 1977, it was estimated that there were 5,900

[10] For example, see the HMO Act of 1973 and the subsequent amendments of 1976 (Public Law 94-460) and 1978 (Public Law 95-559).

programs for alcohol-related problems offered in a variety of facilities, including alcoholism treatment and rehabilitation centers, halfway houses, community mental health centers, mental hospitals, veterans hospitals, and military alcoholism units (84). During 1978, there were about 400,000 admissions to some 3,215 drug abuse treatment units (58). As with alcohol abuse, drug abuse programs are provided in out-patient clinics, day treatment centers, hospitals, residential settings and prisons (57). Many community mental health centers have developed a comprehensive abuse treatment system which offers a wide range of preventive and treatment services. Typical services include information and education, individual, group and family counseling, crisis counseling, outreach and referral, diagnostic evaluation, psychological services, rap sessions, drop-in services, detoxification, medical services, job counseling and placement, vocational rehabilitation, legal assistance, residential placement and half-way houses.

By far, a drug-free regimen or abstinence seem to be the preferred treatment for substance abuse. The identification of alcohol problems is not clear-cut, and therefore difficult to treat, since signs and symptoms of problem drinking may not be overt but latently manifest in domestic violence, marital tension, poor job performance, occupational instability, school delinquency, low self-esteem, and irresponsible behavior. In the acute addictive stage, detoxification, which consists of gradual withdrawal, is the primary management technique. Behavioral therapy, psychotherapy, family counseling, occupational and vocational rehabilitation are provided in comprehensive treatment programs for substance abuse disorders. Drug therapies such as Antabuse and methadone have become increasingly popular in recent years.

By and large, control of drug abuse with treatment and stringent governmental policies has not been as effective as expected. Legislation prohibiting the production, possession and sale of drugs in the United States and the setting forth of harsh penalties for their distribution, as in the case of New York State under the Rockefeller regime, have not dramatically curbed the drug problem. Although availability and access to drugs on the open market were reduced, it led to greater underground demand for procuring drugs, and perhaps, an increased rate of criminal offenses as hard-core addicts strived to fulfill their habit-forming needs. The high relapse rate of those treated by hospitalization and methadone detoxification suggests that prevention may be a more realistic approach to control drug abuse than eradication of illegal drugs.

Recent strategies to reduce the incidence and prevalence of alcohol-related problems have been directed toward primary prevention, particularly: 1) increasing public and professional awareness of alcohol-related problems; 2) reducing risk factors; 3) improving health status, and 4) improving service delivery (88, 91). The Preventive Division of NIAAA has targeted interventions toward individuals' knowledge, attitudes and behavior regarding drinking (host); content, distribution and availability of alcohol (agent); and the context in which drinking occurs (environment) (82).

A variety of prevention programs are targeted to specific populations. Youth alcohol prevention projects have developed in response to the rise in teenage alcoholism. These programs emphasize alcohol education in the public schools, intensive teacher training, peer leadership training, public information and parental education (56). Mass media campaigns, often in conjunction with community organizations and prevention outreach, are instituted to demonstrate the problems of alcohol use and inebriation. Alcoholism programs in the workplace for the prevention and early identification of alcohol-related problems have become increasingly popular. There is a strong economic incentive for employee-sponsored alcoholism programs since alcoholism often results in lateness, absenteeism, industrial accidents and loss of work productivity. Under the auspices of NIAAA, occupational alcoholism employee assistance (OA-EAP) programs[11] were developed during the Carter Administration. NIAAA is examining the relationship between the regulatory activity of alcohol beverage control boards on the one hand, and alcohol availability, purchasing practices, and drinking behavior, on the other.

Social workers have generally been case managers or therapists in substance-abuse settings and thus involved in treatment and rehabilitation. Vocational counseling, planning for community after-care, family counseling, staff consultation and education, and program evaluation have been essential dimensions of the social work role. Role diffusion and lack of task specificity between psychologists, psychiatrists, social workers, nurses and recovered substance abuse counselors in the area of patient and family counseling obsfuscate social workers' contribution to the field.

---

[11] For a detailed description of the elements of an OA-EAP program, see Masi D: "Combating Alcoholism in the Workplace". *Health and Social Work*, 4:41, 1979.

Social workers need to move beyond the traditional tasks of assessment and treatment of substance abuse disorders and increase their involvement in preventive and outreach efforts, linkage of clients to community resources and education, problem identification and early diagnosis. Substance abuse is an area of practice that has been neglected by social work. Out of nearly 36,000 staff in drug abuse treatment programs in 1978, only 9 percent were MSW level social workers (58). Similarly, only 7 percent of the nearly 5,500 full-time positions in NIAAA-assisted treatment programs were filled by social workers.

Social workers should be concerned with community-wide reduction of problems, e.g., promoting education and preventive services in industry and providing public information. They can participate in collecting data on the preventive and treatment needs of target populations so as to assess the incidence and prevalence of substance abuse, distribution of resources, eligibility requirements, and attitudes of mental health professionals. Differential sociodemographic and situational contexts of groups prone to abuse suggest the need for interventions tailored to the nature of the problem. For example, services specifically geared to the needs of women, such as child care and vocational rehabilitation, are inadequate. Social work personnel can aid in evaluating the interpersonal, social, vocational, and community functioning of substance abusers in the aggregate, e.g., termination of relationships, employment stability, attendance record, attitudes about drugs, and drinking and drug history.

Accurate diagnosis is often hampered by lack of professional knowledge and training about substance abuse. Consequently, a sufficient cadre of skills is needed to enable workers to make an adequate psychosocial assessment of individuals with these problems. Such training can be provided through courses in the graduate social work curriculum, inservice training and continuing education programs.

There is also a need for social workers to lobby for social reform. On an individual level, social workers and health educators can teach abusers behavioral skills to help them modify their longstanding life habits. The outcomes of these interventions, however, are unlikely to be successful without support measures, incentives and penalties provided at the macro level that encourage people to moderate or give up harmful drug-taking practices. In addition, structural reforms and policy changes might reduce the hazardous costs of substance abuse to both the individual and society. For example, a pharmacological approach has been suggested to prevent alcohol-related problems — the development of a substance that, when added to alcohol, would weaken or eliminate its deleterious effects, induce vomiting at high concentrations, or block its effect on the nervous and hormonal systems (71). Enforcement of drunk driving laws, placement of warning labels on liquor bottles and over-the-counter drugs, and increased public awareness of the dangers of substance abuse have been advocated (39).

Stringent enforcement of drunk driving and narcotic laws requires considerable police efforts. Imposing indeterminate jail sentences involves timely judicial activity. There is no assurance that stiff penalties will deter the rate of recidivism. Experience from England has shown that restricting opportunities to purchase and consume alcohol has failed because people have sufficiently large enough disposable incomes to spend on alcohol (88). Social workers could lobby for insurance companies to promote benefits for both hospital and outpatient treatment as well as encourage states to increase the availability of prevention and treatment programs for substance abuse.

NEW HORIZONS: THE FUTURE OF SOCIAL WORK AND PUBLIC HEALTH

During the last two decades of the twentieth century, great strides have been made in the professionalization of social work. Objectivity, scientific inquiry and rigor in specifying, documenting and evaluating social work practice have been introduced and accepted by a growing segment of the profession. These elements have helped social work to gain professional recognition in the view of other health disciplines. As health service delivery becomes more complex and specialized, there has been a secular shift from a narrow to a broader practice base. The multiplicity of public health roles in social work practice — preventive casework, casefinding, community organization and outreach, consultation, inservice training and staff development, consumer advocacy, program planning and evaluation research, and planning and implementation of health policy — will undoubtedly continue.

Few empirical studies have focused on primary and secondary prevention efforts which entail a population accountability. This lacuna stems from the fact that most social workers do not think in terms of populations as a basis of practice. Yet, documentation for accountability, critical to agency survival, is the name of the game in the 1980's, as health care costs soar and funding for social programs becomes scarcer. Population changes and the caring for the more physically and mentally ill in the community underscore the need for practitioners to focus on large groups of people and plan and implement continual, long-term health care programs.

Experience has shown that epidemiologic methods can be a valuable aid to hospital social workers in identifying and specifying problems, establishing priorities and solving problems. Social work practice in public health, however, must move beyond individually-oriented preventive interventions in hospital settings and revive its focus on the community. As part of its policy to expand and diversify practice, social work needs to participate in large-scale epidemiologic surveys which examine the psychosocial health problems of communities.

There are many practice settings, situations and problems to which social workers could apply public health concepts. In particular, environmental health is one area in which there has been minimal social work involvement. Social work views people as influencing and being influenced by environments in which they live, but has chosen limited areas, e.g., poverty, slums, malnutrition, of involvement.

Communities could benefit by social work participation in reviewing environmental health hazards. Over the past two decades, as the scope of traditional public health has expanded to include concern for the role of psychosocial factors in health-related behaviors, public health turned to social work for its expertise in the psychosocial dynamics of behavior (40). There is no reason why the profession cannot embrace environmental health concerns, except perhaps for a mind-set that draws workers to a clinical, patient-centered approach to intervention. The potential for creative roles is manifold. There are many areas of environmental health that lend themselves to social work analysis. Environmental protection and safety are major policy issues, since the effects of nuclear accidents, and air, water, noise, pesticide and radiation pollutants have been identified as being potentially deleterious to health. Restrictive national economic and energy policies have resulted in high inflation, limited employment opportunities and substandard housing. These conditions affect the biophysical, socio-economic and psychological dimensions of people's environments. As such, they represent stressors that may increase the likelihood of illness, particularly among groups disproportionally burdened such as the poor, elderly, ill and ethnic minorities.

Trauma and natural disasters are other areas that warrant attention. With the eruption of Mount St. Helens, and events such as floods, tornadoes, fires, earthquakes, and air crashes that threaten or extinguish the lives of large groups of people, the effects of these disasters on survivors need to be studied with psychosocial epidemiologic methods.[12] The crisis at Three Mile Island provided opportunity for social workers to display their skills. Major areas of concern to social work would include community perceptions of exposure to the hazard, concerns about the accident, prevalence of physiological and psychological symptoms, repertoire of coping responses and sense of powerlessness.[13] Similarly, the health concerns of Vietnam veterans exposed to Agent Orange and other workplace issues, e.g., corporate health, stress among air traffic controllers, are also appropriate arenas for social work research and intervention.

The recent influx of Cuban, Haitian, Central and South American, Southeast Asian, and Russian refugees has overburdened our country's health, economic and social service sectors. Public assistance systems are strained, Americans' perceive that their employment opportunities and security are being threatened, and service delivery systems are ill-prepared to anticipate the multiple problems of these immigrants. The immigrant problem is of obvious import to social work as the profession has traditionally sided with the disenfranchised and oppressed. Cultural shock, difficulty in securing jobs and homes, language barriers, restricted access to services and a large segment of the population that opposes asylum for political refugees are problems with which social workers must contend. In terms of the need for preventive interventions aimed toward high-risk situations, forced and often abrupt migration represents a major life crisis. What are the effects of social dislocation, social integration, maladaptation, acculturation, language and skill deficits, restricted employment and earning potential, lack of social support, etc. — on physical and psychological health status? Epidemiologic information of this nature should prove useful in developing programs sensitive to the different values, traditions and lifestyles of these diverse

---

(12) Robert Lifton and Erich Lindemann have conducted studies in these areas, but they were not epidemiologically-based.

(13) A study along these lines is currently underway. For example, see Kasl, S., Chisholm, R., and Eskenazi, B. "The Impact of the Accident at the Three Mile Island on the Behavior and Well-Being of Nuclear Workers," Parts I and II, *American Journal of Public Health*, 71:472, 1981.

populations. Social workers dealing with such groups in health settings may have to broaden their ethnic knowledge base, particularly in relation to health values and practices, such as the prevalence of folk medical practice and its parallel use with allopathic medicine.

The increased emphasis in the last decade on consumer responsibility for health — self-help groups, self-care, holistic medicine and life-style change — has paved the way for the development of new models of community-based social work practice. Social workers have begun to serve as professional resource staff to medical self-help groups for people with chronic illnesses. Consumer health education is a fertile area for social practice, yet few social workers are involved in screening, risk-reduction and educational programs in the workplace and community at large. Current research on the role of both social support and stressful life events in health has pragmatic implications for the nature of social work interventions. For example, if one's social network can help mediate or buffer the impact of illness, then social workers can build networks for those who lack a support system.

Social work's participation in primary prevention, the *sine quo non* of public health, needs to be increased. The potential of primary prevention lies in its capacity for reducing long-term medical costs and, more importantly, preventing disability and the loss of the potential contributions of the physically and mentally ill to society. In light of the current tightening of the Federal government budget for human services, provision of proven cost-effective, ambulatory care services is essential.

REFERENCES

1. American Association of Medical Social Workers: *A Statement of Personnel Practices in Medical Social Work*. Washington, American Association of Medical Social Workers, 1951.
2. American Public Health Association: "Educational Qualifications of Social Workers in Public Health Programs." *American Journal of Public Health*, 52:317, 1962.
3. American Public Health Association, Social Work Section: "Standards for Social Work Programs in Public Health Settings." 1981.
4. Appolone, C.: "Preventive Social Work Intervention with Families of Children with Epilepsy." *Social Work in Health Care*. 4:139, 1978.
5. Barnett, E.M.: "Social Work Training Needs." Background paper prepared for the Third National Conference on Public Health Training, Washington, August 1967.
6. Bartlett, H.: "Perspectives in Public Health Social Work." *Children*. 1:21, 1954.

7. Billingsley, A. and Giovannoni, J.: *Children of the Storm*. New York, Harcourt Brace Jovanovich, Inc., 1972.
8. Black, R.: "Support for Genetic Services: A Survey." *Health and Social Work*, 5:27, 1980.
9. Bloom, S.: "Community Wide Chest X-ray Survey III. Social Work." *Public Health Reports*. 66:139, 1951.
10. Boehm, W.: "The Nature of Social Work." *Social Work*. 3:16, April 1958.
11. Bracht, N.: "Contributions of Public Health Social Work to Academic Departments of Community Medicine." *Milbank Memorial Fund Quarterly*. 47:73, 1969.
12. Brantley, D.: "A Genetics Primer for Social Workers." *Health and Social Work*. 5:5, 1980.
13. Buell, B.: "Implications for Social Work Education of a Conception of Prevention." In *Proceedings: Education for Social Work*, Council on Social Work Education, Annual Program Meeting, Oklahoma City, 1960.
14. Burns, J.: "A Social Worker's Role in the Identification and Counseling of Families at Risk for Genetic Disorders." In *Family Health Care: Health Promotion and Illness Care*, R. Jackson and J. Morton (eds.). Berkeley: University of California, Public Health Social Work Program, 1976, pp. 81-98.
15. Breslin, R.: "Delivery of Social Work Service in Newborn Special Care Unit." In Proceedings of *The First National Workshop in the Delivery of Hospital Social Work Services in Obstetrics/Gynecology and Services to the Newborn*, R. Breslin (ed.). Yale-New Haven Medical Center, 1974.
16. Cabot, R.: *Social Service and the Art of Healing*. New York: Moffat, Yard and Company, 1915.
17. Cannon, I.: *On the Social Frontier of Medicine*. Cambridge: Harvard University Press, 1952.
18. Caplan, G.: *Concepts of Mental Health Consultation — Their Application in Public Health Social Work*. Washington, Government Printing Office, Children's Bureau, 1959.
19. Conyard, S., Krishnamurthy, M., and Dosik, H.: "Psychosocial Aspects of Sickle-Cell Anemia in Adolescents." *Health and Social Work*. 5:20, 1980.
20. Cooper, L., Fedun, B., and Margolin, J.: "Rubella — A Lesson in Health Care." In *Changing Perspectives in the Contemporary Health Scene*, Proceedings of the 1969 Annual Meeting of Medical Social Consultants in Public Health and Health Care Programs, Sponsored by Children's Bureau, New York City, May 23-25, 1969.
21. Costin, L.: *Child Welfare: Policies and Practice*. New York: McGraw Hill, 1972.
22. Council on Social Work Education: *Public Health Concepts in Social Work Education*, Proceedings of a seminar held at Princeton, New Jersey, 1962.
23. Cyr, F., and Wattenberg, S.: "Social Work in a Preventive Program of Maternal and Child Health." *Social Work*. 2:32, July 1957.
24. Fedun, B., and Heckman, L.: Developmental Disabilities Center, St. Luke's-Roosevelt Hospital Medical Center, New York, personal communication, 1982.
25. Fischman, S. and Palley, H.: "Adolescent Unwed Motherhood: Complications for a National Family Policy." *Health and Social Work*. 3:30, February 1978.
26. Giovannoni, J. and Becerra, R.: *Defining Child Abuse*. New York: The Free Press, 1981.
27. Gold, J. and Cates, W.: "Restriction of Federal Funds for Abortion: 18 Months After." *American Journal of Public Health*. 69:929, 1979.

28. Hamovitch, M.: "Epidemiology — Its Application for Social Work." In *Public Health Concepts in Social Work Education*. Proceedings of a seminar held at Princeton, New Jersey, Council on Social Work Education, 1962, pp. 97-106.
29. Hall, B.: "The Role of Medical Social Service in the Public Health Program." In *Expanding Horizons in Medical Social Work*. D. Goldstine (ed.). Chicago: University of Chicago Press, 1955, pp. 90-99.
30. Harris, L.: "The Epidemic of Influenza." *Hospital Social Service Quarterly*. 1:11, 1919.
31. Harris, L. and Associates: *Hospital Care in America*. Survey conducted for Hospital Affiliates International, Nashville, 1978.
32. Hawkins, D.: "Enigma in Swaddling Clothes: Sudden Infant Death Syndrome." *Health and Social Work*. 5:21, November 1980.
33. Howell, R.: "Applied Epidemiology and its Use in the Control of Mental Illnesses." In *Public Health Concepts in Social Work Education*. Proceedings of a Seminar held at Princeton, New Jersey, Council on Social Work Education, 1962, pp. 86-96.
34. Insley, V.: "Health Services: Maternal and Child Health." *Encyclopedia of Social Work*. 17th Ed., Volume I, Washington, National Association of Social Workers, 1977.
35. Institute of Medicine, National Academy of Sciences: *Healthy People: The Surgeon General's Report on Health Promotion and Disease Prevention*. Department of Health, Education, and Welfare, Public Health Service, DHEW Publication No. (PHS) 79-55071A, Washington, Superintendent of Documents, Government Printing Office, 1979.
36. Jayaratne, S.: "Child Abusers as Parents and Children: A Review." *Social Work*. 22:5, 1977.
37. Jerrick, S.: "Federal Efforts to Control Sexually-Transmitted Diseases." *Journal of School Health*. 48:7, September 1978.
38. Joffee, C.: "Abortion Work: Strains, Coping Strategies, Policy Implications." *Social Work*, 24:485, November 1979.
39. Kane, R.: "To Our Health . . . Social Work and Alcohol Problems." *Health and Social Work*. 4:3, 1979.
40. Katz, A.: "Public Health Concepts and the Human Growth Sequence of the Social Work Curriculum." *Case Conference*, 14:377, 1968.
41. Katz, A.: "Genetic Counseling in Chronic Disease." *Health and Social Work*. 5:14, 1980.
42. Kelly, D. and Shannon, D.: "Epidemiology Clues to the Etiology of SIDS." *American Journal of Public Health*. 70:1047, October 1980.
43. Kerson, T. "Sixty Years Ago: Hospital Social Work in 1918." *Social Work in Health Care*. 4:331, 1979.
44. Kiely, L., Sterne, R., and Witkop, C.: Psychosocial Factors in Low-Incidence Genetic Disease: The Case of Osteogenic Imperfecta." *Social Work in Health Care*. 1:409, 1976.
45. Lappe, M.: "Genetics and Our Obligations to the Future." In *Bioethics and Human Rights*. Bandman and Bandman (eds.). Boston: Little Brown, 1978. pp. 84-93.
46. Lasagna, L.: The VD Epidemic. Philadelphia: Temple University Press, 1975.
47. Lilienfeld, A.: *Foundations of Epidemiology*. New York: Oxford University Press, 1976.
48. MacMahon, B., and Pugh, T.: *Epidemiology Principles and Methods*. Boston: Little Brown, 1970.

49. Mausner, J. and Bahn, A.: *Epidemiology*. Philadelphia: W.B. Saunders, 1974.
50. Mayer, M.: "Alcohol and the Elderly: A Review." *Health and Social Work*. 4:128, 1979.
51. Mednick, M.: "The Social Worker's Responsibility in Family Planning." In *The Social Worker and Family Planning*, Proceeding of the 1969 Annual Institute for Public Health Social Workers. Rockville, Maryland, U.S. Department of Public Health, Education, and Welfare, Health Services Administration, Bureau of Community Health Services, DHEW Publication No. (HSA) 77-5204.
52. Meyer, C.: "What Directions for Direct Practice." *Social Work*. 24:267, 1979.
53. Miller, P.: "Medical Social Service in a Tuberculosis Sanitorium." *Public Health Reports*. 66:987, 1951.
54. National Center for Health Services Research: *Evaluation of Child Abuse and Neglect Demonstration Projects 1974-1977, Vols. 1 and 2*. Washington, Department of Health, Education, and Welfare, DHEW Publication No. (PHS) 79-3217-1, August 1978.
55. National Institute on Alcohol Abuse and Alcoholism: "Study Examines Alcohol Use, Exercise, Heart Disease Risk." *NIAAA Information and Feature Service*, U.S. Department of Health and Human Services, Public Health Service, Alcohol, Drug Abuse, and Mental Health Administration, IFS No. 84, June 1, 1981.
56. National Institute on Alcohol Abuse and Alcoholism: "Drinking Alternatives Focus on Health Promotion Effort." *NIAAA Information and Feature Service*, U.S. Department of Health and Human Services, Public Health Service, Alcohol, Drug Abuse, and Mental Health Administration, IFS No. 84, June 1, 1981.
57. National Institute on Drug Abuse: *Data from the Client Oriented Data Acquisition Process (CODAP), Annual Data 1977*. Statistical Series E, Number 7, October 1978.
58. National Institute on Drug Abuse: *National Drug Abuse Treatment Utilization Survey*. April 1978. Series F, Number 5, December 1978.
59. National Institute on Drug Abuse, Office of Program Development and Analysis: *A Report to the President and the Congress on the Drug Abuse Prevention and Treatment Functions of the DHEW*, FY 1978, July 1979.
60. Palmisano, P.: "Targeted Intervention in the Control of Accidental Drug Overdose by Children." *Public Health Reports*. 96:150, March-April 1981.
61. Peterson, A. and Nevin, R.: "Crippled Children Services: Present Practices and Trends for the Future." In *Health Care Delivery to Meet the Changing Needs of the American Family*, proceedings of the 1977 Medical Social Consultants' Annual Meeting, St. Denis and Doss (eds.), Maternal and Child Health Services, Bureau of Community Health Services, Department of Health, Education and Welfare.
62. Provine, W.: "Genetic Screening: The Ultimate Preventive Medicine?" *Hard Choices*, 1980, p. 8.
63. Rapoport, L.: "The Concept of Prevention in Social Work." *Social Work*. 6:3, 1961.
64. Redmon, R.: Commentary to "Risk Taking and a Minor Birth Defect." *The Hastings Center Report*. 11:25, 1981.
65. Rehr, H., Berkman, B. and Rosenberg, G.: "Screening for High Social Risk: Principles and Problems." *Social Work*. 25:403, 1980.
66. Reichert, K.: "Application of Public Health Concepts and Methods to the Field of Social Work." Proceedings of the Eleventh Annual Program Meeting, Council on Social Work Education, 1962.

67. Reichert, K.: "Summary With a Theme: How Can We Harmonize Multiple Social Work Tasks?" In *Mothers at Risk*. F. Haselkorn (ed.). Perspectives in Social Work, 1:1966, Adelphi University School of Social Work.
68. Reichert, K.: "Essentials of Social Work Practice in Public Health Programs." Paper presented at the Tri-Regional Workshop for Social Workers in Maternal and Child Health Services, Raleigh, North Carolina, June 1980, mimeographed, in press.
69. Rice, E.: "Concepts of Prevention as Applied to the Practice of Social Work." *American Journal of Public Health*. 52:266, 1962.
70. Rice, E.: "Social Work in Public Health." *Social Work*. 4:82, 1959.
71. Robertson, L.: "Alcohol, Behavior, and Public Health Strategies." *Abstracts and Reviews in Alcohol and Driving*. 2:1, 1981.
72. Rosen, I.: "Social Aspects of Syphilis." *Hospital Social Service*. 3:284, 1921.
73. Schild, S.: "Genetic Counseling as part of a Mental Retardation Service: Implications for Social Work Practice." In *The Social Worker and Family Planning*, proceedings of the 1969 Annual Institute for Public Health Social Workers, Rockville, Maryland, U.S. Department of Health, Education, and Welfare, Health Services Administration, Bureau of Community Health Services, DHEW Publication No. (HSA) 77-5204.
74. Schmidt, W. and DeLint, J.: "Estimating the Prevalence of Alcoholism from Alcohol Consumption and Mortality Data." *Quarterly Journal of Alcohol Studies*. 31:957, 1970.
75. Shapiro-Steinberg, L. and Neamatalla, G.: "Counseling for Women Requesting Sterilization: A Comprehensive Program Designed to Insure Informed Consent." *Social Work in Health Care*, 5:151, Winter 1979.
76. Shaw, J. and Shaw, R.: "Aiding Expectant and New Parents to Accomplish the Developmental Tasks of Parenthood." In *Family Health Care: Health Promotion and Illness Care*. R. Jackson and J. Morton (eds.). Berkeley: University of California, Public Health Social Work Program, 1976. pp. 59-69.
77. Silver, G. and Stiber, C.: "The Social Worker and the Physician: Daily Practice of a Health Team." *Journal of Medical Education*. 32:324, 1957.
78. Spencer, E.: "Public Health Social Work." In *Health and the Community*. A. Katz and J. Felton (eds.). New York: The Free Press, 1965.
79. Standfast, S., Jereb, S. and Janerich, D.: "The Epidemiology of Sudden Infant Death in Upstate New York: II: Birth Characteristics." *American Journal of Public Health*. 70:1061, October 1980.
80. Stites, M.: History of the American Association of Medical Social Workers. Washington, *American Association of Medical Social Workers*, 1955.
81. Upham, F.: *A Dynamic Approach to Illness*. New York: Family Service Association of America, 1949.
82. U.S. Department of Health, Education, and Welfare, National Institute on Alcohol Abuse and Alcoholism: *Third Special Report to the U.S. Congress on Alcohol and Health*. DHEW Publication No. (ADM) 79-832, Rockville, Maryland, June 1978.
83. U.S. Department of Health, Education, and Welfare: "Healthy People." The Surgeon General's Report on Health Promotion and Disease Prevention," Washington, U.S. Government Printing Office, DHEW Publication No. 79-55071, 1979.
84. U.S. Department of Health and Human Services, Alcohol, Drug Abuse and Mental Health Administration: *The Alcohol, Drug Abuse, and Mental Health National Data Book*. DHHS Publication No. 80-938, Rockville, Maryland, January 1980.

85. U.S. Department of Health and Human Services, *Health, United States, 1983,* Washington, U.S. Government Printing Office, 1983.
86. U.S. Department of Health and Human Services: *Alcohol Abuse and Women.* Public Health Service, Alcohol, Drug Abuse, and Mental Health Administration, National Institute on Alcohol Abuse and Alcoholism, DHHS Publication No. (ADM) 80-358, 1980.
87. U.S. Department of Health and Human Services: "Selected Demographic Characteristics of Teenage Wives and Mothers." *Advance Data from Vital and Health Statistics,* Number 61, Public Health Service, Office of Health Research Statistics, and Technology, National Center for Health Statistics, September 26, 1980.
88. U.S. Department of Health and Human Services. Alcohol, Drug Abuse, and Mental Health Administration: National Institute on Alcohol Abuse and Alcoholism Information and Feature Service. Rockville, Maryland. 82:6, April 1, 1981.
89. U.S. Department of Health and Human Services, National Institute on Alcohol Abuse and Alcoholism: *Fourth Special Report to the Congress on Alcohol and Health.* Rockville, Maryland, Summer 1981.
90. U.S. Department of Health and Human Services, Public Health Service: *The Surgeon General's Workshop on Maternal and Infant Health.* DHHS Publication No. (PHS) 81-50161, Washington, U.S. Government Printing Office, 1981.
91. Vischi, T., Jones, K., Shank, E., and Lima, L.: *The Alcohol, Drug Abuse, and Mental Health National Data Book.* DHHS Publication No. (ADM) 80-938, Rockville: Department of Health and Human Services, Public Health Service, Alcohol, Drug Abuse, and Mental Health Administration, January 1980.
92. Weinbach, R.: "Case Management of Child Abuse." *Social Work.* 20:396, 1975.
93. Weintraub, B.: "Health Chief Gives Plans to Cut Costs." *The New York Times,* June 12, 1981, p. 36.
94. Wilner, D., Walkley, R., and O'Neill, E.: *Introduction to Public Health,* Seventh Edition, New York: Macmillan Publishing Company, 1978.
95. Wittman, M.: "The Social Worker in Preventive Services." In *The Social Welfare Forum: Official Proceedings of the National Conference on Social Welfare.* New York: Columbia University Press, 1961, pp. 136-147.
96. Wittman, M.: "Application of Knowledge about Prevention in Social Work and Practice." *Social Work in Health Care.* 3:37, 1977.
97. Yankauer, A.: "The Ups and Downs of Prevention." *American Journal of Public Health.* 71:6 1981.

Chapter 6

COMMUNITY-BASED SOCIAL WORK WITH THE CHRONICALLY ILL*

IRENE SUE POLLIN
MARJORIE McKINNEY CASHION

Today, patients with kidney disease that would have quickly killed them twenty years ago live almost normal lives, thanks to dialysis. Patients with multiple sclerosis, learning of their disease at an early stage, are living with it, even though the disease cannot be cured. And even cancer, once invariably the cause of swift death, now is being treated with increasing sophistication, so that in many cases, the disease goes into remission — not ending the victim's life immediately, but altering it. Increasingly, the evidence accumulates, demonstrating the success of medical science in finding solutions to the problems of disease (18). Ironically, however, this very success is creating an entirely new set of problems — those faced by our new, and growing, population of individuals who are being maintained instead of cured: the chronically ill.

The person afflicted with long-term illness invariably passes into a difficult emotional state. Torn between hope and uncertainty, he keeps telling himself that a miracle drug will be found and he will be cured before he runs out of time; yet he knows that the likelihood of such a timely discovery is slim. And he is nagged by fears and uncertainties. "How long will it be," he wonders, "before I am incapacitated?" "Will I be able to keep any job?" "What should I do if I should want to marry?" "When am I going to die?" "How in the world am I going to cope with this?"

---

*The writer acknowledges with appreciation assistance received in the preparation of this manuscript from Susan Carey, Marjorie Rosner, Arnold Trebach and Linda Roberts.

Helping these chronically ill people and their families find answers to their questions — and work out ways of coping — is a major challenge to the social work profession today. Their existence made possible by relatively recent developments in medicine, the chronically ill find themselves faced with a unique and baffling set of problems. Developed by and for "well people," our society has no place for the chronically ill; the community does not know what to do with them — may seem, in fact, to find them inconvenient, an imposition or embarrassment in an age of physical fitness. Even the doctor who diagnosed the chronic patient's disease may seem suddenly to have lost interest. How can the social work profession help? In profound ways. More than merely answering questions and giving emotional support, the social work profession is challenged today to help the chronically ill by establishing innovative programs, organizations, and services to bridge the gap between what these people need and what society now provides (3,6,8,16).

The task is a formidable one. Even though efforts have been made to deal with the growing needs of this population — for example, efforts such as respite care, "Meals on Wheels" for the bedridden and elderly, and reading groups for the blind, and so on — these efforts have been uneven, their results not enough (7,12). The numbers of chronically ill persons are increasing each day, and with this increase comes a growth in their needs (14,17). The medical profession has helped this group by extending their lives; it is up to the social work profession now to help make these lives both more meaningful and socially productive. It is the purpose of this chapter, therefore, to clarify the needs of the chronically ill and their families, to report on what is being done in the community to meet these needs, and to describe new developments in services to this group, with attention to what needs to be achieved in the future.

DIFFERENCES BETWEEN ACUTE AND CHRONIC ILLNESS

The major difference between acute and chronic illness is implied in the words, "full recovery." When full recovery is promised, there is always hope; without it, there is the danger of despair, and the need for varying degrees of life adjustment on the part of patients and their families. Surgery and life-time medication are maintenance measures, not cures. By-pass heart surgery, often used today for victims of severe heart disease, improves — but does not restore — the quantity and quality of the patient's life; the chronic disease of atherosclerosis continues to develop, and often, depending on the rapidity of the progression of the disease, the surgery may have to be repeated within a few years. It is this very extension of life — of a different quality — which is the cause of new psycho-social problems.

There is a basic lack of understanding within the community, both professional and lay, regarding the differences between coping with a chronic, as opposed to an acute, illness (13). With an acute illness such as pneumonia or appendicitis, the problem tends to come and go with what might be called "merciful speed." In a case of appendicitis, for example, the patient faces the initial physical trauma and hospitalization, and usually recovers. Even when recovery is not achieved and death results, with an acute problem the resolution tends to be quick — hence, in a way, merciful. The patient dies, scarcely having had time to realize his death was imminent; his family is shocked, mourns; and then life goes on. For the chronic sufferer, however, and for his family, the process is slower — and potentially much more painful. The sufferer himself may experience a slow period of physical decline, watching his own deterioration, which comes, often after a series of crises related to the illness, each leveling off at a lower level of functioning. To make matters worse, each crisis and remission often will tend to carry with it increased disability and even fear of death. For example, a child with muscular dystrophy may have to undergo a series of operative procedures, only to maintain his short life in a wheelchair, and each operation will tend to be experienced by the child as a crisis and potential moment of death. Yet, although much on the patient's mind, death does not come — at least not quickly. The chronic illness sufferer has a long time — in fact, years — to come to terms with his condition. But, in return for that time, he and his family must pay a heavy personal price. All of them, patient and family alike, must learn to accept the patient's steadily deteriorating condition and the inevitability of death. In so doing, they have to learn to understand, and work through, their psychological defense mechanisms, guilt, and fear. They have to confront — in a way that for most of them will be a totally new experience — the growing awareness of human frailty and death. They become engaged in a continued struggle with despair.

PROBLEMS OF CHRONIC ILLNESS: HOW THE PATIENT IS AFFECTED

Lack of Sympathy, Understanding, in the Community

One terrible problem that the chronically ill person may face is a negative attitude toward him in the community. It may take the form of attempts to avoid him, or he may even be the target of resentment or anger. One reason for this, ironically enough, may be found in the extraordinarily high level of well-being in society as a whole today. Unfortunately for the population of the chronically ill, community attitudes today are largely focused on health and physical fitness; and this preoccupation emotionally distances the chronically ill person from society. The chronic illness, and the person who suffers from it, are unfamiliar — and frightening — to people today. A mere one hundred years ago, on the other hand, the situation was quite different. Then, illness was a part of everyday life, and extended families, staying together, were better able to cope with it than people of today. In those days, families routinely had many children with the expectation that some would not live to maturity, with the awareness that childbirth often took the life of the mother, and with the understanding that a sixty year old grandparent was "aged."

Today, in contrast, we have a culture with no expectation of illness, little or no idea of what it is like to be ill, and hence very little sympathy for those who are. In large cities, for example, people riding crowded buses tend to resent waiting while the lift mechanism attached to the rear door of the bus, laboriously and slowly, admits a person in a wheelchair. "Why doesn't a person like that stay home?" some will ask. Similarly, in school classrooms where handicapped and chronically ill persons have been "mainstreamed," some students, and even teachers, impatiently will calculate how much time the class loses while they wait for a spastic, or partially paralyzed, person to articulate a question. "Why," they wonder, "is a person like that allowed in this class? He's slowing us down!"

Our technology today is such that people tend to think of themselves as invulnerable. But they are not; and when they see around them reminders of their own social, emotional or physical vulnerability, they find it unsettling. They try to push the afflicted person away. It is as though, guided by superstition, they believe that to avoid the blind is to avoid being made blind, and to avoid the sick is to avoid disease. Today, because the expectation for well-being is even greater than it was in the past, so also is the potential for despair.

Resentment, Rejection on the Part of Those Who Care for the Chronically Ill

A second problem peculiar to chronic illness (as opposed to acute illness) has to do with a tendency on the part of the family and medical personnel to resent, or even reject, the patient. Throughout the history of human society, to be sure, care of the ill has been difficult. But up until this century, strangely enough, illness has been easier to cope with than it is today. One reason is that in the past, illness usually was acute, hence of short duration; and with illness such as that, hope remains right up until the end. As a result, morale remains relatively high. The family and the medical team "pull together," and, within a short time, they are either rewarded with recovery or fail to save the person's life. In either case, they are able to feel that they have acted aggressively and have "done everything possible." In addition, caring for the acutely ill brings greater social rewards. Nursing a sick family member has always been a respected, admired activity. Visiting the sick, at home or in the hospital, restoring them to health, or making them comfortable before they die have always rated high as socially acceptable behaviors. Nuns have been called saints, and doctors have received national awards for devoting their lives to the care of the acutely ill.

Caring for the chronically ill, however, is a great deal more difficult. Morale tends to be lower, and the social rewards are fewer, making the care of the chronically ill an emotionally taxing, often relatively thankless job. The physicians and nurses who cannot bring about cure tend to be frustrated, often secretly wish the patient away, and then are additionally burdened with guilt as a result (11). The family, still in a hopeful stage at first, does not understand why the doctor fails to return phone calls or answer their questions. The questions often are, in fact, unanswerable, and the lack of answers creates a difficult situation — for medical personnel and patients' families alike. Then the family becomes angry, not just at the disease, but at those in the medical profession who not only are unable to bring about a cure, but who seem unable to do anything at all. "Why are we paying this doctor?" the family may ask. "Why isn't he *doing* anything? Is he 'incompetent'?" When something can be done, there can be hope; when nothing can be done, the result is despair, and a feeling of life out of control. As a result of this stress, the family unit itself may be destroyed. For example, a young couple whose child has received a diagnosis of cystic fibrosis may, at first, seek every physician available, looking for a cure. However, after many hospitalizations, difficult daily nursing tasks, and fear of the child's death, a disillusionmennt with the medical profession sets in. The situation affects every aspect of the family members' lives; they cease being able to cope, and they become dependent upon the community for help. Often the relationship between the parents deteriorates under the strain, and not infrequently the result is divorce.

Not only do marriages suffer. Enormous psychological problems will tend to plague each family member and care provider as well. How can a young parent invest himself in a child who may not live to become an adult? And how does he feel about himself if he does not? How do the siblings evaluate themselves in relation to the "sick" family member? To whom can the many feelings of fear, resentment and guilt be expressed? This bleak outlook for a young family can be devastating.

Chronic illness can last for twenty, thirty, or even forty years, and the afflicted person — as well as those who care for him — will experience potentially very serious psychological problems which, if the family is to survive with its psychological health intact, must be confronted, worked through, and accepted.

Financial Problems of the Chronically Ill

Not only does the chronically ill patient have more difficulty with long-term uncertainty, negativity, and rejection by the people around him than does the acute patient, he also tends to have unique, and more serious, financial problems. Whereas for the acute patient the issues may revolve around insurance, and "making ends meet" while he or she is in the hospital, a chronic sufferer's financial burden is much greater and more complex. He (or his family) will be concerned not only with current hospital bills, but with those that will inevitably build in the future (19). A chronic patient may lose his job as a result of frequent hospital admissions. Such an event would put more than a temporary burden on the family; it would require major changes in plans or life-style. A house might have to be sold, a college education postponed or cancelled, or a non-working spouse might have to start looking for a job. In addition, insurance coverage for the future would have to be re-evaluated, and, in all likelihood, changed significantly in approach.

The problems and complications related to insurance can be devastating not only to finances, but also to morale. A typical problem for patients with chronic illness is the "pre-existing condition" clause of many new insurance policies. Health carriers are notoriously reluctant to provide new policies or increased coverage for persons who have received the diagnosis of a chronic disease. A new policy for a patient with a pre-existing condition is enormously expensive, if available at all. Many patients have reported the cancellation of their policies upon such a diagnosis. Added to the shock of catastrophic illness, the termination of insurance constitutes a devastating blow, leaving the patient and his family enraged and impotent.

There are alternative sources for help, though not many. While the patient will have great difficulty taking out more health insurance than he would have prior to diagnosis, he can apply for Medicare and Medicaid. Patients with other government- or business-related insurance will need to apply for whatever major medical or welfare benefits they can obtain, in order to help their families cope. Counselors should be aware that the need to turn to these agencies is, for many people, a trauma in itself. It is a humiliating experience to become embroiled in the massive red tape; it confirms the patient's disability status, leading him deeper and deeper into feelings of worthlessness. A community-based program, however, can do a great deal to alleviate these problems. It can give many patients the assistance they need in locating financial help.

Psychological Problems of the Chronically Ill Patient

On first consideration, it might seem that, because it can bring death quickly, acute illness would cause greater psychological problems than would chronic illness. But the truth, paradoxically, is just the opposite. From the patient's point of view, the psychological trauma that accompanies the chronic disease can be just as bad as, if in fact not worse than, the disease itself. The psychological problems that the patient faces are so extensive, in fact, that it may be convenient to classify them into several different types.

Fear of Death and Physical Deterioration

One of the major psychological problems that the chronic patient must confront, the fear of death and physical deterioration is what, from the patient's point of view, chiefly sets chronic ailments apart from acute ones. Acute patients facing death generally do not have the time to mull over their impending death, to mourn the loss and separation that will occur. Chronic sufferers, on the other hand, often have years to come to terms with these issues.

The announcement of the diagnosis of a chronic disease may cause major psychological trauma for the patient. The impact of chronic illness has been described by a stroke patient's husband as similar to the shattering of a pane of glass. The splintered lines reaching out in every direction from the center of impact are too numerous to count; they literally surround the patient. Indeed, there have been cases where psychotic breaks and hospitalization in a mental institution have occurred after such a diagnosis. Counseling at this critical time can be invaluable. It can help the patient deal with his or her own personal feelings around sickness and death, physical limitations, and changes in family role and rsponsibilities. End stage renal disease (ESRD) is a good example of a disease that brings about the changes that necessitate great adjustments in life style. ESRD effectively destroys kidney function to the point at which major medical intervention, in the form of transplantation or dialysis, is necessary to keep the patient alive. Transplantation, however, does not provide a final cure. Transplant patients must face the fact that a transplant rarely lasts for more than a few years. Nor is a final cure provided by dialysis. Dialysis causes the body to deteriorate over a number of years. Often patients lose their ability to walk, or to remain continent, eventually finding themselves bedridden until they die. This process of deterioration can continue over an indefinite number of years. Some dialysis patients, as a result of other complications, will survive only a few weeks; others, ten or more years.

Personal Issues

After the first shock of accepting the chronic illness and the inevitability of physical deterioration and death, there are still other issues that the patient must work through. These are personal issues, which virtually every chronically ill patient must face; and they include such problems as changes in body image, dependency, isolation, stigma, and shame. When patients and families avoid or deny these issues, there follows a personal and family anxiety which, at worst, can lead to extreme depression, the breakup of the family, and literal abandonment of the patient. Counseling, which can prevent this, is advisable in every case, because patients and families — even their physicians — often fail to recognize the symptoms until it is too late. In some cases of chronic disease, such as multiple sclerosis, there literally is no form of treatment other than counseling. Another disease for which counseling is indispensible is breast cancer. Currently, breast cancer results in the patient's being sent out of the hospital after surgery, still needing to effect in herself major changes in self-image. Removal of a breast, an important symbol of feminine sexuality, as well as accompanying body changes such as loss of hair from chemotherapy, must be confronted intellectually and emotionally. Individual and group tnerapy is helpful to these women in coping with "here and now" issues. It is not enough — indeed, it is often a cause of outrage — when the physician tells the woman that she should be grateful to be alive. Some women do not want to live if they are not physically intact; they believe that their boy friends may not want to marry them now, or that their husbands may never respond sexually again.

Feelings of Loss

Still another problem that the chronically ill patient must face has to do with his inevitable feelings of loss. In most cases, there are numerous feelings of loss to be dealt with — loss of life, loss of limb, loss of future, and loss of control. In her well-known book, *On Death and Dying*, Elizabeth Kubler-Ross discusses the stages of mourning and loss, as well as the acceptance of death. The chronically ill patient also must go through mourning and loss — and acceptance of the face that he must begin to adapt his life to his disease. He may have many years ahead of him, but now he must live differenttly. The psychological trauma that results from such a realization triggers a period of profound questioning, with a reevaluation of self, personal values, and relationships. As one patient has said, "I am not constantly preoccupied with my mortality, but a fundamental assumption has been permanently altered." Such individuals must pass through the critical first phase of a "different" self, and regain control of their lives by adjusting to a new fundamental assumption. Spouses and other close family members often do not understand this, generally because they too are experiencing changes.

PROBLEMS OF CHRONIC ILLNESS: EFFECTS ON THE FAMILY

Psychological Problems Within the Family System

Personal Issues

The psychological trauma of a chronic illness is almost as powerful for the family as it is for the patient. The basic issues with which the family members must cope are similar to those faced by the patient, but are viewed from their perspective. The issue of body image is difficult for the spouse in one way, for the children in another, and for the parents in yet another. For example, one multiple sclerosis patient's spouse experienced difficulty in accepting the fact that his wife, formerly sexually attractive, had become a cripple. For a time, he was unable to respond to her sexually — and, as a result, had to struggle not only with what he saw as his impotence, but with anxiety and guilt as well. In the same family, the teen-aged daughter also had problems. At first, embarrassed about her mother's condition, she kept her friends away from her home because she did not want them to see her mother crawl up the stairs. Nor was the difficulty limited to the immediate family. The patient's mother and sister, upset and frightened by the disease and approaching death of the patient, and not knowing how to deal with their feelings, avoided the afflicted woman altogether, thereby multiplying their problems, and hers. Family therapy was necessary there, and was received. Fortunately, the help of an experienced counselor was obtained, and the problems of this family were relieved.

Interpersonal Relationship, Communication, Problems

Another source of strain on the family system occurs as a result of the patient's fear of abandonment and his attempts (often unconscious) to relieve it. Fear of abandonment often causes the patient to "force" family members to demonstrate repeatedly how much they care. This "forcing" can take the form of repeated requests for attention and/or irritability and apparent lack of appreciation whenever some attention in fact is received. ("Why didn't you come to see me yesterday? I guess you've been too *busy*! . . . Well, your *sister* has managed to see me every day! Why can't *you* do that?") This sort of thing can create enormous difficulties, because family members tend not to understand this fear, and to experience the patient's persistence only as hostility. In the absence of counseling intervention, the situation can have tragic results. By forcing the issue, the patient unwittingly can turn her fear of abandonment into a self-fulfilling prophesy.

Further difficulties occur if, as a result of these and other stresses within the family, communication breaks down. This can happen, paradoxically, as a result of the family members' loving, caring — and desiring to protect each other, rather than to express negative feelings. Anger, a feeling which the family members will tend to be afraid of, will be felt by everyone, but will be incorrectly focused. It is rarely communicated directly because, in addition to being feared, the anger is seldom understood. The patient and family are angry at the disease; yet they tend to focus their anger on the physician, hospital, and other treatment personnel, all clearer targets than the amorphous disease, and also, in a strange way, more "logical" targets for the receipt of blame. Interestingly, both family and patient will tend to avoid aiming anger at family members, at least directly; yet it will come out in other ways. It may erupt, for example, in the form of a patient's resentment of his wife's "bad driving," which she does for the husband who no longer can manage the car; or, the anger will emerge in another family member's annoyance at the stoke patient's "slowness" in getting into an elevator as he visits the physician's office.

The most intense communication problems (and apparent hostility) can occur between loving married couples. The spouse's wish to return to health and full functioning is continually frustrated. "She could do better if only she *tried*," goes the complaint. Yet the complaint is inappropriate, and only a garbled expression of the real feeling. The real feeling is anger at the situation which they all share, and it is kept unspoken. All that is expressed is a kind of "camouflage" tension and hostility among family members. Arguments over trivia become the order of the day. "Loving" and "caring" are traded for a wish for release. Yet, in general, no one in the family will understand this. "Why doesn't my husband *talk* to me?" the wife will ask. The answer, which the counselor working with the family can help them see, is that he is terrified to tell her that he is just as frightened by the disease that is killing her as she is. He sees the visible deterioration of her body and thinks about her approaching death, and he feels such panic and fear that he is unable to express his love; he is virtually unable to communicate at all.

Children also are affected profoundly by chronic illness, and, for the sake of their mental health, they should not be "protected" by misguided attempts to "shield" them from what is happening. The reason, of course, is that it really is impossible to keep the truth from the child altogether. The child *will realize* the sickness or absence of a family member. And he will need to have the situation explained — as well as an opportunity to work through his feelings, just as would an adult. This working-through of feelings is not only as important for the child as it is for the adult; it may even be, in fact, more important. This is because a child can easily misunderstand what is going on, and develop potentially serious and long-lasting problems later on, as a result. For example, a very young child may come to believe that her stricken parent no longer loves her. Or she will struggle in vain to understand what is going on in terms familiar to her — like the young child of a cancer patient who once said to a counselor, "My mommy is broken." Problems could also develop for an older child. The older child may worry that he will be unable to attend college as a result of his father's disability. Still another possibility would be that an eldest son could become severely disturbed because he may tell himself that, as the only other male in the family after his father's death, he may need to take care of everyone else in the future, thus sacrificing his own youth.

Obviously the concerns of patients and families must be addressed from other than the conventional standpoint. Here is an opportunity for social work to fill a gap in services. Filling this gap — and providing help for these patients and their families — should be considered the challenge of the 'eighties.

BEYOND THE HOSPITAL: THE SEARCH TO FILL PSYCHO-SOCIAL NEEDS OF THE CHRONICALLY ILL AND THEIR FAMILIES

Where Help is Usually Not Available and Why

As the preceding paragraphs have suggested, the diagnosis of chronic illness marks the beginning of a time of struggle and turmoil, both for the patient and his family. For all of them, the financial and psycho-emotional problems can be devastating. It is natural, then, for the patient and his family to look for help in dealing with these problems. Those who are lucky are those who get referred, quickly, into the network of psycho-social health services available in their community (and to the social workers within it who can help them). Those who are not lucky are the ones who do not get a referral, and do not find their way into the health services network until later on, or not at all. In any case, because of the rather haphazard (or unplanned) way in which the system (network) is structured, making the right connections — for almost every patient — is, at the present time at least, a matter of luck. If, for one reason or another, the patient is unlucky, and the "right referrals" are not made, he "falls through the cracks" in the system, seeks help in the wrong places, and winds up trying to deal with the psycho-emotional trauma of his illness virtually alone.

One source from whom the chronically ill patient will tend to look for help, and not find it, is the physician who made the diagnosis. The unfortunate fact is that the psycho-emotional aspect of chronic illness is an area in which many medical practitioners do not take an interest. All too often today, the physician who makes the diagnosis is a specialist, and behaves as a specialist in the narrowest sense of the term. He restricts his interest to the medical problem, and doesn't have the time — or the emotional energy — to concern himself with the patient's emotions. One patient of the author's for example, described an experience with her oncologist, who said that he had "no feelings one way or another" about whether or not she got counseling. He told her that if she wanted someone to talk to, it would "be all right" with him, but he did not want to know about it; his concern was "purely medical".

Other sources to which the patient might turn in his search for psycho-emotional help are in the hospital where he received diagnosis or treatment. Here, in fact, some fortunate patients' search for help is met with some measure of success. This occurs in hospitals that have trained people on the staff — in sufficient numbers to be able either to give the chronic patient who comes to them enough time to work through his problems, or to refer him to someone who can. In many hospitals, however, this first alternative is impossible. And even the second, making a referral, is difficult, because hospital social services tend to be overcrowded with in-patient cases, and little time is available for directing the recently discharged chronically ill patient to an appropriate community service. As an unfortunate result, many patients often are forced to fend for themselves.

A third source to which the chronic patient might turn in vain is, paradoxically, the one by whom he might have had the greatest hope of being helped — the psychiatrist. While this is not always the case, the fact is that conventional psychiatry often is not successful in treating medically ill persons. The general model of psychiatric medicine involves the treatment of the personality. Psychiatry does not deal in physical sickness; it probes more deeply than that. Thus, when the woman sitting in front of the therapist is dying of cancer, it is simply not appropriate to ask her to explore her feelings about her father. Her immediate problem must be addressed; her life is coming to a premature end, and she is not prepared.

This is not to say that psychiatry should be avoided by the chronically ill patient. Once a patient has dealt with his primary/priority agenda, and has come to grips with it, she may well want to explore more deeply buried issues of personality development. The important thing is to recognize the difference between the two levels of concern. In an urgent situation, such as the reaction to a diagnosis of a terminal illness, the immediate symptoms and issues must get attention, and rapidly.

Sources Where Help Usually is Available: The Mental Health/ Social Services Network Within the Community

The world of the chronically ill might well be described as a kind of "halfway world." In it, patients with chronic disease live, in and out of hospitals, as their illnesses dictate. But, thanks to the advances of modern medicine, by far the larger proportion of the time for most chronic patients is spent out of the hospital, back in the community. The victim of kidney disease, connected to a dialysis machine, for as much as six hours in a day, may find life even more precious now than it was before, and want very much to live at home with his family and return to work. And the patient with cancer, going into long remissions and living with her disease for twenty years or more — this patient too may regard her extended life as precious, and want to return to her job and family.

Clearly functional, and with rich contributions to make to family and society, these individuals are, none the less, victims of disease. Although no longer needing twenty-four hour hospital care, they still are not cured. They want to live as normally as possible; yet they must cope with restrictions, often requiring medication, wheelchairs, special transportation, and flexible work hours. In addition, although they may have jobs, their income may be reduced. Certainly, for such individuals, permanent hospitalization is not the solution. It is neither possible, nor is it advisable, in terms of these patients' needs and ability to function.

But what about the restrictions that bind them? In their "halfway world," these people are neither completely well nor desperately ill; they can live comfortably in the community — only if special services are provided to fill their special needs. The question we must consider, then, is this: Is our society able and willing to make the accommodations necessary to provide for the needs of the chronically ill?

The answer is a qualified "yes." Slowly — and with the help and leadership of the social work profession — society is, in fact, beginning to make the accommodations necessary to provide for this special group. To be sure, the community cannot replace the family, but it can provide services that augment or supplement family care, and make it possible for patients to stay out of hospitals and live almost normal lives.

Although the changes are coming at a slow rate, the fact is that what is happening today in the area of community-based health care for the chronically ill is nothing less than a revolution. Focused on freeing the patient from chronic hospitalization, while not allowing her to become an unmanageable burden on the family — these changes are visible all around us in the community today; one has but to look around to see the signs of them. There are nursing homes, home care services, homes for the aged, mental health centers, hospices, and community health agencies, all attempting to bridge the gap between hospital and community. Even within these modes, one can see the formation of other, smaller groups in attempts to fill existing needs not being met elsewhere.

What is happening, in short, is the formation of a vast network of community-based health care and support services for the chronically ill. It is the purpose of this section to describe the components of that network — nothing the advantages and disadvantages, with which today's concerned health care professional must be familiar, in order to be able to deliver the highest quality — and best informed — services to her patients.

Out-Patient Hospital Groups

One component of the community based health care and support services network, and the first one with which many patients come in contact, is the out-patient hospital group (9,20). Charging varying fees, these groups take in patients from two sources. They have patients referred to them by members of hospital staffs. In this case, the patients begin meeting with the group, usually, while still in the hospital, and later, after discharge, continue the association as out-patients. In addition, patients who have not been hospitalized may be referred to a group by medical service providers in the community. The purpose of the out-patient hospital group tends to be, generally, to educate the patient in the area of health awareness, nutrition and life style, and specifically, to help the patient deal with the adjustment problems following his partiular illness and its treatment. In these groups, discussions may include topics such as diet, the importance of exercise, and the avoidance of "negative, or self-defeating behaviors." A major advantage of groups such as these is that they enable the patient to meet and talk with other patients, thus deriving emotional support, and the sense that he is not alone. Another main advantage is that these groups are usually led by a social worker, or nurse clinician, who can manage the group well, facilitate discussions and, more importantly, refer patients who need it to additional sources of help within the network.

Community Mental Health Centers

A second component in the community-based health care and support services network is the community mental health center (15). These organizations are generally publically funded and non-profit making. Fees are charged on a sliding scale, determined by family income; and partial coverage through insurance plans is possible. Counseling, which is provided by trained professionals, including social workers,psychologists, and psychiatrists, is done individually, in groups, and other kinds of therapies, including group, couples, and family. Major advantages of the community mental health centers include their wide availability, their flexible services, and affordability. A disadvantage for the chronically ill patient, however, is that these centers do not provide special training for medically related problems.

Nursing Homes

A third component in the community-based health care care network is the nursing home. Having undergone major changes since the mid nineteen-sixties, the nursing home now offers a very desirable alternative for some patients seeking out-of-hospital health care (4). It should be noted, too, that these changes that have brought about the improvement in nursing home care are largely the result of the evolution or developments in the social work profession itself. As many of us are aware, like most other health care professionals, social workers rarely involved themselves in nursing home care prior to 1965. Neither our society nor its health care professionals gave much priority at that time to the needs of the chronically ill and elderly. The nursing home took care of the complicated medical problems, but once the chronically ill patient was settled in a nursing home, the physician and other health care profesionals tended to pay little attention to him. The result was that the patient usually spent the rest of his life there, gradually becoming alienated not only from family and friends, but also from high quality medical care. During the last fifteen to twenty years, however, social workers have moved aggressively into the area of care for the chronically ill. Even today, it must be said that many nursing homes still are not addressing the psycho-social needs of their patients to the extent that the need exists. But the trend towards improvement has begun and, spurred by continued demands from the social work profession and the community, nursing home directors continue to study their patients' needs and improve services — some of them having already, in fact, achieved a level of excellence.

Nursing homes vary as to affiliation and funding. Some are private; some are state-affiliated. Fees, too, vary widely and, since up-to-date information is desirable, telephoning the particular nursing home in which one is interested is usually best. The advantages of nursing home care are many. There the patient has the security of competent nursing care, on a twenty-four hour a day basis, easy access to physicians and medical facilities, nutrition plannned by trained dieticians, the fellowship of other patients, and the potential for a close, collaborative relationship between patient and support staff. In addition, an increasing number of nursing homes today have one full-time, in-house social worker on staff to help patients cope with psycho-social problems. As with the community mental health center, however, the nursing home has a disadvantage in that special training for medically related problems is often not provided.

Hospices

Another important component in the community-based health services network — and one wherein the social work profession has been able to be substantially more effective than in the nursing home — is the hospice (1). To be eligible for care in a hospice, a patient must be terminally ill (usually defined as having six months or less to live). Inspired by the English concept of "death with dignity," proponents of the hospice movement are emphasizing the value of the remaining life of the terminal patient, and attempting to make that time meaningful and pleasant. Recently the number of hospices in the United States has grown very rapidly. Privately funded for the most part, non-profitmaking, and with fees on a sliding scale depending on family income, hospices offer the terminally ill patient a multitude of psycho-social services. Complete medical care is provided, of course — as well as patient home-care, and social work, with special training for medically related problems, and counseling and support services attempting to meet all family needs. There is, in addition, a Hospice Society Referral Service enabling the health care professional and her patients to locate a suitable hospice with optimum ease.

Church Related Services

Another component in the community-based health services network that the chronically ill patient (and his counselor) should know about is that provided through religious and church-related organizations. During the last few years, the church has been getting increasingly involved in counseling programs. Although many of the clergy are trained counselors, time limitations and the large number of those in need of help who turn to their churches, make it impossible for the clergymen to assume this role totally. As a result, the church has developed broader-scope counseling programs. These have some problems, however: For one thing, they are generally run by untrained volunteers who, though well-meaning, often disappoint the patient, not meeting his expectations. Still, these groups can be helpful and they do have a place among the resources available to the chronically ill. The churches have a special attraction in that they typically are free — or, if a fee is charged,it is low, and determined on a sliding scale basis. In addition, these church-related groups have the advantage of being able to provide a particularly non-threatening, comforting environment for the patient and his family. The church programs tend not to offer the patient support from others who share physical symptoms similar to, or as serious as, his in many cases; but they do provide support from others generally affected by the problems of living with chronic illness, and there is much value in that.

Voluntary Health Agencies

A sixth component in the community-based health services network — and no doubt the one with which people are most familiar — is the voluntary health agency (5). Including such well-known organizations as The American Cancer Society, The Lupus Foundation, and The Multiple Sclerosis Society, the volunteer health agencies evolved in an interesting way. They began, for the most part, as fund-raising groups, formed to support research and provide concrete helping devices such as wheelchairs or prostheses. Over a period of time, however, they became recipients of thousands of phone calls from patients and families. People wanted answers to innumerable questions about serious disease. Where could help be found in the community? Who would help them with financial difficulties? To whom could they turn for help with physical problems? What about emotional problems? To these and many other questions that people were asking, there was no one trained to provide answers. In fact there was no one to answer questions at all, except the office clerks, secretaries, and volunteers who did fund-raising over the telephone. Thus it was that, for a time, office personnel and untrained volunteers began counseling people on an informal basis, and the organization itself recognized a new direction into which to grow.

Not originally set up for the purpose of filling psycho-social needs, but motivated by the knowledge that these needs were not being met elsewhere, the volunteer health agencies soon decided that within their patient services mandates, they had an obligation to address these issues. Accordingly, these organizations undertook programs of tremendous expansion — both in services to be provided, and in acquisition of funds to support these services. Fortuitously, the political and economic climate at the time favored the development of these organizations, and thus it was that, during the Kennedy and Johnson administrations, volunteer health agencies obtained massive funding from the federal government.

As they now operate, the volunteer health agencies provide extremely valuable services to patients and families. They serve also as a valuable source of information for social workers seeking to learn more about a particular disease and its effects, or about support groups and other services to which patients may be referred. The volunteer health agencies are privately funded, non-profit making organizations, and they charge no fees. They provide educational pamphlets and brochures that answer the questions that patients and families tend to have; they provide group counseling, which can be extremely valuable to many patients; and they provide referrals, as needed, to other services. A major shortcoming in what these organizations have to offer to the chronic patient, however, is that they do not provide special training for medically related problems; another shortcoming is that they do not offer counseling on an individual basis.

As a result of the same momentum of volunteering and fund-raising during the sixties that sparked the growth of the volunteer health agencies, and as part of the volunteer health agencies, a great number of smaller peer support groups came into being. During that period the Department of Health, Education and Welfare awarded numerous federal grants for the development of pilot projects in a number of cities around the country. Self-help groups flourished, and new ideas, plus some old ones whose "time had come," bore fruit in the formation of excellent peer group organizations such as "Make Today Count" for cancer patients, and The Stroke Club. Another excellent organization that counselors should know about is "Gut Line," the physician volunteer program of the American Digestive Disease Society. Through this program, anyone in the United States can call in and speak to a physician for five minutes, getting in essence, a free consultation. Further, it can be totally anonymous if the patient wishes. This program has been so successful that the organization is presently opening numerous chapters around the country. It is a classic example of what can result from a marriage between the medical profession and a volunteer health organization. Other extremely valuable organizations are Alcoholics Anonymous, and the more recent Special Olympics, which have shown tremendous growth and have mobilized energy and interest from all sectors of the community.

These groups and others like them which began in a burst of volunteerism, have become increasingly valuable resources in recent years. Counselors and social workers should know about these groups and what they have to offer, in order to be able to refer patients to them when appropriate. It is also necessary, however, for health care professionals to know about the potential shortcomings of peer and volunteer groups. One is that such groups often try, without success, to use untrained, lay volunteers to do work which can be done well only by trained professionals. These attempts often have unfortunate results. An interesting development in this regard occurred, however, when some groups tried to get around the problem of the inadequacy of the untrained volunteer. Taking advantage of the "mind set" of volunteerism, several organizations attempted to enlist the aid of "professional volunteers," or professionals working in the field who were willing to give their time free of charge to perform professional tasks. Several organizations began to use professional volunteers to run treatment groups for people with particular diseases. Peer groups such as these have been found useful by many chronic disease sufferers because they can share experiences with people who, they feel, "understand."

In spite of the fact that there have been a few cases inwhich the use of the "professional volunteer" has worked out well, as a general rule the practice is inadvisable because such arrangements tend not to work well, or not to last very long, because of personality conflicts or "hidden agendas" on the part of some of the personnel. To see the reason for this, it is important to be clear what a volunteer gets out of giving his time. Volunteerism is a business much like any other except that the payment is not money. If all parties understand this, relationships can proceed. However, if this is not understood, relationships get muddy, and help is precluded by interference from hidden agendas. The way that a "hidden agenda" operates can be seen in the following illustration. The helping person may have, without knowing it, a need to control. In a helping relationship, such a need may be manifested as a "need to save" or a "need to be needed." The way that this hidden need can interfere with the helping process is that it can cause the helping person to encourage the patient to become dependent. A counselor may tell a patient, for example, "If you need to, call me at any time, even late at night." Although such an offer may at first glance seem quite generous, stemming from profound and genuine concern for the patient, it may not be what it seems at all. For the counselor to suppose it possible to "be there" for the patient *at all times* is unrealistic; calling at night, the patient might find the counselor not available, and his feelings of inadequacy and abandonment in such circumstances might intensify rather than decrease. The truth is that the helping person who would make the unrealistic offer of perpetual help may not in fact be thinking of the patient's needs at all, but of his own. And, although such a phenomenon can occur when the counselor is being paid, the incidence tends to be far greater among counselors working as volunteers. At all times, then — but especially when working "without pay" — helping persons should engage in continual monitoring of their own needs and motives.

This is not to say, however, that participation in a small peer or volunteer group cannot be of value to the patient. On the contrary, such groups can be of great benefit — to some patients, at some times. What is necessary, though is that the counselor understand the differences between professionally run and volunteer or peer groups, and use careful judgment in recommending participation in the latter for their patients. As a rule, professional counseling is the best option for patients and their families in all cases; but there are some cases in which participation in a volunteer or peer group is advisable *in addition* to professional help. This is because patients — particularly the young — benefit tremendously from social interactions with, and acceptance among, peers. For example, children with muscular dystrophy are truly limited in their mobility and totally dependent upon others. They tend to get major benefits out of sharing experiences with others like them. An argument can be made that this kind of peer support and acceptance during the early developmental period and then "mainstreaming" the child into the normal school system is significant in developing ego strength so the growing child can deal later on with the community.

One young girl of fifteen, for example, was comfortable enough after such an involvement to "dance" and lead a parade as a cheerleader. This, of course, was done from a wheelchair. She did not deny her illness, or deceive herself as to its seriousness. She perceived herself as capable. Such an attitude on the part of the patient can help to educate the community; as she perceives herself, so will she be perceived by others. Helped by the peer group, such a patient can overcome her anger at her misfortune, and regain her desire to get the most out of life.

Another type of case for which participation in a peer group is advisable is that in which the patient is a child and he is not seen by a counselor until the teen years or later. In this case, too, counseling alone may not be sufficient. It is for this type of patient and family that the social activities provided by the special interest volunteer organization can be valuable. If a patient and family is in, or has had some form of, professional counseling, it might be appropriate for the to go into a group at a voluntary health organization as a semi-social peer support experience. Often these organizations have planned social programs which include free or discounted admission to special events.

There are other types of cases, however, wherein participation in a peer group would be a potentially serious mistake. A young multiple sclerosis patient, for example, might find herself sitting in a peer group with persons who are using canes or sitting in wheelchairs. While she may be experiencing few or minor symptoms at the time, what she is seeing is her future self. Unless she is prepared for it, this experience can be unpleasant and frightening. It may be disturbing psychologically, and could, potentially, cause her to withdraw into the world of the "sick" before necessary. Some patients do become totally involved with the advanced illness of "their" people, in fact, and withdraw completely from interactions with those who are well. In circumstances such as these, there is no substitute for professional counseling.

Home Care Agencies

Another resource in the community based health care network that can play an important part in the lives of some patients and families is the home care agency (2, 10). These agencies charge a negotiable fee, in return for which they send a trained medical social worker, who provides patient and family counseling, as needed, in the patient's own home. The main advantage of this kind of arrangement is that because the patient and family are seen in the home environment, they do not have to travel. A disadvantage, however, is that by having the counselor visit his home, the patient may be unable to have the privacy he needs during the counseling sessions.

Private Medical Practice Based Social Services

Another valuable resource in the community based health services network is that of the social service offered as part of a private medical practice. Within a complete health service team, including physicians and nurses, as well as social workers, these medical practice based social services are private, charging fees on a sliding scale; and they offer the patient and family many advantages in terms of providing complete, "holistic" health care, centered at a single location, and featuring both medical and psycho-social services, provided by a team of professionals who communicate effectively and work well together. In such practices, patients enjoy the additional advantages of being able to have individual, group, or family counseling as needed. A disadvantage, however, is that, although a growing trend, the social service offered as part of a private medical practice represents a relatively recent innovation in health care; as a result, practices incorporating such services are not yet widely available in the community.

Private Practitioners

Another relatively recent development in the health services network available in the community is the private practitioner social worker. Working out of her own office, and charging fees on a sliding scale, the private practitioner is an independent (often self-employed) social worker who offers complete counseling services — on an individual, group, or family basis — to help patients and their families cope with the effects of chronic illness. She facilitates communication between patient and family and physician, acts as "patient advocate," and, of course, provides special focus on medically related problems as needed. In addition, because she is independent, (i.e., not obtaining her salary from a private physician, hospital, or other organization), she is in a position to make really good, reliable referrals. The only real disadvantage patients will experience in utilizing the services of the private practitioner is that in some states, the law does not permit third-party payment of her fees through insurance plans, and in those states as a result many patients are unable to afford the private practitioner's services.

THE ROLE(S) OF THE SOCIAL WORKER IN COMMUNITY HEALTH CARE TODAY

The advent of new knowledge, changing philosophies of illness and its relation to mental, emotional, and environmental stress brings a growing awareness of the vital role of social work in treating the chronically ill. The multifaceted functions of the social worker demand in her a unique combination of skills in the health care area. Combining knowledge of human behavior, community resources, systems theory and group dynamics on the one hand, with assessment and treatment skills on the other. The social worker is uniquely equipped as a health care professional in treating the whole person. Skills in observing, diagnosing, and reporting social and psychological stresses which contribute to human dysfunction are vital in patient assessment and planning for both treatment and prevention of illness. The combination of skills that she needs in order to perform her task with maximum effectiveness must enable her to play, at one time or another, four main roles: that of Community Educator, Counselor, Broker between Other Services, and Patient Advocate.

Social Worker as Educator

In the role of educator, the social worker is an integral part of the total helping process. Sensitivity to the needs and feelings of the patient, as well as of the family, will aid the social worker in contributing important information in a timely and acceptable manner. The mother of a cystic fibrosis child recently vented her frustration in a group saying, "I tried to sign up for a seminar recently which was advertised as being 'for care providers.' I was told I wasn't one. I'm the mother of a sick child . . . What am I if not a care provider?" Through formal presentations to *all* the special interest groups, the social worker has a special educational opportunity. The informal education process is inherent in all professional interactions. Perhaps the most important teaching activity of all, however, involves work with individual clients. The emphasis here is on supplying the patient with knowledge about his disease, and of teaching him ways of coping with it, as well as with the world around him, as he faces it with decreasing abilities and strength.

Social Worker as Counselor

As service provider or counselor, the social worker draws upon a knowledge base of normative social functioning, patterns of interpersonal relationships within the family and social environment, and psycho-social factors influencing reactions to illness and treatment. In this role, her job is to listen, understand, and give support as the patient struggles to come to terms with his condition. Throughout this process the counseling should be focused upon keeping the patient functional as long as possible, thus delaying as long as possible the onset of permanent disability, with its negative psychological effects. The counseling must be done, as always, sensitively, with the idea that when at last the patient is forced to go on disability, he will not feel that he has failed. As always, in counseling persons with chronic diseases, these have to be a balance favoring the current situation crisis.

Social Worker as Broker Between Other Services

In her role as broker between other service providers, the social worker functions as an information source and communications link. The linkage role incorporates the social worker's knowledge and use of community resources and the health care system. As linker, the social worker must first ascertain patient and family needs, determine the resources available to meet the identified needs, assess the system through which the patient must maneuver in determining resources, and finally, negotiate an arrangement between the patient and the resources. Her job here, essentially, involves possessing information (and/or knowing where to get it quickly), and making referrals. Thus, it is an important job — in that as part of it the social worker has the responsibility of knowing and selecting the best practitioners in her network to whom to refer patients.

In her role of broker, the social worker must be as knowledgeable as possible regarding all services which could apply to the patient and family needs. She must, for example, have a basic familiarity with disability insurance benefits. She needs to understand the nature of the illness or disease that the patient has, as well as what services might be offered by agencies or foundations in the geographic area to aid the patients and families affected by the disease — the American Cancer Society, for example, or The Cystic Fibrosis Foundation. And lastly, she must know the names and reputations of skilled health care practitioners in her area to whom to refer patients.

After making the referral to the physician or other service provider, the social worker continues to work with the patient, in the role of Patient Advocate.

Social Worker as Patient Advocate

The Medical Crisis Counselor social worker, at almost every level of involvement with agency or private practice, almost always serves in the role of patient advocate, particularly if the patient has been known from the time of early diagnosis. Even if the patient is seen in short term treatment, several months, many patients maintain some form of contact over the years. It is not unusual for former patients or family members to be seen later on, as various new problems arise in their daily lives. These problems may take the form of difficulties with insurance disability, psychological aspects of retirement, decreased sexual functioning, adolescent children, or changes in physicians' services. The social worker, if she understands the client's total picture, can then act as advocate and resource person. And, in that role, she can provide the family with answers to questions such as these: "Where can we get a wheelchair?" "What would be a good nursing home?" "Why is my daughter acting this way?" Or "Why does the doctor seem less interested than he was before?"

The social worker's most important role as patient advocate, however, is as provider of essential information (with the patient's permission) to various other persons in the network of services, most notably the physician. Information regarding the patient's emotional/psychological condition can be crucial, for example, in the physician's decision as to whether or not to prescribe certain drugs. As a case in point, recently, the author learned of a situation that illustrates very well what can happen when a patient advocate is not involved. It was the case of a young girl who, although not *apparently* so, was a borderline psychotic. Her physician, a neurologist, focusing on *other aspects* of the girl's condition, did not note the predisposition to psychosis, and prescribed Prednisone, a drug which — as physicians and trained medical crisis counselors know — is a behavior altering drug, not advisable for use with psychotic patients. After receiving this drug, the young girl suffered a psychotic break, had to be hospitalized, and has at the time of this writing still not been "brought back" from her psychosis. In this case no social worker was involved, or even informed about the situation, until it was too late. If a social worker trained as a medical crisis counselor had been involved soon enough, there is a very great chance that the psychotic episode could have been avoided.

This illustration is intended to show — not that the physician was careless or incompetent, which, in fact, he was not — but that the tremendous benefits of the advances made in medicine in recent years have a price. As medical practice becomes increasingly specialized, and medical treatments more refined, the medical practitioner becomes virtually inundated with information. Not only does he find himself responsible for keeping up with current research in his own field, but also to varying extents in other fields as well; in addition he must continually try to stay up to date on new drugs and their contraindications and side effects; and, sometimes most difficult of all, he must be careful to note the ideopathic situation of each patient (including pre-existing conditions, other drugs being taken, presence of allergies, etc.). And, for each patient, the complex interplay of all these bits of knowledge must be factored into every decision that the physician makes relating to treatment and drug prescriptions. It is clear, then, that the task of information management that the physician faces is enormous. In addition, making matters worse, in many situations the physician is pressed for time — and/or he is dealing with a patient who, for one reason or another, is nonverbal, and hence not a good source of information. Thus, it is clear how important a role the social worker can play as patient advocate. By being familiar with the particular patient's medical and psychological condition, and by being informed as to the nature of the illness, as well as the usually prescribed drugs and their side-effects, the patient advocate can facilitate communication between physician and patient. And in so doing, she can make the physician's job easier, and enable the patient to feel more secure.

ISSUES ON COMMUNITY CARE OF THE CHRONICALLY ILL TODAY: WHAT STILL NEEDS TO BE DONE

As the previous paragraphs have shown, the development of community service agencies, and the expansion of the role of the social worker constitute the two most important new developments in health care for the chronically ill. As part of these same developments, there is a growing tendency for professionals to have as their ideal a concept of "total health care." "Total health care" is coming to be understood by health care providers and their patients as a broad spectrum, holistic type of care, addressing not only the patient's medical needs, but also his psycho-social needs, and those of his family. In providing for these needs, the health care service providers and agencies work together, ideally, as a team. Communicating and cooperating with each other as well as with the patient, these care providers may be thought of as "surrounding" the patient, giving him and his family the optimum kind of support that is possible only through coordinated, team efforts.

This concept of "total health care" provided by a coordinated team of professionals constitutes the ideal in modern health care. Unfortunately, however, in many cases the reality with which chronically ill patients are confronted falls far short of the ideal. There are several reasons why this is so. For one thing, changes in the working relationships between social workers and physicians are being effected at an extremely slow rate. That is to say, although growing numbers of physicians today are aware of the potentially great value of having social workers involved in the care of their patients, they are none the less slow to bring them into their practices because of administrative or economic difficulties. The reasons for this are not far to seek. The fact is that, even though he may well understand that symbiosis with a social worker may be an excellent way to improve patient care, the average physician today does not have the kind of practice that can afford to pay a social worker. Such a physician would be reluctant to bring a social worker into his practice because, already hard-pressed to keep his fees low, he would see a social worker as an unjustifiable added expense. This would be true for the most part, however, only for the average family practice physician and many internists. Such physicians would tend to have very little need for the services of a social worker. Typically, physicians in practices such as these get to know their patients well and will tend to feel that they are providing necessary emotional support themselves. Furthermore, in acting as family physicians, they will be dealing primarily with acute, or less serious, illnesses, and therefore the number of patients that such a physician will have at any one time with serious, or chronic, illnesses will tend to be small enough for him to manage pretty well by himself.

Even though the family practice physician generally is not in a position to benefit greatly from having a social worker on his staff, there are others who are. Typically the specialists — oncologists, neurologists, nephrologists, and gastroenterologists in particular — can benefit immeasurably by having a social worker on staff. For such physicians, in fact, the addition of the social worker not only enables the physician to improve the quality of his patient care, it turns out to be cost-effective as well. The way the arrangement works, ideally, is that the social worker becomes part of the physician's office staff (on a full-time basis if possible, or on a regular, part-time basis if necessary), and she provides counseling and educational support services, right in the medical offices, during the regular schedule. This is cost-effective because it frees up a sizeable portion of the physician's time, enabling him to see more patients. And it results in improved overall health care in that it insures that the patient's psycho-social needs and those of his family are provided for, *without* his having to spend additional time, energy, and money in locating a counselor, making an appointment, and traveling to the counseling sessions. The patient, thus, is assured not only of getting skilled counseling, but of getting it conveniently. The result, in many cases, will be improved morale on the part of patient and family and, as is increasingly in evidence today, improved morale not only makes day-to-day living more pleasant, in some cases it also is a factor in lessening disease symptoms.

Another way whereby the physician and the social worker may collaborate is that wherein the physician, not having a social worker as part of his staff, refers a patient to a private practice social worker, based on his knowledge of her work. The difficulty that may occur here arises from the potential for resistance on the part of both patient and physician. Depending on the extent and closeness of his professional contacts, the physician may have more or less difficulty in locating a social worker for the referral, and he may be reluctant to spend the time it takes to do it. And the patient, fearful of the unknown, and already upset and anxious about his illness — with its potentially enormous costs — may tend to resist the notion of seeking additional professional help. Even after a referral is made, there is the danger that the doctor may lose contact (or may not even establish close contact) with the social worker or the patient. Or, even worse, obliged to make a separate appointment to see the counselor, at a separate location, the patient may get lost in the shuffle. On the other hand, many of these problems can be prevented or minimized by direct, informal telephone contact and brief memos which may be kept in the patient's file for future reference. Even though the doctor and the social worker may not be operating from the same physical plant, they can be collaborating, and the patient will understand and be reassured by this fact.

Today, however, both of these arrangements whereby the physician and the social worker collaborate are, unfortunately, more the exceptions than the rule. Teamwork, and the "total approach" to health care are slow in coming because, although their potential benefits are increasingly well-known today, not enough has been said or written about practical ways of facilitating such arrangements. It is up to forward-thinking physicians and social workers to change this.

A second reason why the care which many chronically ill patients receive today falls far short of the ideal has to do with problems with insurance policies. To be sure, the entire rationale underlying insurance for the chronically ill in the community today needs to be reviewed and changed. At present, not only do such insurance policies fail to address the needs of the chronically ill, they actually add to the already enorous stresses suffered by this group. The author has seen many patients and families nearly devastated when, in addition to the terrible problems of adjusting to the effects of chronic illness, they were obliged to spend entire days in frustrating struggles with insurance companies.

In their eagerness to minimize costs, insurance companies go to great lengths to avoid providing for total health care. Almost invariably, as a result of these cost-cutting attempts, one of the first things to be eliminated is counseling. The fact is, though — and it is up to enlightened health care professionals to convince the insurance companies of this — that comprehensive health care, including counseling, can lower medical costs in the long run. For example, a patient who requires frequent hospitalizations because of his inability to cope with insulin injections can be helped to deal with the problem, and minimize the costly stays in the hospital, by counseling. Home nursing care or care in hospices, also much resisted by penny-saving insurance companies, are additional alternatives in total health care that are cheaper than hospitalization. Moreover, there are some diseases for which counseling, the only treatment possible, is also the only treatment *not* covered by many insurance policies. With multiple sclerosis, for example, the reduction of stress brings about the reduction of symptoms; and the reduction of symptoms, in turn, increases the patient's ability to function. Nonetheless, the costs of counseling for such patients are currently being borne, largely, by the patients themselves.

In spite of the fact that for the most part insurance laws and policies have not kept up with recent developments in the care of the chronically ill, there are some signs that evolutionary change may be beginning to come to the field of medical insurance. In Fairfax, Virginia, for example, Blue Cross and Blue Shield is currently performing an interesting experiment — a pilot project. It is paying for "alternative treatment" to in-patient care (such as day hospitalization, wherein the patient sleeps at home) for 100 patients with certain chronic diseases. The preliminary costs appear to be low, and the patients like the feeling of freedom and control over their lives.

More studies and experiments such as this must be done, so that the relative costs of different treatment modalities can be compared and evaluated. It is the opinion of this author that comprehensive care will ultimately be demonstrated to be more cost effective, and *better for the patient* that the current limited, but expensive, services available.

Clearly, insurance companies and their chronically ill patients and families would benefit from short-term, low-cost, medically related counseling. Such community-provided services, if properly offered, would assist patients and families in functioning better, and cost the insurance companies less for both medical and psychotherapeutic treatment. It is up to today's concerned health care professionals to convince the insurance companies that they should stop trying to save pennies on total health care, only to spend, as often as not, dollars on hospitalization.

Another important issue in health care today — and a third reason why care for the chronically ill often falls short of the ideal — has to do with the shortage of skilled professionals working in this area. In many cases, patients receive substandard care because of a lack of training on the part of the care providers. Some of these providers may even be professionals, but in many cases, although they were trained, they were not trained to treat the special problems of the chronically ill. In any case, although the care provider's intentions may be good, the care he provides is not. Particularly unfortunate is the situation wherein a professional who lacks training in the care of the chronically ill takes a job in this field, tries to "learn by doing,' and winds up making too many mistakes. In such situations, patients and families often believe they are getting an "expert," but then have a bad experience and want no more contact. The Candlelighters, a volunteer peer support group for the parents of children with cancer, will not allow mental health professionals to become involved in their organization because of such experiences.

Our awareness that the care given the chronically ill is not always of high quality, coupled with our chagrin at the dissatisfaction felt by groups such as the Candlelighters, should stimulate us to solve the problem of the shortage of trained personnel immediately. Doing this, however, may not be easy. One reason is there is not yet a sufficient number of high-quality training programs designed to prepare social workers to care for the specific medical and psychosocial needs of the chronically ill and their families. We in the profession of social work have, in the care of the chronically ill, a newly emerging specialization. And, we are challenged to develop more and improved programs to train (and re-train) health care professionals to work in that field.

Moreover, although such programs are still in the early stages of development, we know what they must consist of — because we know the skills and knowledge that are needed by those who care for the chronically ill. Even for someone who has had training, such a job is difficult, and emotionally taxing; a large portion of this special training must consist, therefore, of special psychological preparation. The social worker interested in working with the chronically ill and handicapped must be secure, self-reliant, emotionally mature, and well integrated. She must confront the many issues of death and physical disability before she begins to work with patients and families. She should have some medical knowledge, particularly related to the prognoses, and she must be able to work well with the physician and other health care team members. In addition, she must be prepared to help the patient and family psychologically, emotionally, and intellectually. To do this, she needs to learn to use an aggressive, direct approach, to help the patient see and understand the issues created by his medical situation. She needs to have a "bio-psycho-social" perspective, and to be able to use all of the social worker's tools — in casework, group work, education, and consultation — with equal ease. The shifts in focus and methods will be constant, from patient to family to community. Sometimes she will need to provide individual therapy, sometimes group, or couples therapy. At all times, flexibility in approach is vital, and her training program must prepare her for it.

Although this medical-psycho-social specialization is still in its infancy, it has acquired a name: Medical Crisis Counseling. Moreover, training programs, such as the one sketched above, designed to prepare medical crisis counselors, are now being developed. One of these is in the School of Social Work at the University of Maryland. This program, which will be offered for both full-time and part-time students, will provide course work and supervised fieldwork, enabling the student to become a licensed medical crisis counselor. This will be done, moreover, either as part of a social work degree program or through Continuing Education.

One reason offered for why the shortage of personnel adequately trained in the care of the chronically ill is a problem difficult to solve is that the development of good, up-to-date training programs takes time and effort, and is now just beginning. The second reason, possibly even more serious, is the lack of money to pay for high-quality, total health care. As a result of the rising cost of health care in general, combined with widespread budget-cutting, and the difficulties perpetually created by insurance companies, the cut-backs in federal funding for health care and health care agencies that came about during the Reagan Administration have dealt a blow to the community health care network that is very serious indeed. It is clear, at the time of this writing, that, generally speaking, high-quality services from highly trained professionals deserve and require proportionate remuneration; therefore, if cut-backs in funding take the form of lower salaries and reduced benefits for health care workers, then the best ones will either lack the motivation to enter this important field or, having entered it, they will lack the motivation to stay. In either case, the result will be that the shortage of adequately trained personnel will — in spite of the development of good training programs — remain an unsolved, serious problem.

To minimize this problem, at the very least, it is incumbent upon health care professionals everywhere to devote as much of their energy as possible to the education of the public as to the value of providing adequate support for total health care. If this is done — and only if this is done — can sufficient pressure be brought to bear on legislators to act on behalf of their constituents, and return quality health care to the status of high national priority that it deserves.

The issue of education of the public regarding chronic illness and the need for high quality total health care is of critical importance also in respects other than financial. It is up to today's health care professional to concern herself with another problem faced by the chronically ill: intolerance and prejudice on the part of the public. The intolerance and prejudice that the chronically ill and handicapped suffer at the hands of the public are so pervasive and potentially damaging, in fact, that reflective observers have begun to recognize, just as they did on behalf of blacks and women during the last twenty years, that the chronically ill and handicapped population constitute an oppressed minority. They are variously resented, patronized, ignored, or feared — largely as a result of stereotyped thinking and ignorance.

Happily, a movement to set this injustice right has already begun. To some extent, certainly, public attitudes have started to modify, as a result of educational efforts already made. Signs of these changes can be seen, for example, in the increasing numbers of building entrances, toilet facilities, public transportation vehicles, and accessways which have been redesigned and equipped for use by the handicapped.

But physical equipment is relatively easy to change. More difficult to modify are human attitudes. These tend to persist, and, although sometimes the affronts that negative attitudes cause can be slight, each taken by itself, nonetheless when a patient faces many of them every day, throughout the days, weeks, months, and years of her illness, the cumulative effect can be seriously undermining psychologically. For example, in a Philadelphia newspaper recently, a young woman who uses a wheelchair to get around described her resentment of the fact that sales clerks in stores frequently behave either as if they do not see her, or as if she were a child, or incompetent. "Recently," she wrote, "I went into a dress shop with a girl-friend (who can walk). I told the clerk I was looking for a plaid skirt. The clerk turned to my friend and said 'What size does she wear?"

But being treated by strangers as if they were children or incompetent is not the worst kind of thing that handicapped persons must face. The worst treatment is that which can come from those who know them. Not uncommon, for example, is the tendency of friends — and even family — to taper off or discontinue relationships with a chronically ill or recently handicapped friend. This creates a sense of rejection and abandonment that is very real, and potentially devastating psychologically. Equally — if not even more — serious is the tendency of employers to terminate the afflicted person's employment prematurely, or to refuse to hire him in the first place, on the grounds that "sick or handicapped workers cannot do a good job."

The truth, though, is quite the opposite. As more and more employers and co-workers are beginning to realize, persons with chronic illness or handicaps in many cases, can do an excellent job. Sometimes some modifications may be necessary at the work-place. For example, sound-amplification equipment may be added to a telephone used by someone with a hearing loss. Or, a worker with cerebral palsy may use computer assistance in order to speak to other workers. Sometimes, also, it may be necessary for adjustments to be made in the employee's working hours. In any case, though, modifications are, in fact, possible. Moreover, they often can be made with much less difficulty than employers expect — as well as with much greater than anticipated benefits in terms of high morale and productivity on the part of the employee, and, in many cases, the saving of time and money on the part of the employer who, keeping the handicapped employee on the job, does not have to hire, or train another worker.

In order to bring about real progress for the chronically ill and handicapped today, concerned health professionals must consider one of their greatest challenges to be the modification of people's attitudes. To meet this challenge, health professionls must keep in mind the fact that the rejection and prejudice from which the chronically ill suffer at the hands of the public has its source in two main factors. First is the intellectual component, that is, lack of knowledge about chronic illness — its causes, treatment, and effects, including what afflicted people cannot do, as well as, more importantly, what they can do. To reduce prejudice and rejection stemming from ignorance is relatively easy. The solution, clearly, is information dissemination. The second factor in the public's rejection and prejudice against the chronically ill, though, is more difficult to deal with. This factor is fear. It is, after all, not only the patient or the family who suffer from the human problems of fear and denial, but everyone. We all fear physical deterioration and infirmity; they remind us that we too are on a journey toward death.

Old age can be another unpleasant reminder. We all love old people who look great and are socially active. Yet we shun nursing and old age homes. It is the same fear, ironically, that causes people to avoid taking advantage of the frequent checkups and other features of preventive medicine. Women tend not to want to know — or even think — about breast cancer, until it happens. And few people want to think about all the deforming or fatal diseases that their children could inherit. This fear of death, then, is universal and very human. If health care professionals do not as a rule exhibit the rejecting or prejudiced behavior that this fear gives rise to, however, it is because most of them have had the opportunity to confront and work through this fear as a part of their training and/or experience. We have, as the saying goes, "been through it." The situation is similar for the chronically ill. By the time they begin moving about freely among the public, they too have had an opportunity to confront and deal with their feelings about disease, their fear of death. And, for the lucky ones, their families, too, have "been through it." Just as for the health care professional and for the chronic patient himself, the family member too may have the opportunity to learn about the disease, and to confront and work through his feelings. In virtually every case, this process is neither rapid nor easy, neither totally intellectual nor totally emotional; and many times the process is facilitated by a skilled counselor.

The public, on the other hand, has had no such help. They have had no counselor, no experience with prolonged illness, and no time to confront their feelings about death; they have not "been through it." Nor should these facts be surprising. It is well known that the American public today is, generally speaking, healthier and more physically fit than any human group ever was before. And, although many of them will tend to have had some experience with illness, and even death, for the most of them it tends to have been non-serious illness, or acute illness, and rapid death. The truth is, though, that, with relatively rare exceptions, the greater proportion of the public has not had personal, in-family, *prolonged* exposure to illness or serious handicaps; they have not, therefore, learned about, or confronted their feelings about, disease and death. To do so was not, in fact, necessary — during the years before medical science had made the advances which extended the lives of people with serious illness and created the population of the chronically ill. It wasn't necessary, that is to say, twenty years or so ago. It is now.

How can the public learn about serious illness? How can they confront their feelings about infirmity and death? To be sure, to do so is difficult; unless chronic illness strikes an individual himself, or a member of his family, he is unmotivated to think about it, or about the issues it raises. Invariably, the appropriate reaction of the well to the ill is an uncertain, unpredictable phenomenon. It is influenced by education, life experiences, and exposure to or experience with serious illness. It is, after all, much easier to respond to concrete issues which we can visualize and understand, than to deal with that gray area of unknown problems, of which the chronically ill patient is a good example. Even with experience, however, most people avoid dealing with such examples. As children, most of us can remember being told not to stare at someone walking with difficulty or looking different. For most people that reaction of looking away and turning their thoughts elsewhere — that *avoidance reaction* — continues to be made, long after they have ceased to be children, long after they are old enough to "handle it." And so the avoidance response continues being made, again and again, until the individual at last acquires the exposure to illness, life experience or education that will enable him to grow past this child's level of reacting.

The way to speed up this process by which the individual grows is clear to see, although not easy to implement. It is through education. But to be effective, it must be education not just at the level of information-dissemination, but touching the feelings as well. Moreover, because the "student body" comprises the entire general public, the modes used must include all possible media.

Happily, efforts to achieve this massive public consciousness-raising have already begun. The chronically ill and the handicapped and their families are mobilizing themselves as a political force which is becoming increasingly influential. They are attracting the attention of legislators, who are actively responding by passing legislation that provides for the needs of the handicapped — ranging from the simpler accommodations such as ramps on buildings and access to buses, to the more complicated issues such as public education for children with physical and mental handicaps. In addition, a growing number of advocates for the disabled are involving themselves in the task of stimulating public interest and awareness of the problems of the handicapped and chronically ill. As part of this effort, these advocates are eliciting the support of public figures — actors and athletes and the like — to come forward and talk about their own problems, or share their concern for the problems of others.

It is up to concerned health care professionals to join — and be prepared to take leadership roles in — this massive and overdue effort at public education. The process of consciousness-raising and sensitivity-development must be made just as pervasive in our society as the tolerance and prejudice that we are attempting to displace.

In the final analysis, the best way to develop appropriate services for persons in the community who require long-term health care is to focus on their special requirements and give them what they need. The chronically ill will tell the community what they need and the community may be surprised to discover that the requests will not be unrealistic or impossible. Perhaps one reason we have not listened well thus far is that in the past we have considered the chronically ill to be a burden — a dependent, non-functioning group in our society. They have been seen as "patients" who have given up their civil rights. It is this kind of intolerance that health care professionals, in particular, need to avoid in dealing with the ill and the disabled. If one asks what chronically ill persons want from their community, one of the first things they will say is "independence." Human services professionals must make every effort to grant this request, and to continue listening with understanding to what is being said.

REFERENCES

1. Ames, R.P.: Starting a Hospice Requires Tenacity, High Standards. *Hospital Progress*, 61(2):56-59, 1980.
2. Axelrod, T.B.: Innovative Roles for Social Workers in Home Care Programs. *Health and Social Work*, 3(3):48-66, 1978.

3. Bergman, A.S. *et al.*: Social Work Practice and Chronic Pediatric Illness. *Social Work in Health Care*, 4(3):265-74, 1979.
4. Davis, J.S. and Gibbin. M.J.: An Area Wide Examination of Nursing Home Use, Misuse and Non-Use. *American Journal of Public Health*, 61( ):1145-1155, 1971.
5. Domanski, M.: Comprehensive Care of the Chronically Ill Cancer Patient: An Inter-Agency Model *Social Work in Health Care*, 5(1):59-70, 1979.
6. Editors: Options for the Chronic Patient. *Canada's Mental Health*, 24(1):1-46, 1976.
7. Ewalt, P.L. and Honeyfield, R.M.: Needs of Persons in Long Term Care. *Social Work*, 26(3):223-31, 1981.
8. Goldman, R.H. *et al.*: The Family & Home Hemodialysis: Adolescent Reacting to a Father on Home Dialysis. *International Journal of Psychiatry in Medicine*, 10(3):235-54, 1980-81.
9. Johnson, E.M. & Stark, D.E.: A Group Program for Cancer Patients and Their Family Members in an Acute Care Teaching Hospital. *Social Work & Health Care*, 5(4):335-49, 1980.
10. Lavor, J: Long Term Care and Home Health Care: A Challenge to Service Systems. *Home Health Care Services Quarterly*, 1(1):19-73, 1979.
11. Lorber, J.: Good Patients and Problem Patients: Conformity & Deviance in a General Hospital. *Journal of Health and Social Behavior*, 16(2):213-25, 1975.
12. Lythcott, G.I.: Improving Access to Health Care of the Nation's Underserved. *Public Health Reports*, 93(6):637-41, 1978.
13. Milner, C.J.: Compassionate Care for the Dying Person. *Health & Social Work*, 5(2):5-10, 1980.
14. Nagl, S.Z.: Epidemiology of Disability Among Adults in the United States. *The Milbank Memorial Fund Quarterly*, 54(4):439-67, 1976.
15. Nuehring, E.M. & Ladner, R.A.: Use of Aftercare Programs in Current Mental Health Clinics. *Social Work Research & Abstracts*, 16(1):34-40, 1980.
16. Power, P.W. & Sax, D.S.: The Communication of Information to the Neurological Patient: Some Implications for Family Coping. *Journal of Chronic Diseases*, 31(1):57-65, 1978.
17. Public Health Service: *Chronic Conditions & Activity Limitation, United States*. Vital & Health Statistics, Series 10, Washington: DHHS.
18. Sherwood, Sylvia (ed.): *Long Term Care: A Handbook for Researchers, Planners & Providers*. New York: Spectrum Publications, 1975.
19. Simanis, J.G. & Coleman, J.R.: Health Care Expenditures in Nine Industrialized Countries, 1960-76. *Social Current Bulletin*, 43(1):3-8, 1980.
20. World Health Organization: Controlling Hypertension: Current Care & Mutual Aid through Neighborhood Clubs, *WHO Chronicle*, 32(1):448-50, 1978.

Chapter 7

SOCIAL WORK PRACTICE IN OCCUPATIONAL HEALTH: AN EXPANDED VIEW

SUSAN MOINESTER

Industrial social work has been defined as the utilization of social work expertise to serve the needs of workers and to participate in the formation and implementation of the social welfare goals of the setting (17). Industrial social welfare services are provided under a variety of auspices (sponsorships) including industry, trade unions, community and government agencies, as well as private consulting firms. In 1978, the Project on Social Work in Industrial Settings, a joint effort of the National Association of Social Workers (NASW) and the Council on Social Work Education (CSWE), identified over 200 industrial social work practitioners. These masters-level professionals were either employed directly by a company or trade union, or they were working as consultants to such a setting (17). It is believed, however, that this figure underestimates the actual number of social workers in occupational health practice, particularly those who work as consultants.

The overwhelming majority of industrial social workers are involved in the provision of mental health-related sevices. The development and recent proliferation of these programs is based upon labor and industry's acceptance of two parallel assumptions: (1) that work is a primary contributor to man's economic, social, physical, and psychological well-being; and (2) that mental illness "is without a doubt the nation's costliest health problem . . ." (43).

The first assumption, the notion of centrality of work to the human experience, is certainly not new. Although only recently reflected in health and social service delivery, the subject has been explored from religious, philosophical, sociological, political, and economic perspectives for centuries. In purely physical terms, work is a major focus of adult life simply by virtue of the amount of time that one spends at work. Most people spend considerably more non-sleep time at work than at home. As William Faulkner noted, "You can't eat for eight hours a day nor drink for eight hours a day nor make love for eight hours a day — all you can do for eight hours a day is work. Which is the reason why man makes himself and everybody else so miserable and unhappy" (39).

Freud identified love and work as the most significant themes of adult life. He noted that one's "work at least gives him a secure place in a portion of reality, in the human community" (14). The work ethic is at the core of individual and societal values. "Work means being a good provider, it means autonomy, it pays off in success, and it establishes self-respect or self-worth" (35).

The social purposes of work have been extensively explored. Employment has traditionally been the test of participation in society: "it develops the capabilities, confidence and self-esteem an individual needs to be a responsible citizen . . ." (43). The relationship between work and self-esteem has been summarized in the following manner:

> . . . working for a living is one of the basic activities in a man's life. By forcing him to come to grips with his environment, with the actuality of his personal capacity — to exercise judgment, to achieve concrete and specific results, gives him a continuous account of his correspondence between outside reality and the inner perception of that reality, as well as an account of the accuracy of his appraisal of himself. . . . In short, a man's work does not satisfy his material needs alone. In a very deep sense, it gives him a measure of his sanity (43).

In regard to the second assumption, it is well-documented that mental health problems represent an exposure to industry in terms of absenteeism, low productivity, accidents, and high turnover rates. Additional expenses include disability and medical payments, hospitalizations, and social agency and transfer costs. It has been estimated that fifteen to thirty percent of the work force is seriously handicapped by emotional problems. These problems are believed to be the cause of approximately twenty to thirty percent of all employee absenteeism (43). "Some studies suggest that at least sixty-five and possibly as much as eighty percent of the people who are fired from industry are dropped from their jobs because of personal rather than technical factors" (43). Alcohol and drug abuse in the workplace contribute significantly to these statistics. It is estimated that eight to ten percent of the labor force has an alcohol problem. While alcoholism used to conjure up notions of a skid-row bum, and drug abuse brought to mind images of dingy street corners and dark alleys, these images no longer hold true. It is now known that most alcoholics are employed (36) and that "in a society that pops pills regularly and reaches for the instant feel-good cure, people are not leaving their habits at home" (40).

Estimated annual costs to industry of alcoholism alone vary from eight to fifteen billion dollars. Two-thirds of this total is attributable to loss of work time (21). Health and welfare services provided to alcoholics and their families have been estimated to cost on the average of two billion dollars annually. An additional three to three and one-half billion dollars has been attributed to property damage, medical expenses, increased insurance costs, and lost wages (43).

The General Accounting Office of the Federal Government has developed a formula which demonstrates an annual cost impact of $3,000 per acoholic employee. "The U.S. Postal Service, for example, with more than 700,000 employees and a budget of approximately ten billion dollars annually has an estimated 56,000 employees with alcohol problems with a cost impact of 168 million dollars per year" (21). In a study on alcoholism in the industrial setting, the Stanford Research Institute estimated the annual cost to be approximately $6,000 per alcoholic employee (21). If these figures are used in the example of the Postal Service, the cost would be an astronomical 336 million dollars per year.

THE WORK-RELATEDNESS OF DISEASE

Industrial mental health programs vary greatly in regard to setting, client population, focus, and services offered. They all, however, share a common goal. This can be simply stated as the maintenance of workers on the job or the return of workers to the job. The basic premise is that "individuals express their personal and family problems, their fears, insecurities, frustrations, loneliness and alienation at work and through their work" (43). These problems and the resulting symptomatology can become an obstacle to maintaining functional work performance and therefore can place one's job in jeopardy.

Most industrial mental health programs are crisis-oriented. Treatment is primarily short-term and task-oriented, which reflects the limited nature of the treatment goal. An ecological approach is utilized, which seeks to identify the straw that broke the camel's back, rather than the fundamental cause of a worker's problems. Problems that are not amenable to this treatment module — such as chronic conditions — are generally referred to community agencies. The primary purpose of treatment is to help the worker to adjust to his work world. The parameters that are considered include relationships in the workplace, the ability to adhere to routine, and the performance of assigned tasks. "Approaching the patient through his role as a worker and assessing the interlock between the work situation and pathology, frames and expediates the diagnostic process" (43). Treatment goals are modest and focus on functional ability — the capacity to work — rather than on intrapsychic factors. Intervention is active and directive and based upon the precepts of mutual trust through confidentiality (3).

The motivating philosophy behind the development of industrial mental health programs, including industrial social welfare programs, is that individuals with even severe emotional disorders can function well on the job: mentally ill people can work. The thousands of successful programs in existence today attest to this fact. However, the overwhelming majority of industrial programs and the mental health professionals who staff them, admit to having deliberately "sidestepped the issue of the causal relationship of work to mental illness . . ." (43). This decision has been attributed to the absence of a clear understanding of the nature of the relationship. It can also, however, be ascribed to the sensitivity of the key issues in light of their economic, social and political implications. These programs have been criticized, as they "reflect a preoccupation with specific client problems and fail to address the issues of occupational mental health within the larger context of job satisfaction and occupational and union mental health services." (6).

Research in the area of work satisfaction provides overwhelming evidence that job characteristics play a significant role in the mental and physical health of workers (6). It has been observed that worker's personality disorders, including alcoholism and drug abuse, may stem partially from unpleasant or hazardous working conditions. Moreover, worker alienation or "blues" is not limited to blue-collar workers. It has been found to exist among white-collar workers and middle management as well. In fact, a survey of working conditions found the greatest discontent among young, well-educated workers in low-paying, dull, clerical positions (6).

An area that is currently receiving a great deal of attention is occupational stress — psychosocial stress at work. While some of the research in the field has focused on the manifestation of outside stresses within the workplace, the overwhelming majority has explored the role of work and the workplace in producing stress. Studies have demonstrated the role of work-induced stress in the development of a variety of mental and physical health problems, including heart attacks and peptic ulcers.

Seen in this light, the goal of helping the worker (client) to adjust to his work world must be reexamined. Given the presence of unhealthy conditions within some work environments, the question has been raised as to whether "mental health programs in industry might . . . help individuals to adapt to intolerable work conditions" (6).

> To all this some people reply that man is adaptable, which is of course true. He is adaptable, but you can say equally that he is deformable. He adapts, but he gets deformed. Again, it seems highly likely that stress can be a question of life or death (19).

HISTORY OF SOCIAL WELFARE PROGRAMS IN INDUSTRY

For a number of social workers, findings such as these signalled the need for a redefinition of appropriate modes of intervention to protect and promote health within the workplace. These approaches must "address both the individual and environmental causes of emotional disability . . . for the use of traditional treatment modes in industry fail to take into account the environmental dimension" (6). While presently a fledgling field of practice, social workers' efforts in the area of occupational safety and health have a very rich and varied history. The "discovery" of this field dates back nearly a century making it one of the earliest social work specializations. During the Industrial Revolution, businessmen began to hire welfare or social secretaries in an effort to deal with labor problems and to bring order and efficiency to industry. One function of these professionals concerned physical conditions in the workplace. Many social secretaries were instrumental in inducing employers to provide safe work equipment and in inducing the workers to use them. In many instances they also stimulated action for better environmental conditions such as ventilation, sanitation, lighting, safety, and other physical conditions affecting the worker.

The recent resurgence of industrial social welfare programs can be linked to a number of political, social, and economic forces. Many of these are strongly reminiscent of the conditions that precipitated the development of health and welfare services in industry nearly a century ago. Some of the major forces are outlined below.

Along with increased recognition of the power wielded by industry has come increased pressure for accountability. The public is demanding that business assume a significantly increased measure of social responsibility for the quality of life in America. This relates to conditions within the confines of the workplace as well as the surrounding community. For the first time, people are demanding the "right to know" about the materials they work with. Workers are organizing around safety and health issues and legislation has been enacted to control exposures at the work site. Interested citizens and entire communities are demanding a voice in the corporate decision-making process. Consumerism has reached its zenith and has added a new dimension to community relations: whether to open a factory in a neighborhood or move one has become a matter of public debate (2).

Increased expectations and concern for the quality of life in the workplace has been a major motivational factor in the recent proliferation of industrial social welfare programs. The growth in social services "is taking place in the dynamic atmosphere of the post-industrial era, at a time when alienation from work is said to be growing, when workers have expectations of attaining a higher quality of life both inside and outside the workplace, when a large number of workers have broken families, and when resources seem readily available to foot the bill for such programs" (30).

In addition, as a result of recent legislation concerned with the employment of various population groups — including women, minorities, and the disabled — professional and programmatic responses are often needed to insure job maintenance for these new groups of workers. Two examples of significant legislation in this area is the Affirmative Action program created by Section 503 of the Rehabilitation Act and the nondiscrimination program created by Section 504 of the same Act. The former program requires every business with a government contract to take affirmative action to hire qualified handicapped people. The nondiscrimination program requires that organizations with a government grant may not refuse to hire qualified handicapped people. This includes those with histories of alcoholism and drug addiction.

Regardless of industry's motivation for instituting occupational programs, the mandate for social work involvement remains clear. "Simply stated, our goal is to provide the range of services necessary to enhance the functioning of those who come for help" (2). The nature and scope of these services constitute the remainder of the chapter.

OCCUPATIONAL SAFETY AND HEALTH: BASIC CONCEPTS AND PRINCIPLES

Interest in occupational health and safety was partially stimulated by the recent passage of federal legislation — the Coal Mine Health and Safety Act of 1969 and the Occupational Safety and Health Act (OSHAct) of 1970. This legislation was in itself a response to several issues that became prominent during the lates sixties. These included the increase in the reported injury rate in industry; the new and newly acknowledged evidence for the occupational origin of much disease; the rapid rate of technological change; the rise of the environmental movement with its concern for the effect of toxins on ecological systems; and finally, the changing character of the work force, wherein job health and safety issues have become a higher priority for workers and their representatives.

But what is the nature of the dimensions of occupational health and safety problems? Due to the newness of this information, a brief discussion of key concepts and issues is warranted.

Safety hazards are those aspects of the work environment which may cause burns, electrical shocks, cuts, bruises, sprains, broken bones, or the loss of limbs, eyesight, or hearing (5). Generally, the harm is immediate and violent in nature and is often associated with industrial equipment or the physical environment.

Health hazards typically include toxic and carcinogenic chemicals and dusts, often in combination with heat, noise, and other forms of stress. Other health hazards include physical and biological agents. These health hazards can be absorbed through the skin, taken into the digestive tract through the mouth, inhaled into the lungs, or they can interact with the body through the senses. The results of these interactions can be respiratory disease, heart disease, cancer, neurological disorders, systemic poisoning, or a shortened life expectancy due to general physiological deterioration. The exposure can be acute (high dose, one time) or chronic (low dose over a long period of time), and can result in either an acute or chronic disorder or disease. Some illnesses have a long latency period (such as mesothelioma) before they manifest themselves, and many can result from even a very brief exposure. For the most part, these disorders and diseases can be "difficult or impossible to diagnose early or with certainty" (5). This can be attributed to many factors including long latency periods and the gaps in the present knowledge of workers, employers, and physicians as to the work-relatedness of disease.

Unlike safety hazards, the effects of health hazards may be slow, cumulative, irreversible, and complicated by nonoccupational factors such as smoking. Moreover, chemical, physical, biological, and stress hazards are often found in combination and their effects may not be merely additive but intensified (synergistic). "Carbon monoxide and heat, amphetamines and overcrowding, asbestos and smoking, and promoters of cancer are all examples of agents whose effects can be synergistic" (5). Most combination effects such as these are still unknown and may remain unrecognized until adverse effects are accidentally encountered, as in the case of barbiturates and alcohol (5).

The Magnitude of the Problem

More than 97 million people are exposed each day to occupational health hazards and are at risk of developing job-related adverse health effects. These effects range from classical occupational diseases, such as asbestosis, to the more subtle psychological and behavioral effects of job stresses. The Public Health Service estimates that 390,000 new cases of occupational disease appear annually (5). It has further been estimated that as many as 100,000 deaths occur each year as a result of occupational disease (5).

Additional research suggests that occupational factors may play a more significant role in the causation of the nation's major health problems and diseases than is presently recognized.

> Two million people die every year in the United States. Heart disease, the leading cause of death (accounting for 38.7% or about 750,000 deaths) is only 25% 'explained' by known physiological and environmental factors, such as excess weight, hypertension, serum cholesterol, and cigarette smoking. An unknown but quite possibly substantial proportion of the 75% of heart disease risk that is presently unaccounted for could be related to work and its attendant hazards, particularly stress (5).

As the incidence of infectious diseases has declined, cancer has increased in importance and is now the second leading cause of death, with an annual toll of 300,000. The cancer rate has increased sharply with industrialization: in 1900, 3.7 percent of all deaths were attributable to cancer. By 1968, the number had risen to 16.5 percent. "One in four American and Canadian citizens now living will eventually have cancer. One in five will die from it. Each year over 750,000 new cases are discovered. Each day more than 1,000 people die from this condition" (38). While improved diagnosis and longer life expectancy are partially responsible for this increase, there is substantial evidence that the true incidence of cancer has in fact been rising.

Research conducted in Great Britain suggests that more than 80 percent of cancer is of environmental origin and "therefore, theoretically, preventable" (5). A Task Force of the Department of Health and Human Services recently reported that:

> There is abundant evidence that the great majority of malignant neoplasms — probably over 90 percent of the total — are induced, maintained or promoted by specific environmental factors. Many of the known environmental causes of cancer are physical and chemical agents that directly concern the environmental health professions. Carcinogenesis must therefore be regarded as one of the most significant potential consequences of environmental contamination (5).

The degree to which occupational factors are implicated in the 80 or 90 percent of cancer that is environmentally caused is not currently known. Cancer researchers and environmentalists agree that probably one-half of all cases are complicated by occupational factors (34). "Although there is controversy on the exact figures, scientists from throughout the Department of Health and Human Services estimate that as much as 20 percent of cancers are caused by occupational factors" (5). Another federal estimate indicates that "20 to 40 percent of cancers today and in the near future are related, at least in part, to occupation" (38). Moreover, it is expected that the incidence of cancer characterized by a long latency period may rise significantly over the next twenty to thirty years. This increase is related to the production of petrochemicals, which has doubled every five years since the end of World War II.

The rates of increase in the incidence and mortality of cancer is sharper in blacks, particularly males, than in whites. For example, esophageal and bladder cancers are increasing among blacks although they are declining among whites. Furthermore, recent research indicates that a black person with cancer is more likely to die than a white person with the same type of cancer (42). The difference in cancer rates and mortality between white and black people have generally been attributed to environmental and social factors rather than to any natural characteristics of the races (42).

> Proportionately more blacks have been exposed to environmental pollutants that have been linked to cancer especially since World War II. Also, black workers are concentrated in those industrial sectors with the highest levels of exposure to occupational carcinogens. For example, approximately 22 percent of the steel industry's work force

> is made up of black workers and 91 percent of them are employed in the coke oven operations. In these jobs, workers are exposed to multiple cancer-causing agents and to several agents known to enhance the effects of chemical carcinogens, especially on the respiratory tract. Studies have shown that the lung cancer rate for non-white coke oven workers is 5-10 times the rate experienced by other steel workers. This difference is accounted for by differing work area distribution, in that more non-whites are employed in the higher risk (topside of oven) jobs (42).

Occupationally-related cancer is not limited to the workers immediately exposed to carcinogens in the workplace. Whole communities are affected when these toxins are discharged or escape from manufacturing plants into the water, air, and soil of the surrounding neighborhoods. Frequently, people who work in industrial plants also live near them and are thus placed in a position of double jeopardy.

In addition to cancer, much of the respiratory disease that afflicts workers is known to be job-related. Chronic respiratory diseases have become major causes of death and disability in the United States. Emphysema and chronic bronchitis are the fastest growing diseases in the country. The incidence of these diseases has doubled every five years since World War II and now account for the second highest number of disabilities under Social Security.

Another significant health issue is posed by reproductive hazards in the workplace. Although known as early as 1775, threats to male and female fertility and the problems of birth defects resulting from occupational exposure to toxic materials have, until recently, been virtually ignored by scientists, industry, and regulatory agencies (42). Exposures to lead, benzene, carbon disulfide, and a number of other chemicals have long been known to be dangerous during pregnancy, resulting in birth defects, miscarriages, and increased infant mortality (42).

A current dilemma revolves around the practice of excluding women of child-bearing age from high-paying jobs in areas of potential toxic exposures. In some cases, in order to retain such jobs, women have been required to provide evidence of infertility, such as voluntary sterilization. There is little evidence to suggest that of this type of exclusion is practiced in low-paying jobs with similar exposures. However, research indicates that the male reproductive system is also at grave risk from many toxics (1). In a recent government supported study, polychlorinated biphenyl (PCB) was found in 100% of human sperm samples and the amount of PCB correlated with the decrease in the number of viable sperm. Figures from ongoing studies indicate that the average sperm count of American males has decreased thirty percent in the past 30 years (1).

Job-related health problems are not restricted to industrial or agricultural workers. White-collar workers and corporate executives are affected as well. For example, dentists are currently being studied for the possible effects of X-radiation, mercury, and anesthetics on their having the highest rate of suicide of any professional group and excess diseases of the nervous system, leukemia, and lymphatic malignancies. Operating room nurses have been found to have several times the miscarriage rates of other nurses, and give birth to a larger proportion of children with congenital deformities. Other examples include the excess cancer, respiratory, and cardiac disease experienced by cosmetologists as well as the high incidence of coronary heart disease among administrators.

Strategies for Prevention and Control

"The recognition that occupational factors are associated with these disorders as well as with a significant fraction of the chronic, degenerative diseases, which are incurable by definition, is important because most occupationally-related diseases could be prevented by reducing exposure to physical, chemical and biological hazards in the workplace" (42). The recent increase in the activities of the federal government, as well as of labor, management and public interest groups, demonstrates growing recognition of the importance of health and safety and of the concepts of early detection and prevention of occupational illness and injury. Federal involvement culminated in the passage of the Occupational Safety and Health Act of 1970 (OSHAct). The OSHAct imposes on almost every employer in the private sector an unprecedented "general duty" to " 'furnish to each of his employees employment and a place of employment which are free from recognized hazards that are causing or are likely to cause death or serious physical harm to his employees' " (5). In addition, the employer is required to comply with occupational safety and health standards promulgated and enforced under the OSHAct by the newly established Occupational Safety and Health Administration (OSHA) in the Department of Labor. OSHA is authorized to enter any workplace without advance notice and impose penalties upon the discovery of violations. The Act allows any worker to register a complaint and to call for an inspection while protecting him from discrimination for using the provisions of the Act. It further mandates that employers keep records of work-related deaths, injuries and illnesses, as well as exposures to toxic materials or harmful agents. These records must be made available to the government and the worker.

To assist the Secretary of Labor in enforcing the OSHAct, Congress established the National Institute for Occupational Safety and Health (NIOSH) within the Department of Health and Human Services. NIOSH is a research body which is responsible for developing and recommending occupational safety and health standards to OSHA. The Agency is required to publish a list of all known toxic substances and the concentrations at which these substances exhibit toxic effects. In order to obtain this information, NIOSH is authorized to conduct research and to undertake experimental programs in occupational safety and health.

The OSHAct has provided a stimulus to labor unions in collective-bargaining activities with regard to job health and safety. Since its inception, there has been a significant increase in safety and health provisions in collective-bargaining agreements and in their implementation through national and local union health and safety committees.

Legal action taken by public-interest groups, unions, and employer groups has played a vital role in the implementation of the OSHAct. "Many of the positive steps taken by OSHA have been in rsponse to this legal action or fear of future legal action" (5). Lobbying, testifying, advocacy, and political activities have also helped to shape the course of the government's occupational health and safety efforts. Various groups representing management, labor, health and safety professionals, and the public interest have brought pressure to bear upon the federal government through legislation and administrative agency testimony and publicity efforts.

Thus is it apparent that modes of intervention in the area of occupational health can and should assume many different forms under a wide variety of auspices. It is, moreover, widely accepted that the resolution of health and safety issues is dependent upon the continued voicing of all points of view. To date, however, the number and weight of these voices have not been balanced. While management and labor have always been active in lobbying and advocacy efforts, management has had much greater access to expert testimony on technical, medical, or scientific matters.

The small but effective groups of experts made available to labor by some public-interest and professional groups in the past few years re-

> mains inadequate to counterbalance industry expertise. . . . It is clear that the interests of working people have not been adequately represented (5).

The Information Gap

The OSHAct has thus far fallen short of its potential for reducing occupational injury and disease, for fostering the internalization of the social costs of health and safety hazards, for encouraging technological innovation, or for stimulating job redesign (5). The adoption of health standards has proven to be a highly adversary and time-consuming process which is complicated by the lack of a firm data base and by strong commercial interests. In addition, inadequate levels of OSHA compliance manpower has resulted in a low probability of a firm being inspected. "Moreover, even if employers are cited, the fines are often far too low to serve as an economic incentive to improve working conditions" (5).

A major factor in the limited effectiveness of the OSHAct and OSHA has been the inadequate generation, transmission, and utilization of occupational safety and health knowledge. The generation of information, in particular, has proven to be an insurmountable problem as it is "simply impossible" (5) to research and establish safe levels of exposure for every chemical product in commercial use. To begin with, there are approximately 12,000 materials known to be toxic in commercial use today. In addition, most human exposure to chemicals is to mixtures which may result in multiple etiology of disease or in synergistic efffects. Moreover, there is often a latency period of 20 years or more between exposure to occupational health hazards and the appearance of disease. These problems are compounded by the fact that on the average, 2,000-3,000 new chemicals enter the workplace each year for which no standards have been established.

Additional problems exist in the dissemination of occupational health information. Few mechanisms exist to insure that information is made widely available and is equally accessible to all interested and implicated groups.

> Differential access converts information into a bargaining advantage for the knowledgeable party, and compounds the difficulties of public and private decision-makers who must evaluate the merits of a bewildering variety of conflicting claims. Thus the phenomenon of differential access to information transforms the problem of improving

> our understanding from the purely scientific and technical realm of information generation, dissemination and utilization to the 'political' arena (5).

The effects of the dissemination problem can be diminished through training, technical assistance, publication, and distribution of information.

The recognition and control of occupational hazards has been further hampered by a lack of utilization of existing knowledge by decision-makers. This aspect of the occupational health information problem is illustrated by the following example:

> The debate surrounding the industrial use of asbestos proceeded largely on the assumption that asbestos was an essential raw material without close substitutes for many uses, such as in shipbuilding. Given this assumption, the terms of the debate were confined to the choice of an appropriate asbestos exposure standard and the costs of meeting it in terms of filtration and ventilation equipment and the like. Yet, while this controversy raged, the Swedish shipbuilding industry had for some time been using what are thought to be safer substitute materials in place of asbestos. These materials completely eliminate the necessity of exposing shipyard workers to asbestos, at least in the construction of new ships. It seems clear that we have many lessons to learn from other countries with regard to superior technologies for improving the level of occupational health and safety (5).

Social workers are gradually entering the field of occupational health and safety. Supported by a profession which sanctions involvement in activities that range from casework to class advocacy, a handful of social workers have obtained employment in key sectors concerned with health and safety issues — the government, industry, unions, and public-interest groups. Information about the number and functions of this small group of social workers is extremely limited. The material that is available, however, indicates that the majority of these people are engaged in collaborative efforts with medical and scientific personnel in activities that relate primarily to the issue just discussed — that of the generation, dissemination, and utilization of occupational health information. This area of practice will be explored more fully in subsequent sections.

EMPLOYEE ASSISTANCE PROGRAMS

The interest of management in the rehabilitation of troubled employees has resulted in a growing movement in the work environment: the Employee Assistance Program (EAP) (15). The overwhelming majority of industrial social workers are currently employed in some form of EAP, either based in industry, labor unions, community agencies, or other organizations.

Employee Assistance Program is a generic term used to describe the variety of policies and procedures utilized in a working population to control alcoholism, drug abuse, and certain mental health problems that adversely affect job performance. EAPs have been described as meaning many things to many people (36) because they are characterized by their tendency to adapt themselves to local needs, conditions, and auspices. EAPs do not represent a new concept, but rather an attempt to gather and organize existing information from a variety of sources into a cohesive body of knowledge. This can perhaps be evidenced by glancing at the three predominant models of EAPs: (1) employee alcoholism programs; (2) employee alcohol and drug programs (substance abuse); and (3) comprehensive Employee Assistance Programs. The goal of EAPs should also seem quite familiar by this point: to restore an employee to normal work behavior and productivity. "By offering an alternative to being fired, EAP can help the employee to be a better producer for his employer as well as to function better as an individual" (15).

The EAP concept is believed to have evolved most directly from scattered attempts by industry, over the course of the past forty years, to rehabilitate alcoholic employees. Initially, these programs developed very slowly due in part to the stigma attached to alcoholism. As the extent of the problem and its enormous cost to industry became known, programs began to develop more rapidly.

During the past decade, however, it became apparent to some groups that many of the problems encountered by employees are not alcohol-related. "Although it has been estimated that 50 percent of the problems faced by employees in industry are alcohol-related, 50 percent are not, and there are no programs or resources to deal with these other problems" (15). In an effort to respond to the needs of employees with non-alcohol-related problems, many existing and developing programs assumed a "broad brush" or comprehensive employee assistance approach. The legitimacy and utility of the various approaches has become a major professional controversy. Some prominent observers have criticized the broad brush policy as "an attempt to legitimize the 'alcohol worker' as a professional change agent or consultant, thus eschewing the former image of social worker or do-gooder" (36). Nonetheless, it appears that the trend in EAPs is toward the development of comprehensive services. A recent survey conducted by the National Association of Labor-

Management Administrators and Consultants on Alcoholism (ALMACA) found that only 15 percent of existing EPAs addressed alcohol and drug problems while 72 percent were comprehensive in nature and addressed alcohol, drug, mental health, marital, and other employee problems (29).

Regardless of the type of services provided, all EAPs share several fundamental assumptions. First, it is recognized that an employee's problem is his own concern unless job performance is impaired. Most problems, however, eventually manifest themselves in poor job performance. In addition, EAPs require that supervisors carry the responsibility of evaluating and documenting job performance. The supervisor's objective is to identify declining performance without having to diagnose the nature of the underlying problem. Once identified, these employees may be either treated directly by the social worker or other EAP personnel, or they may be referred to services outside the workplace. If treatment is provided by EAP staff, they must be equipped with the skills necessary to help the employee to identify, focus on, and evaluate the nature and scope of his problem. Generally, problems involving serious emotional problems, marital difficulties, and complex legal or financial problems require services outside of the workplace. EAP staff often work closely with such resources to ensure that the employee is using the service and to evaluate the appropriateness and effectiveness of the services provided.

While the types of services offered by EAPs vary, the vast majority of successful programs share common components although with differing degrees of emphasis. These include — written policy, labor-management involvement and commitment, company-wide information and education program, supervisory training, uniform identification and referral procedures, availability of treatment resources, and follow-up procedures. Programs differ considerably in regard to the location of the program in the organizational structure; the nature of the relationship between the EAP and outside treatment facilities; and whether they subscribe to the "individual model" or the "environmental model" (36). While the overwhelming majority of practitioners and programs subscribe to the individual model, both groups consider themselves to be practitioners of EAPs. The following is an outline of the two approaches, sketched as extremes, which would form the basis of an alcoholism EAP.

Individual Model

1. The excessive use of alcohol is considered dysfunctional to the individual.
2. The causes of alcoholism may be largely sought within the individual's own psychological makeup.
3. The prescribed treatment for alcoholism is some form of rehabilitation that focuses on the individual's psychological makeup such as casework or psychoanalysis.

Environmental Model

1. The excessive use of alcohol is considered, under certain conditions, to be functional for the individual. Alcohol is seen as offering relief from monotony, stress, or feelings of powerlessness. Also the "drunk" role may be part of a broader social role that is important in the industrial peer group situation.
2. The causes of alcoholism may be sought not only (or even mainly) in the individual, but also in the social context (economic or political disadvantage) and in the specific organizational context (the nature of some kinds of work, or the structure of some types of organizations).
3. The recommended treatment may not be for the individual but for society and for the specific organization within which alcoholism is found. A reorientation of the worker to the means of production may be more relevant than psychotherapy.

These fundamentally divergent philosophies have been shown in practice to result in radically different approaches to the problem of substance abuse and mental health disorders in industry. To begin with, there is basic disagreement over who owns the problem — is it the worker, industry, or society? These differences result in variations in the way that EAPs are marketed and implemented. For example, in the individual model, the EAP consultant's goal is to institute a program in any industry that is prepared to develop basic procedures, namely documentation, coercion, referral, and follow-up. In the environmental mode, the consultant's goal is to change the organization of an industry such that it does not promote mental health disorders.

More commonly, the EAP consultant operates at some point between the two extremes. This midpoint is determined by a number of factors, principally the consultant's philosophy and the industry's orientation and permissiveness. These variations will be examined in subsequent sections. On the basis of the foregoing discussion, however, it should be clear that EAP is not a single, simple theoretical and practical package. It is, rather, a title for a vast variety of approaches and services. While most industrial social workers are employed in EAPs, they still represent only a fraction of the total number of professionals and paraprofessionals engaged in this field. The rapidity with which masters level social workers are entering EAPs and the success of their program efforts attests to social workers' unique qualifications for this area of practice.

SOCIAL WORK PRACTICE IN INDUSTRIAL SETTINGS

Program Auspice

While information is scarce, it appears that most industrial social workers are employed in programs that operate under the auspice of company management (25). Employment in labor settings is seen with almost equal frequency. In terms of geographical distribution, it was found that the highest number of programs were located in the Midwest (31%), followed by the New York City area (20%), and New England (15%) (2). The Midwest was found to be a center of management-initiated programs, while the Northeast, particularly New York City, was noted for considerable trade union activity.

Program Structure and Setting

Within the category of programs operated under the auspice of management, a broad variety of structural arrangements can be found. Two predominant models, however, emerge. In the first, social workers and other program staff are employed by management as employees or consultants. All services are delivered on-site at the workplace. In the second model, services are provided through a contractual agreement between the company and either a private practitioner or one who is employed by a community facility, such as a family service agency or a community mental health center. In the latter case, the service may be provided at the agency, or the social worker may be stationed at the work site.

To date, most management-sponsored social welfare programs have been instituted by large manufacturing industries. On the average, the ratio of employees to social workers is approximately 8,000 to 1 (25). Over 70 percent of the U.S. work force, however, is employed by companies with fewer than 1,000 workers (20). These small companies lack the resources of larger firms and typically have not been able to offer social welfare services to their employees. A third structural arrangement — the consortium — provides small and medium-sized companies with many of the benefits of employee assistance programs at a fraction of the cost. In such an arrangement, a number of companies join together and contract for services as a group. Consortiums have been gaining popularity and are employing an increasing number of social workers.

For each of the above program models, a decision must be made as to where services are to be delivered — at the work site or in the community. Both approaches have inherent advantages as well as disadvantages. Ease of access is the primary motivation for providing services on-site. The development of trust and the reduction of social distance has been found to improve utilization. Practitioners that operate within the workplace have the advantage of being seen working in the shops, at union meetings, and in management seminars. They have the opportunity to talk with people informally in the cafeteria, the parking lot, and in the halls as well as in their offices. As a result of the increased familiarity, they tend to be more readily accepted as a nonthreatening, helping resource. In addition, when services are delivered on-site as opposed to at a community mental health center, there is generally less of a stigma attached to utilization. On the other hand, it is widely accepted that physical distance from the workplace offers the client greater protection in terms of confidentiality. Furthermore, outside consultants are generally perceived by employees as being less enmeshed in organizational constraints and consequently are less likely to be pawns of company management. In recognition of the advantages of these two approaches, many management-sponsored programs offer services both on-site and in more neutral surroundings in the community.

Industrial social welfare programs that are conducted under the auspices of management are most frequently located in the company's Medical or Personnel Departments. There are benefits offered by either of these locations. For example, the concept of confidentiality is generally well established in the Medical Department and there is no stigma attached to being physically ill. On the other hand, the medical model tends to focus on issues of health and illness, and often this is not the nature of workers' problems. Frequently, they are in need of assistance in coping with problems of everyday living, such as legal and financial difficulties. Personnel Departments may be more receptive to requests for concrete services and client advocacy as they generally do not operate on the basis of the medical model. Personnel Departments, however, play a key role in organizational decisions regarding hiring, promotion, and dismissal and therefore client confidentiality becomes a central issue. Workers may be reluctant to utilize needed services on the basis of their perception of, and prior experience with the personnel function.

The titles of social workers employed in such settings are as varied as the services offered. The most common titles reflect the employee assistance function. These include Employee Assistance Counselor, Employee Assistance Coordinator, Employee Assistance Representative and Employee Assistance Program Manager. Some titles reveal the existence of programs whose sole or primary focus is alcohol and/or substance abuse, for example, Substance Abuse Program Director. Still other titles, such as Special Projects Coordinator, provide little information about the nature of services offered. Only rarely do social workers retain titles that reflect professional affiliation rather than program function such as Industrial Social Worker. This is an indication that in industry, as in more traditional settings, social workers and social work as a profession are defined not by the title that they hold but by the services that they provide.

Program Services

ALCOHOL ABUSE PROGRAMS. Many industry-sponsored employee assistance programs began as rehabilitation services for employees with alcohol problems. Stimulated by articles in national publications regarding the pervasiveness and the cost to the employer of alcoholism in industry, programs for alcoholic employees began to proliferate as early as the 1950s. Today, many observers continue to maintain that alcoholism is industry's greatest and costliest single program. As mentioned earlier in this chapter, it is estimated that eight to ten percent of the labor force has a problem with alcohol. Moreover, although contrary to popular belief, it is now known that most active alcoholics are employed. The average worker with an alcohol problem is usually in early middle age and has generally been a valuable and skilled worker until affected by drinking. He or she is found on any level of company organization, from laborer to executive. "By the time a work problem becomes apparent, multiple social problems have developed including financial difficulties, threat of divorce or actual separation, disturbed children and many others" (21).

On the basis of such information and often personal experience as well, many companies have elected to continue, or to initiate programs that focus either exclusively or primarily upon the alcoholic worker. This design can also be at least partially attributed to the success of industrial programs in rehabilitating alcoholics. In fact,

FIGURE 1 Mental Health

	No. of Cases	*Percentage*	
At Intake			
Very Good	3	0.9	5.9
Good	17	5.0	
Up and Down	127	37.1	
At 12-Month Follow-Up*			
Very Good	44	15.2	53.8
Good	112	38.6	
Up and Down	84	29.0	
Unsatisfactory	35	12.1	

*Denotes adjusted percentage

FIGURE 2 Rating of Job Performance

	No. of Cases	*Percentage*	
At Intake			
Excellent	4	1.2	15.5
Good	49	14.3	
Fair	145	42.4	
Poor	144	42.1	
Total	342		
At 12-Month Follow-Up*			
Excellent	71	24.3	67.1
Good	125	42.8	
Fair	60	20.5	
Poor	36	12.3	
Unknown	50	—	
Total	342		

*Denotes adjusted percentage

FIGURE 3 Employee Participation in Health Counseling Program

	Participated (211)			Did Not Participate (86)		
	B*	A**	%C***	B	A	%C
Absenteeism (average days per employee)	51	27	−47	42	40	− 5
Disability days (average days per employee)	30	14	−53	23	26	+13
Disability income ($) (average per employee)	764.00	448.00	−41	597.00	769.00	+29
Medical Benefits ($) (average per employee)	1,446.00	957.00	−34	978.00	1,231.00	+26
Days of hospital confinement (average per employee)	10	5	−50	7	6	−14

*Before
**After
*** % Change

the highest recovery rates for alcoholism are found in programs in offices and factories, rather than clinics or hospitals (20). It is not uncommon for good industrial programs to achieve rehabilitation rates of 70 percent or better (21). In addition to improved mental health and job performance, alcohol rehabilitation has been shown to result in reductions in absenteeism, disability, medical payments, and hospitalizations. An example is provided by a recent study of 342 employees in an alcoholism assistance program conducted by the International Harvester Company (12).

Treatment effectiveness is largely attributed to the use of a technique called "constructive coercion." Rather than focusing on the question of whether alcoholism is a symptom of anything else, the occupational alcoholism program insists that the employee make a decision — he must either get help with his drinking or face job loss. "The threat of income loss and the status of holding a job means more to many alcoholics than any other consideration. The average alcoholic will have given up his family several years before he will lose his job" (21).

The majority of industry-sponsored alcohol abuse programs are conducted at the work site, and consist of two fundamental parts. The first part generally includes intake and then referral to a treatment program. Follow-up contact is maintained for a variable period of time. Detoxification is provided in a hospital if necessary. Some industrial programs offer in-house counseling. In these cases the treatment is typically short-term and task-centered (44). Referrals are made for cases which require long-term therapy that cannot be provided in the work setting. Many of the programs that provide in-house treatment also offer counseling of the family members of the worker as part of the treatment process. Some occupational alcoholism programs have taken this treatment aspect one step further and have begun to provide services to members of an employee's family who have drinking problems, upon their request (20). The rationale for this service is based upon the recognition that the employee whose family contains an active alcoholic will often exhibit deteriorating job performance (20).

The second part of industry-sponsored occupational alcoholism programs generally consists of training and education. Supervisors are educated in the key aspects of the program and are trained in the technique of constructive coercion — getting employees to the rehabilitation unit. In addition, a publicity campaign is usually launched to inform all employees about alcoholism as a disease and about the availability of a program for controlling it.

In spite of the abundance of management-sponsored occupational alcoholism programs, a relatively small number of social workers are employed in these programs. Two primarily explanations for this phenomenon have been advanced. To begin with, occupational alcoholism programs have traditionally been staffed by recovered alcoholics. This is particularly true of the alcoholism rehabilitation programs established prior to 1970. Many of these programs have met with considerable success and some companies remain reluctant to replace these "trusted and valued employees" with mental health professionals, particularly those with no prior experience in industry. "Management sees no evidence that they need to employ so-called 'professionals' to obtain satisfactory results — the present staff, with some short training, is producing results" (13).

This situation is complicated by the fact that social workers entering industry are often unprepared for the heavy emphasis placed on the alcoholism component of service programs. Social workers have admittedly been reluctant to establish initial contact with an alcoholic as the preferred approach is based upon confrontation and coercion (2). Since the effectiveness of this approach has been well proven, social workers wishing to enter the world of work must become more familiar and comfortable with this client group and more adept at utilizing this manner of client contact. "Practitioners need to understand that alcoholics recover and that new treatment models have emerged that can be incorporated into the social work repetoire" (2). Thus, while there is no doubt that here is a role for social workers in the administration, planning and servicing of occupational alcoholism programs, this field presents the profession with a distinct challenge: "the need to understand the physical as well as psychosocial dimension to the disease, and to learn how to develop diagnostic and intervention skills to work effectively with the problem that 'denial' presents for practice" (17).

SUBSTANCE ABUSE PROGRAMS. The magnitude of the problem of drug abuse in the workplace was not recognized on a national basis until about 1970. Since that time many corporate occupational alcoholism programs have expanded their service base to form a substance abuse orientation. Until quite recently, most of these substance abuse programs retained their traditional alcoholism focus. Within the past few years, however, drug addiction on the job has become more visible and subsequently a less sensitive subject for industry and labor.

> According to employee counselors at companies around the country and treatment center personnel and government researchers, drug addiction almost always accompanies alcoholism. They say the combined addictions are affecting at least 10 percent of the U.S. work force and are costing businesses millions a year (40).

Poly-addicted workers are being seen with increased frequency in occupational substance abuse programs. Since the mid-1970s, a significant increase has been noted in the drug use of workers between the ages of 18 and 25. The most commonly used drug among this age group is believed to be marijuana, but the use of cocaine and angel dust, an animal tranquilizer known as PCP, is becoming increasingly more widespread (40). In addition, alcoholism is generally coupled with drug use in this group: "there are very few straight alcoholics among the young" (40).

While drug abuse is found among people of all types and levels of employment, some studies suggest that certain patterns of drug use can be discerned. For example, illegal drugs such as marijuana, cocaine, angel dust, and heroin have been found to be the most frequently used drugs among blue-collar workers. Among white-collar workers, addiction to prescription drugs is most common. In a study of white-collar workers in several federal agencies, a researcher noted that "some people had two or three prescriptions for Valium, Librium, and minor tranquilizers" (40).

The services provided by social workers in substance abuse programs tend to resemble those provided in occupational alcoholism programs. These include intake and then referral to a treatment program — either outpatient counseling or hospitalization. Follow-up on service utilization and effectiveness is often provided. In a few cases, treatment may be provided on-site, but this is even less likely to be found in instances of drug abuse than in cases of alcohol abuse. Training and education of supervisors is generally a vital aspect of substance abuse programs, as the company disciplinary process is the source of the majority of treatment referrals. It has been noted, however, that the employed drug abuser is not as difficult to recognize as the early stage alcoholic. This worker can usually be identified within several months after being hired as he will display bizarre symptoms or some form of antisocial behavior, such as thievery. Managers with a substance abuse problem pose a unique set of difficulties, as addiction among this group is the hardest to discover and treat.

> Management is not as visible as lower-level employees. They can go into their offices and shut the door. Also co-workers feel they should protect the person. They feel he's having a hard time and that he'll get over it, but this doesn't solve the problem (40).

BROAD BRUSH PROGRAMS. Significantly more social workers are employed in corporate substance abuse programs than in occupational alcoholism programs. This group still reflects, however, only a fraction of the total number of social workers employed in industrial settings. The vast majority of occupational health social workers are involved in providing comprehensive services in broad-based employee assistance programs (EAPs) or in multi-service centers. This can be at least partially attributed to the fact that it is widely accepted among social workers that a general social service approach is preferrable to a substance abuse-only program (2). Many industrial practitioners maintain that a strong substance abuse identification can contaminate an entire social service department.

> People are afraid that they may be labelled as alcoholics if they are known to use the service. They will stay away in droves and the service may find itself working with a population of involuntary referrals from supervisors who may be using it as an end-of-the-line disciplinary tool (2).

The range of services provided by comprehensive EAPs can be illustrated by an examination of the Counseling Department at the

Polaroid Corporation (22). A description of the functions of the Polaroid Corporation's Counseling Department provides insight into the range and nature of the problems seen in EAPs. The primary focus of the Polaroid counseling staff, which consists of four social workers, is to assist employees and their families with personal problems. The objective is to help workers with problems of living — personal, job, family, or social problems which can hamper one's effectiveness and hinder his or her stability. Counselors help employees "know themselves better so that they may plan more satisfying work lives and careers" (22).

The kinds of presenting problems seen at the Counseling Department are representative of most broad-based EAPs. They fall into three major areas of involvement: problems related to work, those related to self, and those that are related to others, particularly the family. In the category of work-related difficulties, the most common problems include job dissatisfaction, conflict with supervisor, poor performance, absenteeism, disruptive relationship with peers, and anxiety about job performance. Job dissatisfaction and conflict with supervisor are the problems with the highest incidence at Polaroid.

In the area of problems related to self, the most common complaints include depression, anxiety reactions, severe emotional disturbance, alcoholism, and compulsive gambling. Of these diagnostic categories, depression and anxiety reactions are found most frequently.

The most common presenting problems associated with significant figures in a person's life were found to be as follows: marital problems, parent-child problems, aging parent problems, pre-marital concerns, pregnancy counseling, and concern with spouse's behavior, including alcoholism, mental illness, and depression. In the experience of the Counseling Department, marital problems are the most frequent presenting complaint for this category and for all categories. In the search for a reason for this phenomenon, "speculation leads us to believe that the changing family roles and the emergence of the women's movement has caused pressures on marriages requiring responses from counseling resources everywhere" (24).

The Counseling Department, like most EAPs, functions on the basis of the recognition of the interdependency of these three essential areas of life relationships (Figure 4). It is accepted that when one area is affected, it diminishes the person's ability to function, and

PRESENTING PROBLEMS

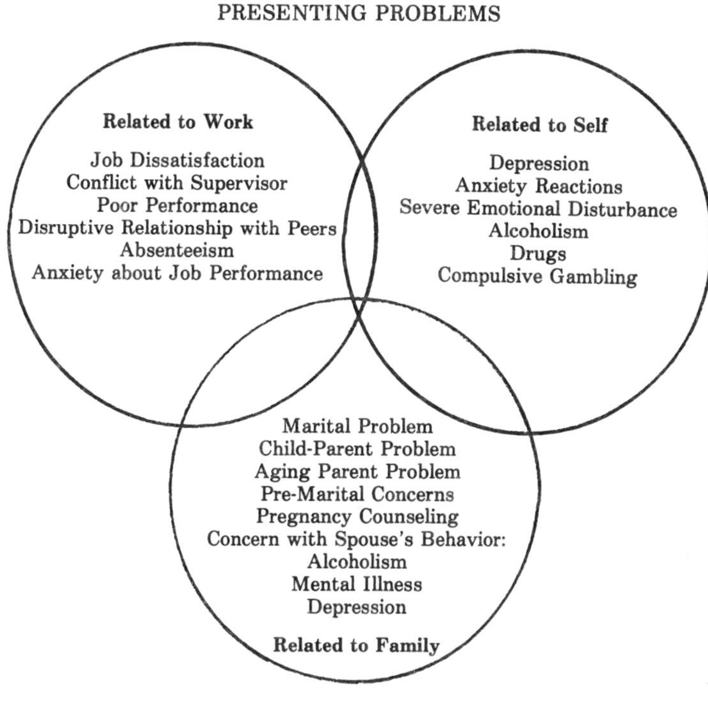

FIGURE 4

all three areas are affected. As such, "support of one of the areas of a person's life relationships can provide the base from which we can explore and can take some corrective actions in another area" (22).

The Counseling Department also offers a retirement counseling program. Many companies, like Polaroid, are increasingly coming to see these types of programs as a means through which they can respond to their aging population. The services offered by the Polaroid Pre-Retirement Program are fairly representative of programs nationwide. These include: (1) counseling sessions at least once a year for people aged 60 to 65; (2) liaison between pre-retirees and available resources inside and outside Polaroid; and (3) meetings for pre-retirees and spouses on benefits, taxes, and so forth. There is also a Post-Retirement Program wherein contact is maintained with retired employees at their request.

In addition to the provision of counseling-oriented services such as casework, crisis intervention, information and referral, and case-centered consultation, many social workers in industry-sponsored programs have administration and planning responsibilities. This is partially due to the fact that the vast majority of programs, whether substance abuse only or full-service EAP, are small and employ only one or two professionals. In these instances, social workers are generally responsible for the provision of treatment and group facilitation services to workers and/or their families. They are also responsible for program development, administration, and evaluation — to the extent that services are evaluated. In the relatively small number of programs that utilize a larger social work staff (three or more), it is not uncommon to find a social worker whose major responsibilities are administrative. It is rare, however, for a social worker to be in such a position if the program is not staffed either solely or primarily by social workers.

INDUSTRIAL RELATIONS. A growing number of social workers employed in industry are expanding their role beyond the provision of assistance to employees with personal and interpersonal problems. "Developments in corporate social responsibility, and the impact of new affirmative action legislation have led to increased policy involvement on the part of social workers" (2). This generally encompasses consultation to management on both internal policies as well as external relations. Industrial relations typically demand a set of skills and knowledge entirely different from those that are traditionally required by social workers in more common industrial roles. Many of these jobs place social workers in pivotal organizational positions and sanction them to effect policy (thereby promoting social change). Armed with the skills to evaluate, diagnose, and to intervene in a system, social workers may be the professional group most appropriately equipped for the task. A few short case examples may serve to clarify the nature of social work involvement in corporate decision making.

> A large manufacturing company in New England with progressive employment and personnel practices had invested heavily in recruitment and placement of women engineers. They found, however, that resignation rates were high and transfer requests frequent. The affirmative action officer — a social work practitioner — was consulted and problem analysis led to intervention on a structural, group, and personal level. Social work training suggested examination of environmental factors that might contribute to the negative situation. The women, new to the setting, lacked role models and were excluded from tradi-

tional informal information and support networks. A tendency developed to take criticism personally and to internalize it as inadequacy or inferiority.

The structural analysis led to a structural response: put the women together — two, three, or four to a department — to reinforce and support each other, and arrange workshops and training sessions for managers and supervisors to sensitize them to the dysfunctional systemic patterns that were inhibiting the contribution and work performance of this group of employees.

At a group level, a support network of women engineers from all parts of the company was put together. On a personal level, where necessary or desirable, counseling was offered to individuals for whom the structural and group developments were insufficient to alleviate the sense of isolation and peer rejection they experienced (2).

My job, especially the primary portion of it dealing with affirmative action for the handicapped and veteran, can best be described as serving as a consultant to personnel managers and other management people around the country. I personally do not hire or promote anyone. I attempt to suggest to personnel managers how they and their facilities can comply with the requirements of the law. I attempt to help those personnel managers and others feel more comfortable with disabled people and with rehabilitation professionals. In addition, whenever a complaint of discrimination is filed by an individual with the U.S. Department of Labor, I am charged with investigating that complaint, recommending a settlement if it appears we are guilty, or defending the company's policies to the Department of Labor if it appears there was not discrimination (13).

OCCUPATIONAL SAFETY AND HEALTH. The smallest group of social workers employed in industry are those who focus on issues of occupational safety and health (25). Although information is scarce and difficult to obtain, there is some evidence to suggest that in at least several instances, social workers in industrial settings are engaged in activities related to the recognition and control of safety and health hazards in the work environment. In most cases, they work with industrial hygienists, or other safety and health professionals (25). Planning, program and policy development, program-centered consultation, and administration are the services that are most commonly provided by social workers in these roles. Training and education, focused on the prevention of injury and illness, is also frequently an area of social work involvement. In addition, some in-plant safety and health programs have research and evaluation components. As social workers gain expertise in these areas, they are assuming increased responsibility for these functions.

Occupational safety and health is a relatively unchartered area in terms of social work intervention. This can be at least partially attributed to the newness of this area of concern as well as to its highly controversial nature. It was not until the 1970's that environmental health issues, such as nuclear energy, air pollution, and soil and water contamination, became focal points of widespread public awareness and concern. Aided by the passage of the OSHAct in 1970, some researchers and observers turned their attention to the workplace as a source of environmental toxins and as well as a hazardous environment in its own right. A new population "at risk" was defined — the industrial worker, and information on the recognition, control and prevention of illness in industry became more readily available. This created, essentially, a new body of knowledge that was quite foreign to social workers.

Controversy over issues such as "safe" levels of exposure and the cost versus the benefit of protecting the health of workers, also proliferated. Occupational safety and health quickly became one of the nation's leading political hot beds. The area promises to become even more highly charged in the 1980's, as more information becomes available on the toxicity and often carcinogenicity of materials found in the workplace. Social workers, for the most part, have been reluctant to enter this tense arena. This marks a departure from a professional heritage that sanctioned class advocacy and political activity as effective and often preferred modes of intervention in the promotion of one of social work's "major objectives — the alleviation of social problems" (33).

Class advocacy, however, is certainly not the only appropriate mode of intervention. Due to the complexity of the problem of occupational illness and injury, multiple levels and types of intervention are possible and necessary to further the goals of the individual and the organization. Collecting data on the incidence of accidents and illness, documenting exposures, educating and training workers and employers, and developing policy and programs are examples of some of the activities that social workers can, and to some extent, do engage in under a variety of auspices. The organizational context is a major determinant of the mode of intervention selected. For example, it is unlikely that a social worker employed by industry would choose to organize workers on health and safety issues as a strategy to promote change in corporate policy and procedures.

Regardless of the program auspice or the types of services that are delivered, the primary professional contribution of social work to the area of occupational health lies in the professional's ability to work simultaneously and effectively with both the organization and the individual.

> A professionally trained social worker becomes involved on more than one level: clinical assessment and intervention skills are matched by knowledge of organization theory and behavior and principles of systems management and communication. The social work perspective takes into account the environmental influences as well as the psychological factors that impinge on an individual (2).

While this type of multilevel response can be found in industry-sponsored programs, it is characteristic of the often increased flexibility of programs conducted under the auspice of organized labor.

SOCIAL WORK PRACTICE IN ORGANIZED LABOR SETTINGS

Program Auspice

The interest and involvement of labor unions in the personal and family needs of its members has traditionally been manifested in three different strategies for service delivery. To begin with, labor leaders have been instrumental in encouraging management to take a more active and responsible role in protecting the mental health of its workers (6). These leaders see industry's increasing emphasis on technical specialization as being incompatible with the basic human needs of workers. In many cases, labor has obtained extended mental health benefits for its members through collective bargaining. These benefits have included insurance coverage for diagnostic services, in-patient and out-patient therapy, drug costs and other services for problems related to mental health. Since the 1960's, private insurance coverage for mental disorders has greatly expanded, but most insurance companies still insure for only severe emotional disorders that require hospitalization (6).

Some unions have also developed their own information and referral services to encourage workers to use community mental health services. For the most part, however, unions have not been satisfied with community-based services, as they generally are not attuned to the needs of workers. Some observers have attributed this gap to the fact that "there is usually insufficient involvement of unions in the planning of community mental health programs" (6).

The third strategy consists of the provision of mental health treatment services directly by the union. Some unions, as early as the 1940's, began hiring social workers to provide counseling services to meet the personal and family needs of its members. These services formed an integral part of an evolving occupational social welfare system. This system is composed of those benefits and services, above and beyond wages, that are directed at the health and social needs of union members.

The goal of mental health programs conducted under the auspice of organized labor is identical to that of all employee assistance program: maintaining workers on the job or returning them to work wherever possible. This is the essence of the work rehabiitation philosophy, which "sees the world of work as the context and partner in the rehabilitation process" (43). The work setting is used as a vehicle through which to find the worker whose personal or family problems are creating an obstacle to job performance and within which to deliver services designed to "help the patient to adjust to his work world" (43).

Union-sponsored employee assistance programs are based on what unions maintain to be "essential differences between union and company to be effective it must be jointly sponsored by labor and management. Organized labor maintains the position that no employee assistance program can be effective unless both labor and management recognize the importance of the program in terms of the bottom line — human happiness, and its relationship to stability and productivity" (32). According to Perlis, this understanding should be reflected in the formation of a "human contract" which is developed jointly by labor and management and consists of the principles, policies, programs and procedures of the EAP. This "human contract" should concern itself with those personal and family problems that are not covered by the union contract. These fall into five major categories: (1) familial (marital problems, child-parent relationships, in-law problems); (2) health (alcoholism, drug abuse, hypertension); (3) consumer (landlord-tenant problems, debt counseling); (4) legal (contracts, accidents, buying, selling); and (5) financial (supplementary assistance, Food Stamps).

Social workers are recognized by many union leaders as being the preferred professional group for the delivery of services to address the problems. "What every joint union-management committee needs in every department, on every shift, depending on the number of employees involved is a professional trained in industrial social work" (32). Organized labor is increasingly coming to trust and appreciate social work's professional code of ethics which is based upon respect for the value systems of other groups.

Program Structure and Setting

Some unions use their welfare funds to purchase services in the community for their members on a prepaid or reimbursement basis. "Those agencies — and social workers — who understand the special needs of workers and their families, the nature of work settings, and the need to reach out and make linkages with the work world will be the professional sources to which . . . unions will turn" (16). More frequently, union-sponsored social welfare programs are located directly in the health and benefit programs (2). The advantages of being located within a union facility are illustrated in a description of the Personal Service Union of District Council 37 of the American Federation of State, County and Municipal Employees.

> The Personal Service Unit is housed in union headquarters where members are accustomed to come for many purposes — meetings, classes, inquiries about benefits, and so forth. The building is familiar, almost home territory. To some extent, members feel it belongs to them. Their dues pay for it and for union staff salaries. Union services are a right. Generally members of District Council 37 perceive the union as benign, as being on their side. There is a feeling of union brotherhood, in which the Personal Service Unit is included. These features, as well as the informality of the setting, serve to lessen some of the sense of strangeness and social distance often felt by working class people in social agency waiting rooms and offices. Users of services are referred to as 'members in need' rather than clients (16).

PROGRAM SERVICES. The services delivered by social workers in union-sponsored EAPs are similar to those provided in corporate programs. In both instances, "social work intervention is strongly focused on enhancing . . . coping capabilities, adaptive skills, knowledge and use of resources" (16). The range of services delivered by union-sponsored programs may in some instances, be slightly broader than services provided in industry-based programs. Descriptions of union EAPs emphasize goals of helping members with any problem that is dysfunctional and of providing "a large array of services in 'response' to its membership's demands" (11). George Bailey, the Director of the Social Service Program of the International Ladies' Garment Workers' Union (ILGWU), in describing the program, refers to "the tremendous variability and intensity involved in the work. The presenting requests may involve a broad range of areas: mental health or interpersonal, physical health related, job related, financial, legal or consumer, housing, union claims or eligibility for public programs" (7).

The increased range of services often available in union-based programs may result from differences in clients' expectations, in the sponsoring organization's goals as well as from differences in the nature of the social worker's primary commitment. In unions, social services are perceived by members as a right — their entitlement as a member. Social workers strive to "provide assistance whatever the problem" (11) in response to workers' (members) "demands" — a word that is never used in connection with the corporate programs.

> One practitioner came to earth with a thump in the early days of his employment when he told a client that he would do something about a problem and was smartly reminded "that you better get this done and you better get this done fast or I'm going to tell the union leader that you're not good for nothing (2).

In addition, social workers in industry-sponsored EAPs are faced with the difficulties inherent in being bound by a "powerful organizational identity. . . . There is the constant pressure of the potential (or actual) conflict between an individual worker's needs, the professional responsibility to these needs, and the organization's goals of expansion and profit maximization" (2). In industry-sponsored programs, the answer to the question of whose agent is the social worker remains unclear. Some observers insist that the social worker "must maintain primary commitment to the client" (2) even though this may conflict with their loyalty to the work setting. It is further maintained that the social worker "is always the advocate of the patient" (43) in terms of protecting his confidentiality and in negotiating with systems and institutions. The difficulties inherent in assuming such a posture, while employed in an industry-sponsored program, are readily apparent. It is suspected that, to a large extent, social workers employed by industry are limited in the services that they can offer to employees by the threat posed by the concept and practice of client advocacy.

The dilemmas inherent in union settings stem less from a possible conflict of values and motives than from organizational maintenance and membership needs.

> For example, if a member is confronted with mandatory job counseling and the threat is treatment or termination, how does the social worker reconcile this referral with notions of client/member self-determination? Or if an approaching election brings a flurry of directives affecting programming, how does a practitioner maintain professional integrity when asked unexpedtedly to expand service goals or to assist in other ways in the survival needs of the leadership (2).

Social work practice in union-sponsored EAPs tends to be relatively consistent across union settings. The services offered by the ILGWU Social Service Department are fairly representative (7). These include: (1) individual and group counseling conducted in-house. The approach that is utilized focuses on quick assessment, problem identification, mutually defined goals, and short-term contract for work; (2) counseling and collaboration with local union officials or Union Health Center staff. This may include medical or psychiatric evaluations; and (3) ongoing linkage service with community agencies. This may involve collaboration, referral or advocacy.

The ILGWU Social Sevice Program also offers group facilitation services which are characteristic of most union programs. These services can be categorized by function: informational, training and therapeutic.

Informational groups are usually one-session presentations to new members, unemployed members and pre-retirement and retirement groups. In an effort to further the goal of prevention, other kinds of sessions such as seminars on physical and mental health-related topics, are currently being explored.

Training groups are conducted for union staff on how to identify and refer job-related problems such as alcoholism. As most referrals to any EAP are performance-based, training supervisors is an essential program component. Union staff are also trained in methods of increasing their effectiveness as providers of service to union members. Therapeutic groups, in the case of ILGWU, have primarily focused on the treatment of alcoholism.

While the provision of counseling and related services to members and their families comprise the core of social work activity in union settings, a variety of other functions are routinely performed by social service staff. One of the most prevalent activities consists of consultation to the union, or to management, on internal and external policies.

> Social workers are engaged in internal consciousness-raising regarding employees' and members' service needs in the community as well as on the job. Are workers late because of the transportation system? Are women hampered by child care arrangements that limit their contribution to the workplace? Are working people debilitated by their physical surroundings at home, lack of heat, or improper sanitary conditions? What is the lighting situation in neighborhood streets? Should an effort be made in the arena of education or recreation? Social workers have sensitivity to and familiarity with workers' personal and family lives, and can document needs and provide feedback to the executives and union leaders of host organizations (2).

Social workers in union-based programs are also involved in program and policy development. Ongoing needs assessment and information gathering is an essential aspect of the social work process. Statistics on utilization and types of presenting problems are routinely collected. The case-by-case analysis of individual service needs can be used to document the pervasive nature of a problem whose resolution requires systematic change. "Hence, out of insights from individual service, systematic changes can take place that enhance the functioning of the organization" (2). This is the essence of the "case to cause and back to case" principle of social work practice. In employee assistance programs the majority of research and evaluation activities are conducted for program planning and policy development purposes. Some unions also conduct research activities that include analysis of proposed legislative benefits and program analysis to determine differential impact on union members (4). These activities, however, rarely constitute a significant portion of program functions.

The provision of linkage services with community agencies has already been described as an integral function of employee assistance programs. In addition to these information and referral activities, social workers in union as well as industry-sponsored EAPs engage in the development and use of community resources.

> Monitoring and evaluating community resources is an important responsibility for many practitiones in industrial and trade union settings for which they are exceptionally well prepared. Their background, training and prior experience in community organizing, interviewing, and communication is invaluable (2).

SOCIAL SERVICE DELIVERY THROUGH CONTRACTOR AGREEMENTS

A third model for the delivery of employee assistance services involves the formation of contractual agreements with community agencies, individual private practitioners, or consulting firms. In this model, services are either provided on-site at the workplace, or at the agency or consultant's office. The advantages and disadvantages of this approach to social service delivery becomes evident upon examination of several well-respected and representative programs.

Community Agencies

The Xerox Corporation is generally considered to be the pioneer in the area of the provision of employee services by staffs of family agencies. In 1970, the company, in collaboration with Family Services of Rochester, New York, began offering in-plant social services to all Xerox employees with personal and family problems (23). The company provided funds to Family Services so that the agency could assign a full-time staff member to the work site. Through this purchase of service arrangement, employees could also choose to see a counselor at any of the agency's offices. Providing a choice in treatment sites proved to be essential to the program's success. It was found that "although employees are responsive to the accessibility of the counselor's presence at the plant, they are also relieved to discover that the service is a confidential one which can be kept separate from the employer-employee relationship" (23).

In addition to the advantages that community-based service delivery offers to the employee, this structural arrangement can be of benefit to the social worker as well. Being part of a community-based agency reduces the sense of professional isolation experienced by social workers in "the unfamiliar and often intensely competitive circumstances" (2) that are typically found in industry. In a community agency social workers are surrounded by other professionals trained in the helping field who share common values. These support groups are not available to the industrial practitioner.

For counselors who are part of a service agency, having time away from the work site also allows for activities such as case-centered consultation and in-service training. This is an integral component of the contractual service delivery model as it "guarantees application of the agency's collective knowledge and experience" (23) to employee problems. Thus, through the company's support of existing community services, not only is immediate professional counseling made available to employees, but the quality of the services provided are assured as well.

Although adequate information is scarce, it appears that when employee assistance services are provided to a company through a contractual agreement with a community agency, the range of services tends to be narrower than under the previously described program structures. Services are generally limited to information and referral, crisis intervention, casework and group work with employees and their families, and training in relation to the utilization of employee assistance services. Activities such as consultation to management or unions on internal or external policies, community relations and other common types of "indirect" services are less likely to be offered by consultants than by in-house staff. The extent to which program and policy development as well as research and evaluation activities, are incorporated into ongoing program function varies greatly from one program to the next. This decision is largely dependent upon the support of management and the possession of the necessary skills by the consultants.

Health Service Organizations

In the past, industry and labor primarily contracted with family service agencies and community mental health centers for the delivery of employee assistance services. With the recent burst of interest in EAPs, however, it has been estimated that "about 100 independent mental health organizations have been formed to service corporate clients" (26) within the last few years alone. In addition, a variety of diagnostic health service firms including hospitals and health maintenance organizations (HMOs — prepaid group medical practices, which are being used by an increasing number of companies in lieu of medical insurance benefits) are entering the occupational programming market. Some of the larger health service groups offer many advantages to the company that is interested in implementing an employee assistance program.

> They (the companies) remain closely affiliated with HMOs and thus have access to huge staffs of psychiatrists, social workers, chemical dependency counselors, and licensed consulting psychologists. This enables them to offer the type of thorough treatment that in-house staffs are rarely equipped to give (26).

Even some companies that have in-house EAPs are now beginning to utilize the medical expertise of large health service groups through contractual agreements.

Consulting Firms and Private Practitioners

In addition to community agencies and health service groups, many companies, both large and small, contract with private consulting firms or individuals to provide services to troubled employees.

The number of consultants in the area of EAPs has skyrocketed within the past five years (particularly within the last two) as people with degrees in everything from psychology to business administration and even history and English (29) display their eagerness to offer a service that industry is so willing to buy. Some concern has been expressed about the effect that this rapid expansion will have on the field and upon the quality of services provided to industry and labor. It is still too early, however, to determine the outcome of this recent flurry of activity.

For the most part, social workers who serve as consultants to industry and labor are prepared to offer the full range of employee assistance services. Crisis intervention, information and referral, short-term treatment, task-oriented casework, family and groupwork and case-centered consultation comprise the bulk of the services delivered.

These services are provided either on-site — often in connection with the Medical and Personnel Department — and/or at the consultant's office. Training and education programs, particularly those oriented towards the promotion of health or "wellness" are rapidly becoming a focus of EAP activity. These programs foster the concept of assuming responsbility for one's own health and emphasize the role of factors such as nutrition, exercise, stress, drinking and smoking in personal health and job performance. Such lifestyle-oriented education programs are increasingly being seen as an integral function of a full-service EAP; one that complements and enhances the treatment functions.

An example of a consulting firm that offers a somewhat different approach to servicing the needs of industry and labor is provided by Human Effectiveness Systems (HES). The HES social work program focuses on "leadership training and organizational development to maximize individual and organizational effectiveness rather than being primarily designed to offer direct services to the troubled individual employee" (10). The goal of intervention is the establishment of a therapeutic environment that supports growth and change. This program, in its focus upon the organization — the workplace — rather than the individual as the target of treatment, builds upon several concepts integral to the EAP environmental model previously discussed. As such, it serves to broaden the traditional definition of industrial social work practice. In this expanded view of the social worker as a change agent, the target of the change effort shifts from the individual to the organization. For HES staff members, the purpose of treatment is not to help the worker to adjust to this work world. The objective of intervention is always the development of a healthy work community that fosters individual as well as organizational effectiveness and growth.

PRACTICE IN GOVERNMENT SETTINGS

A significant portion of industrial social workers are employed in a wide variety of government agencies in some form of direct or indirect delivery of employee health-related services. The majority of these social workers are engaged in the delivery of employee assistance services to the employees and families of city, county, state, and federal government agencies. The first, and for many years the only such program, was the management-sponsored counseling service of the Social Security Administration established in 1944 (18). Social service programs were as slow to develop in government agencies as they were in private industry: in 1959, there were only 50 programs in major corporations in the United States and they all dealt exclusively with alcoholism (20).

The single factor that provided the greatest impetus for the development of programs in government and industry, was the passage of the Federal Comprehensive Alcohol Abuse and Alcoholism Prevention, Treatment and Rehabilitation Act (the Hughes Act) in 1970. One of the key provisions of the Act mandated the Civil Service Commission to establish an office, now called the Office of Personnel Management, for the development and maintenance of appropriate prevention, treatment and rehabilitation programs for alcohol abuse and alcoholism among federal employees. In 1971, federal agencies were mandated to establish employee assistance programs. The Department of Defense and each of the military services also required such programs for military and civilian employees. These developments had an immediate impact on private industry as well, in terms of the proliferation of occupational alcoholism – employee assistance programs. By 1971, approximately 300 major corporations had employee assistance programs; by 1973 the number had grown to 600; and by 1975 it had reached 2,250.

A small group of social workers are employed by a number of federal agencies in capacities other than service delivery in government EAPS (24). Many of these agencies such as the National Institute on Drug Abuse (NIDA), have direct impact upon health-related programs in labor and industrial settings. NIDA sets standards and guidelines and provides funds for drug abuse programs in a wide variety of settings, including industry. Social workers are increasingly assuming more visible roles in federal agencies such as NIDA, and are bearing greater responsibility for decision-making by engaging in activities that include — but are not limited to — planning, program and policy development, research and evaluation, and distribution of agency funds through grants, contracts, etc. Thus, while not directly involved in service delivery to labor and management, "industrial" social workers in government decision-making positions have perhaps the most significant opportunity to bring their unique set of skills, knowledge and values to bear in determining the direction and development of social service delivery in the world of work.

Other social workers are linked to the world of work through direct involvement in federally funded projects. Grants and contracts are the most common forms of awards and these are typically made to non-profit organizations for the development or the maintenance of unique research or service delivery programs. One example of such a project is the Employment and Training Program of the Vera Institute of Justice in New York City (25). The Institute recently received an 18-month grant from the United States Department of Labor to provide personal and vocational counseling and education and training to males and females age 16 to 21 who have histories of criminal justice involvement. The masters level social worker employed on this project is responsible for direct service delivery. The services most frequently provided are casework, groupwork and crisis intervention. The social worker is equally responsible for program and policy development, program-centered consultation, and the supervision of staff.

Another example of a federally funded service project tied to the world of work is the Occupational Health Program (OHP) at the University of Tennessee College of Pharmacy in Memphis (24). The OHP is presently in its third year of funding by the Occupational Safety and Health Administration of the Department of Labor. The primary purpose of the Program is to provide training and technical assistance in the recognition, control and prevention of health hazards to employers and employees in Tennessee. The OHP focuses its public service efforts on groups that traditionally have not had access to technical resources in occupational health — small businesses, trade unionists, unorganized workers (94 percent of the workers in Tennessee are unorganized), minorities, and women. The OHP also works in conjunction with the Southern Poison Center in responding on a 24-hour basis, to all telephone requests for information and technical assistance on exposures to toxic substances in the workplace.

The Occupational Health Program is staffed by four industrial hygienists, an occupational health nurse, and a masters level social worker. The social worker, who is the Assistant Director of the Program, is primarily responsible for administration, planning, program and policy development and all program evaluation and quality assurance activities. Grantwriting is another major focus of activity, along with the development and dissemination of training and informational materials. The social worker, in essence, serves as a direct link between the technical expertise of the OHP staff and the needs and demands of the Program's target groups. The success of the OHP to date has been largely attributed to this unique combination of professional expertise in the physical and social sciences which is reflected in all aspects of program development and service delivery.

IMPLICATIONS FOR FUTURE PRACTICE DIRECTIONS

Over the course of the past decade, social work practice in occupational health has demonstrated its viability and growth potential. The rapid expansion of this diversified field of practice, however, has also resulted in perpetuation of numerous functional inconsistencies in the nature and method of service delivery. These "growing pains" serve as additional obstacles to the specialization's continued development and acceptance as a key profession in human service programming in the labor and industrial community. The existence of these developmental problems signalled the need for direction and support from graduate schools of social work education and from professional organizations such as the National Association of Social Workers (NASW).

In recognition of the need for professional guidance and out of a commitment to further the development of industrial social work education and practice, the Council on Social Work Education (CSWE) and NASW jointly formed the Project on Social Work in Industrial Settings in 1977. The work of the project in its two years of operation (March, 1977-October, 1979), comprises the most systematic and comprehensive effort undertaken by either group in the area of industrial social work to date.

The project established an Advisory Committee that was comprised of representatives from labor and industry, as well as social work education and practice. The Committee formulated recommendations to CSWE and NASW on the direction of future education and practice in industrial social work. A major focus of the Advisory Committee's recommendations was graduate level and continuing education. It was recommended that the CSWE revision of the curriculum policy statement for graduate education include a requirement that content on the significance of work and work institutions be included in all portions of the core graduate curriculum (17). The Committee also recommended that training for practice in industrial social work be at the masters level and beyond, and should include at a minimum, an overview course and a field placement in a labor or industrial setting (17).

> The group pointed out that many other helping professionals in industry have advanced degrees, e.g., psychologists and psychiatrists, rendering stiff competition in the field. Corporate concern for professional licensing lend added weight to the argument for advanced degree training (17).

The Committee went on to recommend that continuing education should be considered a primary component of a total industrial social work education program. Given the small number of social workers who have prior experience in the world of work, continuing education provides an appropriate mechanism for preparing interested practitioners for entry into the field. It has become apparent that social workers practicing in more traditional settings are becoming increasingly interested in this field. Moreover, as the field expands and there is an increased demand for social workers, many of the new positions will be in settings establishing new programs. Practitioners will be required to be skilled in both direct practice and program development, as well as to understand the special dimensions of practice in occupational health. Through continuing education, many of these experienced and skilled social workers could acquire the body of knowledge necessary for successful practice in the complex and demanding world of work.

Suggestions were made for appropriate components of an industrial social work curriculum:

> There appears to be general consensus among educators and practitioners that social work students need an overview introduction to the world of work and its organization structures as well as specific skills in needs assessment, cost benefit analysis, systematic data collection and organizational maintenance. Another question to consider, however, is whether all students moving into this field should have

> counseling skills and whether those with such practice skills need training in program development, outreach and program management. Although there seems to be general agreement that students in these settings need to know about every aspect of practice, restraints within individual school curricula make this difficult (17).

While the proposed curriculum is quite broad and diversified, there is no mention in the project's report of occupational safety and health. Although there are social workers employed in a wide variety of settings who are addressing this public health issue in their practice, schools of social work, for the most part, do not provide any preparation for intervention in this area. It is anticipated that in the 1980's enormous growth in public awareness and concern over environmental and occupational health hazards will prompt increased activity on the part of government, industry, and other organizations. The need and demand for social work involvement in this area will also increase as the distinction between private troubles and public issues becomes less apparent. The profession's contribution to the field of occupational health will be severely stunted unless the graduate schools take the initiative and begin to prepare students for intervention in the world of work.

The Committee also made several recommendations to the NASW which amounted to "a formula for incorporating industrial social work in the practice component of the professional superstructure" (17). The Board of Directors of NASW was asked to appoint an ad hoc task force on social work practice in labor and industrial settings as a first step in the development of a practice specialty group. The ultimate goal of such action would be the development of an official practice special group or council, the same approach that is being taken by school social workers, mental health and health social workers, and clinical social workers.

The Committee encouraged NASW to serve as a liaison to corporations, corporate trade associations and trade unions. It was also recommended that NASW serve as a national information clearinghouse on industrial social work with responsibility for developing communication channels for sharing information among professionals in the field. This would serve to reduce the sense of professional isolation presently experienced by these practitioners as well as to expand the limited body of information available on this area of practice.

Unresolved Issues

Across all settings and types of services delivered, three unresolved professional issues continue to trouble occupational health social workers. The first of these — the question of "Whose agent are you?" — has already been explored to a limited extent. How this question is answered is directly affected by the nature of the sponsorship — auspice — under which the service is provided.

> For example, in the event that the social worker is asked to evaluate an employee's work-caused emotional disability for workmen's compensation, the social worker's assessment might be affected by whether he or she is employed by management, labor, or an outside social agency that has contracted to provide this service (8).

Some observers maintain that those social workers who provide services to industry through contractual agreements are at a distinct advantage in terms of this issue. They suggest that private practitioners are less likely to be identified as part of the management structure. In addition, they can more easily maintain a sense of professional objectivity as they are not directly employed by either management or labor (8). On the other hand, it is agreed that "professional objectivity is an important prerequisite for all social work practice, regardless of the nature of the sponsorship" (8). Nonetheless, according to the CSWE/NASW Project on Industrial Social Work, social workers, regardless of their auspice must maintain primary commitment to the client, even though this may clash at times with their loyalty to the work setting.

While controversy over this issue will continue, most parties agree that the employer-employee relationship is a symbiotic one: neither can exist without the other. The challenge to social work is to maximize collaboration between these two groups through mutual respect for differences, and to find an equilibrium that optimizes the interests of both parties (2). One of the lessons learned by the examination of the rise and fall of the welfare secretary, is that for industrial social work to survive as a specialization, it must be welcomed as a benefit by the worker, the union (where one exists) and the employer. This goal can only be achieved by the development and demonstration of effectiveness in problem solving through the maintenance of professional objectivity.

A second major dilemma involves the issue of professional commitment or focus: Should it be the individual, the work environment, or both?

> Social workers may be accepted as counselors, but many asked whether there is not a larger involvement encompassed by the professional perspective — for example, a commitment to the quality of life stemming directly from our professional values? Does the profession's vision of social change invoke commitment to humanize the workplace. If it does, how can it be done effectively? If it does not is the social worker faced with increasing susceptibility to co-optation, to losing the commitment to the social change characteristic of the social work profession? For example, if the treatment goal of job maintenance doesn't turn out to be in the best interest of the client, at what point does the practitioner help the client to leave the workplace. Or if the employing organization is about to lay off 500 workers, is it the social work function to 'defuse' the situation? Or if the employing organization institutes a speed-up in production, does the practitioner treat the individuals who respond to stress as failures or victims? (2)

This is a topic of heated debate, as evidenced by the now classic exchange between Leo Perlis and Theodore Walden reported in the *NASW News* in 1978. Perlis maintains that the role of the social worker is to help the client solve his or her personal and family problems. He states:

> It is pure fantasy to suggest at this stage of development that there is a role for social workers in union and corporation determination of the four-day week, or flex-time, . . . or affirmative action, or corporate and union community responsibility, or insurance coverage, or organizational change (31).

Perlis goes on to state that such involvement may be threatening and is certainly diversionary and counterproductive to the development of an industrial social work program in the workplace.

Theodore Walden presented an opposing viewpoint in which he chose a systemic perspective which takes into account the effects of the workplace on job performance, as well as on the worker's personal and home life:

> To passively accept a position in which social workers can respond only to the residual aftermath of non-work related personal or familial dysfunction is to relegate the profession to a reactive stand capable of dealing primarily with effects and hardly ever with diseases. It is akin to providing medical treatment for those who contract black lung disease without ever mounting an effort to correct the environmental conditions which produce noxious elements. It is much too heavy a price to pay in instances where workers may be the unwitting victims of industrial or union abuse. . . . Social work has more to offer than employee assistance programs, as important as they are. As a con-

> science to remind industry and unions of social responsibility, and as advocates for workers' rights, social workers need desperately to be able to challenge industrial and union practices which violate the human condition and to seek changes designed to upgrade the quality of life" (41).

This question was also raised by the CSWE/NASW Project on Social Work in Industrial Settings in terms of the need to define the social work relationship to the industrial production process.

> Are social workers simply adjusting people to the demands of existing processes, or is there a role for social workers in job enrichment and redesign? What would be the basis for intervention? How can the integration of humanistic principles with engineering practice be achieved? (2).

The dilemma of professional commitment is further implied in social work involvement with high-risk populations at the workplace. In addition to being defined by the nature of the job, the term high risk refers to those vulnerable or marginal members of the labor force. These workers are vulnerable because of a disability of some kind or because of a social issue, such as the day care problems of women workers. Another example is provided by women who are pioneering in jobs previously performed by men and thus may be placed at risk. Aside from the issue of acceptance by male co-workers, the question of job safety often arises: if the job is safe for men, is it safe for women? Furthermore, if the job is safe for women generally, is it safe for pregnant women? If the job is found to be unsafe for pregnant women, the question then becomes whether the worker should be temporarily reassigned or whether the job should be redesigned so as to accommodate any worker.

The CSWE/NASW project does not offer any guidance for solving this dilemmma. It does, however, report that "these kinds of social issues present fertile fields for social work intervention" (2). This perspective grows out of a broad conceptualization of the profession which affirms that "a major objective of social work is the alleviation of social problems" (33). It is further asserted that in addition to those strategies already being used by social workers in labor and industrial settings, the social worker involved with social issues could assume the role of class advocate: "one who argues for, defends, maintains, or recommends a cause or proposal" (28). Moreover, class advocates seek to "change those systems and institutions within society which are not responsive to the needs and aspirations of individuals and social units, and to their participation in society" (37).

NASW not only sanctions this role, but maintains that "the professional social worker is ethically bound to take on the advocacy role if he is to fulfill his professional responsibilities" (28). In describing "The Common Base of Social Work Practice", Harriett Bartlett gives full recognition to "the other side of the profession . . . those who work broadly with social conditions, programs and social policy", towards the goal of social change: "modifying organizations and making them more effective in solving social problems" (9). Thus social workers have a professional sanction for all levels of interaction in the world of work. The majority are presently functioning in the role advocated by Perlis: that of helping the client (the employee) to solve his personal and family problems. However, it is no longer "pure fantasy" to suggest that social workers can be effective in other areas such as affirmative action, corporate and union responsibility, and organizational change. A number of social workers currently do, in fact, bear responsibility in these areas, and their accomplishments have gained the respect of both management and labor. This is not to imply that one type of practice is preferable to another. Rather, the point to be made is that the profession should not set premature limits on areas of endeavor because of their complexity or their inherently political nature.

Seen in this light, perhaps the answer to the dilemma of professional focus would be a dual commitment: to the individual and to the environment. Undoubtedly, a great many social workers will shun the class advocate role and will continue to deal with the personal and family problems of their clients exclusively on a case-by-case basis. On the other hand, a growing number of social workers will opt for a systemic perspective. In this view, the focus of social work assessment and intervention is the interactions and transactions between people and their social environment, and the outcome is likely to involve organizational change. If properly conceived and conducted, these two approaches could not only complement, but intensify the efforts and outcomes of the other.

The third and final dilemma concerns what has been described as "the intrinsic conflict between the values of industry and those of social work" (8). Throughout the history of the profession, social workers have consistently emphasized this dicotomy in the conceptualization of the individual and his worth, and in ways of dealing with him and his problems. The following statement provides a representative example:

> Concern for the well-being of people, individually and collectively, historically has been social work's trademark. Industry, on the other hand, places its primary value on production and profits. Its people are viewed as a commodity having only instrumental value for the industry's central purpose (8).

Industry, on the other hand, perceives social workers as fuzzy-thinking do-gooders who see industry as interested only in profits and as exploiting its employees. This is the perception of many businessmen who have come to know social workers through serving on boards of social agencies and through contact with the services delivered by social workers (13).

Whether these portrayals are accurate becomes inconsequential. The issue that is of overriding importance is that the American work force is a severely underserved population. Stresses inherent in the nature of work, combined with inadequate access to community-based social services are taking their toll upon the worker in the form of increased physical and mental health problems and upon industry in terms of decreased productivity and profits. The value of occupational health social work lies in the practitioner's ability to simultaneously recognize and objectively mediate between the needs of the individual worker and those of the organization. The goal is to maximize the health and development of the worker and the organization.

If social workers operate from the perspective that industry maintains blatant disregard for human life and is inherently exploitive of labor, the broad-based goal of occupational health social work practice cannot be achieved. It is apparent that when one acts on the basis of such a strong, negative stance, professional objectivity cannot be attained. This situation, in turn, strengthens industry's perception and distrust of social workers and increases their reluctance to employ or work with them. The victim of this circular conflict is the worker, who, as a result of "image problems" (13) on both sides of the issue, remains underserved.

One strategy that has been proposed for dealing with this dilemma advocates accepting the irreconcilability of the two positions and making the necessary adaptations rather than trying to change the nature of an intolerable situation.

> Given the basic incompatibility between the goals and values of industry and those of the profession, it might be less constraining to challenge industry from without than within. Perhaps the profession should *not* enter the world of industry directly but should channel its

efforts through existing social agencies such as community mental health and family service organizations (8).

Another approach to this dilemma calls for the reexamination of social work's knowledge and image of industry. To be successful in industry, social workers will have to come to terms with "the economic facts of life about the free enterprise system" (13). Profit is the only way to insure survival in the tumultous business world and, therefore, is not necessarily a curse but a blessing. Moreover, industry, for the most part, "is not bloated with profits. Rather it is struggling to remain competitive with foreign-made products, to replace aging plants, and to continue to provide jobs and income for people. Money does not flow magically from government printing presses, despite the illusion. It has been produced. All too often, social work's rhetoric does not carry a recognition of that fact" (13).

Social work in industry at the turn of the century failed because the welfare secretaries never developed the trust of the workers nor the confidence of the employers. For industrial social work to survive as a specialization in its present state, it must demonstrate a willingness to deemphasize the issue of values and to focus upon needs: those of the worker and the organization.

To quote, once again, the words of Leo Perlis:

> Here, faulty motivations are less important than proper arrangements. What difference does it make if the employer thinks first of profitability, as long as he does the right thing for his people? He may not get much credit in heaven, but he certainly will get more production in the plant (32).

REFERENCES

1. A Plague on Our Children: NOVA. *WGBH Transcripts*, 1979.
2. Akabas SH, Kurzman PA, Kolben NS: *Labor and Industrial Settings: Sites for Social Work Practice*. New York, Council on Social Work Education, 1979.
3. Akabas SH: Mental Health Program Models: Their Role in Reducing Occupational Stress. *Proceedings — Reducing Occupational Stress*. U.S. DHEW, NIOSH, 1978.
4. Antoniades R: Amalgamated Clothing and Textile Workers Union, AFL-CIO Social Services Department. *Labor and Industrial Settings: Sites for Social Work Practice*. New York, Council on Social Work Education, 1979.
5. Ashford NA: *Crisis in the Workplace: Occupational Disease and Injury*. Cambridge, MIT, 1976.
6. Austin MJ, Jackson E: Occupational Mental Health and the Human Services: A Review. *Health and Social Work* 2:93, 1977.
7. Bailey G: *Social Service Delivery for Union Members and Their Families: An Innovative Approach*. Presentation to the American Public Health Association, 107 Annual Meeting, 1979.

8. Bakalinsky R: People vs. Profits: Social Work in Industry. *Social Work* 25:471, 1980.
9. Bartlett H: *The Common Base of Social Work Practice*, Washington, NASW, 1970.
10. Boone D: Human Effectiveness Systems. *Labor and Industrial Settings: Sites for Social Work Practice*. New York, Council on Social Work Education, 1979.
11. Draft F: District Council 37: American Federation of State, County and Municipal Employees, AFL-CIO Health and Security Plan, Personal Services Unit. *Labor and Industrial Settings: Sites for Social Work Practice*. New York, Council on Social Work Education, 1979.
12. Eggum PR, Keller PJ, Buron WN: Nurse/Health Counseling Model for a Successful Alcoholism Assistance Program. *Journal of Occupational Medicine* 22:8, 1980.
13. Fleming CW: Does Social Work Have a Future in Industry? *Social Work* 24:183, 1979.
14. Freud S: *Civilization and the Discontents*. New York, Norton, 1962.
15. Googins B: Employee Assistance Programs. *Social Work* 20:464, 1975.
16. Hellenbrand S, Hasser R: Social Work in Industrial Social Welfare. *Changing Roles in Social Work Practice*. Philadelphia, Temple University, 1977.
17. Kolben NS: *Final Report — CSWE/NASW Project on Social Work in Industrial Settings*. New York, CSWE, 1979.
18. Kuhl DT: Social Security Administration, Office of Human Resources Personnel Counseling Branch. *Labor and Industrial Settings: Sites for Social Work Practice*. New York, Council on Social Work Education, 1979.
19. Levi L: Psychosocial Stress at Work: Problems and Prevention. *Proceedings Reducing Occupational Stress*. U.S. DHEW, NIOSH, 1978.
20. Masi D: Alcoholism in the Workplace. *Health and Social Work* 4, No. 4:41, 1979.
21. Masi FA, Spencer GE: Alcoholism and Employee Assistance Programs in Industry: A New Frontier for Social Work. *Social Thought*, 3:19, 1977.
22. Miller L: A Counseling Service in Industry: Polaroid. *Social Thought* 3:37, 1977.
23. Mills, E: Family Counsiling in An Industrial Job-Support Program. *Social Casework* 53:587, 1972.
24. Moinester, SC: Discussion of Author's Position as Assistant Director of The University of Tennessee Occupational Health Program.
25. Moinester, SC: *National Survey of Industrial Social Workers*. The University of Tennessee Occupational Health Program, 1980. Unpublished.
26. More Help For Emotionally Troubled Employees. *Business Week*: March 12, 1979.
27. Nathan M: The Social Secretary. *World's Work* 4:2100, 1902.
28. National Association of Social Workers — Ad Hoc Committee on Advocacy: The Social Workers As Advocate — Champion of Social Victims. *Social Work* 14:17, 1969.
29. National Association of Labor-Management Administrators and Consultants on Alcoholism (ALMACA): *Occupational Employee Assistance Programs — What Do They Look Like?: A National Survey*. ALMACA Education and Training Committee, 1979.
30. Ozawa MN: Development of Social Services in Industry: Why and How? *Social Work* 25:464, 1980.
31. Perlis L: Industrial Social Work — Problems and Prospects. *NASW News* 23:8, 1978.
32. Perlis L: Social Services in the World of Work. *Social Thought* 3:31, 1977.
33. Reid WJ: Social Work for Social Problems. *Social Work* 22:374, 1977.

34. Robbins A: *Blacks and Occupational Health.* Reprinted Statement of Director, National Institute for Occupational Safety and Health, U.S. Department of Health and Human Services, 1980.
35. Rosow JM: *The Worker and the Job — Coping with Change.* Englewood Cliffs, Prentice-Hall, 1974.
36. Shain M, Groenveld J: *Employee Assistance Programs.* Lexington, Heath, 1980.
37. Silverstein M: Social Work and Social Change. *Journal of the Otto Rank Association.* Summer, 1975:45.
38. Silverstein M: *The Case of the Workplace Killers — A Manual for Cancer Detectives on the Job.* United Auto Workers Union, 1980.
39. Terkel S: *Working.* New York, Avon, 1972.
40. Traush S: Drug Abuse in the Workplace — Business's Undercover Problem. *The Commercial Appeal* (Daily Newspaper) Memphis, November 18, 1980.
41. Walden T: Industrial Social Work: A Conflict in Definition. *NASW News* 12:9, 1978.
42. Walker B: *Occupational Health.* Reprinted Statement of Director, and Directorate of Health Standard Program, Occupational Safety and Health Administration, U.S. Department of Labor, 1980.
43. Weiner, HJ, Akabas SH, Sommer JJ: *Mental Health Care in the World of Work.* New York Association, 1973.
44. Weissman A: Industrial Social Services: Linkage Technology. *Social Casework* 57:50, 1976.

Appendix I

PSYCHOSOCIAL ASPECTS OF HEALTH CARE
The Hospital's Responsibility*

prepared by the
American Hospital Association

This statement was developed by the Joint Committee of the American Hospital Association and the American Psychiatric Association as a first step in assisting hospitals in acknowledging the need for recognition of the psychosocial factors in illness and the human dimensions of medical care services needed to enhance the quality of patient care. The statement was approved by the American Hospital Association in 1969 and was published as the S59 leaflet. The S59 leaflet is superseded by this statement.

The care we give must be human, and it must be comprehensive. Comprehensiveness means another thing besides a combination of social and medical forces. It means a giving in our system of everything our people need in the proper place and at the proper time. . . . The word "care" in English has a double meaning. It means on the one hand a sevice we render to the sick; in the other meaning that we are fond of the sick, that we care for them as human beings . . . The community instinctively wants "care" in both of its English meanings. But in the modern society the greatest pressure from those we have most poorly served is for an expression from us that we really care to give care while caring.

—Edwin L. Crosby, M.D.
Rene Sand Memorial Lecture
June 1969

---

*Published 1976, American Hospital Association. Reprinted with Permission.

Because no illness is limited to its physical manifestations, recognition of the psychosocial elements of illness is imperative. When a patient is hospitalized, his primary illness is often compounded by increased anxiety, reactions to separation from family and familiar surroundings, fear of the unknown, and inability to understand what is happening to him. In addition, certain cultural and ethnic beliefs affect his attitude toward his illness and the attendant hospitalization.

Psychosocial factors in illness can delay recovery or, in extreme cases, can destroy the patient's ability to survive. It is essential, therefore, that these factors be recognized early. To accomplish the goal of early recognition and help, hospital personnel must be sensitive to the emotional problems that patients bring with them.

The atmosphere in which care is given affects a patient either favorably or unfavorably. Both the physical environment and the attitude of hospital personnel and other persons — patients, visitors, volunteers — may contribute to this atmosphere.

Top-level administration, with the support of the governing authority, establishes the "climate" of the hospital. A policy should be developed affirming the hospital's intent to provide care that meets psychosocial as well as physical needs of patients. This means that care should be provided in such a way that patients' anxieties and emotional concerns are identified and ameliorated to the degree possible. Further, it means that staff objectives and performance should reflect awareness of the impact of staff actions on the patient.

Orientation and in-service training programs are essential for both salaried and volunteer hospital personnel who have contact with patients and community if the hospital is to implement the foregoing policy.

Among those persons who have the most influence in creating the appropriate hospital climate are members of the medical staff and members of the supervisory staff. The medical staff has profound influence on other health professionals; medical staff leadership and example can accomplish much to create a climate in which the patient is recognized as a person who has many needs related to himself and to his family. Supervisory personnel can exert influence both through example and through in-service training programs.

To ensure that the policy on meeting psychosocial needs of patients is carried out, consideration should be given to including as a part of utilization review and other medical care appraisal activities an analysis of how well the psychosocial problems of the patient — whether an inpatient, an outpatient, or a home care patient — have been dealt with. Consideration also should be given to the development of a mechanism for investigating complaints of patients or their families, in order to identify and correct the underlying causes.

Many resources are available in the development of programs directed toward providing staff with knowledge and skill to help them in their interpersonal relationships with patients. Some physicians on the staff may have a special interest and competency that will prove especially helpful. Hospitals having organized psychiatric, social work, and chaplaincy programs can call on their own professional staffs.

Sometimes it will be necessary to call on other community resources for help in developing staff education programs. Such resources include, but are not limited to, community mental health centers, state and private psychiatric hospitals, and appropriate social agencies.

Recognition of the human dimensions of medical care services enhances the quality of patient care, tends to promote comprehensive health care, and can improve employee morale by increasing the employee's sense of his own worth and his confidence in his ability to serve.

The American Hospital Association believes that all hospitals have an obligation to examine their present policies and practices in the light of the need "to give care while caring."

Appendix II

NATIONAL HEALTH POLICY STATEMENT, 1979*

Prepared by the National Association of Social Workers

BACKGROUND AND BASIS FOR CONCERN

Professional social workers practice throughout the health care system and experience daily the strengths and limitations of the health system on the lives and health status of the American people. Their practice also encompasses relationships between the health care system and the social service, educational, and income maintenance systems. This provides an intensive and varied fund of experience and knowledge which enables NASW to contribute to the formulation of national health policy through the legislative processes of the federal government.

The National Association of Social Workers has a social responsibility to participate fully in the development and implementation of national health policy. This responsibility is deeply rooted in the collective professional experience of the 80,000 members of the association.

National Health Policy in the Context of National Social Policies The development of national health policy requires recognition of its relationship to other national policies which affect the health, security, social well-being, and functional capacities of the American people. The need for such policies is based on two premises. One is that each person is a whole being whose requirements for development, sustenance, and productivity must be viewed as a total entity. The other is that the fulfillment of individual potential is an expression of the collective responsibility of society.

Development of an adequate and effective national health policy must, therefore, be accompanied by development of other national social and economic policies, directed to the essential needs of all people and their society:

1. Each person should have a minimum material standard of living which meets the standards of healthful living and provides opportunities for educational and social self-fulfillment.
2. Each person should be assured equitable access to education, training, employment, housing, transportation, and all public services without regard to race, religion, sex, age, or ethnic status.
3. Each person should have available educational and social services, based on the allocation of adequate resources, to support good health and well-being.
4. Each person should be protected from commercial encouragement of personal life styles which are unhealthy, self-destructive, or wasteful of human potential.

Rapidly rising costs have made ill health a potential for economic catastrophe for any family. As health costs have continued to soar, they have consumed resources that should be more equitably distributed in the provision of other human services. In addition to the financial drain on the economy, many persons are not receiving the health care they need either because of age, income, marital status, attachment to the labor force, or geographic inaccessibility. Little of the health resources is allocated to preventive care. Treatment of acute illness is frequently more complex and expensive than necessary. Long term care of the physically and mentally disabled, and health care for the rural and urban poor, are also neglected.

National Health Care Program — The federal government has traditionally provided direct health care benefits to certain classes of beneficiaries. Federal health policy began in 1798 when health care for merchant seamen became a federal government responsibility. Since the 1930s, a multitude of proposals for health care have occupied major segments of legislative, administrative, and judicial processes. Subsequently, the federal government has become increasingly involved in financing health care.

At the present time, the federal government provides most of the funds for health-related research in the country. It provides more than one-half of the funding for medical schools and substantial portions of funding for schools of dentistry, nursing, and for a variety of training programs for allied health technologies. The federal government funds a major portion of the cost of national, state, and regional health planning activities. In addition, it provides loan guarantees for a substantial share of health-related facilities construction. Finally, the federal government provides more than one-quarter of all funds spent directly on health services for the American people, largely through Medicare, Medicaid, the armed services, and the Veterans Administration.

Recent Proposals — Recent legislative proposals on the subject of health have been directed primarily at funding mechanisms. These proposals have varied extensively in perspective, approach, and characteristics. Some have reflected a desire to preserve the major features of the existing health care system. Others have proposed major changes in the structure and operation of the system. Some proposals have reflected the orientation of a national professional society or association of health care facilities. Others have reflected political and bureaucratic attempts to find compromise solutions acceptable to a majority of legislative representatives. Most recently, creation of a national health **service** has been proposed. Unlike national health **insurance** proposals, this approach involves direct government operation of the health care system. NASW considers that all proposals should be analyzed on the basis of the principles listed below.

STATEMENT OF ISSUES

The issues which must be addressed in the development of a national health policy pertain to:

- decisions on whether the program will be voluntary or compulsory;
- the extent of coverage and access;
- the scope of the program and its comprehensiveness;
- the role of various levels of government;
- the relationship of public and private sectors;
- setting standards for quality of care and professional competence;
- funding and payment mechanisms;
- cost containment strategies;
- degree of involvement in education;
- research and planning;
- the relationship to environmental controls and personal life styles.

POLICY STATEMENT

Principles of a National Health Care Program:

a. Population Coverage and Access

Any national health care program must cover the entire resident population of the country. To insure equality of opportunity for health care, all population groups should be served within the same national health care program, to the maximum extent possible. Groups now receiving care through separate programs should be incorporated into the program.

Any national health care program must provide equal access to all health care services in the program. Services should be based on a comprehensive assessment of individual health care needs in the context of family, community, and available health resources. Services should be provided irrespective of race, ethnic origin, religion, age, sex, language,or geographic residence. Under no circumstances should there be separate categories, arrangements, or services which distinguish consumers on the basis of income, assets, or any measure of socio-economic status.

b. Health Services

The scope of the program should be comprehensive, including services which maintain optimum health, prevent illness and disability, ameliorate the effects of unavoidable functional incapacities, and provide supportive long-term and terminal care. Priority must be placed on prevention of illness and dysfunction and the promotion of health. Health services are psychological and social as well as medical in nature. Services related to physical and mental illness and disabilities, now covered in independent programs, should be provided on the same basis as other health care services.

Any national health program should be based on the best available scientific knowledge, professional expertise, and health-related technology as placed within prescribed priority needs. All services provided within the health care program should be coordinated with, and reinforced by, adequate and timely provision of basic financial security, social services, education, and employment opportunities. Services should be provided in ways which recognize and enhance the integrity of each person in the context of family and community.

c. Organizational Structure and Process

There should be a national framework for policy formulation, funding, and program accountability. Health care delivery planning and management should take place on a decentralized community level in accordance with demographic and socio-cultural needs. Delivery systems should reflect: (a) variability to meet the needs of the local community; (b) continuity and linkage in levels of care (preventive, primary, secondary, tertiary, and long-term care); (c) opportunity for choice by consumers; (3) inclusion of qualified social workers in the planning and delivery of preventive, secondary, and tertiary services, along with other health professional providers; (e) services oriented to the comprehensive needs of the individual and family unit, regardless of economic, racial or ethnic origins. The health care program must incorporate mechanisms for integration and coordination with other human services in the community.

The structure and process of any national health care program must insure optimum consumer involvement and participation of consumers at all levels.

d. Standards of Organizational and Fiscal Accountability

The federal government must establish organizational and fiscal standards and assure accountability for any national health care program. There must be standards of organizational and fiscal accountability appropriate to each decentralized level of administration. Appropriate mechanisms for the participation of health care personnel and health care consumers in the creation of organizational and fiscal standards should be provided at each level. Such standards should be designed to enhance the provision of health care services on private, and flexible basis. Conversely, such standards should not impose arbitrary requirements on professional-consumer relationships.

e. Funding

Any national health care program must be publicly funded on a national basis and provide for long-term stability of operation through the mechanism of progressive taxation. The scope of population coverage, benefits and participating health personnel should not depend upon temporary fluctuation of annual appropriation in the type or amount of funds available to the program. To control administrative costs, funding should be organized to utilize the most efficient procedures for collection and distribution.

Funding methods should not involve payments by consumers at the time of, and in partial payment for, individual receipt of health service.

Funding methods must not serve to differentiate among groups in the population.

f. Payment Mechanisms

Methods of payment for institutional-based health care services must support and insure provision of the scope, quantity, and quality of services required by the unique needs of each consumer in accordance with accepted standards.

Payment to professional personnel must provide a fair and equitable income in relation to mutually acceptable standards of quantitative and qualitative performance.

Payment for all services should be based on appropriate cost-finding methods and standards. Alternative methods of reimbursement need to be devised. Whatever method or combination of methods of payment are devised, qualified social workers must be included as reinbursible providers.

Payment mechanism should provide incentives, both economic and professional, which strengthen illness prevention programs and develop improved systems of delivery.

Payment methods should not include sub-contract relationships except when necessary to provide unavailable services.

g. Cost Containment

Cost containment should be applied through public regulation, subject to the nature of the health service principles previously described. Increasing costs in health care arise from multiple factors. It is important that cost containment policies be based on accurate information and addressed to appropriate targets. Public regulation must be designed to control costs because the health care industry does not respond to open competitive market mechanisms.

Cost containment should identify and eliminate those costs brought about by: (1) unnecessary expansion of health institutions, (2) duplicated, expensive equipment, and (3) unnecessary medical procedures.

Development of "prospective" or predetermined schedules of rates of reimbursement through negotiation between health care providers and payers and appropriate official representatives should be encouraged. Agreed-upon rates must be accepted as full payment for all purchasers of care. Integrated health care delivery systems such as HMOs should be encouraged and supported when practical.

h. Standards of Professional Competence and Ethics

Any normal health care program should establish national standards of professional competence set by the professions and subject to consumer and peer review. Accountability activities should aim at the improvement of professional competence; recognition and protection of consumers' rights; improvement in the health service delivery system and elimination of incompetent and unethical performance. Responsibility for evaluation of the competence of professional health service performance should be assigned at varying levels of structure. The criteria on which evaluation is based should be determined by professional peers. The evaluation review process, however, should be accomplished through mechanisms incorporating multidisciplinary professional and consumer participation.

i. Health Personnel Education, Training, Licensure, and Certification

National health policy shall include assurance of an adequate supply of competent health service personnel based on priority needs and the best available estimates of the future health care needs of the population. Standards must be developed as a means of reversing the deficit of health personnel, particularly primary care providers, in rural areas and urban ghettos and in institutions serving vulnerable populations, such as the aged, the mentally and physically handicapped, and minorities. Education and training of health-related personnel should be viewed in the context of societal support for equal access to a variety of education programs, with special emphasis on training of minorities and women in professions where they are currently underrepresented.

Financing for basic education of health personnel should be separate from financing for a national health care program. However, financial support for continuing professional education and technical training should be provided within the health program.

Assessment of educational programs should be made relative to their impact on the scope, competence, cost-effectiveness and ethical quality of professional and technical practice. Assessments should also be made of the extent to which educational specialization within and among the health care professions and technologies has contributed to, or detracted from, the provision of competent, comprehensive and integrated health care services.

National policy should strive for uniform national licensure and certification standards, with regular periodic updating of requirements.

j. Research

National health policy must include provisions for the discovery of new knowledge and the creation of new technology as basic resources for improvement of the health status of the American people within identified program priorities. Financing for an advanced program of health-related research and technology development should be separate from financing for a national health care service program. Health-related research policy should continue to support basic biomedical, psychosocial, and other clinical research and technology. Research policy should support exploration of human behavior which integrates healthy physical, psychological, and social adaptation. It should also encourage epidemiological research to identify populations which, because of personal, environmental, and societal factors, are at risk. In addition, research policy should encourage critical analysis of the benefits, limitations, and consequences of health management, organization, knowledge, and technology.

k. Health Planning

National health planning must include a commitment to the previously stated principles, especially: (1) development of an adequate, integrated and efficient health care system; and (2) development of a health-sustaining society and healthy personal life styles of the population; (3) coordination with other planning services, and (4) assurance of distribution of resources and personnel to medically underserved areas and to targeted minority groups.

A national health planning program should be viewed in the context of planning a society whose members are insured basic financial security, equal opportunity and adequate social, educational, and supportive services.

Health and planning functions should be performed at national, state, regional, and community levels, and supported by adequate regulatory powers of government. Health planning processes should include participation of a broad range of consumer and provider representation.

l. Health and Safety of Human Environments and Personal Life Styes

National health policy must advance public health principles which protect human environments, products, and services that are safe and healthful, in accordance with standards based on scientific knowledge and reasonable use. It is vital to insure that all by-products of industrial and energy production, and those of human functioning, do not endanger the health of present or future populations.

National health policy also must encourage and assist, through the development of appropriate education and social support mechanisms, personal life styles which promote and maintain optimum health. It must, in addition, discourage the exploitation of personal life styles which are destructive of health.

Appendix III

STANDARDS FOR SOCIAL WORK IN HEALTH CARE SETTINGS*

**Prepared by the
National Association of Social Workers
Health Quality Standards Committee**

**Approved by the Board of Directors,
National Association of Social Workers,
at its meeting on June 19, 1981**

*Published 1981, National Association of Social Workers, Inc. Reprinted with Permission.

TABLE OF CONTENTS

PREFACE

The health care system in the United States today is complex and multidisciplinary in nature. It includes a network of services such as diagnosis, treatment, rehabilitation, maintenance, and prevention to individuals of all ages and with a range of needs. These services are provided in a variety of settings, including general and specialty hospitals, nursing homes, community health and mental health centers, hospices, and public health programs.

Professional social workers are particularly well-equipped to practice in the health care field because of their broad perspective on the range of physical, emotional, and environmental factors which impact on the well-being of individuals. Social work is defined as the system of organized activities carried on by a person with particular knowledge, competence and values, designed to help individuals, groups or communities toward a mutual adjustment between themselves and their social environment.

Social workers have been involved in the health field since the turn of the century. The social work profession's earliest concerns in the health field were with making health services available to the poor and with improving social conditions that bred infectious diseases such as tuberculosis. Later, social work's role in health expanded. By the 1950's, as comprehensive health care delivery began to develop, social workers took their place beside other health professionals concerned with the delivery of quality health services. Today, social workers can be found in every component of the health system.

The Health Quality Standards Committee, in developing these standards, has recognized that both core and specialized aspects of social work practice in health care must be defined and described. The first section of this document represents an initial effort to define core administrative standards meant to be applicable to many health care settings and organizational arrangements, and to establish professional expectations for high quality social work practice. The standards are based upon the consensus of many social workers across the country. The intention of the Committee is to build upon these standards for social work practice in specialty interest areas within the health care field.

Chauncey A. Alexander, ACSW
Executive Director, NASW

PRINCIPLE

Every health care setting shall have social work services as an integral part of the organization. The social work services shall include services to individuals, their families and significant others; to special population groups; to communities; and to special health-related programs, services, and educational systems.

In order to provide comprehensiveness and continuity of care, social work services shall encompass:

1. the promotion and maintenance of physical and psychosocial well-being;
2. the promotion of conditions essential to assure maximum benefits from short and long term care services;
3. the prevention of physical or mental illness and;
4. the promotion and enhancement of physical and psychosocial functioning, with attention to the social and emotional impact of illness or disability.

CORE STANDARDS

STANDARD 1

EVERY HEALTH CARE ORGANIZATION SHALL MAINTAIN A WRITTEN PLAN FOR PROVIDING SOCIAL WORK SERVICES. THIS PLAN SHALL HAVE BEEN DEVELOPED BY A SOCIAL WORKER WITH A GRADUATE DEGREE FROM A SCHOOL OF SOCIAL WORK ACCREDITED BY THE COUNCIL ON SOCIAL WORK EDUCATION (CSWE). THIS PERSON SHALL HAVE HAD RELATED EXPERIENCE IN HEALTH CARE AND SHALL BE LICENSED OR CERTIFIED IN ACCORDANCE WITH STATE AND/OR PROFESSIONAL STANDARDS.

Interpretation

A written plan for the provision of social work services must be developed by a graduate level social worker experienced in health care. A contractual arrangement for the plan's development may be made with a graduate level social worker from an outside organization such as a social work department of an accredited hospital, an accredited graduate school of social work or an undergraduate social work program, a community social and/or health agency, a health department or public health agency.

The preferred plan for all sites for the delivery of social work services is an organized program under the direction of a graduate level social worker. An acceptable alternative approach would be a written contractual arrangement for the provision of social work services.

The decision regarding which type of plan to adopt shall be determined by the nature of the program required for the health care organization and the populations served.

STANDARD 2

SOCIAL WORK SERVICES SHALL BE PROVIDED UNDER THE PROFESSIONAL ADMINISTRATIVE DIRECTION OF A SOCIAL WORKER WITH A GRADUATE DEGREE FROM A SCHOOL OF SOCIAL WORK ACCREDITED BY CSWE. THIS PERSON SHALL BE ACCOUNTABLE FOR THE PROVISION OF THE SOCIAL WORK SERVICES, AND SHALL BE ADMINISTRATIVELY RESPONSIBLE TO THE CHIEF EXECUTIVE OFFICER OF THE ORGANIZATION.

Interpretation

There shall be a clearly defined administrative plan that delineates the duties, functions and responsibilities of the social work director. The overall program, and the accountability, coordination, and fiscal management of the social work services shall be assigned to the social work director. The provision of social work services shall be planned, organized and implemented by the director in consultation with administrative, medical and other professional representatives. Responsibilities for program planning, staff supervision, and delivery of services may be delegated by the director to other appropriate staff members.

The director's responsibilities should include the following:

- Development of the social work program policies and procedures;
- Planning for the budget, space and deployment of social work personnel to assure appropriate and adequate services;
- Assurance of quality care in the program;
- Assurance of adequate documentation of services in the records;
- Evaluation and appropriate revision of the social work services;
- Selection, supervision and evaluation of the social work program personnel;
- Provision of orientation and continuing education to the program personnel;

- Participation in the education of other health care personnel;
- Participation in the education of social work students and health care students;
- Participation in program and policy formulation within the organization on administrative and clinical levels;
- Participation in the development of social and health care programs in the community;
- Maintenance of liaison with the community, outside agencies and groups;
- Participation in the development, implementation and review of all research to which social work can make a contribution.

STANDARD 3

THE SCOPE, OBJECTIVES AND ORGANIZATION OF THE SOCIAL WORK PROGRAM SHALL BE CLEARLY DELINEATED.

Interpretation

The written plan for the structure of the social work program, or contracted social work services, shall be clearly delineated in terms of its relationship to the overall organizational setting. The goals and objectives shall reflect the needs of the client population, the overall agency, and the community. The objectives shall clarify the scope and limitations of the program, and the method of providing the services.

The relevance of the social work program and its goals and objectives shall be regularly reviewed and evaluated. Responsibility for assuring this regular review and evaluation rests with the director.

STANDARD 4

THE FUNCTIONS OF THE SOCIAL WORK PROGRAM SHALL INCLUDE SPECIFIC SERVICES TO THE CLIENT POPULATION AND THE COMMUNITY, IN KEEPING WITH THE OVERALL MISSION OF THE ORGANIZATION. THIS SHALL INCLUDE DIRECT SERVICES, CONSULTATION, EDUCATION, POLICY AND PROGRAM PLANNING, QUALITY ASSURANCE, ADVOCACY AND COMMUNITY LIAISON. WHEN THE ORGANIZATION ASSUMES A TEACHING AND RESEARCH FUNCTION, THE SOCIAL WORK PROGRAM

SHOULD PARTICIPATE IN THOSE FUNCTIONS. RESEARCH ACTIVITY, SOCIAL WORK FIELD INSTRUCTION AND OTHER TEACHING RESPONSIBILITIES ARE APPROPRIATE AND RECOMMENDED FUNCTIONS FOR ALL SOCIAL WORK PROGRAMS.

Interpretation

Specific services to the client population shall include but not be limited to:

- Assessment of needs for social work services;
- Admission planning, discharge planning;
- Direct services and treatment to individuals, families and groups;
- Case-finding and outreach;
- Information and referral;
- Client advocacy, within and outside the organization, including attention to fiscal constraints;
- Protection of clients' rights and entitlement, including the right to redress;
- Short and long term planning;
- Promotion and maintenance of health and mental health;
- Preventive, remedial and rehabilitative measures;
- Provision for continuity of care, including guarantee of access and effective utilization.

Services to the community shall include but not be limited to:

- Identification of unmet needs and unserved groups;
- Identification of and service to at-risk populations;
- Consultation and collaboration with outside organizations and professionals concerning client population care and the promotion of health;
- Community liaison services;
- Community planning and coordination activities;
- Psychosocial/health education and promotion.

Since the services to the client population and the community are interrelated and may overlap, the above classifications of functions are not restricted to the particular areas mentioned.

Consultation regarding the social, environmental, psychological, and cultural factors that affect health maintenance should be provided to those involved in the client's care. This may include the agency and its staff, the community, outside agencies and professionals, and significant others.

STANDARD 5

A SUFFICIENT NUMBER OF QUALIFIED SOCIAL WORK PERSONNEL SHALL BE AVAILABLE TO PLAN, PROVIDE AND EVALUATE SOCIAL WORK SERVICES.

Interpretation

The size of the social work staff shall be related to the scope and complexity of the program and to the nature of the population(s) to be served. Staff composition shall also be related to the ethnic and cultural composition of the client population. Needed services shall be based on and related to established indicators of risk.

In addition to the director, the social work personnel may include other administrative/supervisory staff and qualified social work practitioners.* Qualifications for these staff personnel include:

1. Graduate level social worker — a social worker with a minimum of a graduate degree from a school of social work accredited by CSWE.
2. Baccalaureate level social worker — a social worker with an undergraduate degree from a social work program accredited by CSWE.

There may also be social service aides, technicians, or associates on the staff who are closely supervised. There shall be sufficient and appropriately trained or experienced support personnel, such as clerks, secretaries and other technicians to enable the effective and efficient provision of social work sevices. Volunteers may be used within the program under social work supervision.

STANDARD 6

SOCIAL WORK SERVICE PERSONNEL SHALL BE PREPARED FOR THEIR RESPONSIBILITIES IN THE PROVISION OF SOCIAL WORK SERVICES THROUGH APPROPRIATE EDUCATION, ORIENTATION, CONTINUING EDUCATION AND TRAINING PROGRAMS, SUPERVISION, AND REGULAR EVALUATION.

---

*For a more detailed description of the qualifications and functions of various levels of social work personnel, refer to NASW "Standards for Classification of Social Work Practice."

Interpretation

The education, training and experience of personnel who provide social work services shall be related to each individual's expertise, knowledge and skills required for providing services. This information shall be documented in the staff member's personnel file. All new personnel shall receive from the organization and the director of social work services an orientation of sufficient duration and substance to prepare them for their functions and responsibilities.

Personnel providing social work services shall participate in relevant continuing education, including in-service training. The organization, social work director or qualified designees should contribute to providing this education. The education programs shall be partially based upon findings from the review and evaluation of the social work services. Outside educational opportunities shall be provided whenever feasible. The extent of participation in continuing education shall also be documented.

Each staff member shall be regularly evaluated for his/her job performance. This evaluation is to be shared between the evaluator and the staff member.

Social workers who teach in university-affiliated health care settings should qualify and be processed for appropriate faculty rank according to the by-laws and procedures of the university.

STANDARD 7

SOCIAL WORK SERVICES SHALL BE GUIDED BY WRITTEN POLICIES AND PROCEDURES.

Interpretation

There shall be written policies and procedures concerning the scope and conduct of social work services. The director of the social work program is responsible for assuring that the development and implementation of the policies and procedures are carried out in collaboration with other appropriate clinical and administrative representatives. Such policies and procedures should be subjected to timely review, and revised as necessary. They shall be dated to indicate the time of the last review, communicated and implemented. Social work program policies and procedures shall be consistent with all of the organization's rules and regulations, especially those relating to records of care, and with legal requirements. The policies and procedures shall relate to at least the following:

- Types of services and treatment available;
- Identification of patients, clients and families potentially requiring social work services;
- Confidentiality;
- Consultation and referral procedures;
- Relationship to other agency services and outside agencies;
- Maintenance of required records, statistical information, and reports;
- The role of the social work department/service in preadmission planning and discharge planning;
- Social work functions resulting from federal, state, and local requirements;
- Continuing education;
- Teaching and research programs;
- Professional accountability;
- Personnel policies and professional qualifications.

STANDARD 8

A WRITTEN STATEMENT OF THE PERSONNEL POLICIES AND PROCEDURES OF THE AGENCY, THE SOCIAL WORK DEPARTMENT AND THE NASW CODE OF ETHICS SHALL BE AVAILABLE TO EACH STAFF MEMBER.

Interpretation

Personnel policies that relate to the social work program shall be presented in written form and explained to the new employee. Written job descriptions and qualifications as well as affirmative action and grievance procedures shall also be available to staff. If the social work program is part of an organization, the staff should have knowledge of and access to its personnel policies.

STANDARD 9

ADEQUATE DOCUMENTATION OF SOCIAL WORK ACTIVITIES MUST BE PROVIDED IN A RECORD OF CARE OR IN THE PROGRAM SERVICE RECORD. CONFIDENTIALITY MUST BE SAFEGUARDED.

Interpretation

Social work entries in a record of care shall be clearly and concisely written, permitting regular communication with the personnel involved in the client's care. All entries should be dated and should have the social worker's signature and/or identification.

Entries by social work personnel should include, but not be limited to, information regarding the client and his/her family, a social appraisal and observation, plans for social work services and corrective measures, and any action taken. Any results, referrals to other resources, and a final summary of problems and services shall also be incorporated.

Notes, reports and summaries dealing with services and program planning for specific populations shall be regularly entered in the manner consistent with the organization's policies and reporting and record maintenance.

STANDARD 10

THE QUALITY AND APPROPRIATENESS OF SOCIAL WORK SERVICES PROVIDED SHALL BE REGULARLY REVIEWED, EVALUATED, AND ASSURED.

Interpretation

The social work director shall be responsible for assuring that social work services are reviewed and evaluated for appropriateness and effectiveness. This shall be done at least once each year, and shall involve the use of the records of care and pre-established criteria and standards. Such criteria and standards shall relate to the indicators of need for services and to the effectiveness of required social work interventions. Contracted social work services shall be reviewed and evaluated in the same manner.

The review and evaluation of social work services should be performed within the organization's quality assurance program. It shall be documented and shall include feedback and implementation of corrective measures. Where interdisciplinary or multidisciplinary assessments of care are performed, the social work program shall participate.

STANDARD 11

THERE MUST BE ADEQUATE BUDGET, SPACE, FACILITIES, AND EQUIPMENT TO FULFILL THE NEEDS OF THE PROFESSIONAL, EDUCATIONAL, AND ADMINISTRATIVE ASPECTS OF THE SOCIAL WORK PROGRAM.

Interpretation

Offices of the social work staff must be readily accessible to individuals and their families, and other personnel. Privacy for interviews, conferences, telephone calls, and recording is essential. Standard office equipment should be provided.

There should be a clearly defined budget for the department.

GLOSSARY

Baccalaureate level social worker — a professional with an undergradute degree from a social work program accredited by the Council on Social Work Education (CSWE).

Client population — individuals or groups of individuals receiving social work services or who are targeted as at-risk populations in need of services.

Graduate level social worker — a professional with a minimum of a graduate degree from a school of social work accredited by the Council on Social Work Education (CSWE).

Health — in these standards, a term broadly defined to include the physical, psychosocial, and environmental well-being of the client population.

Organization — the central agency or business in which the social work department or program may be a part or unit. Also called organizational setting or structure.

Quality assurance — activities designed to assess services systematically, to determine whether they comply with what are believed to be adequate services, and to correct any observed deficiencies.

Record of care — a centralized documentation of the needs, services provided and relevant information on the client and/or client population.

Social work — the system of organized activities carried on by a person with particular knowledge, competence and values, designed to help individuals, groups or communities toward a mutual adjustment between themselves and their social environment.

Social work program/department — a specified unit established for the provision of social work services independently or within another organizational structure.

Written plan — the operational document that formulates and outlines the purpose and structure of the social work program and the services to be provided.

STANDARDS FOR SOCIAL WORK IN PUBLIC HEALTH SETTINGS

These standards have been prepared by the Social Work Section of the American Public Health Association in collaboration with the Health Quality Standards Committee of the National Association of Social Workers. They refer to the organization of the social work components of a public health program and the practice of social work within that program.

Definition of Public Health: A commonly used definition of public health is one formulated by C.E.A. Winslow in 1920. "Public Health is the science and art of: (1) preventing diseases; (2) prolonging life, and (3) promoting health and efficiency through organized community effort for:

(a) The sanitation of the environment
(b) The control of communicable infections
(c) The education of the individual in personal hygiene
(d) The organization of medical and nursing services for the prevention and treatment of diseases
(d) The development of social machinery to insure everyone a standard of living adequate for the maintenance of health . . .

so organizing these benefits as to enable every citizen to realize his birthright of health and longevity."

Earlier statements of standards of social work practice in public health (*Am.J.Pub.Health*, 1962) referred primarily to practice in official public health agencies. Since that time there has been an expansion of public health services in the curative and rehabilitative areas, and an increase in collaborative efforts by the public and private sector in implementing health programs with public health goals. The use of the phrase, "public health programs," in this statement of standards, therefore, does not refer to a specific agency or setting but rather to the policy base of a program. A public health program may be operated by the voluntary sector, e.g., Visiting Nurse Association, as well as by the public. A public health program, such as a comprehensive program for children and youth, may be one of many administered by a health agency whose primary goal may be curative rather than preventive, e.g., a children's hospital. The phrase, "public health program," may also refer to a tax-supported agency operating independently as an adjunct to the official state or local department such as a comprehensive health center or a health systems agency.

STANDARD 1

THE SOCIAL WORK COMPONENT OF A PUBLIC HEALTH PROGRAM SHALL PARTICIPATE IN PLANNING FOR THE PROTECTION OF COMMUNITIES FROM HEALTH HAZARDS, THE PROMOTION OF IMPROVED PERSONAL HEALTH CARE AND THE PREVENTION OF ILL HEALTH.

Interpretation

Public health social workers focus activities on the promotion of positive health behaviors in the lifestyle development of individuals, families and groups, enhancement of the environment and risk avoidance.

They use the epidemiologic approach in solving community health problems. They assess the health needs of the target population and determine the association of social factors with the incidence of health problems. They plan interventive strategies on the five levels of prevention:

(1) health promotion
(2) specific protection
(3) diagnosis and prompt treatment
(4) limitation of disability
(5) rehabilitation

Their emphasis is to reduce the social stress associated with the health problems, and to determine social supports which will promote well-being and provide protection against ill-health. Even though the social worker's point of entry into a health problem may be in the pathogenic phase, s/he has responsibility to study the extent and distribution of the health problem in the community and to participate with multidisciplinary members of the public health team in reducing the incidence of the health problem and the severity of its impact.

STANDARD 2

THE SOCIAL WORK COMPONENT OF A PUBLIC HEALTH PROGRAM SHALL PARTICIPATE IN PLANNING TO ASSURE THAT ALL PERSONS AT-RISK IN THE TARGET AREA HAVE ACCESS TO HEALTH SERVICES.

Interpretation

Public health is concerned with the physical, emotional and social well-being of the community; the boundaries of the community being determined by political, geographical, legislative and programmatic factors. Social workers in public health programs participate with other staff members in assuring that all persons in the target population have access to health care and social services which facilitate the provision of health care. Social work planning activities should include persons at-risk who do not seek health care.

STANDARD 3

THE SOCIAL WORK COMPONENT OF A PUBLIC HEALTH PROGRAM SHALL COLLABORATE WITH OTHER DISCIPLINES IN PROVIDING FOR CONSUMER PARTICIPATION IN THE PLANNING AND DELIVERY OF HEALTH SERVICES.

Interpretation

Social work promotes and advocates for consumer participation in the planning and delivery of health care and the effective integration of health and nonhealth social services. Social workers participate in the identification of consumers and consumer groups with potential for leadership in these activities and provide guidance in the implementation of consumer involvement in the planning process.

Appendix IV

SOCIAL WORK CODE OF ETHICS*

as adopted by the 1979
National Association of Social Workers
Delegate Assembly effective
July 1, 1980

PREAMBLE

This code is intended to serve as a guide to the everyday conduct of members of the social work profession and as a basis for the adjudication of issues in ethics when the conduct of social workers is alleged to deviate from the standards expressed or implied in this code. It represents standards of ethical behavior for social workers in professional relationships with those served, with colleagues, with employers, with other individuals and professionals, and with the community and society as a whole. It also embodies standards of ethical behavior governing individual conduct to the extent that such conduct is associated with an individual's status and identity as a social worker.

This code is based on the fundamental values of the social work profession that include the worth, dignity, and uniqueness of all persons as well as their rights and opportunities. It is also based on the nature of social work, which fosters conditions that promote these values.

In subscribing to and abiding by this code, the social worker is expected to view ethical responsibility in as inclusive a context as each situation demands and within which ethical judgment is required. The social worker is expected to take into consideration all the prin-

---

*Published 1980, National Association of Social Workers, Inc.
Reprinted with Permission.

ciples in this code that have a bearing upon any situation in which ethical judgment is to be exercised and professional intervention or conduct is planned. The course of action that the social worker chooses is expected to be consistent with the spirit as well as the letter of this code.

In itself, this code does not represent a set of rules that will prescribe all the behaviors of social workers in all the complexities of professional life. Rather, it offers general principles to guide conduct, and the judicious appraisal of conduct, in situations that have ethical implications. It provides the basis for making judgments about ethical actions before and after they occur. Frequently, the particular situation determines the ethical principles that apply and the manner of their aplication. In such cases, not only the particular ethical principles are taken into immediate consideration, but also the entire code and its spirit. Specific applications of ethical principles must be judged within the context in which they are being considered. Ethical behavior in a given situation must satisfy not only the judgment of the individual social worker, but also the judgment of an unbiased jury of professional peers.

This code should not be used as an instrument to deprive any social worker of the opportunity or freedom to practice with complete professional integrity; nor should any disciplinary action be taken on the basis of this code without maximum provision for safeguarding the rights of the social worker affected.

The ethical behavior of social workers results not from edict, but from a personal commitment of the individual. This code is offered to affirm the will and zeal of all social workers to be ethical and to act ethically in all that they do as social workers.

The following codified ethical principles should guide social workers in the various roles and relationships and at the various levels of responsibility in which they function professionally. These principles also serve as a basis for the adjudication by the National Association of Social Workers of issues in ethics.

In subscribing to this code, social workers are required to cooperate in its implementation and abide by any disciplinary rulings based on it. They should also take adequate measures to discourage, prevent, expose, and correct the unethical conduct of colleagues. Finally, social workers should be equally ready to defend and assist colleagues unjustly charged with unethical conduct.

THE NASW CODE OF ETHICS

I. The Social Worker's Conduct and Comportment as a Social Worker

A. Propriety — The Social worker should maintain high standards of personal conduct in the capacity or identity as social worker.

1. The private conduct of the social worker is a personal matter to the same degree as is any other person's, except when such conduct compromises the fulfillment of professional responsibilities.
2. The social worker should not participate in, condone, or be associated with dishonesty, fraud, deceit, or misrepresentation.
3. The social worker should distinguish clearly between statements and actions made as a private individual and as a representative of the social work profession or an organization or group.

B. Competence and Professional Development — The social worker should strive to become and remain proficient in professional practice and the performance of professional functions.

1. The social worker should accept responsibility or employment only on the basis of existing competence or the intention to acquire the necessary competence.
2. The social worker should not misrepresent professional qualifications, education, experience, or affiliations.

C. Service — The social worker should regard as primary the service obligation of the social work profession.

1. The social worker should retain utlimate responsibility for the quality and extent of the service that individual assumes, assigns, or performs.
2. The social worker should act to prevent practices that are inhumane or discriminatory against any person or group of persons.

D. Integrity — The social worker should act in accordance with the highest standards of professional integrity and impartiality.

1. The social worker should be alert to and resist the influences and pressures that interfere with the exercise of professional discretion and impartial judgment required for the performance of professional functions.

2. The social worker should not exploit professional relationships for personal gain.

E. **Scholarship and Research — The social worker engaged in study and research should be guided by the conventions of scholarly inquiry.**

1. The social worker engaged in research should consider carefully its possible consequences for human beings.
2. The social worker engaged in research should ascertain that the consent of participants in the research is voluntary and informed, without any implied deprivation or penalty for refusal to participate, and with due regard for participants' privacy and dignity.
3. The social worker engaged in research should protect participants from unwarranted physical or mental discomfort, distress, harm, danger, or deprivation.
4. The social worker who engages in the evaluation of services or cases should discuss them only for the professional purposes and only with persons directly and professionally concerned with them.
5. Information obtained about participants in research should be treated as confidential.
6. The social worker should take credit only for work actually done in connection with scholarly and research endeavors and credit contributions made by others.

II. The Social Worker's Ethical Responsibility to Clients

F. **Primacy of Clients' Interests — The social worker's primary responsibility is to clients.**

1. The social worker should serve clients with devotion, loyalty, determination, and the maximum application of professional skill and competence.
2. The social worker should not exploit relationships with clients for personal advantage, or solicit the clients of one's agency for private practice.
3. The social worker should not practice, condone, facilitate or collaborate with any form of discrimination on the basis of race, color, sex, sexual orientation, age, religion, national origin, marital status, political belief, mental or physical handicap, or any other preference or personal characteristic, condition or status.

4. The social worker should avoid relationships or commitments that conflict with the interests of clients.
5. The social worker should under no circumstances engage in sexual activities with clients.
6. The social worker should provide clients with accurate and complete information regarding the extent and nature of the services available to them.
7. The social worker should apprise clients of their risks, rights, opportunities, and obligations associated with social service to them.
8. The social worker should seek advice and counsel of colleagues and supervisors whenever such consultation is in the best interest of clients.
9. The social worker should terminate service to clients, and professional relationships with them, when such service and relationships are no longer required or no longer serve the clients' needs or interests.
10. The social worker should withdraw services precipitously only under unusual circumstances, giving careful consideration to all factors in the situation and taking care to minimize possible adverse effects.
11. The social worker who anticipates the termination or interruption of service to clients should notify clients promptly and seek the transfer, referral, or continuation of service in relation to the clients' needs and preferences.

G. **Rights and Prerogatives of Clients — The social worker should make every effort to foster maximum self-determination on the part of clients.**

1. When the social worker must act on behalf of a client who has been adjudged legally incompetent, the social worker should safeguard the interests and rights of that client.
2. When another individual has been legally authorized to act in behalf of a client, the social worker should deal with that person always with the client's best interest in mind.
3. The social worker should not engage in any action that violates or diminishes the civil or legal rights of clients.

H. **Confidentiality and Privacy — The social worker should respect the privacy of clients and hold in confidence all information obtained in the course of professional service.**

1. The social worker should share with others confidences revealed by clients, without their consent, only for compelling professional reasons.

2. The social worker should inform clients fully about the limits of confidentiality in a given situation, the purposes for which information is obtained, and how it may be used.
3. The social worker should afford clients reasonable access to any official social work records concerning them.
4. When providing clients with access to records, the social worker should take due care to protect the confidences of others contained in those records.
5. The social worker should obtain informed consent of clients before taping, recording, or permitting third party observation of their activities.

I. Fees — When setting fees, the social worker should ensure that they are fair, reasonable, considerate, and commensurate with the service performed and with due regard for the clients' ability to pay.

1. The social worker should not divide a fee or accept or give anything of value for receiving or making a referral.

III. The Social Worker's Ethical Responsibility to Colleagues

J. Respect, Fairness, and Courtesy — The social worker should treat colleagues with respect, courtesy, fairness, and good faith.

1. The social worker should cooperate with colleagues to promote professional interests and concerns.
2. The social worker should respect confidences shared by colleagues in the course of their professional relationships and transactions.
3. The social worker should create and maintain conditions of practice that facilitate ethical and competent professional performance by colleagues.
4. The social worker should treat with respect, and represent accurately and fairly, the qualifications, views, and findings of colleagues and use appropriate channels to express judgments on these matters.
5. The social worker who replaces or is replaced by a colleague in professional practice should act with consideration for the interest, character, and reputation of that colleague.
6. The social worker should not exploit a dispute between a colleague and employers to obtain a position or otherwise advance the social worker's interest.

7. The social worker should seek arbitration or mediation when conflicts with colleagues require resolution for compelling professional reasons.
8. The social worker should extend to colleagues of other professions the same respect and cooperation that is extended to social work colleagues.
9. The social worker who serves as an employer, supervisor, or mentor to colleagues should make orderly and explicit arrangements regarding the conditions of their continuing professional relationship.
10. The social worker who has the responsibility for employing and evaluating the performance of other staff members, should fulfill such responsibility in a fair, considerate, and equitable manner, on the basis of clearly enunciated criteria.
11. The social worker who has the responsibility for evaluating the performance of employees, supervisees, or students should share evaluations with them.

K. **Dealing with Colleagues' Clients — The social worker has the responsibility to relate to the clients of colleagues with full professional consideration.**

1. The social worker should not solicit the clients of colleagues.
2. The social worker should not assume professional responsibility for the clients of another agency or a colleague without appropriate communication with that agency or colleague.
3. The social worker who serves the clients of colleagues, during a temporary absence or emergency, should serve those clients with the same consideration as that afforded any client.

IV. The Social Worker's Ethical Responsibility to Employers and Employing Organizations

L. **Commitments to Employing Organizations — The social worker should adhere to commitments made to the employing organization.**

1. The social worker should work to improve the employing agency's policies and procedures, and the efficiency and effectiveness of its services.

2. The social worker should not accept employment or arrange student field placements in an organization which is currently under public sanction by NASW for violating personnel standards, or imposing limitations on or penalties for professional actions on behalf of clients.
3. The social worker should act to prevent and eliminate discrimination in the employing organization's work assignments and in its employment policies and practices.
4. The social worker should use with scrupulous regard, and only for the purpose for which they are intended, the resources of the employing organization.

V. The Social Worker's Ethical Responsibility to the Social Work Profession

M. Maintaining the Integrity of the Profession — The social worker should uphold and advance the values, ethics, knowledge, and mission of the profession.

1. The social worker should protect and enhance the dignity and integrity of the profession and should be responsible and vigorous in discussion and criticism of the profession.
2. The social worker should take action through appropriate channels against unethical conduct by any other member of the profession.
3. The social worker should act to prevent the unauthorized and unqualified practice of social work.
4. The social worker should make no misrepresentation in advertising as to qualifications, competence, service, or results to be achieved.

N. Community Service — The social worker should assist the profession in making social services available to the general public.

1. The social worker should contribute time and professional expertise to activities that promote respect for the utility, the integrity, and the competence of the social work profession.
2. The social worker should support the formulation, development, enactment and implementation of social policies of concern to the profession.

O. Development of Knowledge — The social worker should take responsibility for identifying, developing, and fully utilizing knowledge for professional practice.

1. The social worker should base practice upon recognized knowledge relevant to social work.
2. The social worker should critically examine, and keep current with emerging knowledge relevant to social work.
3. The social worker should contribute to the knowledge base of social work and share research knowledge and practice wisdom with colleagues.

VI. The Social Worker's Ethical Responsibility to Society

P. Promoting the General Welfare — The social worker should promote the general welfare of society.

1. The social worker should act to prevent and eliminate discrimination against any person or group on the basis of race, color, sex, sexual orientation, age, religion, national origin, marital status, political belief, mental or physical handicap, or any other preference or personal characteristic, condition, or status.
2. The social worker should act to ensure that all persons have access to the resources, services, and opportunities which they require.
3. The social worker should act to expand choice and opportunity for all persons, with special regard for disadvantaged or oppressed groups and persons.
4. The social worker should promote conditions that encourage respect for the diversity of cultures which constitute American society.
5. The social worker should provide appropriate professional services in public emergencies.
6. The social worker should advocate changes in policy and legislation to improve social conditions and to promote social justice.
7. The social worker should encourage informed participation by the public in shaping social policies and institutions.

Appendix V

STATE COMPARISON OF LAWS REGULATING SOCIAL WORK, 1983*

*Published 1983, National Association of Social Workers, Inc. Reprinted with Permission.

TABLE I—Year of Enactment, Type, and Administration

State (In Order of Enactment)	Year of Enactment		Type[1]	Name of State Regulatory Agency	Location Within State Government	Number of Board Members	
	First	Amended				Total	SW
1. Puerto Rico	1934	1940	L	Board of Examiners of Social Workers[2]	Independent Board	7	7
2. California	1945	1981[28]	R	Board of Behavioral Science Examiners	Department of Consumer Affairs	11	2[3]
	1968	1973	L				
3. Rhode Island	1961		R	Board of Registration of Social Workers	Department of Social Welfare	5	4
4. Oklahoma	1965	1980	L	State Board of Licensed Social Workers	Independent Board	5	4
5. New York	1965		R	State Board for Social Work	The State Education Department	10[21]	9
6. Virginia	1966	1975[10]	L	Virginia Board of Social Workers[10]	Dept. of Health Regulatory Boards	5	5
7. Illinois	1967		R	Social Workers Examining Committee	Dept. of Registrations & Education	7	7[6]
8. South Carolina	1968		R	State Board of Social Worker Registration	Independent Board	7	7
9. Maine	1969	1978	R/L	State Board of Social Worker Registration	Dept. of Business Regulation	8	7
10. Michigan	1972	1975	R	State Board of Examiners of Social Work	Dept. of Licensing & Regulation	7	5[7]
11. Louisiana	1972		L[8]	State Bd of Bd Certified Social Work Examiners	Dept. of Health & Human Resources	5	5
12. Utah	1972	1977	L	Board of Social Work Examiners	Department of Registration	5	5[17]
13. Kansas	1974	1980	L	Behavioral Sciences Regulatory Board[24]	Independent Board	7	2
14. Kentucky	1974	1976	L	State Board of Examiners of Social Work	Div. of Occup. & Prof., Dept. of Finance	7	6[9]
15. Arkansas	1975	1981	L	Social Work Licensing Board	Independent Board	7	6[12]
16. South Dakota	1975		L	Board of Social Work Examiners	Dept. of Commerce & Consumer Affairs	5	4[13]
17. Maryland	1975	1983[27]	R	State Board of Social Work Examiners	Dept. of Health & Mental Hygiene	5	4[14]
18. Colorado	1975	1981[29]	R/L[11]	Board of Social Work Examiners	Dept. of Regulatory Agencies	7	3[15]
19. Idaho	1976		L	State Board of Social Work Examiners	Dept. of Self-Governing Agencies	5	5[16]
20. Delaware	1976		L	State Board of Social Work Examiners	Independent Board	5	3[18]
21. Alabama	1977		L	Alabama Board of Examiners in Social Work	Independent Board	7	7[19]
22. Oregon	1977	1979	R	State Board of Clinical Social Workers	Dept. of Human Resources, Health Division	7[25]	4
23. Massachusetts	1977		L	Board of Registration of Social Workers	Independent Board	7	4[22]
24. Tennessee	1980		R	Advisory Council—Board of Certification	State Licensing Board for Healing Arts	—	—[23]
25. Texas	1981	1983[29]	R	Council for Social Work Certification	Texas Board of Human Resources	9[26]	6
26. Florida	1981		R	No Board	Department of Professional Regulation	—	—

27. Montana	1983	R	State Board of Social Work Examiners	Independent Board	5	4[30]
28. North Dakota	1983	L	Board of Social Work Examiners	Independent Board	6	4[31]
29. North Carolina	1983	R	Certification Board for Social Work	Independent Board	7	4[32]
30. New Hampshire	1983	R	Board of Examiners of Psychologists	Independent Board	7	1[33]
31. Virgin Islands	1983	R	Board of Social Work Licensure	Independent Board	5	4

TABLE I—YEAR OF ENACTMENT, TYPE, AND ADMINISTRATION

[1]R = Registration or certification title: L = License to practice

[2]1940 also established a College of Social Workers of Puerto Rico, comprised of all social workers licensed in Puerto Rico. (P.R.)

[3]Two Clinical Social Workers; (Two Registered Social Workers) Cal.

[4]Two Licensed Social Workers; Two Lic. Social Work Associates; one public member. (Okla.)

[5]Four with MSW Degrees; three with undergraduate degrees. (Ill.)

[7]The Board shall have at least two Certified Social Workers; one Social Worker and one Social Worker Technician. (Mich.)

[8]Law actually grants "right to practice and use the title" but prohibits only misuse of title. (La.)

[9]Two each Certified Social Workers, Social Worker and persons licensed for independent practice. (Ky.)

[10]Legislature dismantled Board of Behavioral Science Examiners in 1983 (Va.)

[11]Act establishes registration of MSW or BA + 2 years level *and* licensure of other levels. (Colo.)

[12]Three Certified Social Workers; Two Master Social Workers;; One Social Worker; One public member.(Ark.)

[13]Two certified Social Workers; one Social Worker, one Social Work Associate. (S.D.)

[14]Appointments of one person required from each of the three lists from Md. Chapter, and Metro D.C. Chapter, NASW; (Md.)

[15]Requires at least one member engaged in "Direct services" and one member in "education, training, or research in Social Work." (Colo.)

[16]Three Certified Social Workers; Two Social Workers. (Idaho)

[18]Three Licensed Clinical Social Workers; one 'general public' member. (Del.)

[19]Four licensed Certified Social Workers; Two licensed Graduate S.W.; One licensed Bachelor S.W. (Ala.)

[20]Three clinical social workers; one public citizen; one consumer of clinical services. (Ore.)

[21]Law probides "not less than seven" CSW and requires one consumer representative. Ten persons currently appointed. (N.Y.)

[22]Four social workers, representing each of the licensed levels, three persons to represent the general public. (Mass.)

[23]Advisory Council: three Master Social Workers. (Tenn.)

[24]Board regulates both Psychologists & Social Workers: Two Certified Psychologists; Two Social Workers; Three Members of general public. (Kansas)

[25]Four Clinical Social Workers; two public members; one consumer member. (Ore.)

[26]Three Certified Social Workers; Three Social Workers or Social Work Associates; Three public members. (Tex.)

[27]Sunset review reenactment expanded coverage to public employees (Md.)

[28]Act amended to end RSW registration level in 1983. No new registrations issued. (Cal.)

[29]Re-enactment following "Sunset review."

[30]One each social worker member employed in private practice, state social service agency, medical or social welfare field, and social work education. (Mont.)

[31]Two Licensed Social Workers and Two Certified Social Workers (N.D.)

[32]Two Certified Social Workers and Two Certified Clinical Social Workers (N.C.)

[33]A single Certified Clinical Social Worker is added to an existing state board of psychologists (N.H.)

TABLE II—Levels of Practice Regulated—Renewal Periods

	Title	Initials	Education	Experience Required	Current Employment Required	Exam Required	Renewal Period
ALABAMA	Independent Practice		MSW	+2[17]		YES	2 years
	Certified Social Worker	LCSW	MSW	+2 yrs.		YES	
	Graduate Social Worker	LGSW	MSW		NO	YES	
	Bachelor Social Worker	LBSW	BSW	[18]	NO	YES	
ARKANSAS	Licensed Certified Social Worker	LCSW	MSW	+2 years		YES	2 years
	Licensed Master Social Worker	LMSW	MSW		NO	YES	
	Licensed Social Worker	LSW	BSW			YES	
CALIFORNIA	Licensed Clinical Social Worker	LCSW	MSW	+2 years[3]	NO	YES	Annual
COLORADO	Licensed Social Worker II	LSWII[11]	MSW	+5 years		YES	2 years
	Licensed Social Worker	LSWI	MSW	+2 years	NO	YES	
	Registered Social Worker	RSW	MSW or BA	+2 years		NO	
DELAWARE	Licensed Clinical Social Worker	LCSW	MSW	+2 years	NO	YES	2 years
FLORIDA	Clinical Social Worker	LCSW	MSW	+3 years[24]	NO	YES[25]	2 years
IDAHO	Independent Practice	—	MSW	+2 years		NO	Annual
	Certified Social Worker	CSW	MSW		NO	YES	
	Social Worker	SW	BSW[14]			YES	
ILLINOIS	Certified Social Worker	CSW	MSW		NO	YES	2 years
	Social Worker	SW	BA	+2 years	YES	YES	
KANSAS	"Specialties"		MSW	+2 years		YES	
	Master Social Worker	MSW	MSW		YES[4]	YES	2 years
	Baccalaureate Social Worker	BSW	BSW			YES	
KENTUCKY	Independent Practice		MSW	+2 years		YES	
	Certified Social Worker	CSW	MSW		NO	YES	3 years
	Social Worker	SW	BSW			YES	
LOUISIANA	Board Certified Social Worker	BCSW	MSW	+2 years	NO	YES	Annual
MAINE	Independent Practice		MSQ	+2 years		YES[20]	2 years
	Certified Social Worker	CSW	MSW			YES	
	Registered Social Worker	RSW	BSW		NO	YES	
	Associate Social Worker	ASW	BA or	+2 years 6 years		YES	

MARYLAND	Independent Practice		MSW	+2 years		YES	
	Certified Social Worker	CSW[10]	MSW	+2 years		YES	2 years
	Graduate Social Worker	GSW	MSW		NO	YES	
	Social Work Associate	SWA	BSW			YES	
MASSACHUSETTS	Independent Clinical Social Worker	ICSW	MSW	+3 years		YES	[21]
	Certified Social Worker	CSW	MSW			YES	
	Social Worker	SW	BSW or BA	+2 years	NO	YES	
	Social Work Associate	ASW	AA/BA			YES	
MICHIGAN	Certified Social Worker	CSW	MSW	+2 years	NO[6]	NO	Annual
	Social Worker	SW	MSW or BA	+2 years	YES[7,6,13]	NO	Annual
	Social Worker Technician	SWT	2 yr. BA or	1 year	YES[8,6]	NO	
MONTANA	Licensed Social Worker	LSW	MSW	+2[26]	NO	YES	2 years
NEW HAMPSHIRE	Certified Clinical Social Worker	CCSW	MSW	+2[27]	NO	NO	—
NEW YORK	Certified Social Worker	CSW	MSW[4]		NO	YES	2 years
NORTH CAROLINA	Certified Social Worker	CSW	BSW		NO	YES	2 years
	Certified Master Social Worker	CMSW	MSW		NO	YES	
	Certified Clinical Social Worker	CCSW	MSW	+2[28]	NO	YES	
	Certified Social Work Manager	CSWM	BSW	+2[28]	NO	YES	
NORTH DAKOTA	Licensed Social Worker	LSW	BSW		NO	YES	2 years
	Licensed Certified Social Worker	LCSW	MSW		NO	YES	
	Independent Practice		MSW	+3	NO	NO	
OKLAHOMA	Independent Licensed Social Worker	LSW	MSW	+2 years	NO	YES	Annual
	Licensed Social Work Associate	LSWA	BSW	+2 years	NO	YES	
OREGON	Registered Clinical Social Worker	RCSW	MSW	+2 years	NO[19]	NO	Annual[19]
PUERTO RICO	Social Worker		BA-MSW[1]	+2 years	NO	NO	None
RHODE ISLAND	Registered Social Worker	RSW	MSW		NO	NO	Annual
SOUTH CAROLINA	Registered Social Worker	RSW	MSW[5]		NO	NO	Annual
SOUTH DAKOTA	Independent Practice	CSW-PIP	MSW	+2 years		YES	
	Certified Social Worker	CSW	MSW			YES	
	Social Worker	SW	BSW		NO	YES	
	Social Work Associate	SWA	AA-BA			YES	2 years
TENNESSEE	Independent Practice	—	MSW	+5 years	NO	NO	Annual
	Master Social Worker	MSW	MSW		NO	NO	Annual

TABLE II—Levels of Practice Regulated—Renewal Periods—Continued

	Title	Initials	Education	Experience Required	Current Employment Required	Exam Required	Renewal Period
TEXAS	Private Practice		CSW	+ Exper.[22]		NO	Annual
	Certified Social Worker	CSW	MSW		NO	YES	Annual
	Social Worker	SW	BSW			YES	Annual
	Social Work Associate[23]	SWA	HS/BA	+ SW exp.		YES	Annual
UTAH	Independent Practice[15]	—	MSW	+ years		YES	Annual
	Certified Social Worker	CSW	MSW		NO	YES	
	Social Service Worker	SSW	BSW			YES	Annual
	Social Service Aide	SSA					
VIRGIN ISLANDS	Social Work Associate	SWA	AA/BA		NO		
	Social Worker	SW	BSW or BA	+2	NO		
	Certified Social Worker	CSW	MSW		NO	NO	
	Certified Independent Social Worker	CISW	MSW	+2	NO		2 years
VIRGINIA	Clinical Social Worker[16]	CSW	MSW	+3 years	NO	YES	
	Social Worker	SW	MSW	+3 years		YES	2 years

TABLE II—LEVELS OF PRACTICE REGULATED

[1]Act provides eligibility for either of BA + 2 years post graudate study (MSW), BA + 1 year post graduate study + 2 years experience, or BA with Social Work major (BSW) + 3 years of experience. (P.R.)

[2]1972 amendments provide eligibility for MSW, BSW + 3 years of experience, BA + 5 years experience, and 1 year Social Work Master's study + 1 year other MA study—2 years experience. (Cal.)

[3]One year of experience must be in a hospital, clinic, or agency and providing psychotherapy. (Cal.)

[4]Master's or equivalent degree in Social Work. (N.Y.)

[5]Or membership in NASW on May 29, 1968, (effective date of Act). (S.C.)

[6]Legal resident or employed in the state (Mich.) (Kansas).

[7]Or has the equivalent of 4,000 hours of voluntary service. (Mich.)

[8]Or has the equivalence of 2,000 hours of voluntary service, was previously certified, or has AA in Social Work. (Mich.)

[10]Only Certified Social Workers may practice independently. (Md.)

[11]Only LSW-11 with 4 years experience may practice independently, other two levels have title protection only. (Colo.)

[13]Employment not required if person has an accredited BSW or MSW, or was previously certified. (Mich.)

[14]BA in "related fields. . . approved by the board" recognized. (Idaho).

[15]Includes specialty license as "Clinical Social Worker." (Utah).

[16]Previous titles continued temporarily. (Va.)

[17]Experience required in 2 years full time or 3 years part time; 4 years full time or 5 years part time for specialty license. (Ala.)

[18]For six years from May 23, 1977, an LBSW may be granted applicant with BA and two years of full time continuous employment as a social worker. (Ala.)

[19]Renewal requires one to have been "actively engaged" in practice during registration period. (Ore.)

[20]Applicant must submit evidence of qualification to practice independently. (Maine).

[21]Period for renewal to be set by Board. (Mass.)

[22]Dept. to establish procedures including "the number of years of acceptable Social Work experience." (Tex.)

[23]The SWA certificate was open for application for two years only ending August 1983. (Tex.)

[24]The MSW must have "a major emphasis or specialty in direct patient or health care services," and be CSWE accredited. Doctoral degree need not be CSWE accredited. (Fla.)

[25]Exam to be "prepared by dept. or State professional organization." (Fla.)

[26]MSW or "doctorate" required plus 3,000 hours in psychotherapy, in past 5 yrs. Three references also required (Mont.)

[27]"2 years or 3,000 hours of post-masters supervised, paid clinical experience." (N.H.)

[28]The Certified Clinical S.W. requires the CMSW license; the Certified S.W. Manager requires a CSW license (N.C.)

TABLE III —Continuing Education Provisions

The authorizing provisions included in the legislation are listed below, for states that have acts which specify some form of continuing education requirement for the renewal of a license or certificate. Specific regulations should be obtained from the respective boards.

ALABAMA	*Section 12.11* At the time of license renewal each applicant shall present satisfactory evidence that in the period since the license was issued, such applicant has completed the continuing education requirements specified by the Board. At the time of license renewal, the Board may, in its discretion, waive the continuing education requirement upon a showing by an applicant that prolonged illness or other extenuating circumstances prevented completion of such requirement. A waiver shall not be granted to any applicant twice in succession.
ARKANSAS	*Section 10(d)* At the time of license renewal, each applicant shall present satisfactory evidence that in the period since the license was issued, he has completed the continuing education requirements as required by the Board.
COLORADO	*Section 12-63.5-111* Every person seeking a renewal of a certificate shall show evidence to the board that he has been engaged in at least fourteen classroom clock hours of continuing education under the sponsorship of an accredited school or a program approved by the board. The board has the authority to revise the criteria so that time, content, and appropriateness of continuing education activities may be kept current, effective, and relevant. Any revision of criteria regarding time, content, or appropriateness of continuing education must be made known by inclusion in the annual notice of renewal of licensure and registration.
DELAWARE	*Section 378* At the time of the license renewal each applicant shall present satisfactory evidence that in the period since the license was issued, he or she has completed continuing education requirements as developed and specified by the Board.
FLORIDA	*Section 490.007(2)* Each applicant for renewal shall present satisfactory evidence that in the period since the license was issued, the applicant has completed continuing education requirements set by rule of the department or, in the case of psychologists, by rule of the board. Not more than 25 hours of continuing education per year shall be required.
KANSAS	*Section 23(b)* Except as otherwise provided in KSA 75-5356, as amended, a license may be renewed by the payment of the renewal fee set forth in this act and the execution and submission of a signed statement, on a form to be provided by the board, attesting that the applicant's license has been neither revoked nor currently suspended and that applicant has met the requirements for continuing education established by the board.
KENTUCKY	*Section 335, 130(4)* The board may, at its discretion, require continuing education as a condition of license renewal. (Enact. Acts 1974, ch. 279 & 13.)
MAINE	*Section 7060* . . . Every 2nd renewal shall be contingent upon evidence of participation in a continuing professional education course or program as approved by the Board.
MARYLAND	*Section 848(E)* At the time of renewal, the board may require the licensee to produce evidence of keeping abreast of new developments in the applicant's area of specialization in the field of social work. This requirement shall be standardized for all licensees within each category and within each specialization.
MASSACHUSETTS	*Section 136* At the time of license renewal, each applicant shall present satisfactory evidence that in the period since the license was issued, he has completed the continuing education requirements specified by the board.
MONTANA	*Section 9(2)* Application for renewal must be made upon a form provided by the department. A renewal license must be issued upon payment of a renewal fee set by the board and upon submitting proof of completion of continuing education requirements.

TABLE III —Continuing Education Provisions—Continued

NORTH CAROLINA	*Section 90B-9(b)* All certificates issued hereunder shall be renewed at the times and in the manner provided by this section. At least 45 days prior to expiration of each certificate, the Board shall mail a notice for certificate renewal to the person certified for the current certification period. Prior to the expiration date, the applicant must return the notice properly completed, together with a renewal fee established by the Board and evidence of completion of the continuing education requirements established by the Board under G.S. 90B-6(g), upon receipt of which the Board shall issue to the person to be certified the renewed certificate for the period stated on the certificate
NORTH DAKOTA	*Section 12(5)* At the time of renewal the board shall require each applicant to present satisfactory evidence that the applicant has completed the continuing education requirements specified by the board.
OKLAHOMA	Section 8.B on independent practice requires that the licensee "3. Shall continue to meet continuing education requirements set by the Board." (Effective after October 1, 1980).
SOUTH DAKOTA	*Section 25* Attendance at post graduate work as may be prescribed by the board, is a further requirement for renewal of said license. In no instance may the board require a greater number of hours of annual continuing education study than are available at courses approved by the board and held within the state. The board shall be allowed to waive the continuing education requirement in case of certified illness or undue hardship.
TEXAS	*Section 50.023(b)* The department shall notify each person certified of the date of the expiration of a certificate or order of recognition issued to him, the amount of the fee for renewal, and the continuing education provisions that are required for its renewal for one year. The notice shall be mailed by United States mail to the person certified at least 30 days in advance of the date of the expiration of the certificate or order of recognition.
UTAH	*Section 58-35-8* At the time of license renewal the social work licensure board may require a licensee to produce evidence of having upgraded themselves in their area of practice or expertise. This requirement may be satisfied through professional learning or practice.
VIRGINIA	*Regulations—Section IV-B* Renewal applications may contain questionnaires on continuing education, inspection of practices, and other related professional matters. The continuation of a license is contingent upon the completion of these questionnaires.
VIRGIN ISLANDS	*Section 520 Duties of the Board* (b) Promulgate rules and regulations that set standards for professional practice and continuing education requirements for certified independent social workers, certified social workers, social workers, and social work associates.

INDEX

N

O

P

Q

R

S

W

X